THE
MANY FACES
OF
SUICIDE

THE MANY FACES OF SUICIDE

INDIRECT SELF-DESTRUCTIVE BEHAVIOR

edited by

NORMAN L. FARBEROW, Ph.D.

McGRAW-HILL BOOK COMPANY

New York / St. Louis / San Francisco
Auckland / Bogotá / Düsseldorf / Johannesburg / London
Madrid / Mexico / Montreal / New Delhi / Panama / Paris
São Paulo / Singapore / Sydney / Tokyo / Toronto

Library of Congress Cataloging in Publication Data
Main entry under title:

The Many faces of suicide.

  Includes index.
  1. Self-destructive behavior. I. Farberow,
Norman L. [DNLM: 1. Suicide. 2. Violence.
HV6545 M295]
RC569.5.S45M36   616.8′582   79-18799
ISBN 0-07-019944-2

123456789 DODO 89876543210

The editors of this book were Lawrence B. Apple and Suzette H. Annin. The de-
signer was Elaine G. Gongora, and the production supervisor was Sally Fliess. It was
set in Caledonia by Bi-Comp.
It was printed and bound by R. R. Donnelley & Sons.

The pronouns "he" and "his" have sometimes been used in a purely generic sense in
this book to accommodate the text to the limitations of the English language and
avoid awkward grammatical constructions.

TO
KARL A. MENNINGER
Whose pioneer efforts in this field
are responsible for most of the ideas
developed in this book

The planning, literature searches, and review editing of this volume were supported by contract number 271-77-3414 from the National Institute on Drug Abuse to Documentation Associates Information Services Incorporated, Los Angeles, California.
Assistance of the staff of Documentation Associates in preparation of this volume for publication is gratefully acknowledged.

The views and opinions expressed herein do not necessarily reflect the views of the Department of Health, Education, and Welfare or the National Institute on Drug Abuse.

CONTENTS

CONTRIBUTORS

Kalle A. Achté, M.D.
Professor of Psychiatry
Psychiatric Clinic
Helsinki University Central Hospital
Helsinki, Finland

Douglas A. Bernstein, Ph.D.
Professor
Department of Psychology
University of Illinois, Urbana
Champaign, Illinois

Theodore H. Blau, Ph.D.
Professor
Department of Psychiatry
University of South Florida School of
  Medicine
Tampa, Florida

Marcelline M. Burns, Ph.D.
Research Psychologist
Southern California Research Institute
Los Angeles, California

Sandra B. Coleman, Ph.D.
Director, Research and Evaluation
ACT (Achievement through
  Counseling and Treatment)
Philadelphia, Pennsylvania

John C. Connelly, M.D.
Director
Alcoholism Recovery Program
C. F. Menninger Memorial Hospital
Menninger Foundation
Topeka, Kansas

John L. Delk, Ph.D.
Professor
Department of Psychiatry and
  Behavioral Sciences
University of Arkansas for Medical
  Sciences
Little Rock, Arkansas

William J. Filstead, Ph.D.
Assistant Professor and Director of
  Evaluation Research
Department of Psychiatry and
  Behavioral Sciences

Northwestern University
Chicago, Illinois

Calvin J. Frederick, Ph.D.
Chief, Disaster Assistance and
  Emergency Mental Health
National Institute of Mental Health
Rockville, Maryland
Associate Clinical Professor of
  Psychiatry
George Washington University, School
  of Medicine
Washington, D.C.

Gilbert Geis, Ph.D.
Professor
Program in Social Ecology
University of California, Irvine
Irvine, California

Sylvia L. Ginsparg, Ph.D.
Assistant Clinical Professor
Department of Psychiatry
St. Louis University Medical School
St. Louis, Missouri

Alan M. Goldstein, Ph.D.
Associate Professor of Psychology
John Jay College of Criminal Justice
City University of New York
New York, New York

Henriette Groot, Ph.D.
Psychology Service
Veterans Administration Medical
  Center
Long Beach, California
Associate Clinical Professor
Department of Psychology
University of California, Los Angeles
Los Angeles, California

Herbert Hendin, M.D.
Director, Center for Psychosocial
  Studies
Veterans Administration Medical
  Center
Montrose, New York
Professor of Psychiatry
New York Medical College
New York, New York

Ted L. Huston, Ph.D.
Associate Professor
College of Human Development
Pennsylvania State University
University Park, Pennsylvania

Jennifer James, Ph.D.
Associate Professor
Department of Psychiatry and
  Behavioral Sciences
University of Washington
Seattle, Washington

Samuel Z. Klausner, Ph.D.
Director
Center for Research on the Acts of Man
Professor
Department of Sociology
University of Pennsylvania
Philadelphia, Pennsylvania

Igor Kusyszyn, Ph.D.
Associate Professor
Department of Psychology/Counseling
  and Development Center
York University
Toronto, Canada

Edward Lichtenstein, Ph.D.
Professor
Department of Psychology
University of Oregon
Eugene, Oregon

Robert E. Litman, M.D.
Co-Director
Suicide Prevention Center
Professor
Department of Psychiatry
UCLA Medical School
Training and Supervising
  Psychoanalyst
Southern California Psychoanalytic
  Institute
Los Angeles, California

Alexis M. Nehemkis, Ph.D.
Psychology Service
Veterans Administration Medical
  Center
Long Beach, California

Clinical Associate
Department of Psychology
University of Southern California
Los Angeles, California

Christopher V. Rowland, Jr., M.D.
Assistant Clinical Professor of
  Psychiatry
Peter Bent Brigham Hospital, and
Harvard Medical School
Cambridge, Massachusetts

Melvin L. Selzer, M.D.
Private Practice, Psychiatry
San Diego, California

Michael A. Simpson, D.P.M.
Associate Professor
Department of Psychiatry
Temple University School of Medicine
Philadelphia, Pennsylvania

Reginald G. Smart, Ph.D.
Associate Research Director in
  Evaluation Studies
Addiction Research Foundation
Toronto, Canada

M. Duncan Stanton, Ph.D.
Director
Addicts and Families Program
Assistant Professor of Psychology in
  Psychiatry
University of Pennsylvania School of
  Medicine
Director of Family Therapy
Drug Dependence Treatment Center
Veterans Administration Medical
  Center
Philadelphia, Pennsylvania

Hans Toch, Ph.D.
Professor of Psychology
School of Criminal Justice
State University of New York
Albany, New York

J. Thomas Ungerleider, M.D.
Associate Professor of Psychiatry
Neuropsychiatric Institute
University of California, Los Angeles
Los Angeles, California

FOREWORD

Interest in or curiosity about the behavior of our fellow man is the basis for many features of our culture. Gossip, numerous news items, crowds at fires, and accidents are examples. Most of us regard some of the actions of others as examples of poor judgment, at best, or as irrational behavior, in the extreme instance. Many of us also believe that people are motivated to behave, at least most of the time, in a manner that is in some way useful to them.

This book presents a discussion of some types of behavior by individuals, or groups of people, that may be considered irrational by others. Norman Farberow, an authority on suicidal behavior and Principal Investigator of the Central Research Unit, Veterans Administration Wadsworth Medical Center, has asked a number of authors to offer material on indirect self-destructive behavior (ISDB). He states that ISDB is "distinguishable from direct self-destruction by at least two criteria, *time* and *awareness*. The effect is long-range and the behavior may span years; the person is usually unaware of or doesn't care about the effects of his behavior, nor does he consider himself a suicide" (p. 17).

Certain stress-seeking behavior, and a variety of seemingly irrational responses to medical treatment by persons suffering from somatic illness, appear more rational when viewed as types of indirect self-destructive behavior. The history and literature on partial suicides go back to Durkheim in 1897, reappear in Freud's work on the concept of a death instinct, and reach fruition in the work of Karl Menninger. It was Menninger who developed Freud's concept of the death instinct and described its manifestation in indirect self-destructive behavior. Faberow also reviews the other modern literature on the subject. The book is deservedly dedicated to Karl Menninger, who of all persons in modern times has done most to direct our attention to these phenomena.

To my knowledge, this is the first attempt to organize and examine the kinds of behavior that may be listed under the rubric of indirect self-destruction. There may be some who will disagree about the activities which have been included. As a matter of fact, the authors of two of the chapters disclaim or at least question whether their areas are most appropriately conceptualized as indirectly self-destructive. Lichtenstein and Bernstein believe that cigarette smoking, at least in its milder phases, is better explained with other concepts. Geis and Huston find their Good Samaritan interveners acting in a self-enhancing, socially lauded, although recognizedly high-risk way, when they rush to the aid of an unknown victim of a crime. Actually, it does not take too much stretching of the imagination to see how some phenomena need to be practiced to an extreme (as in cigarette addiction) before they become self-destructive, or may be seen as the opposite side of the same coin, as when high-risk, self-enhancing behavior can pass beyond the point of being a socially acceptable, reasonable action. Klausner describes this area in much more detail in his discussion of stress-seeking behavior and how it is mediated and controlled by the society in which it occurs.

Some readers may raise questions about other kinds of behavior which were not included but which could be readily seen as indirectly self-destructive. Anorexia nervosa, malingering, invalidism, asceticism, sexual deviations are a few which come to mind, and I'm sure there are many more which could be included. But the book does not claim to be exhaustive. Rather, it is a description of the "state of the art," with many items in it both directly and indirectly related to the general topic of indirect self-destructive behavior. There is some evidence that persons who engage in indirect self-destructive behavior have certain personality traits in common. In particular they may employ counterphobic activity as a defense against depression. There is also information that makes more rational some irrational behavior, such as that of patients who flout the physician's orders, of persons who ignore sensible adherence to safety regulations, of people who repeatedly engage in drunken driving, and others.

This is an excellent book which tells where we are in this familiar "new field," and which points the way for future explorations.

Jack R. Ewalt, M.D.
Director, Mental Health and
  Behavioral Sciences Service
Department of Medicine and Surgery
Veterans Administration
Washington, D.C.

ACKNOWLEDGMENTS

Dr. Dan Lettieri, Chief, Psychosocial Branch, Division of Research, National Institute on Drug Abuse served as Project Officer for the contract which supported the preparation of this volume. His wise counsel throughout the project was invaluable. Ms. Mary Macari and Dr. Greg Austin of Documentation Associates monitored all the financial, managerial, and correspondence tasks related to the project, including the typing and indexing of the manuscript. Eunice Pierce, Ruth Jensen, Leslie Metour, and Arana Greenberg also helped in the typing. The Veterans Administration and the Los Angeles Suicide Prevention Center have provided a comprehensive base for development of the work in this area. Pearl, my wife, continues to be an inexhaustible source of support and encouragement.

Grateful acknowledgment is made for permission to use excerpts from the following copyright material:

S. S. Asch, "Wrist-scratching as a symptom of anhedonia: A predepressive state." *The Psychoanalytic Quarterly,* Vol. 40, 1971. Reprinted by permission of The Psychoanalytic Quarterly.

J. Curlee, "Women alcoholics." *Federal Probation,* Vol. 32, 1967. Reprinted by permission of the Administrative Office of the United States Courts.

W. G. Dahlstrom and G. S. Welsh, *An MMPI Handbook.* Minneapolis: University of Minnesota Press, 1960. Reprinted by permission of the University of Minnesota Press.

Kingsley Davis, "The sociology of prostitution." *American Sociological Review,* Vol. 2, 1937. Reprinted by permission of The American Sociological Association.

Nanette J. Davis, "The prostitute: Developing a deviant identity." In J. M. Henslin (ed.), *Studies in the Sociology of Sex.* New York: Appleton-Century-Crofts, 1971. Reprinted by permission of James M. Henslin.

John L. Delk, "Why they jump: A psychological study of skydivers." *Parachutist,* Vol. 12, 1971. Reprinted by permission of John L. Delk and the United States Parachute Association.

Emile Durkheim, *Suicide: A Sociological Study,* trans. by J. Spaulding and G. Simpson. Springfield, Ill.: Free Press, 1951. Copyright 1951 by The Free Press, a corporation. Reprinted by permission of Macmillan Publishing Co., Inc., New York, and Routledge & Kegan Paul Ltd., London.

Sigmund Freud, "Inhibitions, symptoms and anxiety." In Vol. 22 of *The Standard Edition of the Complete Psychological Works of Sigmund Freud,* trans. and ed. by James Strachey. London: The Hogarth Press, 1959. Reprinted by permission of The Hogarth Press.

Harold Greenwald, *The Call Girl.* San Diego: Decision Books, 1978. Reprinted by permission of Harold Greenwald.

J. S. Kafka, "The body as transitional object—A psycho-analytic study of the self-mutilating patient." *British Journal of Medical Psychology,* Vol. 42, 1969. Reprinted by permission of the British Psychological Society.

Samuel Z. Klausner, ed., *Why Man Takes Chances: Studies in Stress-Seeking.* Bureau of Social Science Research, Washington, D.C., 1968. Reprinted by permission of Samuel Z. Klausner.

A. MacLennon, *Women: Their Use of Alcohol and Other Legal Drugs.* Addiction Research Foundation of Ontario, 1976. Reprinted by permission of the Addiction Research Foundation of Ontario.

Karl A. Menninger, *Man against Himself.* New York: Harcourt, Brace, 1938. Reprinted by permission of Harcourt Brace Jovanovich, Inc.

Karl A. Menninger, *Man against Himself.* New York: Harcourt, Brace, 1938. printed by permission of Viking Press, Inc.

Karen E. Rosenblum, "Female deviance and the female sex role: Preliminary investigation." *British Journal of Sociology,* Vol. 26, 1975. Reprinted by permission of Routledge & Kegan Paul Ltd.

Hans Selye, "Stress: It's a G. A. S." *Psychology Today,* Vol. 3, No. 4, 1969. Reprinted from Psychology Today Magazine. Copyright © 1969 Ziff Davis Publishing Co.

Hans Selye, "Creativity in basic research." In F. F. Flach (ed.), *Creative Psychiatry,* Vol. 2. Ardsley, N. Y.: Geigy Pharmaceuticals, 1977. Reprinted by permission of Geigy Pharmaceuticals.

Michael A. Simpson, "Self-mutilation and suicide." In Edwin S. Shneidman (ed.), *Suicidology: Contemporary Developments.* New York: Grune & Stratton, 1976. Reprinted by permission of Grune & Stratton and Edwin S. Shneidman.

THE

MANY FACES

OF

SUICIDE

INTRODUCTION

NORMAN L. FARBEROW

QUESTIONS

As the title of this volume indicates, this is not the usual book on suicide examining familiar, albeit tabooed, forms of overt self-destructive behavior by which man inflicts on himself hurt, defeat, and death. Despite their familiarity, such forms of behavior are infrequent, occurring in a very small proportion of our population and usually signaling severe emotional distress or a fully developed psychiatric syndrome. Rather, this collection of writings looks at man's tendencies toward self-injury, self-defeat, and self-destruction from another point of view and with a different set of questions. The areas about which the questions are asked are relatively familiar to all of us. Often, the questions are puzzled voicings about curious kinds of behavior which on the surface don't seem to make much sense. For example:

1. Why did he stop taking his insulin when he knew he had to take it regularly to stay well, or even to stay alive?
2. Why did he go on an eating binge of all those forbidden foods when the doctors had told him over and over how important it was that he observe a strict diet if he wanted the hemodialysis to work?
3. Most kids know what drugs can do to you if you become addicted. Why did the kid take a chance on getting hooked?
4. Why does a person pop phencyclidine (PCP) pills when they're known to be completely unpredictable and might make him violent enough to injure or kill someone?
5. Why does an alcoholic deliberately stop his Antabuse so that he can go on another binge when he knows from bitter experience the pain and depression that follows?
6. Why did he drive so fast on the curving mountain roads when he had known for the last three months how bad his brakes were?

1

7. Why would anyone step out of an airplane and deliberately delay opening his parachute, bringing the margin of safety between life or death down to a fraction of a second?
8. Why take any unnecessary risks?

These are questions about certain actions within areas we all engage in—eating, taking medication, social drinking, social gambling, driving, and risk-taking sports. They refer to certain feelings we have all experienced—excitement, depression, anger, and the-hell-with-it, I-don't-give-a-damn attitudes. They are forms of behavior in which there is neither intention nor awareness of any suicidal outcome. However, heretofore, these feelings and kinds of behavior have not been investigated from the point of view of indirect self-destruction. This volume explores their implications for understanding of both acceptable and harmful behaviors. On the one hand, by their very familiarity and frequency of occurrence they must merge into the normal, acceptable end of the continuum of behavior. On the other hand, if they can be so self-destructive or self-injurious, they must merge into the pathological end of the continuum represented by overt suicidal activity. In other words, these indirectly self-destructive phenomena may well fill the gap between the two ends of the continuum; and increasing our knowledge of their characteristics may contribute much to our understanding of the broader spectrum of man's functioning.

Consider just a few of the possible areas in which increased knowledge of this field might have impact. Addictive behavior, such as drug and alcohol abuse, has been considered a (slower) substitute for overt suicide. Indeed, it was the awareness by Dr. Dan Lettieri (Chief, Psychosocial Branch, Division of Research, National Institute on Drug Abuse) of this view of drug addiction which led to the decision to compile a book representing the state of the art. It is the first time original writings on the relationship between the many forms of addictive behavior and indirect self-destructive activity have been gathered in one place. Will the greater focus on and the intensive exploration of the risk-taking, depression-averting, excitement-seeking, present-oriented, denial-mediated qualities characterizing both drug abuse and indirect suicidal behavior help in our attempts to control and to manage addiction? Perhaps. If not in control and management there may at least be benefits obtained through early identification of potential cases.

Increased understanding of the role of indirect self-destructive behavior (ISDB) in the physical illnesses is also of great potential value. Noncompliance has been identified as a significant problem in medicine for many years. But noncompliance might well be just another form of ISDB, behavior counter to the patient's own best interests and best health. The occurrence of ISDB among people with various psychosomatic illnesses, in which the role of the individual in the condition and progress of his illness has long been recognized as a major factor, frequently has a markedly negative effect on the quality of the wards which treat such illnesses. The flouting of ward rules and the disregard of medical regimen by the patient have often been interpreted by the staff as personally directed. Anger toward and rejection of the patient have been predictable reactions. It might help relieve the staff's feelings of frustration and circumvent their anger if they learned that the patient's behavior is far more likely to be self-directed and an expression of the patient's character and individual dynamics.

If noncompliance and indirect self-destructive behavior is as pervasive as it seems, this might have implications for a society where national health insurance is close to implementation. Should insurance cover people with obvious ISDB when they require medical treatment which might involve extensive hospital and staff expense? Should insurance (drawn from taxes you and I pay) cover behavior which seems "deliberately" gauged to make an illness worse? What should be the viewpoint of both national health and private insurance carriers toward high-risk sports when the risk accepted goes beyond that deemed reasonable and results in injury? Or toward criminal behavior where potential damage to the person becomes actual? These questions make interesting topics for debate.

Another reason for a focused look at indirect self-destructive behavior is that its study might add greatly to our knowledge of overt suicidal activity and therefore assist in our efforts at identification and prevention. The more we learn about the former, the better equipped we should be to treat the latter. For example, we learn from some of the contributors that depression is probably the most significant dynamic in ISDB. Depression has also been identified as the most prevalent and most profound dynamic in overt SDB. Some authors have also conceptualized the ISDB as a substitute activity for direct suicidal tendencies. If depression is a dynamic common to both, but personality characteristics determine whether the resolution of such feelings come out as indirect or direct SDB, it is important to identify those personality features and environmental circumstances which lead in either direction. We also know that substitutes frequently do not work, so that knowledge of a substitute being used alerts us to a heightened potential for more direct acting out.

SUGGESTIONS FOR THE
CONTRIBUTORS_____

The chapters in this volume are original writings. Each contributor was asked to prepare a chapter because he or she was identified through his/her publications as an expert in a particular field. Most had not, however, previously considered their area in its relationship to indirect self-destructive behaviors. Each was asked to organize material around that central theme and was provided with questions and identified areas to cover. The suggestions follow:

1. *Definition*
   (a) Define the behavior within your area which might be indirectly self-destructive.
   (b) What specific actions make the behavior *indirectly suicidal*?
   (c) What is society's attitude toward the behavior area in general? Toward the indirectly self-destructive behavior, if it is different?
   (d) What are the reactions of specific groups or individuals: family, friends, hospitals, personnel, therapist, significant other, etc.?
   (e) Are there demographic characteristics: age, sex, religion, nationality, ethnicity, marital status, etc., which characterize the ISDB?
   (f) Location—does the behavior generally occur in one place, or everywhere?
2. *Characteristics*
   (a) Symptoms
   Physical, neglect of illness; potential physical harm, etc.
   Cognitive, impact on reasoning and thinking ability.
   Significant affects found pre, during, or post activity.
   (b) Dynamics
   Motivation—why does the subject use this particular behavior (conscious or unconscious)?
   (c) Futurity
   Attitude toward, feelings about the future.
   (d) Temporal aspects
   Any characteristic features of pre, during, and post periods?
   Any particular stimuli which serve to initiate the behavior?
   Any results sought after which are reasons for the behavior?
   (e) Coping mechanisms
   Are there any defensive or coping mechanisms which characterize the users of the behavior?
   (f) Communication aspects

Is it purposive behavior? To whom is the communication addressed?

(g) Relationships

Are there interactions with others?

(h) Risk-taking, excitement-seeking

What is the role played by the element of risk?

(i) Personality

Are there any particular personality characteristics? Are there any personality measurements to report?

3. *Relationship of behavior* to overt self-destructive behavior—similarities, differences—and to normal behavior.

4. *Notes*

5. *Bibliography* of additional reading material

OVERVIEW _____

The rest of this book is organized into seven sections. In the first section, on theory and concepts, the introductory chapter by Farberow offers a schema for classifying various conditions in which indirect self-destructive behavior is found. It is a descriptive, empirically based schema which classifies the listed conditions according to actual or probable impact the behaviors have or will have upon the body or self when there is or is not a prior physical illness. The conditions in which ISDB occurs have been selected on the basis of clinical experience, literature, and early research. Although the schema may help in defining ISDB, its parameters, characteristics, and the most useful model to describe it are yet to be determined. A primary concern is whether and how ISDB differs from direct or overt suicidal activity (DSDB). Comparisons of groups showing each type of behavior permits the identification of a number of variables within which striking differences and similarities appear.

The next three chapters in the section delve into the psychodynamics involved. Litman examines the motivations and concludes that ISDB is one kind of defense used to ward off the devastating, pervasive pain of depression. Lack of self-esteem and intense feelings of helplessness and hopelessness are the most common factors leading to depression. ISDB has a positive value in defending against the depression when it substitutes behaviors which enhance self-esteem.

Achté examines the concept of ISDB and its role in most of the major psychiatric conditions and physical conditions, such as masochism, asceticism, psychosomatic illnesses, and drug and alcohol abuse. Some of these had long been recognized as self-injurious and self-defeating but had not been incorporated into the comprehensive schema provided by the concept of ISDB. Achté arrives at the same conclusion as Litman, that ISDB is developed as a defensive mechanism primarily to handle the severe impact of depression on the psyche. Achté also incorporates other dynamics into his schema, especially anxiety and fear of dependency.

Filstead, theorizing from the viewpoint of sociology, reaches very similar conclusions as a result of his study of hyperobese patients applying for a bypass operation. Instead of depression, he calls the feeling despair; but despair is actually the state of mind which produces the depression. Despair means "no hope," and hopelessness is one of the legs of the basic triad—hopeless, helpless, and worthless—which leads to self-destructive behavior. Filstead introduces an additional element when he adds that hyperobese people in their efforts to lose weight and remain thin also have to struggle with a deeper, apparently immodifiable problem. The ISDB helps to suppress the fact of an underlying problem, but then the person has to be made aware that the ISDB itself can become a problem.

The second section looks at ISDB in an area in which it is relatively easily identified, that is, a physical illness which is used against the self. Persons with long-term chronic illnesses have a number of choices as to how they will live their lives. Often the illness requires a radical change in a cherished self-concept, making it difficult to accept a new self-image which now means limited activity, markedly increased dependency, change in life-style, and loss of such things as occupation, hobbies, and sexual interaction. To many, these choices are filled with feelings of anger and bitterness. In some illnesses the degree of change required is not so great, as in diabetes where control is at least moderately easy to establish and physical activities need not be limited. In other illnesses, such as renal failure involving hemodialysis, or the spinal cord injuries, the required amount of change is radical.

As expected, depression and anger are the predominant emotions in these patients, and ISDB clearly serves as a means of rebellion and reestablishment of feelings of control over one's own life. These reactions and motivations appear in all the groups described in this section: Farberow's diabetic and Buerger's disease patients, Goldstein's hemodialysis patients, Nehemkis and Groot's spinal cord injury (SCI) patients, and Ginsparg's coronary patients. The hemodialysis and SCI patients make extensive use of one of the most primitive (and effective) mechanisms to adapt, denial. Their denial has to be massive, for it is difficult to deny the reality of a wheelchair, or of a pulsing dialysis apparatus three times a week. The diabetics and the heart patients also use denial, but more effectively, for the range of tolerance for their disregard of physical health requirements is much greater.

As Nehemkis and Groot point out, it is actually easier for the SCI patient not to be a good patient. He has to work at it if he is to survive and be comfortable. Ginsparg emphasizes the significant element in the progress of the illness of the person's own reaction to his illness. There may be a loss of basic trust in an environment which has suddenly become "hostile," and a loss of basic personal integrity because he no longer can take his body for granted. These are serious losses in the integration of man with his environment, a relationship which most healthy persons never question. Quality versus quantity of life becomes much more than a philosophical question in all of the illnesses described above.

The section entitled Drug Abuse and the one called Alcohol Abuse, Hyperobesity, and Cigarette Smoking represent areas in which the behaviors per se, when carried beyond certain limits, become both the ISDB and the condition. They are all pleasure-oriented, tension-reducing activities. It is the phrase "when carried beyond limits" which is the key, for all of these conditions, except for cigarette smoking, are activities engaged in by practically everyone in society. All require individual control over the degree to which they are practiced. Drugs and alcohol are beneficent when used in moderation. Society attempts to regulate their abuse or mis-use, but with greater or lesser success depending on the arbitrari-ness of the approach. Eating, a vital process, is left up to the medical world to regulate. There are no legal restrictions against overeating, but society exercises some control through dictation of what is phys-ically attractive and healthy. Cigarette smoking has only recently moved toward a level between drugs and alcohol and the level occupied by overeating. With its physical dangers confirmed, the government now assumes the obligation to intervene to the extent of requiring warnings about the dangers to health.

In the drug abuse section, Frederick points out how widespread drug-taking activity in the United States has become and concludes that the use of drugs for self-destructive purposes has been an al-most inevitable consequence. Drug dependency has spread throughout the community and large portions of our society survive the day by extensive use of pills and medications. The step from drug dependency to drug abuse is a small one and especially self-destructive when it involves drugs with unpredictable effects, such as phencyclidine (PCP) and lysergic acid diethylamide (LSD).

Ungerleider examines the relationship between violence and drug misuse and concludes that direct causal relations between ex-cessive drug intake and subsequent violence are very few. It is the amphetamines and PCP which have been found to be most directly related. With most of the other drugs, it is the life-style (crime and prostitution) required to support the habit which has a high potential for violence and so may be self-destructive.

The rise of suicide rates among adolescents and youth in the recent past and their possible relationship to the high level of drug abuse in this age group is examined in the next chapter, by Smart. He reviews the literature and finds solid data and careful methodology hard to come by, with consequent mixed results. It is probably not until drug abuse becomes heavy that the level of self-harm reaches a noteworthy stage.

Stanton and Coleman add another perspective to the understanding of young drug abusers by examining their behavior in the context of family dynamics. The contributors conclude that although the role may be personally self-destructive, it may also serve a significant purpose for the family. The young addict first becomes the scapegoat on whom the anger and disappointments of the family are vented and who is blamed for their problems. But because the family is felt to be more important than its individual members, the addict becomes the sacrifice, used to keep the family together. His own efforts to escape are ambivalent, for he gets some recognition in the attention he receives and reward for his willingness to fill this role. Such paradoxical forms of self-enhancement are not unfamiliar in other types of psychological problems.

In the section on alcohol abuse, hyperobesity, and cigarette smoking, forms of ISDB which have their sources in oral activity are discussed. Some of the dominant personality characteristics which emerge are already familiar, such as the focus on immediate gratification and the low level of frustration tolerance. Both Connelly in his chapter on alcoholism and Burns in her chapter on the female alcoholic point out that alcoholism is a self-generating ISDB in that drinking serves to manufacture excessive guilt, which then is escaped by further drinking. This process is more noticeable in women alcoholics, who are still censured more strongly for drinking than are males. Burns sees woman's role in society—still considerably more limited than man's, although currently undergoing much change—as a major cause of alcoholism in women. The affective reactions to second-class status lead to the familiar dynamic of depression and, in this instance, are seen as the means to forestall or to mitigate it.

But at least there is some measure of choice in drinking alcohol. It is possible to control not only the degree to which it is ingested, but whether or not it will ever be drunk at all. It is even possible to live without ever touching another drop again. The "foodaholic," however, does not have that choice. As Rowland points out, the hyperobese can never escape their addiction but must face it at least three times daily. They have to learn to live *with* the enemy, not *without* it. The motivations are the same in overeating as they are in the other addictions, that is, pleasure, release of tension, and avoidance of conflict and discomfort. The problem of overeating seems to grow autonomously, and the need for a "fix" of food can become as powerful and demanding as the need for a drink or a drug is for an alcoholic or a drug abuser.

Lichtenstein and Bernstein review their considerable experience in working with cigarette smokers and conclude that the concept of ISDB might not be the most useful framework within which cigarette smoking can be understood. They are correct in pointing out that the concept must be highly refined, the parameters identified, and its characteristics specified. The concept of ISDB is still new. Whether it will serve effectively as a model to bridge the gap between pathological and normal behavior is yet to be seen. Cigarette smoking is an interesting activity in which to observe the functioning of ISDB. Smoking obviously has a long-term, cumulative effect. It is systemic and affects many parts of the body. It has been identified as a major contributor to certain kinds of cancer and to respiratory and circulatory diseases. The surgeon general of this country has labeled it "possibly injurious to your health." Its attraction as one kind of social behavior and its strength as an addiction is attested to by the fact that smoking continues to increase, especially among the young, despite well-publicized warnings. It may well be, as Lichtenstein and Bernstein point out, that it is not until severe symptomatic health conditions occur, as in emphysema, heart disease, and Buerger's disease, that the view of smoking as an ISDB becomes more relevant. But it is also true that the relevance of ISDB does not appear for many of the other conditions discussed in this book, such as social drinking, gourmet eating, social gambling, and others, until overinvolvement has produced symptoms.

The next section discusses self-mutilation, automobile accidents, and gambling. These activities contain a high potential for severe physical injury and for serious damage to occupational, social, and mental functioning. Simpson writes about self-mutilation, which, on the face of it, seems more a direct than an indirect self-destructive action. However, we learn that dynamically it is much closer to the indirect forms of self-destructive behavior in its lack of lethal intent, its specialized meanings, its focus on excitement and pleasure. While self-mutilation may take many forms and may be inflicted on many parts of the body, the most familiar form is wrist-cutting, in which the act of cutting often serves the significant purpose of helping the person to regain contact with reality and to come out of a depersonalized state. Blood is often imbued with a special significance, a kind of visible evidence of a sacrificial act which the person must carry out, perhaps to expiate some overwhelming guilt. The pain experienced in the cutting becomes important, too, as indicated by a patient who described the need to transform her unbearable psychological torment into something physical. Once the pain became physical, it was manageable. Menninger has described this kind of behavior as substitutive and partially suicidal. By offering a part of oneself in a self-injurious act, it is not necessary to act out entirely and take (all of) one's life.

The automobile occupies a special place in social and personal functioning in our country. Its use ranges from highly personalized means of self-expression to uncritical acceptance as a part of everyday life. The automobile has been used as an instrument for direct self-destruction (in deliberate crashes into abutments or carbon monoxide poisonings), as a means for indirect self-destructive behavior (as in high-risk, careless driving in a poorly maintained car), and as a weapon of aggression (as when it is deliberately driven at a pedestrian or at another occupied car). Selzer's comments about the pervasiveness of unconscious factors in producing traffic accidents emphasizes the ISDB role that driving an automobile can assume. It is especially evident when the driving is combined with other ISDB, such as in driving while drunk, or when judgment lapses, coordination deteriorates, and risk of self-injury increases markedly.

A more socially recognized and acceptable form of high-risk activity is examined in the chapter by Kusyszyn on gambling. Here, the focus is on gambling with money, rather than with one's life or limbs, but the long-range effects of gambling can be extensive and highly destructive of self and family when uncontrolled. Kusyszyn points out the error in viewing all gambling as the same. There are many forms of gambling and many kinds of gamblers. He charts the variety of such forms and identifies the gambling which is ISDB, especially in classical compulsive gamblers, whose inability to control their activity leads to complete self- and family deterioration. If the gambling is self-actualizing, it can be positive and fulfilling, without hurting anyone. When the gambling provides no forms of self-growth or development and hurts others, it becomes highly destructive.

Criminal behavior as ISDB is considered in the next section. Three of the chapters look at this behavior from the point of view of the offenders, while the fourth examines the Good Samaritans who intervene in a criminal situation. A common theme emerges from the first three: Criminal activity has to be carefully evaluated before the label of ISDB is applied. As Toch points out with adult offenders, most crime actually does pay, and much criminal activity may be self-enhancing in terms of subculture pride, prestige, and power. In addition, it may be true that the members of some subcultures have few if any other options, if they are to survive. In other words, much of illegal behavior may be generated by society.

It is different for the delinquent offender described by Hendin. In the young delinquent the illegal activity is likely to be the intrapersonal reaction to the interpersonal dynamics of the family. By harming themselves, the delinquent youngsters have discovered a powerful weapon of revenge against the parents, who are mortified, disgraced, and stripped of their parental power. Hendin does not neglect society's role, however, and notes the contribution made by socioeconomic status and community values, especially in terms of the form and object of the acting out.

The practice of prostitution as an ISDB is explored by James, who finds that much of the behavior is essentially adaptive. James too includes society's contribution to the development of this occupation, such as the prostitute's early exposure to the subculture in which it was openly practiced, but emphasizes also the intrinsic rewards for the prostitute. In terms of social values it is one of the few areas where financial return for services is equitable and satisfying and also where a continuing sense of excitement can be experienced. Typically, other forms of ISDB are common, especially drug and alcohol use. Most intriguing is the examination of the relationship between the prostitute and her pimp, in which she is able to live out the traditional female role even though the circumstances seem reprehensible to "straight" society.

Probably one of the most unusual groups reported on in this volume is the group of interveners studied by Geis and Huston. Despite all the publicity about crimes committed under the windows of apartment houses or in a crowded street in which onlookers turned away or ignored the pleas of the victims for help, there are apparently some persons who respond to the situation with personal intervention, sometimes at known high risk of self and limb. California provides compensation for those who have suffered injury as a result of intervening. Such interveners often run very high risks, for the crimes frequently involve use of knives or guns. It is interesting that for many this was not the first time; they had intervened before in similar criminal situations. Geis and Huston do not find evidence of ISDB among this group, illustrating that not all high-risk activity need be considered negatively. Rather, high-risk behavior for these people is consistent with and affirms a sense of competence and a positive self-image.

The elements of excitement, challenge, mastery, and control which are repeatedly identified in many of the forms of ISDB discussed in this volume emerge as the most significant factors in high-risk sports. Society loves this area up to a point, says Klausner in his chapter describing stress-seeking by man and the importance it has in the functioning of society. But society is keenly aware of the dangers of such activities when uncontrolled. It therefore sets up constraints to define the limits of high-risk activities, beyond which such behavior becomes unacceptable and attains a level of indirectly self-destructive behavior. Society values stress-seeking behavior in terms of its lending excitement to life, increasing intensity of feelings, and stimulating exploration of the unknown and expansion of the new. Society becomes stagnant without change; it is only the rate of change which must be regulated.

Delk and Blau explore two of the more exciting high-risk sports, sport parachuting and scuba diving, in order to define the personality characteristics and feelings of those who choose such activities. It is interesting to note the addictive quality of the activities, the stress-producing, stress-reducing elements, and the personal sense of reward and pleasure. This individual gratification is then further supported by the identification with an elite group the members of which have shared the same experiences and from which is excluded the vast majority of the world.

PART ONE
THEORY AND CONCEPTS

1

INDIRECT SELF-DESTRUCTIVE BEHAVIOR
Classification and Characteristics

NORMAN L. FARBEROW

Self-destruction occurs in many ways, some obvious, some disguised, but always hastening, in one way or another, one's own death. Freud (1920/1955) declared that no man can realize his own death because he is unable to integrate the fact of his own nonexistence into his timeless fantasies of immortality. In another sense, Freud was accounting for the taboo aspect of death and man's apparent need to deny it by surrounding it with many forms of mysticism, rituals, and disguises. To accommodate the incontrovertible fact of an inescapable progression toward death from the moment of birth, he formulated the concept of the death instinct, describing it as a catabolic process which, most often operating unconsciously, exerted a variable influence in bringing about eventual termination. In its most obvious expression, the death instinct could be seen in the form of overt suicide, or direct self-destructive behavior (DSDB). Although Freud never discussed indirect self-destruction, he implied its existence in his hypothesis of a fluctuating valence which expressed itself in varying strength as time and situations changed. Karl A. Menninger (1938) developed the concept of the death instinct fully, postulating a state of balance between the opposing forces of the life and death instincts, a state that is constantly changing and which, under the influence of diverse patterns of guilt, aggression, and eroticism, may produce a number of self-injurious or self-limiting behaviors. Menninger's formulations in describing self-destructive behavior still apply, even though today many people do not subscribe to the death instinct as a motivating force behind such behavior.

The phenomenon of overt suicide, or direct self-destructive behavior, has been explored for many years. The suicide event at first

15

seemed to be clearly identifiable—a person was suicidal when he talked about suicide, attempted it, or succeeded in killing himself. The study of suicide, however, revealed it to be a complex event, involving much conceptual confusion about *behavior* (verbal or action); *time* (is, was, or will be self-destructive); *intention* (to die, to gamble with death, or not to die but to hurt self); *activity* (passive versus active self-inflicted injury or death); and other factors. Much past effort has been devoted to exploring and examining self-destructive behavior and to constructing a suitable nosology of its various manifestations.

One aspect of self-destructive behavior, though it was identified many years ago, has been especially troublesome in terms of classification. This behavior included what was often called "unconscious" suicidal tendencies because the actor seemed unaware that, or at least denied that, the actions were intended to destroy or injure self. In addition, the behavior did not seem to have any immediate effect upon the person and the results tended more to be long-term and cumulative in nature. This behavior has been called "indirect" self-destructive behavior (ISDB) to distinguish it from the more familiar overt or direct forms of suicide.

Actually, its presence was recognized many years ago by one of the pioneer investigators in the field, Emile Durkheim (1897/1951). In 1897, he said in his classic book, *Suicide*:

> Suicides do not form, as might be thought, a wholly distinct group, an isolated class of monstrous phenomena unrelated to other forms of conduct, but rather are related to them by a continuous series of intermediate causes. They are merely the exaggerated form of common practices . . . the result from similar states of mind, since they also entail mortal risks not known to the agent, and the prospect of these is no deterrent; the sole difference is a lesser chance of death. . . . All such facts form a sort of embryonic suicide, and though it is not methodologically sound to confuse them with complete and full suicide, their close relation to it must not be neglected. For suicide appears quite another matter once its unbroken connection is recognized with acts on the one hand of courage and devotion and on the other of imprudence and clear neglect. [pp. 45–46]

Besides Durkheim, other distinguished theorists have discussed the concept of indirect self-destruction. Menninger (1938) developed the concept to its fullest in postulating different degrees of expression in the interaction of the life and death instincts. One group of behaviors he termed "focal suicide," including in it self-mutilation, malingering, polysurgery, purposeful accidents, impotence and frigidity, chronic suicide (including asceticism and martyrdom), neurotic invalidism, alcohol addiction, drug addiction, antisocial behavior, psychosis, and organic suicide. Meerloo (1968) called the behavior "hidden suicide," Blachly (1973) coined the word "seduction," and Shneidman (1968) used the term "subintentioned death" to describe the death which results from behavior that the person did not consciously intend.

Stress-seeking behavior with its negative and positive potentialities also seems to play an important role in indirect self-destructive behavior, especially when the search for excitement and the degree of risk-taking begins to exceed the boundaries for safety, survival, and self-preservation. Stress-seeking in relation to ISDB may well have special significance, for risk-taking in its positive qualities has played a prominent role in the development of man in the form of mastering fear-provoking situations, facilitating resolutions of developmental conflicts, and fostering the drive for exploration and ambitious achievement. For example, Charles Darwin (1957) theorized and documented pervasive struggle and natural selection to account for evolutionary development. We have already referred to Freud's postulated struggle between Eros and Thanatos, and Otto Fenichel (1945) later analyzed the counterphobic attitude of seeking fear-provoking situations so that, by mastering them, more basic anxieties could be fended off. Erik Erikson (1968) hypothesized growth stages emerging from resolutions of developmental conflicts. D. E. Berlyne (1965) talked of "epistemic curiosity" which drove individuals to explore and change themselves in the process. In social areas, David McClelland et al. (1953) states that where there is an achievement need, there is often a risk-taker. Georg Simmel (1955) felt that conflict and cooperation are interwoven forms of sociation, alternating in priority to produce a war-peace rhythm.

To recapitulate, self-destruction takes many forms. In its most familiar form, we see the overt behavioral manifestations which result in death, injury, or pain consciously inflicted upon the self, or we hear the verbal warning that self-harm is intended or death is planned. The behavior is visible, and the effect is immediate. Indirect self-destructive behavior is distinguishable from direct self-destruction by at least two criteria, *time* and *awareness*. The effect is long-range and the behavior may span years; the person is usually unaware of or doesn't care about the effects of his behavior, nor does he consider himself a suicide.

DESCRIPTIVE CLASSIFICATION
OF ISDB _____

This chapter presents some of the thinking which has emerged from our continuing efforts to explore the dimensions of ISDB and its relationship to direct self-destructive behavior (DSDB). The results of three studies, one of uncooperative diabetics, the second of uncooperative Buerger's disease patients (presented elsewhere in this volume), and the third of ISDB among elderly chronically ill, have been used to begin the delineation of the concept of ISDB and to describe some of the similarities and differences between direct and indirect self-destructive behavior. First, however, it may be useful to present a descriptive framework within which the various forms of indirect self-destructive behavior can be classified, on the basis of the interaction of physical condition (prior presence or absence) and primary effect (on body or person). No claim is made that the classification is exhaustive or complete. It should also be understood that not everyone with the conditions noted is by definition self-destructive, either indirectly or directly. (See Table 1.)

The intersection of the rows and columns produces four main groups. The first group consists of those potential ISDBs in which a physical illness is already present and the person uses it against himself by making it or other physical conditions worse, resulting in serious injury or damage to his body. Examples include the exacerbation of psychosomatic conditions, diabetes, Buerger's disease, Raynaud's disease, cardiorespiratory illnesses, hypertension, physical debilities of the elderly, neurasthenia, hypochondria, invalidism, polysurgery, and malingering. Polysurgery and malingering are included in this category because they are conditions in which the person acts as if there were a prior illness that required surgery and then uses it against himself.

In the same row the second group includes prior physical conditions, generally loss of some part or function of the body, which require an extensive change in self-image or self-concept. In these cases, ISDB is directed primarily against the self rather than against the physical body. Examples of conditions in this group include loss of limb, loss of mobility, and loss of identity among women with mastectomy and among men with castration. Sensory loss, especially vision and hearing, are included in this classification because they too require a change in self-concept and functioning which sometimes is extremely difficult to accept.

The third and fourth groups in the second row comprise those activities in which there is no prior physical condition. These are further divided into two subgroups, one where the injury or damage may have already occurred to the body from self-initiated activities,

TABLE 1 *Indirect Self-Destructive Behavior*

Prior physical condition	Primary effect on	
	Body	Person
Present Prior physical condition exists: individual's activity increases actual or potential damage.	Psychosomatic: Asthma, ulcer, colitis, dermatitis, etc. Diabetes Buerger's, Raynaud's diseases Cardiorespiratory diseases Hypertension Physical debilities of elderly Invalidism Polysurgery Neurasthenia Hypochondria Malingering	Loss of body part or function: Limb (accident) Mobility (stroke, aging) Mastectomy sequelae Sensory loss (blindness, deafness)
Absent No prior physical condition exists; actual or potential damage may result from activity.	*Actual*	
	Hyperobesity Smoking Drug addiction Alcoholism Self-mutilation	Severe sexual disorders Asceticism
	Potential	
	Violent crime; rioting Assassination Repeated accidents; traffic, industrial	Nonviolent crime, delinquency Compulsive gambling
	Stress-seeking, risk-taking	
	Mountain climbing Sports parachuting or skydiving Scuba diving Hang gliding	Games of risk, chance
	Circus artists; trapeze performers Stuntmen Motorcycle, boat and auto racing Violent contact sports (boxing)	Stock market speculation

such as hyperobesity, smoking, drug and alcohol addiction, and self-mutilation; or to the person, such as severe sexual disorders and asceticism; and the second subgroup where the injury or damage is potential to the body, such as violent crime, rioting, assassination, and repeated traffic or industrial accidents; or to the person, as in nonviolent crime, delinquency, and compulsive gambling.

The fifth and sixth groups of activities included in the table are derived from the variable of excitement, which seems to be important to the general population for its positive qualities as well as to ISDB users for its negative experiences. Examples of such stress-seeking, risk-taking activities and occupations include mountain climbing, sports parachuting, scuba diving, hang gliding, circus or stunt performing, motorcycle, boat, or auto racing, violent contact sports, games of risk or chance, and stock market speculation.

At this point, the chart should not be considered any more than a tentative classification of a wide range of conditions and activities which could involve ISDB. Improved categorizations and greater refinement will undoubtedly emerge as other studies are conducted, for example, classifications emphasizing dynamics or functional characteristics (see Litman, Achté, and Filstead, this volume). All the behaviors except the risk-taking ones would generally receive consensus as self-injurious, life-shortening, and self-defeating. The risk-taking behaviors on the other hand, while containing the possibility of instant death or severe injury, also promise excitement, challenge, and stimulation, and are usually entered into with care, preparation, and extensive training. They have been included as ISDBs, however, because they are dangerous and involve a conscious gamble with one's life and limb. The predominant motives seem to be the seeking of excitement and mastery. These qualities, however, in varying degrees and patterns, are also present in most of the other activities. The Russian roulette player whose trigger falls on an empty chamber, the diabetic who chances fatal coma when he stops taking his insulin, the drug addict who thrills at the "rush" of the large dose—all experience the same qualitative feelings. In other words, they are different in degree and relationship, not in kind, and society calls some positive and laudable, others negative and undesirable.

RELATIONSHIP BETWEEN DIRECT AND INDIRECT SUICIDAL BEHAVIOR

From the studies (of diabetics, Buerger's disease, and chronically elderly ill) conducted so far it is now possible to compare the characteristics of direct and indirect self-destructive behavior, noting similarities and differences. We recognize that there is great diversity among overtly suicidal persons, just as there is among ISDB users, and that, in drawing comparisons, we are using modal pictures of each. Table 2 summarizes the characteristics on which they may be compared.

SYMPTOMS. The physical impact of ISDB is most often long-term and frequently permanent so that it is only the end results

TABLE 2   Comparison of Direct and Indirect Self-Destructive Behaviors (Diabetes, Buerger's Disease, Elderly Chronically Ill)

Character-istics	Direct	Indirect
Symptoms Physical and behavioral	Eating, sleeping disorders; fatigability; agitation; listlessness; apathy; weight loss or gain; crying spells; decreased sexual libido; impotence/frigidity.	Physical symptoms of neglect of physical illness, e.g. diabetic acidosis, insulin coma, circulatory pain; gangrene; excessive weight loss or gain; malnutrition; amputation.
Cognitive	Inability to concentrate; decreased mental productivity; poor problem-solving; inability to see alternatives; dichotomous thinking.	No marked changes in cognitive functioning. Shallow, superficial reasoning.
Affects	Depression, anger, guilt, anxiety, excessive mood swings.	No characteristic affects; reactions are subclinical.
Dynamics	Reactions to feelings of severe loss with feelings of worthlessness, inadequacy; poor self-concept; low or no feelings of mastery or control; feeling helpless and hopeless about possibility of change, adding to feeling of worthlessness or inadequacy; overwhelming feelings of psychological pain and exhaustion; desire to obtain surcease, change others' behavior or attitudes; invested in achievement, production, success, recognition.	Motivation is most often gratification from present pleasures; oriented toward self, not others; strong ability for denial; poor social adjustment; many feelings of personal losses; moderate feelings of inadequacy; moderate sense of power and control; actions do not occur under conditions of great stress, more when life seems smooth; little investment in achievement or production.
Futurity	Low sense of futurity, especially under stress; "no" future is the result of someone depriving them.	No future orientation; little maturity, capability for delay; hedonism; present gratification important.
Temporal	Reacting to present stress and/or precipitating cause; results of behavior immediate; short-term impact.	No immediate precipitating stress; results of behavior delayed, cumulative; long-term impact.
Risk-taking, excitement-seeking	Gambling is on all or none basis; ordeal quality—if survive, deserve to live.	Excitement-seeking for sake of stimulation; related to present orientation; adds meaning to existence; attraction of gambling is in the process not the outcome.
Coping mechanisms	Constriction; regression; projection.	Denial; suppression; regression; narcissism.

TABLE 2 (Continued)

Character-istics	Direct	Indirect
Communica-tion	Most behavior is a com-munication; message contains all degrees of conscious and unconscious substantive con-tent, affectual and cognitive, addressed to a person, group, or society.	Most behavior contains no message, directed to someone, group, or society. At most, inferred message is lack of sensitivity or regard for others.
Relation-ships	Generally intense, meaning-ful; dependency; source of self-worth; "lends meaning to life."	Casual; generally uninvested; source of gratification, not confirmation of self-worth; self-centered; detached.

which are clearly apparent. By that time they may appear as severe physical difficulties which have affected the whole body, or systems within the body, such as metabolism and circulation, or parts of the body, such as intestines and skin, or functions of the body, such as mobility and other aspects. Even amputations are not infrequent. The directly self-destructive patient, on the other hand, evidences more or less transient physical symptoms, especially the symptoms of depression, such as eating and sleeping disorders, fatigability, agitation, listlessness, apathy, weight loss or gain, crying spells, and decreased sexual libido. All or most of these conditions disappear when the suicidal crisis is passed.

Cognitively, ISDB patients show no marked changes in their functioning in relation to their self-destructive activity, probably reflective of the lack of any immediate stress. Their reasoning, for the most part, tends to be shallow and superficial. Directly self-destructive people, however, generally show poor cognitive func-tioning as a result of a heightened emotional state, which brings with it decreased mental productivity, inability to concentrate, and difficulty in problem solving. Thinking frequently becomes dichotomized and patients are unable to contemplate reasonable alternatives. They may complain that their thought processes are slowed down.

ISDB patients do not seem to be responding with specific affects to any immediate stimulus. They do not appear emotionally dis-turbed and, in some instances, may even describe feeling good and having a general sense of euphoria. DSD people, in contrast, most often display the dominant affects of depression, either apathy and withdrawal or agitation. In addition, they may express strong feelings of anger, guilt, and heightened anxiety. Mood swings are excessive and the emotional responses are often unpredictable.

DYNAMICS. A sense of great loss is found much more frequently in overtly self-destructive patients, a feeling which serves to reaffirm basic feelings of inadequacy and worthlessness. They gradually become more helpless in their ability to obtain verification of feelings of self-worth, and hopeless that their present painful situation will change. The familiar triad of premonitory feelings, worthlessness, helplessness, and hopelessness, converge to block their future and to consign them to a pain-filled present. They experience overwhelming feelings of psychological and physical exhaustion. It is in response to these feelings that the directly self-destructive person often acts out, looking either for a way in which to manipulate or change others' behaviors and attitudes or for a desperate means of surcease or escape.

ISDB people, on the other hand, do not profess any feelings of worthlessness or helplessness. Their behavior does not occur in conditions of stress, as with the overtly suicidal person, but surprisingly seems to occur more often when life is smooth and functioning well. Their behavior gives them a moderate sense of power and control which helps to overcome many of their feelings of inadequacy. Motivation is directed toward obtaining pleasure from present behavior. Actions are oriented mostly toward the self, not toward others, so that they appear self-centered and narcissistic. They are able to maintain this behavior on the basis of a strong ability for denial.

FUTURITY. Both direct and indirect self-destructive behavior patients have a low sense of futurity. The reasons for this, however, are significantly different for the two groups. When not under pressure or stress, directly self-destructive people are interested in a future which contains success and recognition. By attaining these goals, they are able to prove their own worth and obtain love. The lack of a future found in overtly suicidal persons is the direct result of someone else's action through rejection or abandonment, depriving them of a future they had counted on. With resultant feelings of worthlessness heightened, these persons see no use in struggling further to merit love.

ISDB people, however, have little investment in the future because they are so much interested in the pleasures of the present and the gratifications they can receive from the here-and-now. They are intolerant of the delays and postponements necessary to achieve in the future; they are not really ambitious, although they may talk in grandiose terms.

TEMPORAL ASPECTS. ISDB users generally fail to indicate any specific precipitating stress for their actions, making their behavior seem impulsive and difficult to understand. Usually, the effects of their behavior are small and cumulative, so that any one indirect self-destructive activity of itself does not seem to be significant. However, the long-term impact is extensive in terms of physical condition and/or status or position.

Directly suicidal persons, on the other hand, are generally responding to some immediate stress, most often loss or threatened loss, and the results of their behavior are seen in immediate, direct injury or death.

RISK-TAKING, EXCITEMENT-SEEKING. Closely related to the low sense of futurity described above for the indirectly self-destructive person is the need for and pleasure derived from the excitement of the present. It is as if the stimulation of the activity is sufficient reason for the activity and provides meaning to what otherwise feels like a dull and boring life. The end result is little considered, allowing the user to concentrate on the stimulation of the process.

Overtly self-destructive people gamble too, but with much more focus on the end result, that is, life or death. They abdicate the right to make their own decisions and leave their survival to luck or fate. The excitement is in the unknown outcome, not the process. "Winning" is celebrated with a sense of mastery over death if they survive and over their "significant others" if the self-destructive behavior forces the latter to change.

COPING MECHANISMS. Directly self-destructive persons are generally forced by the storm of their feelings into regressive behavior, which may become immature and passively aggressive. Constriction appears as they focus in on their loss; projection is used when the feelings become unbearable.

Indirectly self-destructive persons cope mainly through denial, blocking out or suppressing what is uncomfortable. They may regress in their self-centered, narcissistic efforts to obtain excitement or pleasure, but their level of maturity is generally low to start with.

COMMUNICATION. The behavior of indirectly self-destructive people contains no message to others, except, perhaps, the message inferred from the evident self-involvement or the pronounced lack of sensitivity and regard for others.

Directly self-destructive people, however, are generally using their actions to declare in loud, clear, unmistakable terms to a person, group, or society their own feelings of hurt and despair, anger and guilt.

RELATIONSHIPS. Indirectly self-destructive people, because they are so self-concerned, have generally been unable to invest much of themselves in a relationship with significant others. They are often loners and have few sources of external support.

The directly self-destructive person is more often concerned with a significant other, and the loss of such a person is felt as utter catastrophe. A dependent relationship is extremely important and the dependency is likely to be intense, for often the DSDB person gains confirmation for existence through the relationship.

SOCIETY AND INDIRECT SELF-DESTRUCTIVE BEHAVIOR _____

Society's attitudes toward indirect and direct self-destructive behavior is another variable on which the two groups might have been compared. It is striking to note that, within the Occidental culture, a number of similar reactions may be delineated, although actually they occur for different reasons. For example, society strongly condemns indirect self-destructive behavior when it appears as violent crime or assassination; overt self-destructive behavior is also often condemned because it is considered self-murder, or sin, or a cowardly and gutless evasion of life. ISDB evokes feelings of anger, frustration, and resentment in others when a person flouts his medical regimen, as if derogating the physician, medical science, and the worth of all that has been done for him. DSDB arouses some of the same feelings, but with guilt and anxiety added. These feelings often wind up, also, as the residue in many survivors of suicides. They are the result of feeling rejected and abandoned, of frustration because further efforts are no longer possible, and of guilt from wondering if more could have been done.

Some ISDB produces sympathy, as in those cases of physical loss of limb, part, sense, mobility, or function of the body. There is at least an effort in society toward tolerance of the behavior of the incapacitated aged, the severely crippled, or the blind or deaf, although the tolerance often verges on condescension. In direct suicidal behavior it is not until we get to the terminally ill that we find more willingness to accept self-destructive actions.

On the other hand, society has admired, glorified, and sometimes even made national heroes of its members who engage in high risk-taking, stress-seeking activities. Crowds gather to watch and applaud the death-defying daredevils in motorcycle, boat, and auto races, circus trapeze and high-wire performances. Mountain climbers and explorers are honored; successful stock market speculation leads to invitations to the financial "wizard" to sit on other industry boards. Society has very few direct suicides which it can so honor, except for those occurring under special conditions such as war (where a man might throw himself on a grenade to save his buddies or volunteer for a suicide mission) or in disasters (where a parent might sacrifice his life to save that of his child). Religious sacrifices, such as dying for the sake of one's faith, or traditional suicide, like the captain going down with his ship, are outmoded and no longer expected and might be viewed today with amusement.

It is in the intervention area that the greatest differences in society's attitude toward indirect and direct self-destructive behavior appears. Societal prerogatives and individual rights clash in this area. Society assumes the right to intervene in an overt suicide attempt, presuming that the individual's capacity to think clearly and to make rational judgments has been impaired and that society's claim to that person's talents and their products is greater than the right of the individual to do with his life as he wishes. In indirect suicide, society does not presume that thinking and judgment have been impaired. As a consequence, it does not intervene while the person wastes his health, his talents, his position, and his life. It's as if these fall within the important area of the rights of the individual, rights which society treasures despite the fact that the price is sometimes inordinately high.

REFERENCES ————————————————————————————————

Berlyne, D. E. *Structure and Direction in Thinking.* New York: Wiley, 1965.

Blachly, Paul H. *Seduction: A Conceptual Model in the Drug Dependencies and Other Contagious Ills.* Springfield, Ill.: Thomas, 1973.

Darwin, Charles R. In Marston Bates and Philip S. Humphrey, *The Darwin Reader.* London: Macmillan, 1957.

Durkheim, Emile. *Suicide.* Glencoe, Ill.: Free Press, 1951. (Originally published, 1897.)

Erikson, Erik H. *Identity: Youth and Crisis.* New York: Norton, 1968.

Fenichel, Otto. *The Psychoanalytic Theory of Neurosis.* New York: Norton, 1945.

Freud, Sigmund. Beyond the pleasure principle. *Standard Edition,* 18. London: Hogarth, 1955. (Originally published, 1920.)

McClelland, David C., Atkinson, John W., Clark, Russell A., and Lowell, Edgar L. *The Achievement Motive.* New York: Appleton-Century-Crofts, 1953.

Meerloo, Joost A. M. Hidden suicide. In H. L. P. Resnik, ed., *Suicidal Behaviors and Management.* Boston: Little, Brown, 1968.

Menninger, Karl A. *Man against Himself.* New York: Harcourt, Brace, 1938.

Shneidman, Edwin S. Orientations toward death: A vital aspect of the study of lives. In H. L. P. Resnik, ed., *Suicidal Behaviors and Management.* Boston: Little, Brown, 1968.

Simmel, Georg. *Conflict and the Web of Group Affiliations.* Glencoe, Ill.: Free Press, 1955.

2

PSYCHODYNAMICS OF INDIRECT SELF-DESTRUCTIVE BEHAVIOR

ROBERT E. LITMAN

Self-destructive behavior injures one's health, hastens one's own death, or increases the probability of bodily injury and premature death. The distinction between direct and indirect self-destructive behavior depends on what the person has in mind as a goal of the behavior. When the primary, conscious goal is self-injury, the term direct self-destructive behavior (DSDB) is accurate. Suicide is the extreme of direct self-destructive behavior. Indirect self-destructive behavior (ISDB) can be defined as that self-destructive behavior where self-injury is not the primary conscious goal but, instead, is an undesired effect. Some examples of ISDB include drug abuse, alcoholism, cigarette smoking, reckless driving, masochistic sexual perversions, noncompliance with medical treatment programs, and, in a broader sense, failure to take optimal care of one's own health.

The concept of indirect self-destructive behavior is broad. It includes relatively harmless errors, self-punishment, and minor risks that merge on a continuum of rising danger with more serious injuries and, finally, death as the outcome.

This chapter concerns the psychodynamics of persons who are self-negligent, self-careless, and on their way to partial or complete self-destruction. In contrast with directly self-destructive persons who consciously seek to injure or kill themselves, victims of indirect self-destructive behavior would probably admit responsibility without admitting intention. The victim might say, "I admit I played a part in causing my death (by automobile accident, lung cancer, fatal asphyxiation, cirrhosis of the liver, drug overdose, diabetic coma), but that outcome was not the goal of my behavior; rather, it was an unfortunate side effect. I was careless or thoughtless, but I enjoyed myself. I took risks and made some mistakes and had some bad luck, but I did not intentionally seek to injure myself or hasten my death."

Whereas direct self-destructive behavior is usually symptomatic of a person in great psychological stress, indirect self-destructive behavior occurs in persons who typically do not show acute stress. ISDB is a life-style, a character trait, a habit. Often, indirect self-destructive behavior seems to be psychologically helpful for a person's well-being, since the behaviors are coping mechanisms over short periods of time; eventually, however, the behaviors tend to hasten disability and death. Value judgments and ethical considerations are involved, because the medical care eventually required to treat the results of indirect self-destructive behavior can significantly increase the health care costs borne by everyone through medical insurance and taxes (Knowles, 1977).

The central thesis of this chapter is: indirect self-destructive behavior (ISDB) is a part of the repertoire of all of us, and is, in fact, ubiquitous. Indirect self-destructive behavior becomes dangerous and life-threatening when it is repetitive and habitual. Life-threatening, chronic ISDB patterns of behavior are usually developed in an effort to defend against or cope with mental pain which threatens to result in depression. Therefore, this chapter will deal primarily with the psychodynamics of depressive illness and of the defenses and coping mechanisms through which people attempt to avoid the pain of depressive illness.

ISDB IN EVERYDAY LIFE_____

From the standpoint of danger and lethality, ISDBs constitute a continuum. At one extreme is death, and at the other are the usually harmless forms of indirect self-destructive behavior in everyday life. I refer to ordinary mistakes, errors, minor accidents, bungled actions, slips of speech, and forgetting that all of us often experience. For these occurrences, Sigmund Freud (1901/1960) confidently offered a set of explanations which everyone could verify for themselves. In my opinion, it was his classic monograph *The Psychopathology of Everyday Life* which more than any other of his works was responsible for the general acceptance of psychoanalysis. Freud perpetually revised this classic of psychology throughout his life, and it has been translated into more than forty languages.

The first example from the book seems especially appropriate for the purposes of this chapter, since it concerns self-destructive behavior. While on vacation in Italy, in conversation with a traveling companion, Freud could not remember the name of the Italian painter Signorelli, and instead, two other names came into his mind; but he knew these replacements were incorrect. Freud's inability to recall the name correctly was a source of dissatisfaction and tension. Finally, someone else produced the correct name; Freud recognized it immediately, and he tried to understand the incident through self-analysis. Several trains of association led Freud from the name Signorelli to certain quite unpleasant recollections which, he realized, he had unconsciously tried to forget. One set of associations and memories involved a patient who had committed suicide, the news only recently having reached Freud. He realized that he had repressed the memory of the patient's suicide, but along with this unpleasant memory, the name Signorelli was dragged into repression as well. Throughout the rest of the book, Freud provided analytic demonstration after demonstration that slips of the tongue, misreadings, slips of the pen, the forgetting of instructions, bungled acts, and certain accidents—all these too—represent: (1) an effort to repress and forget some painful memory or thought; and (2) an effort to substitute something else for what was repressed. Usually the substitution contains disguised elements of the original painful memory or thought.

We call such occurrences—for example, the forgetting of a name or an appointment—"symptomatic" behavior. We note that people in conflict or under stress are more inclined toward symptomatic behavior than they are at other times. If the conflict is transient, the symptomatic ISDB usually is not serious enough to be life threatening, but, instead, the mistakes and bungled actions cause only minor or symbolic damage. The person experiences this behavior as symptomatic and tries to overcome the discomfort and to reach a psychological equilibrium through solving a personal problem, or by other coping mechanisms.

When the psychological pain threatens to become depressive pain, the symptomatic behavior, which is an attempt to repress and substitute for the depressive feelings, usually also expresses some of the depressive feelings and thoughts. For example, a patient of mine would drive his car recklessly for several hours after he had had a fight with his wife. Reckless driving was counterdepressive behavior which helped him overcome a feeling of helplessness and loss of love and to regain a feeling of mastery over himself and his life. When I pointed out to him the very real life-threatening danger of his driving behavior, he admitted to me that at such times he consciously did not care much whether he lived or died. After several hours of reckless driving and the possibility of impact at high speed, the very fact that he had survived helped him feel better. Such a feeling of triumph and mastery through surviving dangerous ordeals is one of the essential psychodynamic features of masochism.

Persons in crisis often resort to indirect self-destructive behavior as a coping mechanism. They may get into fights, drink themselves insensible with alcohol, overeat, or overwork. They often become preoccupied and self-negligent. Persons who are indirectly self-destructive while going through a crisis of change or loss need support and sympathy, and a chance to communicate. Usually, they make a complete recovery.

When painful psychological states, especially depression, are chronic rather than transitory, and the need for repression is also chronic, the symbolic replacement or symbolic partial expression of the problem in its own turn becomes chronic and fixed. We speak of it no longer as a symptom formation or as crisis behavior, but as a character trait or character formation, or as a habit. It has become part of the self. The person has become an "addict" or "drunk driver." Once established as character traits or habits, the behavior acquires an autonomous status. Regardless of the original painful memories and feelings which provoked the habit as a defense, the loss of the habit or character trait later in life is felt as a loss of part of the self. This is a source of further pain, depression, bereavement, and mourning. Many forms of indirect self-destructive behavior that developed as coping mechanisms have often also been a source of temporary pleasure. To give up the ISDB is not an easy task, since it means the loss of pleasure and a reactivation of the painful depression.

CIGARETTE SMOKING IN ANALYTIC HOURS ————————————————————————————

My colleague, Norman Tabachnick, and I enlisted the cooperation of more than twenty psychoanalysts from the Southern California Psychoanalytic Institute in a series of investigations of a relatively minor ISDB, namely, cigarette smoking, in a relatively elegant setting, the private offices of psychoanalysts. Tabachnick and I conceptualized the psychoanalytic interview as an ongoing creative task, interrupted by the patient smoking a cigarette, an act which we felt was self-destructive to the patient and to the patient's psychoanalytic hour. It should be noted that Tabachnick and I are nonsmokers. The methodology of this investigation was quite thorough. Each analyst kept track of twenty consecutive patient hours on a standardized data sheet; two of the hours were tape-recorded and scored on the data sheet by colleagues as a reliability check; and the data were computerized and subjected to tests of statistical significance.

We had hypothesized that cigarette smoking during an analytic hour would be correlated with something: either with getting closer emotionally to the analyst, or farther away; with an increase in the flow of words, or a decrease in the flow of words; with an increase in the resistance, or a decrease of the resistance. However, when the data were first analyzed, no significant relationships emerged. We then separated the analysands into two groups, heavy smokers (over two packs a day) and light or moderate smokers (under two packs a day). This greatly clarified the data. For the heavy smokers, the time of lighting the first cigarette and finishing it, and so on, was stereotyped, repetitive, and unrelated either to content or to feelings. By contrast, for light or moderate smokers, there was a definite correlation between the lighting of cigarettes and change of the feeling tone in the hour. In essence, the light and moderate smokers tended to light a cigarette when they were emotionally distanced from the therapist, and this behavior helped them to feel closer. The process of lighting a cigarette was, for them, a symptomatic action. For the heavy smokers, lighting and smoking cigarettes was a habit, a character trait rather than a reaction.

Although I do not smoke myself, I am a permissive person and have in the past customarily allowed smokers to light up in my office and use the ashtrays. This study convinced me that smoking should be prohibited during analytic hours. Light and moderate smokers, I believe, should express their anxieties in words rather than in the action of lighting and smoking a cigarette; and the heavy smokers would be better off in therapy if they gave up the gyroscopic controlling, stabilizing effect of lighting four cigarettes during the hour, obscuring the underlying feelings of depression and distress by the smoke. However, patients will not give up their cigarettes, even for one hour, without a great deal of protest. When I pointed out to one woman that heavy smoking might shorten her life, she replied, "If you found out that fucking might shorten your life by four years, would you give up fucking?"

ONE-CAR AUTOMOBILE ACCIDENTS _____

Investigation of one-car traffic fatalities indicate that approximately 2 to 4 percent of the deaths represent direct self-destructive behavior and should be labeled as suicide. Presumably, many other one-car automobile mishaps, fatal and nonfatal, represent indirect self-destructive behavior. Again, Dr. Tabachnick and I, with a group of psychoanalytic colleagues, investigated the survivors of serious one-car accidents by means of structured interviews with the drivers in the hospital immediately following the event. Our original theory was that one-car accidents were symptomatic ISDB. More specifically, we hypothesized that in the period immediately prior to the accident, there would have been more stress in the drivers' life situations and personal relationships than usual, and more than those found in a control group consisting of appendectomy patients in the same hospital, matched for age and sex. However, we failed to prove the stress-crisis hypothesis.

The data, which were later published in a book (Tabachnick et al., 1973), show that the great majority of one-car traffic accidents occurred in the late evening or early morning hours, among drivers coming home drunk from parties or bars where they had spent the evening drinking. Moreover, it was found that coming home late drunk was part of their life-style. According to the drivers, they fell asleep, were suddenly startled by another car, or could not remember what had happened. These drivers agreed that to spend the night drinking in a bar and then drive home intoxicated was risky; but this behavior was part of their life-style, and they could see no other way to get home.

Compared to the control group, the injured drivers tended to be more independent psychologically, at least in their exterior behavior. They appeared not to turn to others for help or advice. During the interviews, they would become silent when asked about their personal problems. They liked to take care of things by themselves. They seldom went to doctors (whom they disliked). They did not seem to have a high incidence of mental illness, suffer from intense feelings of loss, or feel that they were incapable or incompetent, although they did have their share of frustrations, including not enough money, disappointment at work, and conflict with friends, relatives, and lovers. In connection with these frustrations, drinking was used as a restorative or a way of dealing with their unsatisfied dependency needs. It seemed to be characteristic of the accident-injured drivers we interviewed that they did not pay enough attention to their dependency needs. They had to appear strong and self-reliant. We believed that they used alcohol to find release and gratification, to avoid feeling bad, and to help feeling good. Furthermore, drinking in a bar satisfied the need for social contact. Thus, for them, the drinking pattern served a number of important needs. However, a risk factor accompanied this behavior—the danger the drinker incurs if he is also a driver. Being ourselves social drinkers who rarely, if ever, drive home drunk, we had to reconsider the relationship of risk-taking to values. The accident driver had found a coping mechanism. Drinking was part of a set of successful psychological defenses, with "successful" meaning that anxiety was well handled, and depressive pain was repressed. In return, the accident driver was quite willing to accept the additional risk which accompanied his drinking, just as the rest of us are ready to accept the risk of driving at all. The fact that other persons are also placed at risk was not considered by the drinking driver.

BONDAGE PERVERSION AND SEXUAL ASPHYXIATION _____

Most self-hanging deaths represent direct self-destructive behavior. However, several times a year in Los Angeles, and 50 to 100 times a year in the United States as a whole, asphyxiation deaths occur as an unintentional complication of partial asphyxiation for enhancement of sexual feelings (Resnik, 1972). There is a well-established culture and appropriate pornography for bondage perversion. In this type of masochism, practitioners are tied up, restricted, and restrained or imprisoned, often humiliated; such elements as cross-dressing, leather, rubber, and whips and other fetishes are involved, in order to induce sexual arousal. Since these expressions of masochism can cause death when something goes wrong with nooses or other devices, and they clearly involve pain and the threat of injury, they must be classified as ISDB.

I interviewed about a dozen bondage practitioners in order to find common elements, especially similar family circumstances and early experiences that might account for masochistic development (Litman, 1972). They all had in common lives of loneliness, isolation, and constriction. All had been depressed from time to time, and nearly all had been on the brink of suicide at one time or another. Yet the details of their sexual desires were somewhat different. Their life histories were quite varied, as were their choices of partners, their political viewpoints, and their occupations. Some of them had read about bondage in the pornographic literature, and it appealed to them. Others had been directly introduced by someone they had met. Some of them had invented bondage for themselves during masturbation. For all of them, however, the perversion was an effort to get some sexual pleasure in a world that seemed empty of loving people. The perversions functioned as defenses against depression and were an effort to hold their personalities together. As Avery Weisman (1967) put it, "As a result, out of the fragments of acts, sensations, organs, meanings and fantasies, they put together a way of life which condenses conflict into deviant sexual behavior" (p. 298).

There are some types of masochism in which defeat, pain, and submission are simulated pretexts for ultimate victory, pleasure, and dominance. Similarly, self-destruction combined with sexual perversion may be a state of being in which one is almost overcome by death. Is it possible to play a game skillfully, and at the same time court defeat? This is a dilemma for these patients.

Here again, behavior which from one point of view appears to be self-destructive appears also to have adaptive and survival values. Masochistic sexual practices seem to carry some pleasure in the short run and are a method for achieving a semblance of closeness across barriers of withdrawal, distrust, isolation, and aloneness.

ISDB IN DIABETIC PATIENTS

My colleague, Norman Farberow (1970), investigated the records of twenty-four diabetic patients with repeated hospital admissions for diabetic acidosis or insulin coma. These patients showed denial and negligence in their attitudes towards their illness. They were also highly dependent persons and openly demanded that they be taken care of. They considered their illness the hospital's responsibility, not theirs. The most frequent descriptive phrases for the group referred to passivity, dependency, hostility, and antisocial behavior. They were also inclined to be suspicious, impulsive, dissatisfied, and complaining; alcohol drinking was a problem for most. In contrast, a comparison group of controlled diabetics were seen as passive, dependent, anxious, and depressed, but also quieter, more cheerful, and pleasant. For the noncooperative group, the ISDB represented character traits rather than symptomatic responses. These particular patients not only refused to acknowledge the disease as part of their own self-image or their own responsibility, but they also seemed to derive a certain pleasure and satisfaction out of the experience of suddenly becoming critically ill and then surviving.

RISK AND STRESS

There is, of course, an inherent conflict in society and in each individual between a desire for peace and stability and an equally strong desire for alteration and change. When people have extra energy, they like to experience thrills and excitement and to take some risks. The stress and the relief from stress are felt as pleasurable. Much depends upon the person's preparation. Stress for which a person feels unprepared leads to regression and painful states of helplessness. Continuing painful helplessness may end in direct self-destructive behavior. On the other hand, stress for which the individual is prepared, and for which a constructive outcome is anticipated, can lead to growth and mastery and increased self-confidence, even though, over the long haul, such stress could be self-destructive. Such deliberately encountered stress situations not only include mountain climbing, hang gliding, scuba diving, and amusement park rides, but also some of the ISDBs I have discussed, such as drunk driving, bondage sexuality, and diabetic coma. Sometimes we encounter persons whose need for excitement and for personal risk seems to be compulsive or addictive. For example, we have read of mountain climbers who felt impelled to attempt more and more difficult and, finally, foolhardy ascents, until they were killed (Klausner, 1968). When the risk-taking becomes compulsive or addictive, we recognize the quality of indirect self-destructive behavior as a defense against depression. Still, the ISDB has value for the person if it protects against direct self-destructive behavior.

PSYCHODYNAMICS OF DEPRESSION _____

A basic depressive response in children was described by Joffe and Sandler (1965). Typically these children looked unhappy, had little interest in their surroundings, and appeared withdrawn, bored, or listless. They felt discontented with what was offered to them and showed little capacity for pleasure. They communicated feelings of rejection and lack of love and showed a readiness to turn away from disappointing objects. Insomnia and various other sleep disturbances occurred, as did autoerotic or repetitive self-comforting activities. The depressive affect was thought to represent a fundamental biological response, as basic as anxiety. It has its roots in a primary psychophysiological state and is a reaction to helplessness in the face of physical or psychological pain.

These observers regarded the basic depressive response as representing a state of helplessness, hopelessness, and resignation in the face of mental pain. "It is not the only possible response to pain or to the anticipation of pain, but a particular one, in which there is a feeling of being unable to restore a wished-for state accompanied by an attitude which is essentially one of capitulation and retreat" (p. 396). The healthy response to pain is protest or fight, rather than flight. However, many children who are called unhappy are not, in fact, manifesting a depressive response. They have not capitulated, but rather show varying degrees of discontent and resentment, and their response to pain is manifested directly, rather than accepted passively.

One source of pain is physical separation of the child from its mother. This has been vividly described as producing depressive reactions in human infants (Spitz, 1946; Bowlby, 1973), and in primates (Harlow et al., 1976). At first, upon separation, the infant goes through a stage of active protest, of crying and searching. This is followed eventually, however, by withdrawal and despair. In this situation, babies fail to thrive in hospitals or in any setting. Often, however, the depressed babies or primate infants are rescued by nurses who give special loving attention, or by other sources of love.

From an evolutionary standpoint, depression as a primary psychobiological reaction has the positive survival value of preserving energy in a situation where nothing constructive seems to be possible anyway. Secondly, verbal and nonverbal posture and attitudes of depression provide powerful communications to persons in the environment, inducing or "releasing" in them rescuing or protecting behaviors.

The psychoanalytic concept of "mental pain" is not entirely clear. The concept of mental pain and the concept of depression are somewhat ambiguous psychologically, because they are truly psychobiological reactions. They are mediated, metabolically and hormonally, through neurotransmitters comprising a variety of chemical and biological substances. We have only an incomplete knowledge of the manner in which these substances operate physiologically, and we can only speculate about their relationship to psychodynamics. It is a matter of great importance to know that there are biological receptors in the brain for opiumlike substances which are produced in the brain and have presumably some role in the experience of pain and in the experience of anhedonia. Brain extracts contain a natural substance called "enkephalin." This substance seems to control in part how much pain a person experiences. It mimics morphine in action and is even found in areas of the brain similar to those where opium and morphine are received (Snyder, 1978).

The mental pain signal can lead, on one hand, to depression, if the person feels resigned to helplessness, or on the other hand, to a number of defenses and countermeasures, including acting out or the taking of drugs and alcohol, as well as a number of healthier alternatives. It is only when these alternatives are not resorted to, or when all coping attempts fail, that a depressive reaction occurs. There is a great deal of controversy about the relationship between aggression and depression, and very little consensus on it. Certainly, in most depressed persons one encounters a great deal of bound-in aggressive energy, which the individual feels unable to express. The appropriate timing and release of aggression in constructive self-assertion is one of the major problems in the therapy of depression.

DEFENSES AGAINST DEPRESSION _____

Individual human development is long and complicated. All of us have histories of traumatic events in our lives; there were times when we felt weak, helpless, insecure, and unsafe, perhaps because we were separated from the persons we loved. Psychodynamically, repetition of past traumatic events threatens our sense of well-being and safety and provokes signals of possible loss. The signals take the form of anxiety, which becomes depression when the threat is overwhelming. Mendelsohn (1974) has reviewed the psychoanalytic concepts of depression.

Over time, we all develop coping mechanisms and defenses against depression. Older persons have developed an ego ideal. To the extent that we can conform to the ideals we have for ourselves, we feel self-esteem. Bibring (1953) and Jacobson (1971) relate the depressive reaction particularly to a decrease or a sudden deflation in a person's self-esteem, a loss of the ideal state of well-being.

Bibring stated that for self-esteem, people need to feel that they are loved and cared for; that they themselves are good and loving people; and that they are strong and competent. The development of self-esteem is often complicated by narcissistic strivings to be a "special" person—a saint or a devil. The need to be special makes a person unusually dependent upon the love of others and vulnerable in self-esteem. This was emphasized by Jacobson, who noted clinically that depressed people feel inferior, weak, and helpless, are dependent on others, and need someone else to idealize and overvalue. There is almost a specific ego weakness in which one is supersensitive or intolerant to frustration, disappointment, and hurt and then blames the loved object or loved person. There is a denial of one's own weakness and inadequacy, and especially of weakness in the love object. Finally, depressed persons often experience, during periods of denial of weakness, a manicky effort to merge into the strength of the loved person or the loved environment, with a consequent ballooning of self-esteem.

Although most investigators believe that depression is primarily a disturbance of feeling and affect, Beck (1967) focuses attention upon certain primary disturbances of thinking in depression. These consist of basic attitudes of pessimism, disillusionment, lack of interest, and a lack of joy directed toward the self and the world. Depressed people see everything as empty and worthless and without pleasure. They put themselves down with negative ideas about the future and with negative feedback cycles: "I feel bad, I note that I feel bad, and that makes me feel even worse."

Masochism and its goals can be mentioned only briefly in this discussion of psychodynamics. Most adults carry with them from childhood a sense of guilt. All of us have had forbidden impulses and have learned to control them, often through guilt. Most of the guilt is unconscious. At times, in a symptomatic way, unconscious guilt may lead to coping mechanisms which consist of minor mistakes or transgressions, with or without minor punishments. Persons who have a greater sense of guilt may need to include some form of punishment, repetitively, as part of their life-styles. In analysis, they may repeatedly tell of dreams in which the analyst is beating them into shape. They may have learned that through punishment, especially, they can achieve love or union with the mother or a temporary feeling of safety and/or ideal tranquility, even a feeling of triumph. My observations tend to confirm Theodore Reik's (1941) brilliant conceptualization of masochism as "victory through defeat." In masochistic behaviors, the person simultaneously gratifies an unconscious sense of guilt, relieves the tension of expected mental pain, and eventually feels a surge of triumph at having survived the punishment or the danger. There is a masochistic component in most indirect self-destructive behavior.

CONCLUSION

Much of the ISDB we are considering has the psychodynamic function of denying or coping with mental pain which might otherwise lead to states of helpless depression. Through the ISDB there is an experience of mastery and victory, tinged with masochism. There may be direct erotic gratification, and, at times, components of aggression and revenge. Essentially, however, the function of the ISDB is to deny helplessness and replace it with coping mechanisms that enhance self-esteem. For example, cigarette smoking reinforces a feeling of security while still allowing one to spit smoke in the face of the world.

Since ISDB increases self-esteem and relieves unconscious guilt, it rather easily becomes not only symptomatic but also characterological. In this volume, the chapters on hemodialysis and spinal cord injury discuss the concept of the "marginal person." Men and women with spinal cord injuries or kidney damage must follow a very precise way of life, with no margin for deviation. Noncompliance causes a high risk of disability or death. Although the rest of us do not like to think about it, in many ways we are all marginal persons, yet we all try to deny it. In denying our ultimate helplessness against death, fate, bad luck, and inner turmoil, we all indulge in ISDB to some extent, and all of us and society must pay the cost.

REFERENCES

Beck, A. T. *Depression.* New York: Hoeber, 1967.

Bibring, E. The mechanism of depression. In P. Greenacre, ed., *Affective Disorders.* New York: International Universities Press, 1953.

Bowlby, J. *Attachment and Loss.* New York: Basic Books, 1973.

Farberow, N. L., et al. Indirect self-destructive behavior in diabetic patients. *Hospital Medicine* 6:123–133, 1970.

Freud, S. The psychopathology of everyday life. *Standard Edition,* 6. London: Hogarth, 1960. (Originally published, 1901.)

Harlow, H., Suomi, S. G., and Delizio, R. Social rehabilitation of separation-induced depressive disorders in monkeys. *American Journal of Psychiatry,* 133:1279–1285, 1976.

Jacobson, E. *Depression.* New York: International Universities Press, 1971.

Joffe, W. G., and Sandler, J. Notes on pain, depression, and individuation. *The Psychoanalytic Study of the Child,* 20: 394–425. New York: International Universities Press, 1965.

Klausner, S. *Why Man Takes Chances: Studies in Stress-Seeking.* New York: Anchor Books, 1968.

Knowles, J. H. Responsibility for health. *Science,* 198:1103, 1977.

Litman, R. E., and Swearingen, C. Bondage and suicide. *Archives of General Psychiatry,* 27:80–85, 1972.

Mendelsohn, M. *Psychoanalytic Concepts of Depression.* New York: Spectrum, 1974.

Reik, T. *Masochism in Modern Man.* New York: Grove, 1941.

Resnik, H. L. P. Erotized repetitive hangings: A form of self-destructive behavior. *American Journal of Psychotherapy,* 26:4–21, 1972.

Snyder, S. H. The opium receptor and morphine-like peptides in the brain. *American Journal of Psychiatry,* 135:645–652, 1978.

Spitz, R. A. Anaclitic depression. *Psychoanalytic Study of the Child,* 2:313–341, 1946.

Tabachnick, N., Gussen, J., Litman, R. E., Peck, M., Tiber, N., and Wold, C. *Accident or Suicide? Destruction by Automobile.* Springfield, Ill.: Thomas, 1973.

Weisman, A. D. Self-destruction and sexual perversion. In E. S. Shneidman, ed., *Essays in Self-Destruction.* New York: Science House, 1967.

3

THE PSYCHOPATHOLOGY OF INDIRECT SELF-DESTRUCTION

KALLE A. ACHTÉ

KINDS OF INDIRECT SELF-DESTRUCTION

In recent years, increasing attention has been paid to indirect self-destruction, as studies have shown that it, as much as direct suicide, may shorten a person's life. In some cases, indirect self-destruction approximates overt suicidal impulses; in other cases, it serves various defensive purposes, and the self-destructive effects are merely a by-product. The same may be true in cases where a person seeks pleasure from an activity that can be valuated as indirectly self-destructive only by looking at the long-term effects. In many cases involving indirect self-destruction, a counterphobic attitude is present—the person plays with the danger of death, as it were, as a means of attempting to control death. Sometimes a person may seek to achieve a goal so intensely and consider it so important that he is prepared to destroy himself indirectly.

Indirect self-destruction generally proceeds slowly and often unconsciously. For example, people may damage themselves by overeating, neglecting their physical fitness, seeking stress, drinking excessively, neglecting to go for treatment when they contract an illness or are chronically ill, and by smoking. In smoking, for example, it has been calculated that a person aged 24 who smokes three packages of cigarettes a day shortens his life by an average of 8.4 years, and that smoking two packages a day shortens his life by more than 5 years (Tamerin, 1971).

Many a masochistic person sabotages his own success in life, adopting the role of an ill-fated martyr, a chronically miserable person who has to be constantly on the defensive. Masochistic persons often have difficulty becoming aware of their masochistic behavior. Meerloo (1968) even hypothesizes that the extreme masochist becomes the victim of manslaughter.

Farberow (1972) views Menninger's (1938) examples of focal suicide, such as self-mutilation, asceticism, and martyrdom, as forms of indirect self-destruction. Gambling, too, may be included in the same group. In a broad sense, psychosomatic diseases can also be subsumed under the concept of indirect self-destructive behavior (ISDB).

Some persons choose occupations or adopt hobbies or interests with which great risks are associated. Risks may be connected with dangerous sports, too, though these may also be accompanied by a certain sense of strengthening the ego, of elegance, and of ability to master oneself and one's body, even in difficult situations (Rechardt, personal communication, 1975). Self-destructive behavior may also appear as an attempt to avoid something considered still more harmful or disturbing. A person who eats himself into obesity may actually be seeking to avoid anxiety-evoking sexual temptation. Taking disproportionately great risks may involve rebellion against the advice of parents, school, and society, all of which force the human being to accept reality. And then again, there are people who are subject to frequent, unexpected accidents. On a wider, more global plane, mankind is threatened by certain forms of self-destruction such as pollution, excessive population growth, and the possible consequences of the armament race.

Indirect self-destruction thus may be given either a narrow or a broad interpretation. In this chapter, it is discussed as a widespread phenomenon, as a symptom of very frequent occurrence, containing both masochistic and self-destructive features met in certain character disorders.

INTENT IN INDIRECT
SELF-DESTRUCTION _____

When assessing the self-destructive features of any behavior it is important to note the purpose of the behavior. In almost every instance of indirect suicide, a conscious intention of self-injury or death will be absent. In some cases, the behavior seems to be a means of controlling tendencies toward severe depression or anxiety. In other cases, the indirect self-destruction may be associated with impulsive behavior; the person thinks only of his momentary gratification and is unable to consider the long-term consequences of his behavior.

NEUROSES OF DESTINY AND
MASOCHISM _____

The concept of indirect self-destruction has practical importance in character disorders associated with an exceptionally severe superego; in these disorders there is a strong inward need for punishment. Such disorders have been characterized as neuroses of destiny because the persons suffering from them seem to be constantly harassed by bad luck. In their own opinion, all the adversities they experience are due to external factors. They do not succeed in anything they do; they may also be socially self-destructive. On the face of it, these people's misfortunes appear to be accidental. Closer scrutiny often reveals, however, that they unconsciously provoke their difficulties. The term "moral masochism" has also been applied to the person(s) who show such behavior. Similar features are also often found in persons who for reasons of principle expose themselves, or persons close to them, to great suffering (Achté et al., 1976).

A masochistic person seeks to gain sexual gratification through submission to personal humiliation and bodily suffering. In mild cases, satisfaction may be derived from verbal reproaches and merely imagined humiliating events. In more serious cases, physical pain may be sought, such as in whipping or binding. The suffering is rendered more meaningful through the fact that the person concerned has actively chosen this position. Every sort of masochism invariably involves a severe conscience, which produces strong feelings of guilt. The person feels that in order to experience pleasure, he has to suffer and atone. In masochism, aggression has been turned inward. It should be noted that mild masochistic features are present in almost all neuroses, but these are not exhibited at the same intense level described above and therefore are not considered a perversion.

Another typical feature of masochism is that the person uses his suffering as a weapon against others. This device is often the only one available to a neurotically disturbed person, inasmuch as his self-esteem is low and he is unable to vent his anger outward without fear of losing the support of others. The only remaining alternative is to use one's self as the object of hatred, which also results in self-punishment. Sadistic persons and masochistic persons often attract one another. Sadistic behavior brings out masochistic activity in the partner in whom it has been latent, and vice versa.

Even more basically, masochism can be seen as a characterological defense mechanism against anxiety-evoking emotions. Masochism can then be regarded as a choice forced upon a person in his efforts to avoid something that seems even worse. It would thus be incomplete to view masochism exclusively as a matter of enjoyment. Despite the fact that the masochistic person has learned to enjoy suffering, it brings him more pain and ill-being than pleasure. In treating him, the most important thing is to realize that, despite the fact that he is irritating because of his treatment resistance and manipulativeness, the masochist is a suffering human being.

The masochistic person experiences punishment even before it comes, perhaps because it will be easier to endure that way. Failure and defeat have unconsciously been arranged beforehand in order to receive the punishment, which in turn relieves the pressure of the severe superego. There are many persons who need to pay the price for success with anxiety or suffering in some other area of life.

Clinical experience suggests that persons with self-destructive tendencies often fail in psychotherapy unless the psychodynamics and psychopathology underlying their paradoxical behavior are sufficiently analyzed. Freud (1933/1964) spoke of a negative therapeutic reaction in the patient who, instead of showing improvement, responds to the therapist's support and interpretations by becoming worse. What seems to underlie such a reaction is a need for punishment, a successful interpretation of which may or may not help the patient, depending on the intensity of this need.

CHARACTER NEUROSIS BEHAVIORS
AND INDIRECT SELF-DESTRUCTION_____

Certain character neurosis behaviors which lead to either direct or indirect self-destruction are associated with acting-out behavior and, in a broader sense, with the aggressive sides of the personality. Various personality types have been described, particularly in the psychoanalytic literature, which are difficult to assign to any of the classical neurosis groups, or to any of the other usual diagnostic categories (Achté et al., 1976). Some of these personality types may be characterized by a pronounced use of such defense mechanisms as acting out, excessive use of reaction formation, counterphobic suppression of fears, and proof of fearlessness by foolhardy behavior. Ferenczi coined the term "Sunday neurosis" for the pains experienced on Sundays and other holidays by people who need to discharge their inward tensions in hard work. All of these may be associated with tendencies toward indirect self-destruction, but it is also important to recognize that such behaviors may have a valuable side of their own.

ACTING OUT

Acting-out behavior is an effort to solve some internal difficulty through action. In the process, it often subjects the person to self-damage. A character disorder frequently underlies the acting-out behavior and its psychotherapeutic treatment may be difficult (Rechardt and Achté, 1973). Traumatic experiences during infancy have resulted in an inability to tolerate anxiety and to act in accordance with a long-term plan. The behavior may take the form of aggressive acting out within the family circle, it may appear within the current employment relationship, or it may show as asocial acting out—in a destructive drinking period, for example.

The treatment of acting-out behavior often requires the use of clearly stated restrictions and prohibitions. However, no results can be expected from the treatment unless rapport is established with the patient. Patients who act out imagine that they control their entire environment; this gives them an unrealistic sense of independence and power. These patients must be shown in their psychotherapy that they are slavishly repeating a given behavior pattern and that they are not really in such control as they imagine. During psychotherapy these patients should be helped to realize that there are other solutions, or at least hope of such solutions. A typical feature of acting-out behavior is that patients frequently experience their own behavior not as a negative symptom but as a personal character trait of which they may even be proud. On the other hand, if a difficult life situation is eliciting the acting out, the focus should be on alleviating the situation and on helping the patient to find alternatives to self-destructive behavior. This will enhance his self-esteem and help him avoid painful feelings of helplessness (Rechardt and Achté, 1973).

ASCETICISM

Many philosophers and mystics have advocated that the body become accustomed to abstinence, thus establishing its control over the spirit. The practice of asceticism is more widespread than is generally realized and the phenomenon is highly interesting in itself. Individual cases may be impossible to explain without a detailed knowledge of the person's personality. In the last analysis, asceticism is an effort to cope with difficulties, anxiety, and guilt by punishing the self. If one is content with very little, one cannot fall from very high. When a person seeks suffering, it may be an expression of an unconscious wish to attain alleviation in some other sector of life. By so doing, he seeks to ward off even worse feelings of depression and anxiety.

According to psychoanalytic theory, self-contempt and self-accusation reflect the parents' attitudes toward, and ways of relating to, the person, ways he incorporates into his personality starting in infancy. History bears evidence that persons who have led ascetic lives are characterized by strong feelings of guilt. Their inward suffering may be so intense that not even the most severe self-torture is enough to bring them peace of mind. They are unable to accept their own normal emotions and thoughts, thinking these are due to the Devil's temptations. They focus on the primary aspect of their being, the body, and try to propitiate their conscience by castigating it. One may ask why the fear of punishment and asceticism so often involve abstinence from eating, drinking, and sexuality. It is as if, when one denies oneself these satisfactions, it is a victory for the self and a revenge on others. Menninger (1938) hypothesizes that some children develop resentment against their parents, the first authorities in their lives, because parents prevent them from fulfilling their wishes. Usually these children learn to hide their hostility in order not to anger their parents and lose their love, without which they are unable to live. Sometimes the hidden rebelliousness of these children, as well as occasional forbidden pleasures, makes them feel guilty. To propitiate their consciences, these children punish themselves in one way or another. The pain caused by hunger is one very efficient way of suffering, as well as a way of hurting the parents, to whom the child's eating is important. These children are able to attract attention, pity, and concern, and at the same time show defiance and feel power. Nevertheless, in these cases there is deep-seated anxiety, and the child often unconsciously associates danger with eating. Sometimes asceticism initially involves aggression that is turned against the self.

PSYCHOSOMATIC AND SOMATIC ILLNESSES _____

When people contract a somatic illness, their attention invariably shifts from the external world and focuses on the self. Depending on the situation, patients may feel anxiety when faced with illness, and use various ego defenses, such as denial, to ward off awareness of the illness. During the initial phase of the illness, everything may take place at an unconscious level so that patients feel only inexplicable anxiety. The more serious they fear the illness to be, the more they may delay consulting a doctor, thus in effect indirectly contributing to their own self-destruction.

The psychological meanings attached to illness vary. For some people an illness may provide an honorable retreat from an overwhelmingly difficult life situation. Others may experience illness as a punishment, while still others will view it as destiny. Patients' earlier courses of life and the structure of their personalities will determine, in combination with the nature of the illness, how they experience the illness. Illness binds the patient's psychic energy. Both the nature of the illness and the psychic meanings attached to the affected part of the body play a role in the behavior. Ferenczi (1950), for example, has stressed that diseases of the eyes and the genitals are likely to be more highly charged emotionally than those of other organs, probably allowing additional functional symptoms to appear in the eyes and the genitals.

Dorpat et al. (1968) have discussed the risk of suicide in depression and somatic illnesses. In a study of 80 suicides, they found that psychosomatic illnesses, especially peptic ulcer, rheumatoid arthritis, and hypertension, occurred relatively frequently in suicides. Among their 80 suicides, 56 cases have a history of 107 somatic illnesses, almost all chronic. Peptic ulcer was two to four times as frequent among the suicides as in the general population, hypertension was two to three times as frequent, and rheumatoid arthritis was five to seven times as frequent. They also found cancer 15 times more often among the suicides than in the general population. Of the suicides, 13.8 percent had undergone a major surgical operation during the preceding year. Hysterectomy and other surgical operations or illnesses that tend to reduce the patient's self-esteem are frequently followed by states of severe dejection with an increased risk of suicide. Fear of dependency, helplessness, and isolation may increase the depth of the dejection. According to Dorpat et al., suicide risk is more often associated with organic illnesses, especially among men. In our culture it is much more difficult for a man to accept the role of a sick, disabled, or helpless person, the end result of many organic illnesses.

In a sense, all psychosomatic disorders can be seen as instances of indirect self-destruction, in which the person uses his body to destroy his organ system. For example, the person with a peptic ulcer ingests his own stomach, so to speak; and hypertension leads to an increased risk of myocardial infarction and apoplexy, and thus to an increased possibility of death. In some of the other somatic illnesses, also, self-destructive tendencies are clear, as in anorexia nervosa in which the mortality rate often exceeds 10 percent.

CORONARY DISEASE AND
CORONARY THROMBOSIS _____

It is not clear how much certain character traits and external stress promote the occurrence of coronary thrombosis. Internists seem increasingly inclined to assume the existence of a relationship between coronary thrombosis and personality characteristics of middle-aged people. Stress-seeking behavior is one such characteristic, and while it certainly has significance for the promotion of society and its culture, it is more likely that for the individual, it serves as a defense against depression and even more difficult emotions. The cardiovascular system responds sensitively to emotional reactions (Cannon, 1932). Blood pressure, pulse rate, minute volume of heart beats, oxygen consumption, peripheral resistance, and coagulation of blood all respond. Psychic stress factors have also been found to cause distinctly pathological heart functions in the form of rhythm disturbances, electrocardiogram (ECG) changes, and even heart failure. Under severe stress, the patient may feel intense anxiety and fear of death, which may be allayed by the doctor's reassuring attitude and by drugs.

Dunbar (1954) was the first to construct a consistent personality profile of the coronary patient. According to her, such patients are diligent people who work hard and compulsively and have a high level of aspiration. They hide their aggressions and other conflicts under a calm surface, often in a rigid way. Basically, this sort of personality derives its origin from insecurity experienced during childhood. Friedman and Rosenman (1971) have hypothesized two personality types, A and B. Personality type A, for whom the risk of coronary disease is particularly great, is competitive, lives in accordance with a rigid timetable, suffers from the slowness of other people, and is very active. Type B, the opposite of type A, is more relaxed and more inclined to take things easy. Type A was found to correlate with heightened blood cholesterol and triglyceride values, heightened diastolic blood pressure, reduced coagulation rate of blood, increased diurnal adrenalin secretion, a more distinct arcus senilis, and a certain degree of motor and vasomotor lability. The matter has not been settled, however, since the work of certain investigators, for instance, Keith et al. (1965), has not confirmed these findings.

In terms of personality characteristics, recent studies have stressed premorbid heightened suspiciousness and inward tension as characteristic of persons belonging to the coronary group. It has been noted that just before falling ill, many infarction patients have experienced prolonged psychic stress, have been in some acute conflict situation, or have gone through a significant change in life. For instance, they have lost a person important to them, or have experienced economic difficulties or marital or sexual conflicts. Groen (1964) has assumed that the determining factor is the attitude the person adopts toward the problem situation. He feels that a compulsive sense of duty and responsibility is typical of the people in Scandinavia, and that it prevents them from finding an outlet for emotional factors or from talking out their problems. These factors, together with an accentuated control of emotions, may contribute to the development of a myocardial infarction.

According to van Hejningen and Treurniet (1966), macho masculine attitudes are typical of many patients who have contracted coronary thrombosis. The patients cannot bear dependency and inactivity, which they feel are infantile. To be passive means to be worthless. They are therefore good workers and have often been described as work addicts. They tend to be highly ambitious and to dominate others at work, at home, and in social intercourse. At the same time they are also impulsive and shift abruptly from activity and independence to passivity and dependence. They discharge their aggressive affects by hard work. At work they tend to assume a solicitous role toward others and try to be, in a sense, fathers and mothers at once.

The fear of dependency and passivity seems to be associated with the restrictions the person experienced in his childhood. Many coronary personality-type people have described an intense wish to grow up and become independent adults as fast as possible. Work was generally the only means available. On the other hand, at a deeper level, repressed desires to be dependent and cared for remained. These wishes are anxiety-evoking, however, so that dependence and independence needs continually struggle against each other.

AGED CHRONICALLY ILL PATIENTS ——————————————

Indirect self-destructiveness seems to be associated with chronic illnesses, particularly in the case of aged patients (Nelson and Farberow, 1976). Mishara and Kastenbaum (1973) suggest that attention from the staff is rewarding, even if negative, and that self-injurious behavior is engaged in precisely because the resulting physical problems attract attention. Rachlis (1970) observed that the elderly person, particularly if chronically ill, suffers from feelings of excessive loss and does not possess the flexibility to adapt to external change. Farberow and Moriwaki (1975) noted, in investigating suicides committed by elderly hospital patients, that these patients had experienced a lifelong history of isolation which had been aggravated both by their chronic illness and by aging. Many an elderly person is inclined to experience old age and chronic illness as a crisis. Diminished self-esteem often plays a central role and, when the crisis grows increasingly serious, may lead to either direct or indirect self-destruction. In their investigation of elderly chronic patients, Nelson and Farberow (1976) found that indirect self-destruction seemed to be a substitute for suicide. This indirect self-destruction manifested itself in part as neglect of the doctor's treatment instructions, poor cooperation, self-injury, and various kinds of risk-taking, as well as in the form of a negative attitude toward one's own recovery.

NEGLECT AND DISREGARD IN THE TREATMENT OF LONG-TERM ILLNESS ——————————————————————————————

Neglect of the treatment of many long-term illnesses represents indirect self-destruction in its purest form. Diabetes is a good example of an illness which lends itself readily to such abuse. What may be said about diabetes applies to all illnesses in which the neglect of treatment directly injures and/or shortens the patient's life. Diabetes mellitus is a disease which requires treatment for the rest of the patient's life. For the treatment to be successful, good cooperation between the doctor and patient is imperative, inasmuch as the regimen of diet and medication must be observed and regular follow-up examinations carried out. The doctor's skills and the patient's personality will determine whether the latter will experience the former as a restricting and prohibiting person or as a cooperative helper. Despite the fact that guidebooks are a great help, they can never replace the personal interaction between the doctor and patient.

Some patients whose illness requires daily insulin injections may have difficulty in performing this self-treatment. This difficulty may sometimes be due to psychological factors, but most often it will be due to the patient's advanced age or some organic illness or disorder, such as blindness, brain injury, or parkinsonism. When it is psychological, the patient's resistance to the insulin injection is most likely a reflection of his passive fears of finding himself at the mercy of other people and losing the feeling of control.

Observing a dietary regimen may be particularly difficult for children and young patients. A young diabetic may use the diet as a means of manipulating or as a means of protest against his parents. When parents feel guilty about their child's illness, a not infrequent fantasy in the children is that if they were to die others would grieve and cry when they realized what they had lost. Contrariwise, the less guilt felt by a young patient's parents and other family members, the greater is the likelihood that the illness will not give rise to disturbances in either the patient or his family.

In their approach to the illness, a middle road for the doctor and the parents seems best. If they assume an excessively authoritative attitude, they may provoke opposition in the young patient and lead him to neglect the treatment. On the other hand, too lax an approach is apt to give rise to a sense of insecurity. It thus seems reasonable to make the diet as unrestricted as possible within the requirements of the illness, since the patient is more likely to follow such a diet than an excessively strict one.

ABUSE OF DRUGS AND ALCOHOLISM _____

For Meerloo (1968), one typical feature of drug abuse is the need to escape and to sleep, often to a point approximating death. Underlying this self-destructive mechanism may be a need to get away from painful emotions, insomnia, and anxiety, and from a difficult life situation. The early sense of well-being with the first use of the drugs is of short duration; before long the person begins to abuse the drug by taking increasingly larger doses. This leads gradually to heightened negative feelings and to severe subjective suffering.

The same applies to alcoholism. A person takes alcohol in an attempt to avoid unpleasant emotions and situations. Often he does not think of the harmful long-term effects of alcohol, but only seeks momentary satisfaction and relief. The deleterious effects make their appearance later.

Both drugs and alcohol may temporarily reduce aggressiveness, relieve guilt feelings, and heighten self-esteem. Anxiety and tension can be made to disappear, and disappointments can thus be denied. In the last analysis substance abuse is due to anxiety and to attempts to deny it. However, when an addictive substance is used for a long time, the benefits obtained from it—i.e., the relief of symptoms and the sense of pleasure—gradually diminish and, at the same time, the deleterious effects grow increasingly pronounced. It becomes more and more difficult to control the alcohol or drugs and to avoid their impact on performance capacity and discharge of duties. The person suffers increasingly from hangover and abstinence symptoms, orientation becomes ever more unrealistic, and, with increasing tolerance, the dosages reach toxicity and have greater detrimental effects on the body.

Drug abusers and alcoholics have a number of personality features in common. Their self-esteem is low, they incline toward high anxiety and low pain tolerance, and they feel vulnerable and dependent. Increased aggressiveness, depressive inclinations, and guilt feelings become more pronounced in these persons (Achté et al., 1976). Psychoanalysts regard drug and alcohol abuse as a regression to oral narcissism.

Aggression problems and conflicts related to depression are seen in the self-destructive use of one's self as an instrument for passive aggression: The person cannot direct his aggression outward for fear that he might be deserted, or because his self-esteem is low, and so turns it inward on himself. It is possible that the masochism associated with drug abuse is basically an attempt to deny one's dependence on others.

Alcoholism and drug addiction have been characterized as slow suicide. In a study in Finland (Achté and Mäki-Mattila, 1967) of the drug addicts who came for treatment of their addiction in 1950, 48 percent died during the following 16 years. In half of the cases the cause of death was a poisoning, and in a majority of the cases the deaths were suicides. The intoxicants most widely used at that time were opiates. The patient's average age at death was 48, and, for those cases where data were available, an average of 11.5 years had elapsed between the first use of the intoxicant and the patient's death.

With an alcoholic it is more difficult to determine cause and effect, and it is impossible to draw a uniform personality profile. Certain traits, however, are most repeatedly cited as typical of the alcoholic's personality (Achté et al., 1976). They tend to have a lower tolerance for disappointment, conflict, anxiety, tension, and discomfort in comparison with the general population. They have lower self-esteem, are emotionally vulnerable, and lack endurance and persistence. Alcoholics are considered orally fixated persons. They are often extremely dependent on their love objects, and this makes it impossible for them to express their hostility directly. Addictive drinking instead becomes a means of indirectly expressing aggression. At the same time the self-destructive effects of deviant drinking on the alcoholic's physique, psyche, and social life serve as self-punishment or as a means of obtaining masochistic gratification, and thus make it possible for him to mitigate his increasingly intense guilt feelings.

ALCOHOL POISONING _____

In a Finnish investigation of the possibility of suicides hidden in deaths in which the mode is listed as accident or as due to unidentified causes, deaths from poisoning formed a crucial group. The number of accidental cases of poisoning was increased not only in Helsinki, but also in the whole country, by the high number of cases of alcohol poisoning. In one study, the hypothesis was advanced that the high Finnish figures for deaths due to poisoning which were certified as accidents or due to unidentified causes actually included a number of suicides (Brooke and Atkinson, 1974). Lönnqvist, however, examined this question in his study of suicide in Helsinki in 1977 and determined that the large majority of the cases of poisoning due to accidents and to unidentified causes were actually the result of causes other than suicide.

However, despite the fact that most deaths due to alcohol poisoning were not actually suicides, they were most often consequences of self-destructive behavior. The majority of cases where death was due to alcohol poisoning involved chronic, excessive use of alcohol by a middle-aged male. In about 40 percent of the cases of poisoning that led to death, the use of alcohol had reached "skid-row dimensions" (Lönnqvist, 1977). It seems apparent, thus, that deaths due to alcohol poisoning form a notably large group of deaths which should be considered an aspect of the wider problem of self-destruction.

THE MYTH OF DRUG AUTOMATISM _____

Drug automatism has been regarded as a train of events, comparable to an accident, in which a person, after taking a therapeutic dose of a drug, forgets and takes the drug repeatedly. In the consequent state of drug intoxication, he finally takes an excessive dose of the hypnotic, without awareness of his actions and without intending to damage himself. The concept of drug automatism was first introduced by Richards (1934). He described three patients who took several sleeping pills and fell asleep and who, after they awakened, did not remember that they had taken the pills. Several other investigators subsequently used the concept of drug automatism to explain cases of self-poisoning. Jansson (1962), for instance, estimated that a quarter of the suicidal attempts made by drugs involved drug automatism. If this estimate were accepted, the deaths due to drug automatism would, of course, notably increase suicide statistics.

Long (1959) was the first to call attention to the fact that the drug automatism described by Richards was based on only three cases, and that these cases did not represent research results but an interpretation of such results. Barraclough (1974) points out that in suicides committed by means of poisoning and in the cases of death classified either as accidental or as unclear, the drugs used do not differ greatly. He asks how it is possible to take "accidentally" a lethal dose of several different drugs, inasmuch as, in most cases, the deaths are due to multiple drug poisoning. Aitken and Proudfoot (1969) investigated 994 hospital admissions for poisoning and found that 2.9 percent of the patients denied the presence of poisoning. The authors' interpretation, in contrast to Richards's, was that what was occurring was not an amnesia due to the poisoning but a psychologically determined repression and denial. Dorpat (1974) stresses that it has not been possible even experimentally to demonstrate that barbiturates, in therapeutic doses, produce amnesia and cause the patient to forget that he has taken them. He also points out that the literature contains no well-authenticated cases of fatal poisoning caused by drug automatism. In contrast, many other psychotropic drugs and alcohol do influence consciousness and the functions of the ego, impairing defenses against the acting out of self-destructive impulses (Dorpat, 1968).

The above observations and critical remarks concerning drug automatism have been based mainly on nonfatal cases of poisoning. In only a few studies have cases of fatal poisoning been explored employing the method of the so-called psychological autopsy. Dorpat (1974) has hypothesized that behind the use of the automatism concept in connection with deaths due to drugs there is often an inclination to deny the existence of self-destructive tendencies. Not only the patient but also his family members, and even the professionals investigating the matter, are likely to have such an inclination. On the other hand, not all deaths from drug poisoning are suicides. Curphey (1968) found in a study of 440 cases of barbiturate poisoning deaths that 90 percent were suicides, 9 percent remained unclear and 1 percent were accidents. Litman et al. (1963) stressed that in "accidental" cases of fatal drug poisoning the victim is often a chronic abuser of alcohol who takes a small dose of a hypnotic while in a state of heavy intoxication. Thus, in the light of recent investigations, it seems that most cases of drug poisoning, particularly when several drugs or large doses are involved, are likely to be suicides rather than accidents.

AUTOMOBILE ACCIDENTS _____

Some automobile accidents may, in fact, be suicides. Lönnqvist's (1977) study did not include any cases of death by automobile accidents that could have been regarded as suicide. Despite the fact that suicides sometimes do occur in connection with automobile accidents, they are not, judging by Näätänen's study (1972), of much significance from the standpoint of the suicide problem. Näätänen's finding is consistent with the corresponding results reported in the United States (Tabachnick et al., 1973). In certain cases, however, a person's method or manner of driving may lead indirectly to his self-destruction.

REFERENCES _____

Achté, K., Alanen, Y. A., and Tienari, P. *Psykitria*, 3rd ed. Porvoo-Helsinki: WSOY, 1976.

Achté, K., and Mäki-Mattila, A. Laakkeiden vaarinkaytto sairaalahoitoon johtaneena tekijana Helsingissä v. 1950. Jalkitutkimus. *Laakaari ja yhteiskunta*, 22:1804–1810, 1967.

Aitken, R. C. B., and Proudfoot, A. T. Barbiturate automatism—myth or malady. *Postgraduate Medical Journal*, 45:612–616, 1969.

Barraclough, B. M. Poisoning cases: Suicide or accident. *British Journal of Psychiatry*, 124:526–530, 1974.

Brooke, E., and Atkinson, M. Ascertainment of deaths from suicide. Public Health Paper No. 58. Geneva: World Health Organization, 1974.

Cannon, W. B. *The Wisdom of the Body*. New York: Hoeber, 1932.

Curphey, T. J. Drug deaths: A problem in certification. In N. L. Farberow, ed., *Proceedings of the Fourth International Conference for Suicide Prevention*. Los Angeles: Suicide Prevention Center, 1968.

Dorpat, T. L. Loss of controls over suicidal impulses. *Bulletin of Suicidology*, pp. 26–30, 1968.

Dorpat, T. L. Drug automatism, barbiturate poisoning, and suicide behavior. *Archives of General Psychiatry*, 31:216–220, 1974.

Dorpat, T. L., Anderson, W. F., and Ripley, H. A. The relationship of physical illness to suicide. In H. L. P. Resnik, ed., *Suicidal Behaviors: Diagnosis and Management*. Boston: Little, Brown, 1968.

Dunbar, H. F. *Emotions and Bodily Changes*. New York: Columbia University Press, 1954.

Farberow, N. L. The development of self-destructive personalities. *Psychiatria Fennica*, 2:279–288, 1972.

Farberow, N. L., and Moriwaki, S. Self-destructive crises in the older person. *The Gerontologist*, 15:333–337, 1975.

Ferenczi, S. *Further Contributions of the Theory and Techniques of Psychoanalysis*. London: Hogarth Press, 1950.

Freud, S. New introductory lectures on psycho-analysis, Lecture XXXII: Anxiety and instinctual life. *Standard Edition*, 22. London: Hogarth, 1964. (Originally published, 1933.)

Friedman, M., and Rosenman, R. H. Type A behavior pattern: Its association with coronary heart disease. *Annals of Clinical Research*, 3:300–312, 1971.

Groen, J. J. Emotional factors in the etiology of internal diseases. In J. J. Groen, ed., *Psychosomatic Research*. Oxford: Pergamon, 1964.

Jansson, B. A catamnestic study of 476 attempted suicides with special regard to the prognosis of cases of drug automatism. *Acta Psychiatrica Scandinavia*, 38:183–198, 1962.

Keith, R. L., Lown, B., and Stare, F. J. Coronary heart disease and behavior patterns. *Psychosomatic Medicine*, 27:424–434, 1965.

Litman, R. E., Curphey, T., Shneidman, E. S., Farberow, N. L., and Tabachnick, N. D. The psychological autopsy of equivocal deaths. *Journal of the American Medical Association*, 184:924–929, 1963.

Long, R. H. Barbiturates, automatism and suicide. *International Counselling Journal*, 26:299–312, 1959.

Lönnqvist, J. Suicide in Helsinki. An epidemiological and social-psychiatric study of suicides in Helsinki in 1960–61 and 1970–71. *Monographs of Psychiatria Fennica*, no. 8, 1977.

Meerloo, J. Hidden suicide. In H. L. P. Resnik, ed., *Suicidal Behaviors: Diagnosis and Management*. Boston: Little, Brown, 1968.

Menninger, K. *Man Against Himself*. New York: Harcourt, Brace, 1938.

Mishara, B., and Kastenbaum, R. Self-injurious behavior and environmental changes in the institutionalized elderly. *Aging and Human Development*, 4:133–145, 1973.

Näätänen, R. *Maantiekuolema: tutkimus liikenneonnettomuuksista*. Porvoo: WSOY, 1972.

Nelson, F. L., and Farberow, N. L. Indirect suicide in the elderly chronically ill patient. In K. Achté and J. Lönnqvist, eds., *Suicide Research.* Helsinki: Psychiatria Fennica Supplement, 1976.

Rachlis, D. Suicide and loss adjustment in the aging. *Bulletin of Suicidology*, 1:23–26, 1970.

Rechardt, E., and Achté, K. Psykoterapia istemurhayrityksiss. In K. Achté et al. *Istemurhat ja niiden ehkaisy.* Porvoo: WSOY, 1973.

Richards, R. A symptom of poisoning by hypnotics of the barbiturate acid group. *British Medical Journal*, 1:331, 1934.

Tabachnick, N., Gussen, J., Litman, R. E., Peck, M. L., Tiber, N., and Wold, C. J. *Accident or Suicide? Destruction by Automobile.* Springfield, Ill.: Thomas, 1973.

Tamerin, J. S. Cigarette smoking as a form of neurotic risk-taking behavior. *Proceedings of the Fifth World Congress of Psychiatry.* Mexico, D. F., Amsterdam: Excerpta Medica, 1971.

van Hejningen, K. H., and Treurniet, N. Psychodynamic factors in acute myocardial infarction. *International Journal of Psycho-Analysis*, 47:370–374, 1966.

4

DESPAIR AND ITS RELATIONSHIP TO SELF-DESTRUCTIVE BEHAVIOR

WILLIAM J. FILSTEAD

This chapter approaches the theme of this volume indirectly. Rather than concentrating on the self-destructive aspects of various kinds of behavior, I have chosen to address, from a sociological perspective, the following question: How does it come about that individuals consider self-destructive behavior as something they might try? To some, this question may seem to be obliquely related to the volume's scheme. However, from the author's viewpoint, this question is central to this theme, for it deals with the essential phenomenological reality of experience upon which behavior is predicated. In simple terms, in order to understand and eventually explain a phenomenon, it is imperative that the phenomenon be understood from the perspective of those persons who have experienced it. Not to follow such a course of action can raise doubts about the credibility of theories that purport to explain behavior but lack this grounding in phenomenological reality (Glaser and Strauss, 1967).

The role of despair in self-destructive behavior will be explored in the following manner: (1) through a review of the relevant literature on this topic; (2) through a presentation of a theoretical model for conceptualizing the natural history of a personal problem; (3) by identifying the phases of despair through the presentation of data collected in a study of obese persons who underwent an experimental operation (jejunoileal shunt) to lose weight; and (4) by identifying how these ideas can be used in understanding the nature of self-destructive behavior.

THE CONCEPT OF DESPAIR _____

The concept of despair is both simple and complex. Perhaps the simplest definition of despair is hopelessness. Many writers have discussed hopelessness with respect to death and dying (Kubler-Ross, 1969; Glaser and Strauss, 1966; Glaser and Strauss, 1968); developmental crises such as childhood (Renshaw, 1974; Robertson and Robertson, 1971; Ekstein et al., 1971); adolescence (Mintz, 1973); aging (Darnley, 1975); other phenomena such as depression (Minkoff et al., 1973; Hampton, 1975); suicide (Pokorny et al., 1975; Beck et al., 1975; Wetzel, 1976); other psychiatric conditions (Beck et al., 1976; Beavers, 1972); and various medical problems (Schmale and Iker, 1971; Moldofsky and Chester, 1970). But in these contexts, hopelessness is often characterized as an intrapsychic phenomenon. This is clear in the work of Maddi (1967), which defines despair as a type of existential neurosis. The psychoanalytic framework has been extensively used to examine the properties of the experience of hopelessness (Sweeney et al., 1970; Green, 1977; Heuscher, 1976), but this framework has been the subject of considerable criticism (Wolstein, 1962; Gaylin, 1968).

From a sociological perspective, the concepts of anomie and alienation are complex terms which embody some of the experiences of despair, but they have been typically studied as consequences of rapid social change, ambiguous social values, or microstructural processes in society, rather than as experiences that are felt by the social actor (Merton, 1938; Seeman, 1959; Cloward, 1959; Cohen, 1965).

While the medical and social science literature dealing directly with the concept of despair is scant, a more formidable body of literary and philosophical work depicts the many facets of despair in a more graphic and experiential manner. For example, the writings of Eugene O'Neill and August Strindberg depict despair as essentially a product of psychological influences. Writers of other periods indicate that despair is more generally associated with social values and social forces. In the twentieth century, for example, there is the literature of the Holocaust and of existentialism (e.g., Beckett and Camus), which has its roots in the ideas of such nineteenth-century philosophers as Schopenhauer, Von Hartmann, and Kierkegaard. This literature is extensive and far beyond the scope of these general comments. It must be said, however, that much can be learned about the experiential nature of despair from an examination of these writings.

In sum, despair, as a concept in its own right, has not been extensively studied in the medical–social science literature. Rather the consequences of despair, namely hopelessness and alienation, have been discussed. What follows is an attempt to define this concept and identify the processes and properties that are associated with it.

Despair can be thought of as a psychosocial state that people experience when they are trying to resolve what has become a serious personal problem—i.e., "a perceived disturbance in the integration of a system about which something must be done" (Katz, 1971)—and realize that there does not appear to be any way to resolve it. There are psychological consequences attendant on repeated failures to resolve problems and the social realities of the reactions of others.

From the perspective of the person experiencing the personal problem, everything possible has been tried that could have resolved the problem, but nothing has succeeded. The person is now at a complete loss, for there is *nothing left to try;* and this is the feeling of despair. The experience of desperation, that is, a willingness to try anything that might resolve a personal problem, "is a harbinger of despair." This "grasping at straws" clearly indicates that conventional strategies for solving the personal problem have failed, thereby heightening one's awareness of despair. The dynamics of this experience will be discussed in more detail later in this chapter.

A THEORETICAL FRAMEWORK FOR CONCEPTUALIZING PERSONAL PROBLEMS _____

In order to understand despair and its implications for behavior, it is necessary to place this concept in a broader context, a theoretical framework which I have chosen to call a "natural history of a personal problem."

The natural-history element of this model refers to the development, course, and results of coping with a personal problem. This framework has been used by some sociologists to conceptualize social problems (Blumer, 1971; Fuller and Myers, 1941; Spector and Kitsuse, 1973). It has the distinct advantage of orienting the researchers and/or clinicians to the temporal dimensions of a personal problem's development, the stages and/or phases the problem may pass through, and the role various institutions, organizations, and individuals may play in shaping the distinctive history of the problem. In short, things take place over time and in sequence, and they usually involve more than one person; therefore, it behooves the researcher-clinician to be sensitive to the role these forces potentially play in a personal problem.

As indicated earlier, the phrase personal problem represents a way of conceptualizing troubles or a "social mess." Katz (1971) has identified three interrelated aspects of a social mess which clearly shape the character of the personal problem. First, the determination of the nature and existence of a personal problem is not independent from the reaction to it: "Often the social mess is defined in the process of selecting an appropriate and efficacious resolution." Second, "an important part of understanding how a mess came about is the understanding of the motivation of the individual deemed to have caused it." Finally, having identified a personal problem, and having made judgments about the motivation of the person responsible for producing it, place constraints on the social actor "to do distinctive work in constructing a way of understanding the source of the social mess and, therefore, how the proposed solution can be efficacious." With these assumptions about personal problems in mind, let us turn to an examination of three perspectives which interact in the process of identifying and responding to a personal problem.

KEY PERSPECTIVES ON THE PERSONAL PROBLEM

Three key perspectives must be kept in mind when studying a personal problem in this natural-history framework. First, there are the generally shared, taken-for-granted societal conceptions about the personal problem (Garfinkel, 1967). These are commonsense notions and folk wisdom. This knowledge emerges from the patterned forms of social interaction which continually add to, modify, and rearrange the assumptions and beliefs that people hold about the social world. While this body of knowledge is ever changing, it has an obdurate character which emphasizes the shared quality of this knowledge among social actors. This commonsense knowledge is particularly important to the study of personal problems because it forms a common foundation upon which both the individual and the various audiences can begin to define each other, regardless of the degree to which this identification process is shared by the parties.

Secondly, there are the various audiences, both public and private, personal or remote, informal and formal, which are encountered by someone with a personal problem. Each audience, be it a parent, spouse, "problem solver," etc., has an impact on and is influenced by the social actor. One of the basic underlying assumptions of the natural-history framework is that *events take place over time*. This processual-temporal dimension calls attention to the need to focus on how the problem, the audiences encountered, and the persons experiencing the problem have made sense of this condition and how the very fact of "making sense of it" (the personal problem) keeps changing and, as a consequence, changes how the personal problem is perceived and understood.

The third perspective to bear in mind is the person's own understanding and explanation of the personal problem. The perspective the social actor brings to bear on the personal problem will be influenced not only by the aforementioned perspectives, but also by the unique manner in which the person constructs social meanings to "make sense" of the personal problem. This perspective is the key organizing principle of this theoretical framework. How and why personal problems arise and develop is intimately related to the experiences in a person's social setting. Truly to understand the personal problem, it is necessary to describe how the person experiencing it "makes sense" out of it, that is, how social actors explain to themselves how the present situation came to exist.

The following questions apply to each of the three perspectives just discussed and should provide direction to researchers and clinicians in comprehending each perspective.

1. *Commonsense societal conceptions about social life.*

   (a) What do the commonsense knowledge, assumptions, and stereotypes say about the specific personal problem under study?

   (b) To what extent is this body of knowledge differentially known, understood, and used by the social actor and by the audiences involved with the personal problem?

   (c) What does this body of knowledge dictate as to courses of action, focus and levels of responsibility for the personal problem, problem-resolution strategies, agents of social control to contact, and the expected outcomes having complied with these guidelines?

2. *The various audiences of a personal problem.*

   (a) What rules are used by the various audiences in making a judgment that a personal problem exists? What factors affect the differential application of these rules? How is the course of the personal problem affected by the rules that the respective audiences invoke to make sure of the personal problem?

   (b) What stages or phases are involved in the personal problem? What "explanations" are used by which audiences to understand and explain this phenomenon? How do these multiple explanations "fit" with each other? Which explanations are judged to be correct and why? What lines of action do these explanations suggest? Do the explanations undergo changes as one moves through the stages of the personal problem? What factors or conditions produce changing explanations?

(c) What are the characteristic elements/properties of each stage of the personal problem? What are the critical junctures in each stage of the personal problem which either facilitate or impede movement to the next stage or maintain the present stage of the personal problem? Which audience appears to be most flexible and which most rigid in its conceptualization of the personal problem?

3. *The social actor's perspective.*

(a) What is the social actor's explanation for how and why the personal problem developed, how and why it reached any particular point of its development, and how the "final" explanation for making sense of the personal problem came about? How has making sense of the personal problem, at any stage of its development, affected a future course of action?

(b) What kinds of activities were tried to resolve the problem and what logic was used to select such activities?

(c) What influences did the various audiences involved in the personal problem have on the social actor's perception of the problem? What meanings and interpretations did the social actor give to these audiences, and how did the process shape the social actor's understanding of the personal problem?

These perspectives are central to the natural history of a personal problem. With this in mind, we now turn to a discussion of the phases of a personal problem, followed by the presentation of the elements of despair. By way of introduction to these two areas, a brief description follows of the research upon which these discussions are based.

THE STUDY OF OBESITY _____

In the course of presenting the elements of despair, examples will be used from a study of persons who underwent an experimental operation to lose weight (Morgan, 1967; Payne et al., 1969; Sherman et al., 1965; Scott et al., 1970). The purpose of using substantive examples is to clarify the phases of despair and how it develops while a person is trying to resolve a personal problem.

The purpose of this obesity research was to describe "how it came about" that a person learned about, considered, went through with, and recovered from the operation, and the subsequent changes this drastic weight loss had on the person's self-concepts and social worlds (Filstead, 1973). In order to understand this process, unstructured interviews were conducted with people who came to the surgeon's office to be "evaluated" as candidates for the operation. I spoke with those who, after having been evaluated, decided they would have the surgery and, finally, I talked with some who were from three months to eight years postoperative. By talking with people along this continuum—from considering the operation to having experienced the effects of the operation—I hoped to be able to capture the natural history of this personal problem.

On a theoretical level, a number of explanations emerged which seemed like plausible answers to the initial question raised by this research. Subsequent analysis and interpretation of the data produced two explanations which encompassed all the answers the patients gave to the question: "How did it come about that you decided to have the surgery?"

First there is the *funnel effect* of a personal problem. That is, the options available to resolve a personal problem are limited by the conceptions and assumptions the person brings to bear on the nature of the problem. Such conceptions and assumptions (e.g., dieting, exercise, counting calories, physician-directed weight-reduction program, diet pills, self-help groups, etc.) prescribe courses of action, locate the focus of responsibility for the problem, and indicate the consequences of not resolving the problem. Such constraints restrict the options that are available as potential solutions. As a person tries various options and fails to resolve the personal problem, and repeats this process many times, there is the gradual but inevitable elimination of all potential solutions. This process leads to the experience of despair. That is, trying what should resolve the personal problem and failing, and even trying potential solutions not generally thought of as ways of resolving the problem but also failing, leads one to the experience of despair. Despair is the feeling that there is no possible way to resolve a personal problem.

PHASES OF A PERSONAL PROBLEM _____

In order for people to experience despair, the personal problems they are encountering must have gone through three phases of development. In the obesity study, the first phase of the personal problem was *identifying* a weight problem. Although these people had been extremely overweight for a number of years, they had not acknowledged that there was a weight problem. Regardless of how much a person is overweight or the length of time such a condition has existed, as long as the person does not identify overweight as a problem—i.e., a condition about which something has to be done—there is no weight problem for that person. This phase is closely related to the denial component of illness, in that a great many people who are identified by others as having personal problems do not identify themselves in such a manner. Such people may or may not engage in problem-solving activities. It is not uncommon to find people who are "trying" to resolve a problem they do not really feel they have. They do this to comply with pressures brought to bear on them by various publics and/or to diffuse the pressure people are placing upon them to do something about the problem.

Once people realize and acknowledge the existence of personal problems, they typically attempt to *do something about the problem.* This is the second phase. At this stage, the task is to find a solution to the problem. What one does about the personal problem is inseparable from what one thinks about the personal problem. How the problem is defined, who are identified as causal agents in the development, continuation, and resolution of the problem, etc., all have bearing on what options are available for problem resolution. During this phase of trying to do something about the problem a person either finds "solutions" that resolve the problem or, failing to do so, embarks upon a search to find such solutions. A critical experience of this phase of the personal problem is failing to resolve the problem according to the traditional strategies that should work to resolve it.

The third and final phase of the personal problem, which leads to despair, is *not being able to do anything to resolve the personal problem.* At this point the nature of the problem changes and, consequently, so does the self-image of the person experiencing the problem. Now the thrust of activity is no longer aimed at the personal problem, but at the inability to resolve it. These people no longer have a weight problem, they have a problem doing something about the weight problem. For the first time there is a conscious realization that solving the personal problem is now more problematic than the problems caused by the personal problem.

These phases of the personal problem are necessary to produce the context in which the person experiences despair. In the discussion that follows, the various properties of despair will be identified.

THE CONCEPTUAL PROPERTIES OF DESPAIR _____

The definition of despair emphasizes the psychological consequences of repeated failures in attempting to resolve a personal problem and the social reality of the reactions of various audiences to this situation. The following quotation from a person who underwent the surgery for obesity describes these two dimensions and how they contribute to the emotional state of despair.

> *Interviewer:* I am trying to get an understanding for the kind of thinking you went through in coming to the decision that surgery was the thing to do.
>
> *Subject:* Well, it doesn't happen immediately. You have to understand that obesity doesn't happen in a week; it's a

lifetime affair. When people are that gross, they have been gross since childhood, and it's something that is constantly on their minds. We also live in a society that rewards slimness, so the farther you are away from being slim, the farther you are going to be out of it. I don't care how well adjusted anybody says they are, when you are constantly out of it, you are going to feel it. At least that is the way I felt. I don't think there is anybody who can always be out of it and yet be happy about that. You've got to feel the pressure and this makes you very aware of who you are and how people around you react to you. You always play the game of whether they are reacting to the fat or to you, and after a while, you realize there is no longer any difference, you are fat and that's the way it is!

Consequently, you spend a life of trying perhaps to become thinner, and, for most fat people who are extremely obese, it works in reverse. Every time you lose ten pounds you gain twenty pounds. And you spend your life on one variety of diet or another. And you spend a life of really deluding yourself of who you are and where you want to be and it just gets to a point where you figure you aren't going to do it—I mean that's all there is to it. You feel that there is just no way you can ever get out of the well you are in. You have to realize that when you have gone on so many diets that you can't remember them all, and that this has been going on for the last ten, fifteen, twenty years, in my case, almost thirty years, and that the result is always the same, you get nowhere; you just keep going up. You really begin to wonder. I mean, I have lost thousands of pounds in my life and have always gained back a few more. And this is the pattern you go through and this is the existence you try and make a go in. This, I think, is the same pattern in all fat people. I don't think you can find anyone who is obese who hasn't been up and down, up and down, and you always go back higher than when you started. Every time you get down you always go back higher than you were. Now, it gets to a point, after this has been going on all your life, of desperation, you know, that you can't do it by diet because you have done all that before and you have tried countless numbers of times, so that there is a way out. It all boils down to a question of how desperate you are as to whether or not you are going to take this way out [surgery].

I think the surgery in itself is an act of desperation. Truthfully, I think that when a person gets to the point of considering surgery, they have run out of any other way to solve their problem, and the surgery offers this hope.

The experiences of this person typify the experiences of those who have undergone the operation. The following discussion specifies the different conceptual properties of despair.

It is clear that *time* is an important feature of despair. How long a person has been trying to resolve a problem is critical to the development of this emotional state. The person experiences despair as the outcome of a *history of attempts* to resolve a problem. The history usually covers a considerable number of years. In some cases, it may have been a lifetime.

> *Interviewer:* You mentioned that you were desperate when you found out about the surgery. Can you describe how you arrived at that point and what it feels like to be there?
>
> *Subject:* Well, it's not the kind of thing that all of a sudden just one day you get desperate. It takes time. It's a gradual thing. Like in my case, as I look back on it, it happened over a period of years. To me, it's the result of having tried to do so many things for such a long time and finding out that nothing works.

Contributing to the temporal dimension in a history of attempts to resolve a problem are commonsense notions about the nature of the particular problem. Commonsense beliefs dictate a variety of *conventional and appropriate ways* to resolve it. Because of the many "possible solutions," it takes a considerable amount of time to try them out. In addition to the variety of potential solutions, a considerable amount of time can pass before people define themselves as having problems with their weight. However, such a recognition can telescope the past in such a way that the past is conceived as a problem, thereby instantly creating a history to the personal problem. Also, at the initial stage of a personal problem one is very optimistic about successfully resolving it. Only after attempting to resolve the problem in the conventional way, and failing (which takes time), does the person become concerned about the ever-diminishing pool of "solutions."

Being unable to resolve the problem in the conventional ways leads the person to consider *unconventional and atypical* solutions. This is the stage of desperation, preceding the feeling of despair. Desperation triggers the search for "anything" that has the "possibility" of resolving the problem. But in time, even the unconventional and atypical solutions prove fruitless.

> *Interviewer:* When you were thinking of the surgery you said you thought there was no other way to solve your problem. Why was that?
>
> *Subject:* I just didn't rule them out. I had tried them all and they had failed. Everything I tried failed. So as far as I was concerned, I hadn't any other ways to consider. There were no

other ways. It was as simple as that. I felt I had done everything and been everywhere. Even after what should have
worked didn't, I tried fat farms, clinics, doctors, quacks, pill
pushers, hypnotists, psychiatrists, every diet you could imagine and nothing ever worked. Nothing was left. I mean when
you have gone through those things there isn't too much left to
choose from, especially after you have been choosing and failing for as many years as I had.

The experience of trying to resolve a personal problem and failing leaves its mark on the person's conception of himself. He becomes very sensitive to the remarks of others and to the situations he
has found himself in. He begins to question his own mental health
and in the process his own identity.

Subject: I felt very guilty about being heavy. It was like I was
robbing myself and my family of the joy of living. I guess I felt
guilty because I really believed I made myself fat and to be fat
in our society is about the worst thing one can do. And I felt
guilty about that.

You look at yourself and all you can think of is that you don't
have any self-respect for yourself. How could you if you let
yourself get that heavy? You think that you must be crazy or
have some underlying problem or else you wouldn't have allowed yourself to get that fat.

A fat person feels a lot of pressure to be slim and look like
the mass-media portraits of life, and you feel this pressure to be
slim from within because you believe it and so do the people
you meet. And you feel really guilty for not doing something
about yourself. You know, it's funny. You may be fat and it
doesn't bother you but you know it bothers others so somehow
you have to allow for or compensate for that or else you are
going to get into trouble with them. Like rather than have
someone make a smart remark or comment on my weight, I
wouldn't go into an ice cream parlor or order a chocolate sun-
dae, because I and they knew what they would think of me
because I would be thinking it about myself. Now imagine
that happening three or four times a day for fifteen-twenty
years or even all your life and no wonder why you got trouble,
or you are withdrawn, or you become shy and introverted.
That's a lot better than having to handle all that flack from
people.

At this stage the person has tried all the conventional and unconventional ways to resolve his or her problem and all have failed.
Such people nevertheless continue to try these potential solutions
over and over again in the hope that something may work this time.

The result of these efforts has been *initial success,* but not a *permanent solution.* In fact, this history of attempts to solve the problem has resulted in a sense of defeat. Now they find themselves *worse off* than before they started, and with each new attempt the problem seems to get worse. Then an attitude of *why try anymore* begins to set in.

> *Subject:* I can remember when I really became serious about doing something about my weight. I had reached a point where losing weight, although it was tough, wasn't half as hard as keeping it off. I could lose but never keep it off. It always went back plus a few more pounds. The more I tried to do about the weight, the more I gained, and I figured why try anymore.
>
> When I would go on diets or start a new doctor, I'd lose four pounds the first week but I'd put back three pounds the next week. Then I'd be only one pound down after two weeks so where would that leave me, especially if I had to lose 150 pounds. I just couldn't seem to get anywhere. No matter how hard I tried, I was always worse off.
>
> *Interviewer:* What do you mean worse off?
>
> *Subject:* I'd weigh more. Like I'd lose 3 pounds a week, go off the diet and gain 5 pounds back. Then I'd start up again and lose 10 pounds and sooner or later, I'd put on 15 pounds, so in the long run I was heavier after each time I started a diet. So why diet?

At this point, the nature of the personal problem is beginning to undergo a change. What began as a concern about a problem caused by excess weight has changed to a concern about excess weight as a problem. The weight problem is now a *central* concern of the person's life. If not on a diet, the person is considering starting one. Another doctor is consulted, another fad reducing program is begun, and new pills are tried. But with each failure the attitude of why try anymore gets stronger and stronger. The pressure to do something about the weight problem comes more from outside social forces than internal desires. One is trying to resolve the problem because one is expected to try. However, the years of trying, the countless failures, the vanished hopes, the steady gain in weight have a synergistic effect which adds a new dimension to the personal problem and makes it even more difficult to solve. Each new attempt to do something about the weight problem is no longer an isolated event. Rather, it is part of the history of the personal problem, which gives it an added dimension of significance. That is why attempts which make no sense to others—for example, going to a psychiatrist or a hypnotist or having a staple put in the ear—may make a lot of sense to the person with the weight problem. For no longer is any action taken to resolve the problem simply an action. It is an extension of a history of actions and, as a result, represents an evolution of potential solutions to resolve this personal problem.

> *Subject:* At one point I had 40 pounds to lose and at the last point I had 140 pounds to lose and that makes a big difference. When you know you couldn't lose 40 pounds, you know damn well that there is no chance at all to lose 140 pounds. And you really don't have a chance! What especially makes a big difference is the fact that by the time I reached 140 pounds overweight, I had so many failures that I just didn't know what to try anymore. You see, every time you start a diet, you realize you have been through this before and you also realize that you are heavier this time than the last time you tried to do something, and you also are at your heaviest period. And that doesn't help matters. You know what happened before and you really don't have too much confidence in your ability to do anything about it. How could you with that history of failures?

This long history of failure with its ever-decreasing pool of "possible solutions," coupled with the steady gain in weight, has reached the point of incapacitating the person in his or her daily activities and causes a shift in approach to the personal problem. By now the person sees himself/herself as different from those who are "just fat"—different from other people and especially from other fat people. No longer do the conventional solutions to this problem apply. Conventional solutions work only for conventional problems and for conventional people. The personal problem is not conventional; it is atypical. The person is not like others; he/she is different. Nothing can be done about the weight problem. This is a significant change in the person's conceptualization of the personal problem. A new factor has been added: the person cannot solve his/her weight problem. Now the person's problem is his *inability to do something about* the weight problem.

> *Interviewer:* What is it like to believe that there is nothing left for you to try so that you can lose the weight?
>
> *Subject:* It's very hard to describe. You know you should lose, you really have done your best to lose, but that hasn't worked. You have tried everything you can think of and at least twice and that hasn't worked. You just feel like dying. I really mean that. I just lived in a shell. I used to go to bed and cry and I would think about killing myself. I thought about that quite a lot because I was so depressed. I used to get up in the morning and think, "What kind of life do I have?" What sense was there to going on like this. I mean I wasn't living. I was alive but that

was that. For all practical purposes I was dead. I just didn't know what I could do to lose weight. There was absolutely nothing left to do and either the weight was going to kill me or I was going to kill myself because of the weight. It was only a matter of time.

Being aware of these forces leads the person to the emotional state of *despair*. Early in the history of this personal problem, the difficulty that confronted the person was finding the *right solution* to the personal problem. Now there is the realization that *there are no solutions*. There is nothing left to try.

In this emotional state, the person sees his/her continued existence as a life and death issue. Life is not worth living as it currently is. The only way one's life can be made worth living is if the personal problem is resolved, but that is not possible. That is the dilemma—an insoluble problem that has to be solved. It is this kind of emotional state which forces the person to make the drastic decision to have surgery. Surgery is the end result of despair.

Interviewer: You said that when you first heard about the surgery, you thought, "What kind of nut would do that?" What made you change your thinking?

Subject: I suppose in my own mind I had become somewhat desperate. I had done all I had thought would have worked and nothing ever did. So I really felt I would try anything that had even the remotest possibility of working. I was at a point of doing anything I had to do to lose the weight. I didn't care how far out it sounded. If there was a possibility of it working I'd try it.

Interviewer: Can you say any more that would describe what you were going through?

Subject: I don't know if I can. I think what happens is that you experience a feeling of hopelessness—that you are in something that is ruining your life and you don't know if you are ever going to get out of it. In fact, you don't even believe there is a way to get out of it. If somebody does show you a way to get out, you calculate your chances and the risks involved and decide whether or not you are going to do it. I don't know if that helps but that's the best I can do. It's hard to explain to someone who hasn't experienced it.

Interviewer: How could I get an understanding of what it is like to be desperate?

Subject: I think if you want to get an understanding of being desperate, you have to look at situations, it doesn't have to be this kind alone, but you have to look at any situation where an individual is forced to make a drastic decision. I mean a drastic decision—something that is going to leave an indelible mark on the person's life. That's what you are going to have to do. And to me the surgery was a drastic decision.

These, then, are the components of despair, and it is within this frame of reference that a person considers the surgery as a "possible solution" to his personal problem.

THE RELATIONSHIP OF DESPAIR TO INDIRECT AND DIRECT SELF-DESTRUCTIVE BEHAVIOR _____

It is clear that the subjects discussed above were aware of their weight problem and its ramifications in other areas of their lives. An important question is how the concept of despair fits into a theoretical scheme which will facilitate our understanding of indirect self-destructive behavior (ISDB). Let me speculate about how this might occur.

The preceding discussion defines despair on the basis of a conscious awareness of the existence of a problem (or "troubles" brought about by a problem), conscious and repeated attempts at resolution that have produced a history of failure, and an awareness that the "identified pool of potential solutions" has gradually diminished. As a result of the preceding processes, the progression into feelings of desperation and despair occurs. This is a conscious process. That is to say, the person is aware of what is occurring and is actively involved in trying to "figure out," "resolve," etc., what is going on in his/her life.

However, with many forms of ISDB this level of conscious awareness may not exist. For example, diabetics who go off their diet, or patients who episodically violate a medical regimen required by other forms of chronic illness, often do not regard their behavior as problematic. Other forms of behavior such as risk-taking may actually produce a sense of euphoria or elation at being able to beat the odds. Despair does not fit into this scheme of things. Yet to others, such actions may be seen as signs of desperation or despair. But how could despair be conceptualized in such behaviors?

One speculation is that behaviors such as those mentioned in the preceding paragraph (for example, violating medical regimens, risk-taking) represent *unconscious* self-destructive motivations. On the other hand, such behavior might have an ability to repress the feelings. For example, by being able to engage in risk-taking behavior, a person can "deny" the need to examine some other facet of his identity or situation. However, removing the facade produced by risk-taking may bring into awareness a problem which needs to be addressed. Depending on the success, or lack of it, the person has in resolving this problem, the feeling of desperation and despair could become a part of this situation.

In essence, despair as defined in this chapter appears to be a significant process in self-destructive behavior. With ISDB, it is suggested that such behaviors may serve as a facade for a variety of psychosocial states or events which, depending on how they are responded to by the person, may lead to desperation and a sense of despair. Furthermore, if the person came to understand ISDBs as mechanisms for suppressing personal troubles, ISDBs may be the very actions which would eventually produce a climate in which the conditions would be set for a self-destructive action to occur.

Assuming that the theory of despair as presented has credibility for a variety of behaviors and social situations, then despair as defined could be an explanatory factor in self-destructive behavior. That is, if in fact the feeling that there is nothing left to try in order to resolve a personal problem is central to despair, then it clearly could be the precipitating event or context which allows a person seriously to entertain self-destructive behavior as a possible solution to the personal problem he or she is experiencing. Therefore, in treating people who are potential suicide risks or who have attempted suicide, it would be important for the therapist, among other things, to begin to get the patient to perceive other viable options available for resolving the problem. The key word is viable. To have some chance of succeeding, the patient in this situation has to define the suggested option, or it is really not an option. Given the history of failure that accompanies such a person, it is not an easy matter to suggest viable options.

Another equally important issue to keep in mind is the stage of the personal problem. If the person feels his or her problem is doing something about the problem and the clinician is still focusing on the substantive problem, there will be miscommunications about what action needs to be taken. Given the significance of the "problem of doing something about the problem" phase of the personal problem to the patient's definition of self and of options for resolving the problem, the clinician needs to be keenly sensitive to this qualitative shift in the nature of the personal problem if intervention is to be effective.

The interface between the experience of being desperate and despair needs to be better understood. We do not know what processes are associated with a person's willingness to try any "solution" that has a possibility (even a remote possibility) of succeeding versus no longer being willing to try anything—because everything has been attempted to resolve this perennial problem. It is almost as if the feeling of despair carries with it the sense of desperateness that is critical to the struggle to find a solution to the problem.

The natural history of a personal problem model stresses three key elements: (1) commonsense cultural beliefs about the problem, (2) the various perspectives audiences and publics can bring to bear on the problem, and (3) the phenomenological view of the person facing the problem. These factors and the questions they raise should heighten the awareness of clinicians to multiple interpretations of reality which need to be understood in their own right with respect to the contribution they make to the process of making sense of the personal problem. A famous sociological dictum of W. I. Thomas's says: "If people define the situation as real, it is real in its consequences." With this dictum in mind clinicians can ask, "How is it that this person doesn't recognize this problem?" rather than assuming they already know the answer. It is important to pay close attention to how people go about the task of constructing meanings for events in their lives. The natural-history model requires such close attention.

Clearly, there are more unknown than known dimensions to self-destructive behavior. In part, this lack of knowledge is due to the tendency not to view the phenomenon in its own right but to explain it with theories and concepts developed without a grounding in this substantive area. The ideas expressed in this chapter stress the importance of comprehending phenomena and people in their own setting before attempting theoretical formulations. Given the task this volume has set for itself, the situation is ripe to begin the study of self-destructive aspects of various kinds of behavior, both indirect and direct, with a framework that builds upon the substantive understanding of this area.

REFERENCES _____

Beavers, R. Schizophrenia and despair. *Comprehensive Psychiatry*, 13:561–572, 1972.

Beck, A., et al. Alcoholism, hopelessness and suicidal behavior. *Journal of Studies on Alcohol*, 37:66–77, 1976.

Beck, A., et al. Hopelessness and suicidal behavior: An overview. *Journal of the American Medical Association*, 234:1146–1149, 1975.

Blumer, H. Social problems as collective behavior. *Social Problems*, 17:298–306, 1971.

Cloward, R. Illegitimate means, anomie, and deviant behavior. *American Sociological Review*, 24:164–176, 1959.

Cohen, A. The sociology of the deviant act: Anomie theory and beyond. *American Sociological Review,* 30:5–14, 1965.

Darnley, F. Adjustment to retirement: Integrity or despair. *Family Coordinator,* 24:217–226, 1975.

Ekstein, R., et al. *The Challenge: Despair and Hope in the Conquest of Inner Space. Further Studies of the Psychoanalytic Treatment of Severely Disturbed Children.* New York: Brunner-Mazel, 1971.

Filstead, W. The Natural History of a Personal Problem. Unpublished doctoral dissertation, Northwestern University, Department of Sociology, 1973.

Fuller, R., and Myers, R. The natural history of a social problem. *American Sociological Review,* 6:320–328, 1941.

Garfinkel, H. *Studies in Ethno-methodology.* Englewood Cliffs, N.J.: Prentice-Hall, 1967.

Gaylin, W., ed. *The Meaning of Despair.* New York: Science House, 1968.

Glaser, B., and Strauss, A. *Awareness of Dying.* Chicago: Aldine, 1966.

Glaser, B., and Strauss, A. *The Discovery of Ground Theory.* Chicago: Aldine, 1967.

Glaser, B., and Strauss, A. *Time for Dying.* Chicago: Aldine, 1968.

Green, M. Anticipation, hope and despair. *Journal of the American Academy of Psychoanalysis,* 5:215–232, 1977.

Hampton, R. *The Far Side of Despair: A Personal Account of Depression.* Chicago: Nelson-Hall, 1975.

Heuscher, J. Inauthenticity, flight from freedom, despair. *American Journal of Psychoanalysis,* 36:331–337, 1976.

Katz, J. Adjudicating Social Messes. Unpublished paper, Northwestern University, Department of Sociology, 1971.

Kubler-Ross, E. *On Death and Dying.* New York: Macmillan, 1969.

Maddi, S. The existential neurosis. *Journal of Abnormal Psychology,* 72:311–325, 1967.

Merton, R. Social structure and anomie. *American Sociological Review,* 3:672–682, 1938.

Minkoff, K., et al. Hopelessness, depression, and attempted suicide. *American Journal of Psychiatry,* 130:455–459, 1973.

Mintz, L. Nihilism and despair, rebirth and repair: A psychoanalytic view of the adolescent crisis. *Journal of the Medical Society of New Jersey,* 70:631–666, 1973.

Moldofsky, H., and Chester, W. Pain and mood patterns in patients with rheumatoid arthritis. *Psychosomatic Medicine,* 32:309–318, 1970.

Morgan, A. Jejunoileostomy for extreme obesity. *Annals of Surgery,* 166:75–82, 1967.

Payne, J., et al. Surgical treatment of obesity. *The American Journal of Surgery,* 118:141–147, 1969.

Pokorny, A., et al. Hopelessness and attempted suicide: A reconsideration. *American Journal of Psychiatry,* 132:954–956, 1975.

Renshaw, D. Suicide and depression in children. *Journal of School Health,* 44:487–489, 1974.

Robertson, J., and Robertson, J. Young children in brief separation: A fresh look. *The Psychoanalytic Study of the Child,* 26:264–315, 1971.

Schmale, A., and Iker, H. Hopelessness as a predictor of cervical cancer. *Social Science and Medicine,* 5:95–100, 1971.

Scott, H., et al. Jejunoileal shunt in surgical treatment for morbid obesity. *Annals of Surgery,* 171:770–782, 1970.

Seeman, M. On the meaning of alienation. *American Sociological Review,* 24:783–791, 1959.

Sherman, C., et al. Clinical and metabolic studies following bowel bypassing for obesity. *Annals of the New York Academy of Science,* 131:614–622, 1965.

Spector, M., and Kitsuse, J. Social problems: A re-formulation. *Social Problems,* 21:145–158, 1973.

Sweeney, D., et al. Differentiation of the "giving-up-aspects"— helplessness and hopelessness. *Archives of General Psychiatry,* 23:378–382, 1970.

Wetzel, R. Hopelessness, depression, and suicide intent. *Archives of General Psychiatry,* 33:1069–1073, 1976.

Wolstein, B. *Irrational Despair.* New York: Free Press, 1962.

PART TWO

PHYSICAL ILLNESS USED AGAINST SELF

5

INDIRECT SELF-DESTRUCTIVE BEHAVIOR IN DIABETICS AND BUERGER'S DISEASE PATIENTS

NORMAN L. FARBEROW

While the past three decades have seen a great increase in studies of overt self-destructive behavior, the study of self-destruction has only recently begun to include the much larger range of behavior by which man aggravates his disease, impairs his functioning, increases his pain, and shortens his life. This may have been because such behavior has more frequently been found near the "normal" end of the continuum of man's activity, and because it has attracted less public attention by avoiding the transgression of the taboos surrounding suicide. Indirect self-destructive behavior (ISDB) seems to serve uniquely personal needs and, at the same time, to frustrate and irritate those obligated for the person's health and care.

To distinguish such behavior from the more familiar suicidal acts which are direct and immediately evident, it has been called indirect self-destructive behavior. It is generally characterized by a long-term and cumulative impact and by the person's denial of any intention to harm himself. Indirect self-destructive behavior appears in many forms. The most obvious are the substance abuses, hyperobesity, compulsive gambling, and disregard of basic requirements for one's own health. Within this last category fall those long-range physical illnesses in which the patient is able largely to control his condition by adhering to a relatively simple medical regimen. Ignoring the regimen, however, will usually result in serious physical symptoms. Two such illnesses in which indirect self-destructive behavior is readily seen are diabetes mellitus and

Buerger's disease (thromboangiitis obliterans and arteriosclerosis obliterans).

This chapter reports two studies—one each on diabetes (Farberow et al., 1970a, 1970b) and Buerger's disease (Farberow and Nehemkis, 1979)—as part of a continuing effort to determine the characteristics and dynamics of those persons who engage in such behavior. The procedures were the same in each study: A case file examination was conducted on an experimental group drawn from a medical and surgical hospital who were identified (by our medical consultant) as uncooperative and noncompliant with their medical regimens and then compared with a matched (man for man) control group drawn from the same hospital on the basis of age (plus or minus six years), race, marital status, and length of illness (within three years). The control cases were also compared demographically with all the cases appearing in the hospital for one year to determine their representativeness. A second part of each study was a clinical investigation, using a prepared interview with and psychological tests on patients currently in the hospital and identified as noncompliant with their required medical regimen.

The results of the two studies are reported below.

DIABETES MELLITUS PATIENTS_____

CASE FILE STUDY

This study was the first in a series of studies on indirect self-destructive behavior and was exploratory in nature. It was meant to determine whether ISDB was a characteristic pattern found in some chronic long-term patients and, if so, what its predominant features were. The study examined the files of twenty-four experimental subjects and twenty-four matched controls. The experimental patients were those who had been admitted to the hospital at least three times because of diabetic acidosis or insulin coma, states that could be taken as prima facie evidence of consistent disregard or neglect of their illness.

The modal ISDB diabetic patient was described as having a mean age of forty-eight years, compared with a mean age of fifty-six years in the baseline group. He was more likely to be separated or divorced than either the matched controls or the baseline group, who were more likely to be married. The implication is that the experimental group experienced more difficulties in establishing and maintaining interpersonal relationships. In the experimental group, the average number of admissions because their diabetes was out of control was 8, while for the controls the average was 2, and for the baseline group the average was only 1.4. The differences between the experimental and the control and baseline groups in this respect indicate how much greater a problem the experimentals present for hospital administration. The average length of illness for the two groups and for the baseline group was nearly ten years. The uncooperative diabetics also tended to have many more related-to-diabetes illnesses (about 1.5 versus 0.71 for experimental and control groups respectively) and more unrelated illnesses (about 2.9 versus 2.0 per patient). The experimental patient was described in the records as uncooperative because he flouted hospital rules, disregarded diet regulations and medical prescriptions, failed to appear for appointments, and made unending demands. Uncooperative patients were characterized by such remarks as "Patient was discovered off the ward, drinking alcohol" and "The meanest man on the ward." In contrast, the cooperative patients were considered to be friendly, quiet or sociable, kept laboratory appointments, and adhered to diet regulations.

The experimental group showed, primarily, denial and negligence in their attitudes toward their illness. They were also highly dependent persons and openly demanded that they be taken care of. Their remarks showed that they considered their illness the hospital's responsibility, not theirs. The most frequent descriptive terms for the experimental group were: passive, dependent, hostile, and antisocial. They were also inclined to be suspicious, impulsive, and complaining. In contrast, the controls were seen as passive-dependent, anxious, depressed, but also quiet or cheerful and pleasant. The anxiety was most often related to realistic worry and tension. In general, they did not seem as involved with the hospital.

The experimental group showed more prior overt suicidal behavior as well as more indirect self-destructive behavior than the controls. Thus at least three patients in the experimental group had been overtly suicidal in the past, compared to none in the control group. In addition, alcohol was a problem among the experimentals (twelve versus two controls). Two patients drove while drunk and one was a drug addict.

CLINICAL STUDY

A clinical study was conducted on twelve "uncooperative" patients from the metabolic ward of the hospital. All were adult, male, mostly in their forties and fifties, and most were either divorced or separated. Length of illness ranged from three to twenty years, and the median number of hospital admissions was twelve. All but two patients had directly related illnesses, and all had from four to ten nonrelated illnesses.

Interview material indicated the same attitudes of denial, rejection of the disease, poor interpersonal relations, and problems with alcohol. The dominant defense mechanism of the patients seemed to be massive denial, as seen in their statements that they had no problems with diet, insulin, alcohol, or hospital staff. They denied emotional problems, but "insisted" on their dependency through declarations that they could not work or take care of themselves. They were described as self-centered, lacking in self-awareness, moderately depressed, and having many feelings of inferiority.

Rorschachs were obtained on nine patients. These emphasized their low frustration tolerance, poor impulse control, and high level of anxiety, frequently accompanied by agitation. There seemed to be two subgroups. In the first, the illness seemed to play no dynamically meaningful role in the patient's behavior but rather was exacerbated as a concomitant of impulse-gratifying activities. In the second, the illness appeared to have been integrated into defensive personality patterns and then deliberately manipulated for personal satisfaction. In a number of the patients an ability to use extensive denial allowed strong tendencies for impulse gratification to seek expression. The other side of the coin was a minimal tolerance for frustration or delay. Future orientation or concern was also minimal.

BUERGER'S DISEASE _____

A second study also focused on patients who notoriously neglect their medical regimen, patients with diagnoses of thromboangiitis obliterans, or Buerger's disease. This is a vascular disease characterized by recurrent inflammation of superficial blood vessels of the extremities which may produce symptoms or signs of occlusive arterial disease in an extremity. Buerger's illness seems to be differentiated from diabetes in that it is more specifically related to and controlled by a single activity, smoking. It is also helped by avoiding undue exposure to cold. Diabetes is more systemic, and its control is therefore more complicated. Treatment involves more than just insulin or diet alone and the patient's personality is a major factor.

This study also was conducted in two parts. In the first part case files of matched cooperative and uncooperative Buerger's disease patients were examined; in the second, interview and psychological test data were used for an in-depth study of patients currently in the hospital. Although the selection of patients in the diabetic study was based on a symptom or physical state (i.e., diabetic acidosis or insulin coma), the selection of the Buerger's disease patients was based on the presence of uncooperative behavior itself. The experimental patients were identified as uncooperative, as judged by a medical consultant, on the basis of neglect of medical advice, refusal to abstain from or markedly reduce cigarette smoking, nonavoidance of contact with cold, and resistance to the hospital regimen. For example, in the hospital the patient refused physical therapy, or was reluctant to exercise related muscles after amputation, or avoided practice with his prosthesis. He was querulous, demanding, and annoying to other patients, insisted on instant relief from pain, and frequently neglected accompanying medical conditions. Matched controls were selected by using the criteria that the patient did observe his prescribed medical regimen, abstained from or markedly reduced smoking, moved to a warmer climate, and even changed his profession to help his medical condition. In the hospital, he observed regulations and seemed eager to be rehabilitated.

CASE FILE STUDY

Each group consisted of twenty-six patients, and both groups were compared with a total sample of all Buerger's disease cases discharged from the hospital during a subsequent year, consisting of twenty-five cases. The modal description of the uncooperative Buerger's patient showed him to be around forty-eight years of age (versus fifty for the baseline group), to have had Buerger's disease for approximately eighteen years (versus sixteen in the baseline group), and to have an average of five additional illnesses, two related and three unrelated, which complicated his treatment program. He was likely to be married and to hold a skilled job when not in the hospital. In personality characteristics the experimental patients were most often characterized as complaining, demanding, and manipulative, or hostile or negativistic. No such descriptions were found for the controls, who were seen as friendly, pleasant, helpful, considerate, grateful, responsible, and reliable. Depression and anxiety, however, did not differentiate the experimentals from the controls.

Alcohol was a more continuing problem for the experimentals, among whom excessive drinking was seen more often than among the controls. The experimentals were arrested for drunk driving nearly three times as often as the controls. Smoking behavior was the most significant differentiator. Nearly all patients in both groups were smokers before the illness was diagnosed. However, all twenty-three of the smokers in the uncooperative group continued to smoke after their illness had begun, whereas only twelve of the twenty-four controls who originally smoked continued to do so. They markedly reduced the amount of their smoking, however.

Prior suicidal behavior did not seem to differentiate the two groups; four to six previous suicide attempts or threats were noted for each group. Other ISDBs—fighting, leaving against medical advice, being absent without leave, or disciplinary discharges—were found almost entirely among the experimentals.

In attitude toward the illness the experimental group showed marked denial, negligence, and a tendency to minimize the seriousness of the illness. They placed the responsibility for their illness on the hospital and its staff in an open bid for dependency gratification. They resented the illness and made frequent demands for relief of pain.

CLINICAL STUDY

Interviews and psychological test data were obtained on twenty-four patients currently in the hospital with Buerger's disease, twelve judged to be noncooperative experimentals and twelve cooperative controls. No attempt was made to match the groups. The files were used by our medical consultant only to classify the patients as either experimental or control. Psychological test data included a semantic differential scale for two items, "my life now" and "my life in the future," the Time Metaphor Test (Knapp and Garbutt, 1958; Wallach and Green, 1961), Attitudes toward Time (Kuhlen and Monge, 1968), Attitude toward Death (Kalish, 1963), and the Rorschach.

The psychological tests and interview material indicated that the uncooperative Buerger patient did not value time nor was he invested in production and achievement goals esteemed in our society. He seemed less driven and without ambition to achieve distant goals. He hated the prospect of a dull life, apparently preferring the excitement and pleasures of the here and now to the promises of a future. The Rorschach indicated that the experimentals tended to be less well organized in their reality orientation, to be looser in their thinking, and to show more sexual conflict. The experimentals were more likely to be dependent-dissatisfied and the controls more dependent-satisfied. The experimentals were also more hostile than the controls and less tolerant of frustration. The uncooperative Buerger patients did not describe feelings of helplessness or hopelessness. Helplessness seems to be derived from the feelings of loss of control and inability to do anything about a situation personally. However, these patients appeared instead to have found a mechanism for maintaining control which was highly effective and frequently gratifying. Thus, Buerger's disease ISDB patients were infrequently depressed. With less investment in relationships with others and in future goals, they interpreted defeat not as evidence of inadequacy but as merely a temporary setback in the pursuit of immediate pleasure. Almost incredibly, then, they saw loss of a limb or function or sense as a temporary discomfort that simply occurred and was to be endured.

COMPARISON BETWEEN DIABETIC
AND BUERGER'S DISEASE PATIENTS _____

Table 1 makes more apparent the various characteristics on which the diabetic and Buerger's disease patients were measured and how they compared on each. Of fourteen variables there were similarities on eight, differences on five, and no comparison was made on one.

In terms of their illness, both indirectly self-destructive diabetics and Buerger's disease patients tended to have their illness longer than other patients with the same illness and to deny, disregard, and neglect their illness more. They often refused recommended or necessary treatment and examinations, got into fights on the ward, left the hospital early against medical advice, disregarded their other illnesses, and abused alcohol. In the hospital they were both characterized as complaining, demanding, aggressive, hostile, suspicious, negativistic, and manipulative. They felt little responsibility for their illnesses and assumed it was the hospital's obligation to take care of them. As a result of their poor interpersonal relations they had few outside supports. They were highly present-oriented, seeking instant gratification. Consequently they had poor work histories, showing little interest in achievement or in working toward a goal. Life held little promise, so satisfaction had to be sought immediately for any desire, need, or impulse.

Age was one of the five variables on which there were differences, the diabetics tending to be younger than their baseline group, the Buerger's disease patients being about the same age. The diabetics also tended to have more illnesses in addition to their principal one of diabetes, probably because their illness is systemic and, when not attended to, affects many other parts of the body. The Buerger's disease patients, on the other hand, did not show any significant differences from their baseline group in the number of other illnesses.

One significant area of difference lay in the attitude of the patients toward the hospital. The diabetics looked upon the hospital as their major source of support and made obvious efforts to remain patients. They were more likely to be dependent-satisfied until there were efforts to move them out of the hospital, at which point they became complaining and demanding. They were more invested in controlling treatment and in forcing the staff to continue with responsibility for their illness. The Buerger's cases were more dependent-

TABLE 1 *Characteristics of Indirectly Self-Destructive Diabetic and Buerger's Disease Patients*

Variables	Diabetes	Buerger's disease
	ISDB patients tend:	ISDB patients tend:
Age	To be younger	To show no significant differences
Length of illness	To be ill longer	To be ill longer (slightly)
Other illness	To have a greater number of other illnesses	To show no significant differences
Attitude toward illness	To deny, neglect, disregard their illness	To show denial, negligence, indifference
Attitude toward hospital	To use hospital as major source of support	Not to like the hospital
Overt suicidal behavior	To show more overt suicidal behavior	To show no significant differences
Other ISDB	To disregard other illnesses; to have drunk-driving records	To refuse treatment, examinations, surgery; to fight; to leave the hospital early against medical advice
Behavior in hospital	To be complaining, demanding, aggressive, hostile, suspicious; to have poor impulse control	To be complaining, demanding, aggressive, hostile, negativistic, manipulative
Outside supports	To have few; not interested in having outside support	To have few outside supports
Futurity	To be highly present-oriented, seeking instant gratification; to have very poor work history	To be pessimistic; to prefer immediate gratification (smoking); to show little interest in achievement or in working toward a goal
Feelings of adequacy, control, mastery	To be manipulative, passive-aggressive, dependent (illness is hospital's responsibility); to use ISDB as outlet for feelings of inadequacy	To be dependent-dissatisfied (forcing others to take care of him)
Risk-taking, excitement	Not obtained	To feel that living a dull life is worse than death
Feelings about and satisfactions from life	To feel life has little to offer	To feel that life offers few rewards or satisfactions
Impulsivity	To show low frustration tolerance, poor control	To be more constricted than impulsive

dissatisfied and tended to be much less interested in controlling others. They did not like the hospital and became concerned primarily when the treatment made inconvenient demands on them. The diabetics were more disorganized, had little frustration tolerance, and used ISDB as a means of establishing some feeling of mastery. The Buerger's patients were more likely to be constricted and in better control of their behavior.

DISCUSSION

Patients characterized by ISDB are most frustrating for staff and hospital. When the same patients return to the hospital time and time again—mostly because they have engaged in what seems like conscious and deliberate disregard of simple requirements for their self-care—the staff understandably feels resentful and rejected. When the staff has been called upon to perform heroic measures to stabilize the patient's illness and reorient him toward better health, it is most upsetting when the patient shows little awareness, much less appreciation, of the hospital's contribution and, instead, acts in a highly self-centered manner that only multiplies the demands on the hospital.

Theoretically, it may be promising that a somewhat consistent pattern emerges from patients with two different categories of physical illness, indicating a possible identifiable syndrome and raising hope of an effective treatment program. Diabetic and Buerger's disease patients are often without outside resources or support, frequently having exhausted family and friends. The patients often have only the hospital as the source of both medical and emotional support. Their frustrating and negating behavior is not directed at alienating it, but rather is the expression of strong denial coupled with a need for immediate gratification of impulses and desires. There may be some small measure of reassurance for the staff that the inconsiderate behavior is not directed personally at them. A rational approach with an appeal to reason in an effort to enlist compliance with the medical regimen has little effect, for the patients see no value in long-range planning which involves delay and postponement of satisfactions. Nor do any of the patients consider themselves suicidal in the sense of intentional behavior directed toward self-injury or premature self-destruction. The results of their present activity will become apparent only in the distant future and therefore need not be regarded in the present. This implies that the best approach is the use of simple, well-structured rules, firmly insisted upon and equally firmly enforced, in order to provide a well-defined framework for care while these patients are in the hospital. Outside the hospital, their continuing care is much more of a problem. Cooperation of family or relatives, when available, can be enlisted.

Among the diabetics, some evidence appeared of a small subgroup who seemed consciously to manipulate their illness for the sake of controlling others. Here, limited insight treatment might be useful; staff and peer confrontation in group psychotherapy might have some impact.

A positive aspect of indirect self-destructive activity is evidence that ISDB patients experience time as passing more slowly than do the patients in the cooperative group. It has been reported that slow psychological time is generally an affectively unpleasant experience (Wallach and Green, 1961). This must be especially irritating to the ISDB user because it lacks the excitement and stimulation which he values so highly. The ISDB user hates a dull life. When time passes slowly, he tends to become frustrated and depressed. ISDB thus serves the useful positive purpose of forestalling any depression which lurks in the background. Perhaps, in this way, ISDB also prevents aggression which, in the framework of poor control and low tolerance, would be more likely to result in delinquency, homicide, or overt suicide.

REFERENCES ————————————————————————————

Farberow, Norman L., and Nehemkis, Alexis M. Indirect self-destructive behavior in patients with Buerger's disease. *Journal of Personality Assessment*, 43:86–96, 1979.

Farberow, Norman L., Stein, Kenneth, Darbonne, Allen R., and Hirsch, Sophie. Indirect self-destructive behavior in diabetic patients. *Hospital Medicine*, 6:123–135, 1970a.

Farberow, Norman L., Darbonne, Allen R., Stein, Kenneth, and Hirsch, Sophie. Self-destructive behavior of uncooperative diabetics. *Psychological Reports*, 27:935–946, 1970b.

Kalish, Richard A. Some variables in death attitudes. *Journal of Social Psychology*, 59:137–145, 1963.

Knapp, R. H., and Garbutt, J. T. Time imagery and the achievement motive. *Journal of Personality*, 26:426–434, 1958.

Kuhlen, R. G., and Monge, R. H. Correlates of estimated time passage in adult years. *Journal of Gerontology*, 23:427–432, 1968.

Wallach, M. A., and Green, L. R. On age and the subjective speed of time. *Journal of Gerontology*, 16:71–74, 1961.

6

THE "UNCOOPERATIVE" PATIENT
Self-Destructive Behavior in Hemodialysis Patients

ALAN M. GOLDSTEIN

Today he will take the drops and eat what he is ordered to eat, and will go to bed early; tomorrow, if I do not watch him, he will forget to take the medicine, will eat some sturgeon (and he is not allowed to eat that), and will sit up playing vint until one o'clock.

Tolstoy, The Death of Iván Ilích

Physicians, psychologists, social workers, nurses—in fact, anyone who has dealt with the chronically or terminally ill—can recognize similarities between Ivan Ilych's behavior and that of their own patients. The "uncooperative" patient presents a serious problem to the medical staff responsible for his treatment. More important, however, his apparent inability to follow the prescribed treatment regimen represents a significant threat to his continued survival. "Uncooperative" behaviors take many forms: an inability to follow a specific diet; missing treatment appointments; a failure to report either changes in physical condition or the appearance of secondary symptoms; a failure to take medication; a refusal to limit physical activities or, conversely, a failure to follow an exercise program.

Such behaviors have been explained from a number of distinct theoretical perspectives. At times the "uncooperative" patient is thought of as being an angry, negative person who is acting out his frustrations through displacement on his family and the medical team. Often, such a patient is viewed as exceedingly "concrete," intellectually unable to grasp what is expected of him. Still others view the patient's inability to follow the prescribed medical regimen as a form of suicidal acting-out behavior, an attempt to put an end to an intolerable, hopeless situation. While such factors may be the sole cause for uncooperative behavior in some patients and contributing factors to such behaviors in others, a review of the literature relative to coping and adjustment behaviors in the chronically and terminally ill fails to provide much support for these points of view.

Instead, I see the "uncooperative" patient as a person who is frightened, overwhelmed, and reaching out for any and all evidence that his condition is not critical and that he will recover, continue to survive, and lead a normal happy life. Like the rest of us, the chronically or terminally ill patient employs a variety of coping strategies designed to make life more bearable by avoiding realities which might prove to be overwhelming if directly confronted. Thus "uncooperative" behaviors employed by such patients are viewed as attempts to minimize or avoid the recognition of one's tenuous hold on life by "proving" to themselves and to others that life-sustaining treatments are not required and, therefore, that they are not as critically ill as others might fear. However, by denying the severity of their condition and the need for treatment, such patients risk their lives through noncompliance with the treatment regimen. They engage in forms of indirect self-destructive behavior (ISDB).

The use of the defense mechanism of denial in chronic hemodialysis patients has long been recognized (Wright et al., 1966; Kaplan De-Nour and Czaczkes, 1968; Short and Wilson, 1969; Glassman and Siegel, 1970; Goldstein and Reznikoff, 1972; Goldstein, 1976). According to Anna Freud (1946), denial represents "the phantasy of the reversal of the real facts into their opposite . . ." (p. 100). It permits the chronically ill patient to "perceive and experience only that which he unconsciously feels he is able to handle at the moment" (Goldstein and Anderson, in press). Through the use of denial, the patient with a chronic or terminal illness can avoid the anxieties resulting from his condition and the implications of his condition for continued survival.

Patients on long-term hemodialysis encounter, at every moment, "reminders" of the severity of their condition and the tenuous hold they maintain on life. Their kidneys fail to function adequately to eliminate waste materials from the blood. Uric acid concentration increases and must be removed by dialysis if the patient is to survive. Once begun, hemodialysis treatments must continue for the remainder of the patient's life or until a successful kidney transplant is made. The patient undergoes dialysis, in the hospital or at home, two or three times a week, each session lasting for approximately six hours. The patient hears the constant hum of the dialyzer and sees his blood flowing through the tubing.

In addition to the stress imposed by the actual dialysis treatment, other sources for psychological stress exist. Friedman et al. (1970) found that income is reduced by 28 percent; social activities decline; sexual intercourse is significantly reduced or totally eliminated; and the quality of personal relationships deteriorates. Levy and Wynbrandt (1975) report a deterioration in family life as well. Similarly, such patients often experience debilitation and physical pain; they worry about additional medical complications; they are unable to plan for the future; and they are confronted with thoughts about death. "Patients who have been with them for months and years die. They know that their life span is limited." They also experience "body image problems . . . caused to some extent by repeated operations and by the lack of urination" (Kaplan De-Nour and Czaczkes, 1974a). While treatment keeps such patients alive, it does not constitute a return to health. In a sense, they are "marginal men" (Landsman, 1975), adrift somewhere between the world of the sick and the world of the healthy. Hampers and Schupak (1967) conclude, " . . . there is perhaps no situation which is as stressful to patients and their families as chronic hemodialysis" (p. 147).

It is clear that the chronic condition brings with it two major sources of emotional stress: the physical symptoms themselves and, perhaps more important, the psychological "side effects" precipitated by both the physical symptoms and the treatment process (Goldstein and Fenster, 1973). Similarly, Pritchard (1974) views the patient as being aware of his condition on two levels: the physical level where the patient experiences the symptoms caused by the disturbances in bodily functioning; and the informational level, where the patient acts as "an observer and evaluator of his illness and the primary concern is with its 'meaning' to him, which in turn influences the way in which he reacts to and copes with it" (p. 64). It is on this, the "informational" level, that the coping mechanism of denial serves its most significant function. While the patient may choose to deny his condition and the need for treatment so as to allow him to cope with the emotional stress caused by his condition, such denial may take the form of an inability to follow the medical regimen. It may show itself in indirect self-destructive behavior such as refusal to follow the low sodium and protein diet; refusal to follow fluid restrictions; refusal to care properly for the shunt; and not appearing for a scheduled treatment session. Scribner (1974) refers to these behaviors as "unconscious suicide." Abram (1974) believes that "the uncooperative patient who will not comply with his dietary or fluid restriction represent(s) a variant of self-destructive behavior—a form of 'passive' suicide or slow death by literally drowning in one's own fluids . . ." (p. 52).

While denial may serve to help the patient cope with a frightening reality, its use becomes counterproductive when it reduces his ability to cooperate actively in the treatment regimen. In moderation, a patient's anxiety may serve to motivate him to be concerned about his condition and to comply with the treatment program. "However, when . . . vague and diffuse fear of the future continues unabated for a prolonged period, the reaction can become serious" (Buchanan and Abram, 1976, p. 41). Thus, denial, originally employed by the patient to allow him to *live* his life, can result in a serious *threat* to his continued existence when it leads to ISDB. According to Wilson et al. (1974), the emotional reaction of the chronically ill patient to his condition may represent the most significant obstacle to his treatment.

Though it has long been established that denial serves a purpose in helping a patient cope with anxiety-laden reality, the mechanism through which denial is successfully carried out has only recently been described. Goldstein and Reznikoff (1971) and Goldstein (1976) relate the use of denial by long-term hemodialysis patients to the adoption by such patients of an external-locus-of-control frame of reference in perceiving the world. According to Rotter (1966), people perceive the source of reinforcement for their actions as falling on a continuum. Those who believe that rewards or punishments occur solely as a direct consequence of their own actions and who feel that they alone determine their own lives and their destiny are described as possessing an internal locus of control. On the other end of the continuum are people who perceive reinforcements as occurring on a random basis, bearing no relationship to their own actions. They possess an external locus of control; they believe that luck, chance, or fate controls what happens to them. By adopting a view of the world in which one's own actions have no consequences in one's life, the chronic hemodialysis patient, or any patient with a long-term illness or terminal illness, can avoid the anxieties associated with a strict interpretation of the medical regimen; such patients avoid the perception that they are constantly walking a tightrope between life and death and that any small deviation from the prescribed treatment program could result in death. Thus, the external locus of control adopted by these patients allows them to engage in denial in order to adapt to harsh reality. As dialysis continues, Wilson et al. (1974) found that patients become increasingly more "external" to help them cope with their condition and its implications. Kilpatrick et al. (1972), however, found that as treatment time continued, patients became more "internal." They explain this contradictory finding by stating that the group sampled after twenty-three months of treatment had changed because "of the deletion from the sample of individuals who have been unable to follow their treatment regimen" (p. 728). The externally oriented patients deny the need to follow the treatment program and die as a consequence. While Foster et al. (1974) correctly claim that "the deliberate abrogation of responsibility for a member of the dialysis group has significant survival value" (p. 96), denial, occurring through an external-locus-of-control orientation, can result in death.

Such deaths have, in the past, been thought of as a direct consequence of suicidal impulses. Abram et al. (1971) report a suicide rate of more than 400 times that of the normal population. Of all the patients he studied, 5 percent ended their lives by "suicide." However, approximately 61 percent of the patients in the hemodialysis group died as a direct consequence of not adhering to the treatment program; for instance, by the "ingestion of large amounts of fluids and foods forbidden by the dialysis regimen." Such behavior is more appropriately viewed as an aspect of denial in that the patient develops an external locus of control to allow him to cope and adjust to life. The patient denies the consequences of his action to "prove" to himself he is not as sick as he fears. In fact, nearly one-half of the patients on dialysis abuse their diets (Kaplan De-Nour and Czaczkes, 1974a) and "consume large quantities of 'forbidden foods'" (Glassman and Siegel, 1970, p. 569). Dietary indiscretions, even of the extreme kind, represent indirect self-destructive behavior designed to help the patient cope with life. In comparing the suicide potential of dialysis diet violators to that of nondiet violators, Steinkerchner (1974) concluded that no differences exist between these groups. Dietary violations among dialysis patients *cannot* be interpreted as a form of suicidal acting-out behavior. Similarly, in describing weight gain, often used as an index of a patient's inability to follow diet and fluid instructions, Foster et al. (1974) believe that "weight gain may be an adaptive attempt to reconstitute a disintegrating body image rather than an unconscious self-destruction of the body" (p. 90). While such behavior clearly may have self-destructive consequences, it has its roots in a desire to adapt and to make life emotionally bearable. The motivation behind such indirect self-destructive actions "is to obtain pleasure from present behavior" by denying that which is threatening or uncomfortable (Farberow, 1977, p. 17).

Research on the personality of the "successful" hemodialysis patient supports the view that ISDB is *not* a form of suicide, but rather represents an adaptive strategy. Beard (1969) and Moore (1976) both found that an ability to cope productively or deal with illness-related anxiety was associated with effective dialysis. Such patients were often described as "mature," "adaptive" or "successful." Anderson (1975) views problems of adaptation as being related to conflicts over dependence-independence—the dependent patient experiencing a more difficult time in coping; patients who do well on dialysis are described by Anderson as being "autonomous." In a sense, part of autonomy consists of the willingness of the individual to take responsibility for the consequences of his actions or, in other words, his possessing an internal locus of control. Again, such patients tend to follow the medical regimen and avoid indirect self-destructive behaviors. Patients whose locus of control is internal have been described as having made positive emotional adjustments to their condition (Galaz, 1972). Similarly, Hagberg and Malmquist (1974) found that a favorable outcome on dialysis was related to a patient's intermittent access to anxiety. Low levels of anxiety appear to motivate a patient to be concerned about his condition and to follow the medical regimen. However, when a patient uses denial and adopts an external locus of control, anxiety is blocked, the medical regimen is ignored, and indirect self-destructive behaviors result.

The view that ISDBs are extensions of coping mechanisms receives additional support from the work of Pritchard (1977). In factor-analyzing the adjustment of such patients, among the factors he identified were: a helpless dependence or lack of self-involvement; a distressing preoccupation with or a wish to escape; and paranoid hostility or a tendency for such patients to view the illness as an unjust enemy. These patients perceived their illness as a chance event or a "nonattributable challenge," a view that would encourage behaviors based upon a similar locus-of-control perception of causation. Again, ISDBs appear to be a reflection of this coping strategy.

Patients receive considerable support in their denial, both from their families and from the hospital staff (Goldstein, 1972; Weisman, 1972; Abram, 1974; Krupp, 1976; Goldstein and Anderson, in press). Family and friends face having to cope with the patient's condition. They often support the patient's denial so as to reduce their own anxieties. Similarly, the hospital staff attempts to defend against their feelings and their unconscious associations with dying and death. They may feel helpless in being unable to return the patient to a state of health and may encourage the use of denial by the patient so as to avoid facing emotion-laden material. In fact, Kubler-Ross believes that the patient's tendency to deny "is in direct proportion with the doctor's need for denial" (1969, p. 32).

Perhaps Tolstoy describes the relationship between physician and patient denial most clearly in *The Death of Iván Ilích.* Tolstoy writes about Ilích, who is unable to obtain a direct, truthful answer about his terminal condition from his physician: "And he was tormented by this lie and by this, that they would not confess what all, and he, too, knew, but insisted on lying about him in this terrible situation, and wanted and compelled him to take part in this lie. . . . he was within a hair's breadth of shouting out to them, 'Stop lying! You know, and I, too, know that I am dying . . .' " (1904, pp. 55–56).

In supporting the patient's denial, the physician may unwittingly contribute to or encourage aspects of denial associated with external locus of control—indirect self-destructive behaviors—even though such overt coping mechanisms may "evoke feelings of anger, frustration, and resentment when the individual flouts his medical regimen, as if he has put down the physician and medical science" (Farberow, 1977, p. 17). Kaplan De-Nour and Czaczkes (1974a) describe the tendency of physicians to overestimate a patient's ability to adjust to dialysis and to follow diet restrictions because of the physician's own need to deny. Similarly, they found physicians used greater amounts of denial on dialysis units where patients were doing less well than on units where patients were more successfully responding to treatment (Kaplan De-Nour and Czaczkes, 1974b). Perhaps when denial in the patient is supported by the medical team, it encourages indirect self-destructive behavior in the patient, leading to a need to use even greater amounts of denial by the physician.

The chronically or terminally ill patient needs a variety of defense mechanisms to help him cope with and adjust to his illness and its physical, economic, psychological, and social implications. If his defenses do not operate effectively, he can be overwhelmed by anxiety and cease to function. Yet, moderate levels of anxiety are related to positive adjustment to the illness and to the treatment regimen. However, attempts to reduce anxiety through the use of denial and the development of an external-locus-of-control framework result in ISDBs which, while originally designed to make life more bearable, may, in fact, lead to a premature death. In reinforcing denial, the patient's family and the hospital staff may, inadvertently, increase the likelihood of ISDBs, while at the same time incorrectly identify such actions as "suicide," "uncooperativeness," "negativism," or "hostility."

Noncompliance with the medical regimen is best viewed as an aspect of denial and external-locus-of-control orientation which takes the form of ISDB. Such patients can be helped to substitute other, "more adaptive" adjustment mechanisms, ones that do not produce overt coping disturbances.

REFERENCES _____

Abram, H. S. The uncooperative hemodialysis patient. In N. B. Levy, ed., *Living or Dying: Adaptation to Hemodialysis.* Springfield, Ill.: Thomas, 1974.

Abram, H. S., Moore, G. L., and Westervelt, F. B. Suicidal behavior in chronic dialysis patients. *American Journal of Psychiatry,* 127:1199–1204, 1971.

Anderson, K. The psychological aspects of chronic hemodialysis. *Canadian Psychiatric Association Journal,* 20:385–391, 1975.

Beard, B. H. Fear of death and fear of life: The dilemma in chronic renal failure, hemodialysis, and kidney transplantation. *Archives of General Psychiatry,* 21:373–380, 1969.

Buchanan, D. C., and Abram, H. S. Psychological adaptation to hemodialysis. *Dialysis and Transplantation,* 84:36–42, 1976.

Farberow, N. L. Suicide: Doesn't everybody? *The Clinical Psychologist,* 31(1):16–17, 1977.

Foster, F. G., Cohn, G. L., and McKegncy, F. P. Psychobiologic factors and individual survival on chronic renal hemodialysis. In N. B. Levy, ed., *Living or Dying: Adaptation to Hemodialysis.* Springfield, Ill.: Thomas, 1974.

Freud, A. *The Ego and the Mechanisms of Defence.* New York: International Universities Press, 1946.

Friedman, E. A., Goodwin, N. J., and Chaudhry, L. Psychosocial adjustment of family to maintenance hemodialysis, II. *New York State Journal of Medicine,* 70:767–774, 1970.

Galaz, A. Psychological Aspects Related to the Adjustment of Hemodialysis Patients. Unpublished doctoral dissertation, University of Oklahoma, 1972.

Glassman, B. M., and Siegel, A. Personality correlates of survival on a long-term hemodialysis program. *Archives of General Psychiatry,* 22:566–574, 1970.

Goldstein, A. M. The subjective experience of denial in an objective investigation of chronically ill patients. *Psychosomatics,* 13:20–22, 1972.

Goldstein, A. M. Denial and external locus of control as mechanisms of adjustment in chronic medical illness. *Essence,* 1:5–22, 1976.

Goldstein, A. M., and Anderson, M. M. A model for social work intervention in thanatology. In E. H. Gerchick et al., eds., *The Role of the Community Hospital in Caring for the Dying and the Bereaved.* New York: Arno Press/MSS Information Corp., in press.

Goldstein, A. M., and Fenster, C. A. The role of the mental health practitioner in long-term medical treatment. *Psychosomatics,* 14:153–155, 1973.

Goldstein, A. M., and Reznikoff, M. Suicide in chronic hemodialysis patients from an external locus of control framework. *American Journal of Psychiatry*, 127:1204–1207, 1971.

Goldstein, A. M., and Reznikoff, M. MMPI performance in chronic medical illness: The use of computer-derived interpretations. *British Journal of Psychiatry*, 120:157–158, 1972.

Hagberg, B., and Malmquist, A. A prospective study of patients in chronic hemodialysis, IV. Pretreatment psychiatric and psychological variables predicting outcome. *Journal of Psychosomatic Research*, 18:315–319, 1974.

Hampers, C. L., and Schupak, E. *Long-term Hemodialysis—The Management of the Patient with Chronic Renal Failure*. New York: Grune and Stratton, 1967.

Kaplan De-Nour, A., and Czaczkes, J. W. Psychological and psychiatric observations on patients in chronic hemodialysis. In D. N. S. Kerr, ed., *Proceedings of the European Dialysis and Transplant Association*, vol. 5. Maastricht, Netherlands: Boosten and Stols, 1968, pp. 67–70.

Kaplan De-Nour, A., and Czaczkes, J. W. Personality and adjustment to chronic hemodialysis. In N. B. Levy, ed., *Living or Dying: Adaptation to Hemodialysis*. Springfield, Ill.: Thomas, 1974a.

Kaplan De-Nour, A., and Czaczkes, J. W. Bias in assessment of patients on chronic dialysis. *Journal of Psychosomatic Research*, 18:217–221, 1974b.

Kilpatrick, D. G., Miller, W. C., and Williams, A. V. Locus of control and adjustment to long-term hemodialysis. *Proceedings of the Annual Convention of the American Psychological Association*, 7:727–728, 1972.

Krupp, N. E. Adaptation to chronic illness. *Postgraduate Medicine*, 60:122–125, 1976.

Kubler-Ross, E. *On Death and Dying*. New York: Macmillan, 1969.

Landsman, M. K. The patient with chronic renal failure: A marginal man. *Annals of Internal Medicine*, 82:268–270, 1975.

Levy, N. B., and Wynbrandt, G. D. The quality of life on maintenance hemodialysis. *Lancet*, 1:1328, 1975.

Moore, G. L. Psychiatric aspects of chronic renal disease. *Postgraduate Medicine*, 60:140–146, 1976.

Pritchard, M. Reaction to illness in long-term hemodialysis. *Journal of Psychosomatic Research*, 18:55–67, 1974.

Pritchard, M. Further studies of illness behavior in long-term hemodialysis. *Journal of Psychosomatic Research*, 21:4–48, 1977.

Rotter, J. B. Generalized expectancies for internal versus external control of reinforcement. *Psychological Monographs*, 80:1–28, 1966.

Scribner, B. H. Panel discussion. In N. B. Levy, ed., *Living or Dying: Adaptation to Hemodialysis*. Springfield, Ill.: Thomas, 1974.

Short, M. J., and Wilson, W. P. Roles of denial in chronic hemodialysis. *Archives of General Psychiatry*, 20:433–437, 1969.

Steinkerchner, J. E. Empirical Analysis of Suicide Potential among Dialysis Patients. Unpublished doctoral dissertation, George Peabody College for Teachers, 1974.

Tolstoy, L. N. The death of Iván Ilích. *Works*, 18. New York: Willey, 1904.

Weisman, A. D. *On Dying and Denying*. New York: Behavioral Publications, 1972.

Wilson, C. J., Muzekari, L. H., Schneps, S. A. W., and Schneps, D. W. Time-limited group counseling for chronic hemodialysis patients. *Journal of Counseling Psychology*, 21:376–379, 1974.

Wright, R. G., Sand, P., and Livingston, G. Psychological stress during hemodialysis for chronic renal failure. *Annals of Internal Medicine*, 64:611–621, 1966.

7

INDIRECT SELF-DESTRUCTIVE BEHAVIOR IN SPINAL CORD INJURY

ALEXIS M. NEHEMKIS AND HENRIETTE GROOT

Before analyzing the problem of indirect self-destructive behavior (ISDB) in spinal cord injury (SCI) patients, we should consider the more direct forms of self-destruction. As Durkheim long ago observed (1897/1951), suicide may be viewed as the exaggerated form of common behavioral practices rather than an isolated discontinuous phenomenon. Below, we review the available statistics on the most extreme form of self-destructive behavior—suicide.

MORTALITY STUDIES OF SPINAL CORD INJURY PATIENTS

Hackler (1977) reported the combined results of two studies conducted at the Richmond Veterans Administration Hospital: a twenty-five-year prospective study of 270 SCI patients, and a twenty-one-year retrospective evaluation of 175 paraplegics. After twenty-five years, the mortality rate was 49 percent, with renal disease accounting for 43 percent of the deaths. Suicide was listed as the cause of death in 5 of the 137 cases, and acute alcoholism was given as the cause of one death, classified as accidental in the study.

Nyquist and Bors (1967) presented mortality and survival data on 2,011 patients treated on the SCI Service at the Long Beach Veterans Administration Hospital during a nineteen-year period from 1946 to 1965. The mortality rate was 15 percent. Direct suicide was the cause of 21 of 258 deaths (8.1 percent) or 1.3 percent of all patients with traumatic myelopathy. There was no correlation between suicide and age or level of injury. Among those methods most frequently employed were drug overdoses and gunshot wounds. Death from undetermined causes was reported in 10.85 percent. Interestingly, the authors noted that 7 of the 28 cases so classified may have hastened if not actually accomplished their deaths with drug addiction and alcoholism. In discussing their finding of a suicide rate of 8.1 percent, the authors acknowledged that this figure almost certainly is a very conservative one as it does not include accidental deaths, undetermined deaths, and the so-called "physiological suicides" (Seymour and Comarr, 1956) resulting from self-neglect and chronic alcoholism, eventuating in decubitus ulcer, secondary amyloidosis, and cirrhosis. The authors felt that these deaths, while difficult to trace, would probably increase the statistics on suicidal death.

INDIRECT SELF-DESTRUCTIVENESS _____

In a report on a nine-year study at the University of Minnesota of the causes of death in 11 of 227 patients with traumatic spinal cord injury, Price (1973) emphasized that too little attention has been given to the personality traits and behavior patterns predictive of self-destructive attitudes resulting in physical deterioration or overt suicide. Five cases were discussed. Two of these were the result of overt suicidal action. Of particular interest, however, were the remaining three cases. One of these patients was described as generally uncooperative and disinclined to follow advice regarding care of his urinary tract, although aware of the added hazard posed by a poorly functioning ectopic kidney. Suicidal wishes were verbalized prior to discharge. Death was due to gram-negative shock secondary to a urinary tract infection. One of the other patients developed multiple decubiti which resulted in osteomyelitis. His nutrition was poor, in part owing to his reliance on alcohol. His kidney function was noted to be severely deteriorated for the last three years of his life and he died in renal failure after developing pneumonia. These three patients were reported to have severe personality problems.

In an early study of the comparative social and personal adjustment of paraplegics and quadriplegics, Seymour (1955) introduced the term "physiological suicide." As examples of the practice, Seymour cited patients who had stopped drinking water, cut their food intake to less than the bare minimum, ingested large quantities of alcohol or narcotics, or were brought into the hospital with massive hemorrhaging decubiti that had been deliberately neglected until it was too late to institute remedial measures. Comarr (1965) reported on a case of self-induced bilateral ischiectomy in an SCI patient due to prolonged sitting.

From the available data, it appears that the problem of ISDB in SCI patients has received only minimal attention and is far more significant than previously suggested.

PREINJURY SELF-DESTRUCTIVENESS————————————

The prevalence of self-destructive behavior among SCI patients raises a question whether we might be dealing with a group which is preselected for self-destructiveness in that the spinal cord injury itself may have been the result of direct self-destructive behavior. Over an eight-year period at San Francisco General Hospital, Hoff and Chapman (1971) found that of 204 patients who were treated for traumatic vertebral fractures, 12 sustained the injury during a suicide attempt. In 7 of these cases, paraplegia (complete or incomplete) occurred immediately after injury. All but 2 patients had significant psychiatric illness (schizophrenic diagnosis) prior to the suicide attempt. Five patients had a history of prior attempts and 8 of the 12 were habitual drug users. Khella and Stoner (1977) reviewed 101 cases of SCI admitted to Philadelphia General Hospital during the past fifteen years. One striking finding was that 66 percent of the injuries were caused by gunshot or stab wounds. More than 60 percent of their patients reported a history of heavy drinking and 30 percent revealed a history of drug addiction prior to the injury and admission to the hospital.

DATA COLLECTED BY PRESENT AUTHORS————————————————————————

A varied, multiple-strategy approach was used to collect information regarding the problem of self-destructiveness in SCI patients. The three methods employed were: (1) a *ward census checklist* to establish incidence of self-destructive behavior, (2) an *autopsy case-file study* to evaluate evidence of ISDB, and (3) *staff interviews* to collect anecdotal information regarding personal experience with self-destructive SCI patients and to corroborate findings from the ward census checklist and the autopsy study.

WARD CENSUS CHECKLIST

Staff members at a major Spinal Cord Injury Center who were thoroughly familiar with the patients on their wards were asked to judge the presence or absence of ISDB in each patient. ISDB was defined to include alcohol or drug abuse, refusal of essential treatment, prolonged sitting, and other forms of self-neglect. The staff members were also asked to indicate for each patient whether or not direct self-destructive behavior (DSDB) was evidenced and whether the patient had ever expressed death wishes verbally.

The results indicated that out of a total of 200 patients, only 8, or 4 percent, had demonstrated DSDB. However, 68 patients had displayed various forms of ISDB, or 34 percent of the total inpatient population. Eighteen patients, or 9 percent, had expressed suicidal ideation. Six of the 68 patients showing ISDB also had a history of suicide attempts, and 14 of the 68 had verbalized suicidal wishes. Two patients showed DSDB but no ISDB.

AUTOPSY CASE-FILE STUDY

The autopsy protocol and clinical summary of all spinal cord injury patients ($N = 52$) who died while on the Long Beach Veterans Administration Hospital rolls between 1971 and 1976 were reviewed. A board-certified pathologist[1] evaluated each case to determine whether indirect self-destructive behavior had contributed to the death and could be documented by the autopsy protocol. The period of 1971 to 1976 was selected for several reasons: (1) neither author was affiliated with the SCI service prior to 1971, (2) the 1977 autopsy reports were not yet available, and (3) mortality statistics dating back longer would be of questionable use in view of the recent advances in the multidisciplinary approach to the care of SCI patients (i.e., gram-negative antibiotics, hemodialysis, etc.).

Table 1 presents the results of the autopsy study. Inspection of these data, in particular a comparison of columns 3 and 4, reveals that the traditional Natural-Accident-Suicide-Homicide (NASH) classification of modes of death is insufficient in that it fails to reflect, in many instances, the important role which the decedent played in effecting his own death. Certification of the death as "natural" on the death certificate implies that the decedent has played no role in bringing about his demise and that death was due entirely to failure of the body's processes. Column 3 shows that 16 out of the 49 cases certified as natural were judged to have had an ISDB contribution to the cause of death.

A further reclassification of the mode of death derived from application of the Lettieri and Nehemkis (1974) eight-step revision of the standard NASH taxonomy is represented in column 5. In this classification system the modes of death (natural, accidental, suicidal) are recast in terms of *suicide, first, second,* and *third* degree for purposes of standardizing certification procedures, simplifying the judgment process, and ultimately clarifying and improving the resultant vital statistics. Four basic dimensions (determined by eight questions) are used in certification judgments: (1) life-style, (2) agents of death, (3) anticipation of lethal consequences, and (4) positively reinforcing aspects of predeath behavior.

From column 5 it can be seen that a noteworthy number of cases certified as natural deaths under the NASH system became

---

[1] The authors are deeply indebted to Dr. Byron Smith for having given generously of his time in assisting them in reaching these conclusions.

TABLE 1 *Autopsy Case-File Study Results*

(1)	(2)	(3)	(4)	(5)	(6)
A 3-71	Septicemia and acute bacterial endocarditis	Yes	Natural	Suicide, 2nd degree	Yes
A 28-71	Bronchogenic carcinoma	No	Natural	*	No
A 58-71	Amyloidosis and chronic pyelonephritis and pulmonary emboli	No	Natural	*	Yes
A 86-71	Adenocarcinoma of urinary bladder	No	Natural	*	No
A 219-71	Amyloidosis, renal failure	Yes	Natural	Suicide, 2nd degree	Yes
A 276-71	Barbiturate intoxication[1]	Yes	Suicide	Suicide, 1st degree	Yes
A 337-71	Bronchopneumonia	No	Natural	*	No
A 382-71	Amyloidosis	Yes	Natural	Suicide, 2nd degree	Yes
A 432-71	Respiratory depression, due to sleeping pills and antihistamines	Yes	Natural	Suicide, 2nd degree	Yes
A 446-71	Renal failure due to blood loss post-operatively	No	Natural	*	Yes
A 453-71	Exsanguination—femoral artery	Yes	Suicide	Suicide, 1st degree	Yes
A 507-71	Bronchopneumonia	No	Natural	*	Yes
A 64-72	Bronchogenic carcinoma	Yes	Natural	Suicide, 2nd degree	Yes
A 112-72	Renal failure	Yes	Natural	Suicide, 2nd degree	No
A 132-72	Bronchopneumonia	No	Natural	*	?
A 301-72	Lymphosarcoma	No	Natural	*	No
A 311-72	Acute pulmonary congestion and edema, severe bilateral	Yes	Natural	Suicide, 1st degree	Yes
A 317-72	Confluent bronchopneumonia, bilateral, severe	Yes	Natural	Suicide, 2nd degree	Yes
A 348-72	Intestinal obstruction with sepsis	No	Natural	*	?
A 395-72	Bronchopneumonia	No	Natural	*	No
A 520-72	Acute bacterial endocarditis with septicemia	Yes	Natural	Suicide, 2nd degree	Yes
A 38-73	Bronchopneumonia	No	Natural	*	Yes
A 74-73	Amyloidosis	No	Natural	*	No

TABLE 1 (Continued)

(1)	(2)	(3)	(4)	(5)	(6)
A 96-73	Acute myocardial infarction	No	Natural	*	No
A 179-73	Bronchopneumonia; respiratory insufficiency	No	Natural	*	No
A 235-73	Squamous cell carcinoma of bladder	No	Natural	*	No
A 250-72	Bronchopneumonia	No	Natural	*	Yes
A 322-73	Chronic pyelonephritis, renal failure	No	Natural	*	Yes
A 481-73	Chronic pyelonephritis with renal failure	No	Natural	*	No
A 457-73	Bronchopneumonia (secondary to morphine overdose)	Yes	Natural	Suicide, 2nd degree	Yes
A 23-74	Amyloidosis, renal failure	Pr.[2]	Natural	*	Yes
A 63-74	Acute and chronic pyelo-nephritis with renal failure	No	Natural	*	No
A 131-74	Peritonitis due to perfor-ated duodenal ulcer	No	Natural	*	?
A 161-74	Meningitis	No	Natural	*	Yes
A 206-74	Acute peritonitis	No	Natural	*	Yes
A 209-74	Acute hemorrhagic gastritis with perfora-tion; cirrhosis of liver; chronic pancreatitis	Yes	Natural	Suicide, 3rd degree	Yes
A 268-74	Bilateral broncho-pneumonia, lung and brain abscess with meningitis	Yes	Natural	Suicide, 2nd degree	Yes
A 432-74	Renal failure secondary to pyelonephritis and amyloidosis	No	Natural	*	Yes
A 450-74	Renal failure secondary to pyelonephritis	No	Natural	*	Yes
A 467-74	Bronchopneumonia, pyelonephritis	No	Natural	*	Yes
A 468-74	Coronary thrombosis secondary to athero-sclerosis, nephritis	No	Natural	*	No

TABLE 1 (*Continued*)

(1)	(2)	(3)	(4)	(5)	(6)
A 80-75	Gram-negative sepsis secondary to operative procedure	No	Natural	*	No
A 166-75	Respiratory failure secondary to panlobular emphysema	Yes	Natural	Suicide, 2nd degree	Yes
A 303-75	Acute and organizing bronchopneumonia	No	Natural	*	Yes
A 339-75	Upper GI bleed, peritonitis with septicemia	No	Natural	*	Yes
A 371-75	Meningitis	Yes	Natural	Suicide, 2nd degree	Yes
A 491-75	Respiratory failure secondary to tracheal stenosis and broncho-pneumonia	No	Natural	*	No
A 181-76	Bacteremia secondary to decubiti	Pr.[3]	Natural	*	No
A 237-76	Bronchopneumonia	No	Natural	*	Yes
A 293-76	Bronchopneumonia	No	Natural	*	Yes
A 352-76	Bronchopneumonia	No	Natural	*	No
A 374-76	Anesthesia death	No	Accident	*	No

Column 1: Case
Column 2: Cause of death
Column 3: ISDB contributed to death as documented by autopsy protocol
Column 4: Mode of death (from death certificate)
Column 5: Mode of death (Lettieri-Nehemkis classification system)
Column 6: Patient judged self-destructive by reputation prior to death

* Not rated—ISDB not judged to be contributory.
[1] Blood barbiturate level 24 hours after admission to an outside hospital in comatose state = 2 mg %; 2–2.3 mg % representing the lethal dose. This 40 y.o. C-5 level quad engaged in auto cannibalism resulting in the loss of digits 2, 3, 4, and 5 of both hands at the 1st interphalangeal joint area and (R) great toe (accessible to his mouth probably because of flexion contractures).
[2] Probable—cannot state definitively on basis of available records.
[3] Probable—because difficult to evaluate as patient had mental changes, confusion toward the end of his life, hence difficult to attribute deterioration to willful neglect.

second-degree suicidal deaths when reclassified using the Lettieri-Nehemkis dimensions. Second-degree suicide is defined by them to include cases of so-called accidental suicide. As Lettieri and Nehemkis observe, "The individual does not consciously intend to die; he is not overtly anticipating the lethal outcome of his actions, although he has at least a moderate awareness of death as a *possible* consequence of his behavior" (1974). The inference is that the decedent does not clearly intend to die because he/she has selected a method of self-injury which is only moderately risky and/or he/she has made provisions for possible rescue. Some case history material will be used to illustrate the reclassification.

CASE A 166-75. This patient, severely affected by chronic obstructive pulmonary disease (COPD), repeatedly defied the warnings of his physicians that continued heavy smoking would aggravate his pulmonary status by contributing to his chronic bronchitis. His history of extended use and chronic abuse of opiates (IM Demerol and Levo-Dromoran) may have further increased his respiratory embarrassment. Because of his COPD the patient had been cautioned several times that indiscriminate and excessive use of oxygen could abolish his respiratory drive which would result in apnea and death. In addition, he subjected himself to the obvious hazard of explosion by smoking while breathing oxygen. He finally died in respiratory distress.

This death is scored as follows on the eight Lettieri-Nehemkis criteria: (1) Death precipitated by actions which are a part of regular life-style—*true*. (2) Death result of naturally anticipated catabolism—*false by definition*. (3) Death result of untimely catabolism—*true*. (4) Death result of foreign catalyst(s)—*true* (tobacco, excessive oxygen, and drugs). (5) Decedent not overtly anticipating lethal consequences—*true*. (6) Decedent at least moderately aware of death as possible outcome—*true* (because of repeated warnings). (7) Behaviors leading to death were positively reinforcing, such that payoff in terms of pleasure offset the element of risk—*true*. (8) Decedent intentionally killed by another individual—*false*. This scoring pattern of 10 111 110 translates to a reclassified mode of death as: *Suicide, second degree*.

CASE A 371-75. This twenty-nine-year-old C-2 level quadriplegic with implanted phrenic nerve stimulator developed a massive decubitus ulcer over the area of the sacrum. He resisted all attempts by the nursing staff to assist in the healing process. The psychologist reported that, although the patient denied suicidal ideation, he admitted looking forward to death bringing "a release of his spirit from his body." He aggravated his condition by not eating properly and by continually lying in a supine position. This resulted in osteomyelitis, which subsequently communicated with the leptomeninges. The resultant contamination from the sacral decubitus produced meningitis, to which the patient succumbed. The scoring pattern is 00 111 110. (Dimension 7 is scored as true in view of the patient's preference for the supine position and the psychologist's report of the ultimately reinforcing aspects of death to the patient.) The mode of death thus is: *Suicide, second degree.*

The above case histories demonstrate the validity of reclassifying these deaths as subintentioned suicides. Figure 1 outlines some of the mechanisms involved in a suicide, second degree. Certain commonly observed behaviors in our patient population were consistently found to cause certain pathological processes leading to eventual death.

Amyloidosis is well documented as a cause of death in SCI patients, known not only to the attending physicians but to the patients under their care, as well. It is also well established that amyloidosis develops as a result of chronic infection such as pyelonephritis and, more specifically, osteomyelitis. In a certain percentage of SCI patients pyelonephritis and uremia are unavoidable end-stage complications of the spinal cord injury. However, patients who refuse adequate nutrition to enhance wound healing contribute to their chronic infection. Similarly, patients who refuse proper positioning develop recurrent decubiti with osteomyelitis as a frequent result and amyloidosis as the end stage of this state of chronic infection. It is remarkable, therefore, how many of the SCI patients, being knowledgeable about this disease process, sabotage the prescribed regimen in such a way as to hasten its development. The following case illustrates the process.

CASE A 382-71. This thirty-one-year-old patient was rendered quadriplegic when he was struck by a car while crossing the street. He had several hospitalizations for decubitus ulcers and osteomyelitis of both hips. A history of psychiatric difficulties was

---

FIGURE 1 The Pathology of Self-Destruction: Some Commonly Observed Mechanisms Indigenous to the Spinal Cord Injury Population

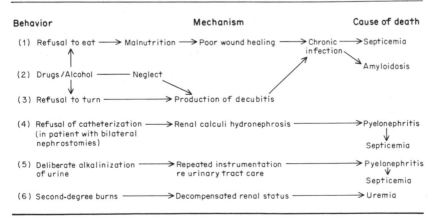

noted in the chart. The patient had been treated with Stelazine. No further information was available. Substantial neglect on the part of the patient was indicated by his refusal to be turned to prevent decubiti and osteomyelitis while in the hospital and by the malnourished state in which he was last admitted. Numerous surgeries were required for attempted correction. His refusal to follow doctor's orders interfered with the healing process. The resultant state of chronic osteomyelitis further resulted in the secondary complication of amyloidosis for many years standing, from which he expired. (Pattern: 10 111 110; mode and degree of death: *Suicide, second degree.*)

Chronic states of infection may also result in septicemia, bacterial endocarditis, and death, as shown in the next case.

CASE A 520-72. Throughout this forty-nine-year-old T-4 level patient's hospital course of twenty-two years, recurrent difficulties occurred involving decubitus ulcers, requiring bilateral above-the-knee amputation, graft rejection, and recurrent decubiti over the trochanteric areas resulting in bilateral disarticulations to arrest osteomyelitis. These decubiti healed or improved significantly upon hospitalization, but exacerbations of the condition always appeared on the patient's return to self-maintenance. It was noted that the patient discontinued necessary analeptic medication and left the hospital against medical advice numerous times. Two years after his spinal cord injury he was hospitalized in the psychiatric unit following a suicide attempt (hanging). The attempt occurred after many months of verbal threats. When he entered the hospital for what was to be his final admission, a physical examination revealed a prominent decubitus over the area of the sacrum with perineal cellulitis and a prominent perirectal abscess. Despite debridement and drainage of the perirectal abscess, the patient developed a bacterial endocarditis: The same coagulase + Staph were isolated from the perirectal abscess as from the vegetative lesions of the heart valves. It is clear that self-neglect was instrumental in both the formation of these decubiti and the perineal cellulitis and perirectal abscess which resulted in recurrent septicemia, endocarditis, and death. (Pattern: 10 111 110; mode and degree of death: *Suicide, second degree.*)

A particularly interesting example of one patient's non-compliance with the medical regimen, for which no reason was apparent, is represented by the fourth mechanism in Figure 1. The following case history illustrates this mechanism and several other forms of ISDB.

CASE A 317-72. In 1968 this sixty-one-year-old male World War

II veteran, 10 percent service-connected for psychoneurosis, was admitted to a county hospital with urinary retention, disorientation, memory impairment, and confabulation. Because of his disorientation and confusion the patient fell while in the hospital, resulting in transverse myelitis. He had had several previous hospitalizations for alcoholism, cirrhosis, impending delirium tremens, and bromide intoxication. After the spinal cord injury, he developed recurrent urinary tract infections, multiple decubiti necessitating surgical correction, recurrent bronchopneumonia, and emphysema. His chart is laden with entries indicating the extent and severity of his uncooperative and self-destructive behavior, such as continued heavy smoking and drinking. Psychological evaluation indicated a passive-dependent, passive-aggressive type of personality with evidence of chronic brain syndrome. His behavior on the ward was described as very hostile and inappropriate. Following numerous episodes of "passing out" and burning his bed, his effects were searched and a number of over-the-counter drugs and unidentified drugs ("street whites") were found in his possession. On a later occasion he was seen by Psychiatry because of his uncooperativeness and his refusal to ingest anything but Coca-Cola. Psychiatric impression was that of a personality disorder, passive-aggressive type. Despite repeated advice about the necessity for acidification of urine, the patient was discovered with a box of sodium bicarbonate by his bedside, which he had been ingesting in unknown amounts while frequently refusing to take ascorbic acid as prescribed. (This use of sodium bicarbonate results in blockage of gastrourinary drainage systems and necessitates repeated instrumentation with attendant likelihood of serious infection.) He remained uncooperative, for example, pulling out intravenous tubes and persisting in smoking even while sedated, and with an oxygen tank at bedside. After discharge to a nursing home, he refused to eat and tipped over his wheelchair, bruising his forehead, face, and neck. The morning he was scheduled for endoscopy for study of a hiatus hernia, he ingested an unknown quantity of rubbing alcohol. Following the ingestion of the alcohol the patient complained increasingly of respiratory difficulty but appeared to be doing reasonably well. Soon thereafter, however, he was noted to have Cheyne-Stokes respiration and cyanosis. He became stuperous with irregular respirations. It is clear that the alcohol ingested precipitated the respiratory insufficiency. At the time of necropsy it was established that confluent bronchopneumonia was responsible for death. (Pattern: 00 011 110; mode and degree of death: *Suicide, second degree.*)

Patients who survive spinal cord injury for at least a decade frequently exhibit a precarious renal status. It is a truism of medicine that a major injury in these patients will result in prompt renal decompensation. The next case illustrates one possible way in which this delicate balance may be irreparably disturbed.

CASE A 112-72. In 1952 this fifty-five-year-old male, with rheumatoid arthritis, fell against a table, sustaining a T-3 fracture and a T-10 complete cord lesion. He was admitted to the hospital on numerous occasions for medical care. In 1962 he was admitted with burns of his right thigh following a spill of boiling water. Ten years later the patient sustained multiple burns to his right thigh on a bathroom heater. This second admission for a burn problem was complicated by gastrointestinal bleeding. The patient was known to have a peptic ulcer diathesis of twenty years' duration. A persistently elevated blood urea nitrogen (BUN) was noted. He was readmitted the following month with acute second-degree burns of both legs, sustained while he was in a shower which, he claimed, he could not turn off. Interestingly, all of this patient's burn injuries involved the insensitive regions of his body (below the level of his cord lesion), suggesting that these episodes may have been subintentioned. On this admission it was noted that his will to live was minimal. He repeatedly asked to be "put to sleep" and was markedly uncooperative in following a bland diet and taking antacids and antispasmodics as prescribed. Active gastrointestinal bleeding required that he have many transfusions. During these episodes of gastric bleeding a markedly elevated BUN occurred and persisted despite the medical measures instituted by Nephrology. His renal function continued to deteriorate; and he expired in terminal uremia due to second-degree burns of both legs with the subsequent decompensation of his tenuous renal function. (Pattern: 001 111 10; mode and degree of death: *Suicide, second degree.*)

From the preceding discussion it is apparent that a number of patients actually employed many behaviors and mechanisms for self-destruction. These patients usually were quite well known to staff because of their self-destructive tendencies. The final column in Table 1 relates information regarding the patients' reputation gathered in the staff survey interviews to the findings of the autopsy study. Again, we see that many of the "natural" deaths were not considered so by the staff who had known the patient. In fact, there is a high degree of corroboration of the pathologist's judgments by the Lettieri-Nehemkis ratings.

The conclusion is inescapable that ISDB is a serious problem on the Spinal Cord Injury Service and, moreover, that it is endemic.

THE CONCEPT OF THE "SLIM MARGIN"[2]

In order to place statistics on self-destructiveness in SCI patients in perspective, we must consider what is required for these patients to maintain good health. From the discussion of Figure 1 it will be apparent that it is far easier for the SCI patient to be self-destructive than not to be self-destructive. Health maintenance requires constant vigilance, considerable self-discipline, and a compulsive attention to matters of health and hygiene; or, simply, the practice of good preventive medicine.

The spinal cord patient is further handicapped by the fact that his sensory system fails to give him the necessary warning signals; for example, the skin area to which circulation is cut off due to pressure will not signal warnings to the brain. Rodgers (1973) discussed the importance of the "symptom threshold" to the surgical patient. The symptom threshold for the paralyzed patient has (in most cases) been radically altered; consequently, he must learn a new set of cues to signal the development of health- or life-threatening conditions, such as, for example, a visible erythema of the skin which may herald the development of a decubitus. The implication of the "slim margin" concept is that often the SCI patient teeters on the brink of self-destruction. If he does not take particular care, and if he does not learn his new cues, it is much easier for him to be self-destructive than not.

The patient faced with this task, moreover, starts out with yet another handicap. More likely than not, the newly injured patient (and he is the one who needs to learn *all* these lessons of survival) is acutely depressed over his loss of function. The severe emotional constriction that accompanies depression may make even more difficult the task of assimilating new cues. In the emotional sphere, also, he has been, at least temporarily, pushed beyond the bounds of normal health. Is it any wonder that SCI patients, either actively or indirectly, wish to do away with themselves?

DSDB IN THE GUISE OF ISDB

As our ward census indicated, many of the patients expressed a death wish verbally as well as behaviorally in the form of direct attempts at suicide. The actual number of suicidal patients probably is considerably greater if we take into account that for some quadriplegics, the only feasible way to commit suicide is by indirect

---

[2] We gratefully acknowledge the contribution of our colleague, Dr. Carol Cummings, to the formulation of this concept.

means. In other words, some of what at first blush looks like ISDB is in actuality intended to be directly self-destructive. An illustrative case is that of a quadriplegic who attempted suicide with a rifle, but because of lack of hand function and unsteady aim, discharged the gun through the roof of his mouth; the bullet lodged in the ethmoid sinus, thereby saving his life. He might, ultimately, have been more successful had he selected one of the mechanisms listed in Figure 1. Resnik (1970) described a case of a clearly intentional suicide attempt enacted by the only means available to the patient, that is, *indirect* ones. The patient was a ten-year-old boy who had undergone quadruple amputations. On the day following the surgical removal of his last limb he refused all food, fluids, and medication by mouth or intravenously, and threw himself from the bed, trying to land on his head.

POTENTIATING EFFECTS OF DRUGS AND ALCOHOL _____

The abuse of alcohol and other drugs poses still a greater hazard for the SCI patient. These commonly used palliatives for grief and trauma also dull the person's awareness of bodily warning signals. A few evenings of overindulgence thus may have serious consequences. The way in which drugs and alcohol may assume a potentiating effect on other types of ISDB is diagramed in Figure 1. The "slim margin" dictates that even here the SCI patient must be extraordinarily cautious.

THE PERSONALITY OF THE SPINAL CORD INJURY PATIENT _____

How well is the SCI patient equipped to deal with the demands and restrictions imposed on him by his injury? In the absence of systematic information we can only record our impressions derived from the case history information. The modal personality is that of a person who tends to be action oriented, extraverted rather than introspective, impulsive rather than compulsive, who externalizes locus of control and uses denial as a major defense mechanism. This type of person has the greatest difficulty conforming to the strict regimen required of the SCI patient and is most likely to run afoul of the slim margin. He is caught in a vicious circle of compounding physical problems, while attempts at escape into drugs or alcohol lead to more frequent and prolonged hospitalization and its attendant restrictions. It is indeed paradoxical that the injury demands the type of behavior that, because of his personality makeup, the patient is least likely to have in his repertoire.

A search of the literature turned up surprisingly few articles relating to personality characteristics and diagnostic classification of the SCI patient. Khella and Stoner (1977) in their fifteen-year follow-up study indicated that all 101 patients were evaluated by a staff psychiatrist and merely stated that "many were found to be psychopathic or sociopathic" (p. 27). The Minnesota Multiphasic Personality Inventory (MMPI) study of a large ($N = 100$) sample of SCI patients by Bourestom and Howard (1965) failed to confirm these observations. The profiles of the SCI sample were within normal limits and their psychopathic (Pd) scores were not elevated. Lyon (1975), in a study of personality factors and life history styles of burn patients and spinal cord patients, differentiated those with self-initiated injuries from those with accidental injuries and reported that the self-initiated group seemed to be "phallic in character" with evidence of deprivation and frustration, whereas the accidental group was more obsessive in character.

Our patients displayed behavior similar to that described by Farberow (1977) in his studies of diabetics, Buerger's disease patients, and the elderly chronically ill. He summarized the characteristics of the indirectly self-destructive person as follows. Cognitively, the ISDB patient shows no marked changes in his functioning in relation to his self-destructive activity. He does not seem emotionally disturbed and his behavior does not seem to occur in response to any immediately identifiable stress. He may even describe himself as feeling good or euphoric. His self-destructive behavior appears to give him some sense of power and control, which helps to overcome feelings of inadequacy (or, in our patients, of helplessness). His motivation is toward the pleasures of the here and now and he tends to be intolerant of the delays and postponements necessary to achieve in the future. He is shortsighted and unconcerned about the long-term effects of his self-destructive activity.

Self-destructive behavior in spinal cord patients appears to have some features in common with the Munchausen syndrome in that patients often display little anxiety but are addicted to hospitalization and to surgery. For both types, diagnostic labeling is problematic, psychiatric or psychological input is often not obtained, and the prognosis for treatment is poor.

THE ROLE OF THE MENTAL HEALTH PROFESSIONAL _____

Perhaps because SCI patients often do not appear to be emotionally disturbed and because the unmistakable red-flag communications of suicidal distress are usually missing, relatively little psychological and psychiatric information exists in the otherwise extensive records of our patients.[3]

It should be noted that, where there was evidence of intervention from mental health professionals, in many of our cases (admittedly the failures, in that they resulted in death) the intervention did not appear to arrest the process of ISDB.

Can the psychologist address himself more effectively to the prophylaxis and treatment of ISDB, or are there factors which effectively stand in the way of treatment and rehabilitation? Perhaps the real issue can be expressed thus: Is the seemingly pervasive tendency to externalize locus of control over matters of health really reflective of the incidence of personality disorder in the SCI population, or does it reflect a shortcoming of our present health care delivery system? Indeed, it appears that for some of the more financially disadvantaged patients there are strong incentives for repeated hospitalization. Moreover, it may be that for all seriously disabled persons, the "patient" role inside the hospital is made more attractive than that of the "disabled" role in the community outside. If it is more difficult for the spinal cord patient to practice the disabled role in the community in at least a minimally rewarding manner, it may be said that "patienthood" can easily become addictive.

A QUESTION OF VALUES _____

As Farberow (1977) has observed, the problem of effective intervention is further complicated by the great difference in society's attitude toward indirect versus direct self-destructive behavior. In the case of indirect self-destructive patterns, especially when the effects of the behavior are small, albeit cumulative, so that any individual act in and of itself does not seem critical, society does not intervene. It presumes that there has been no impairment of the person's capacity to think clearly and to make rational judgments, whereas the converse is assumed in the case of the suicidal person.

Moreover, in the case of the severely disabled person, it may well be that a commonly held, though unstated, assumption of life having little remaining value operates in such a way as to condone, if not encourage, self-destructive behavior. Staff working with the severely disabled are caught in the dilemma, on the one hand, of endorsing the rehabilitation ideal, and, on the other hand, having misgivings that it may not be fair to demand this ideal from a patient who clearly will have greatly impoverished life circumstances.

---

[3] This was more particularly true of the pre-1971 cases. Since then an improved staffing ratio has made psychological services more readily available.

REFERENCES _____

Bourestom, N. D., and Howard, M. T. Personality characteristics of three disability groups. *Medical Rehabilitation,* 46:626–632, 1965.

Comarr, A. E. A self-induced ischiectomy. *Journal of Indian Medical Profession,* 12:5509, 1965.

Durkheim, E. *Suicide.* Glencoe, Ill.: Free Press, 1951. (Originally published, 1897.)

Farberow, N. L. Research in indirect self-destructive behavior. Paper presented at the Psychopathology Section, World Psychiatric Association, Helsinki, Finland, 1977.

Hackler, R. H. A 25-year prospective mortality study in the spinal cord injured patient: Comparison with the long-term living paraplegic. *Journal of Urology,* 117:486–488, 1977.

Hoff, J., and Chapman, M. Vertebral fractures associated with suicide attempts. *Proceedings of the Veterans Administration Spinal Cord Injury Conference,* 18:53–55, 1971.

Khella, L., and Stoner, E. K. 101 cases of spinal cord injury. *American Journal of Physical Medicine,* 56:21–32, 1977.

Lettieri, D. J., and Nehemkis, A. M. A socio-clinical scale for certifying mode of death. In A. T. Beck et al., eds., *The Prediction of Suicide.* New York: Charles Press, 1974.

Lyon, T. Personality factors and life history styles in severe burns and spinal cord injuries. *Dissertation Abstracts International,* 36(3-B):1443, 1975.

Nyquist, R. H., and Bors, E. Mortality and survival in traumatic myelopathy during nineteen years, from 1946 to 1965. *Paraplegia,* 51:22–48, 1967.

Price, M. Causes of death in 11 of 227 patients with traumatic spinal cord injury over a period of nine years. *Paraplegia,* 11:217–220, 1973.

Resnik, H. L. P. Suicide attempt by a 10-year-old after quadruple amputations. *Journal of the American Medical Association,* 212:1211–1212, 1970.

Rodgers, H. The mind of the surgical patient. *Proceedings of the Royal Society of Medicine,* 66:319–324, 1973.

Seymour, C. T. Personality and paralysis, I. Comparative adjustment of paraplegics and quadriplegics. *Archives of Physical Medicine Rehabilitation,* Nov., pp. 691–694, 1955.

Seymour, C. T., and Comarr, A. E. Compulsive polysurgery. *American Journal of Surgery,* 91:849–851, 1956.

8

CORONARY ARTERY ILLNESS AND INDIRECT SELF-DESTRUCTIVE BEHAVIOR

SYLVIA L. GINSPARG

Perhaps the first student of human behavior to observe the importance of psychogenic factors in cardiac functioning was William Shakespeare, who noted, "A light heart liveth long." Since that time, cardiologists, internists, and mental health professionals alike have all observed that serious physical illness may occur in people following a period of depression and reduced ability to cope with the stresses of life.

George Engel (1968) observed that serious physical illness is "commonly preceded by a period of psychological disturbance, during which the individual feels unable to cope." He has designated this the "giving up–given up complex," which is characterized by a feeling of helplessness or hopelessness, a depreciated self-image, a loss of gratification from significant relationships or roles in life, a sense of disruption in continuity, and a reactivation of memories of earlier periods of giving up. Engel believes that the temporary failure of mental coping mechanisms results in the activation of neurally regulated biological emergency patterns which, in turn, may alter the organism's ability to deal with concurrent pathogenic processes and thus lead to the development of physical illness. Lieberman (1965), in a study of elderly subjects, found significant test differences between those he called "death imminent" and "death delayed." He concluded that the psychological changes preceding death are best viewed in terms of the person's "lessened ability to cope adequately with environmental demands," which in turn can hasten or delay death. Weisman and Hackett (1961) studied patients who anticipated their own deaths, even though there was no medical basis for that expectation. The distinguishing feature in these patients was found to be "the absence of living human relationships during the terminal period combined with anticipated reunion, resolution, or release in death." Weisman and Hackett have further developed the concept of an "appropriate death," the circumstances of which "are the opposite of those in which a patient would commit suicide." This concept recognizes personal death as a fulfillment of life and requires the satisfaction of four conditions: (1) conflict reduction, (2) compatibility with ego ideals, (3) preservation or restoration of important personal relationships, and (4) consummation of wish-fulfilling fantasies.

Since depression results from the internalization of anger, it is reasonable to assume that people who have failed to develop adequate channels for the expression of anger are also at risk for the development of serious illness. Dohrenwend (1967), in his attempt to develop a model, suggested that "constraint" in the expression of anger seems to be a significant factor cutting through the various studies. It seems that for a serious physical illness to develop, the anger must be either totally repressed or denied. In some situations the anger may be recognized, but the reality of the situation does not permit discharge, causing the anger to be deflected back upon the self, often as a type of somatic self-punishment. The person who is experiencing a depression either as a result of the loss of a significant object tie or because of internalized anger may be at high risk for the development of cardiovascular illness.

Since the heart is the organ which both provides and symbolizes the essence of life itself, it is a particularly suitable "organ of choice" in those conflicts which represent a "life and death" struggle; that is, for people who feel locked into an intolerable situation from which there is no apparent means of escape.

Daniel Schneider (1967), on the basis of clinical experience, states that in some people the psychic apparatus is not fully developed and therefore fails to act as a buffer to protect the heart from the direct effects of psychic conflict. Such people, furthermore, tend to respond to conflict with terror and rage and are predisposed to a coronary occlusion if the conflict is severe or prolonged.

Stewart Wolf (1967), in collaboration with Bruhn and Adsett, has conducted extensive studies of coronary artery illness over a period of years. They noted that people suffering a myocardial infarction "have been alienated to some degree from their culture or social setting" prior to the infarction. Further, they observed that these people had experienced a significant "emotional drain" before the infarction. Comparing coronary artery patients with healthy matched controls, they found higher Minnesota Multiphasic Personality Inventory (MMPI) depression scores, more long-term frustration in jobs and at home, and an inability to find meaningful satisfaction in leisure and social activities. The patients, furthermore, made little or no attempt to modify their way of life following the infarction. These observations are in keeping with those of Paffenbarger (1966) and others, who found that social and psychological exhaustion correlated significantly with subsequent death from coronary heart disease. Wolf (1967) further concluded that potentially fatal cardiac disturbance may be initiated from the higher centers of the brain in people who are in some way alienated from their environmental supports or otherwise "at the end of their rope." In other words, sudden death can result from neurogenic disruption of cardiac rhythms and can be an adaptive mechanism in a person for whom death appears to be "the ultimate solution" to a pressing problem or difficulty. In a personal communication, Stewart Wolf described how his interest in this whole area of research developed while he was visiting a coronary care unit in Israel where a man was brought in during the night with sudden heart stoppage. A team of cardiologists and internists, working through the night, attempted to save the man's life. When he regained consciousness in the morning, in place of the gratitude one might have anticipated, he angrily reproached the medical team, saying, "For two years I have been trying to find a way to die. Now that I finally managed to die legitimately, you had to save me."

Dassberg et al. (1964), also studying patients in Israel, reported a disproportionately high evidence of myocardial infarction among patients hospitalized for depression. Morton Reiser (1950–1951), in this country, also noted a link between coronary occlusion and depression.

Catherine Bacon (1954) observed in her analytic patients that cardiac pain frequently occurred coincident with the emergence of an acute conflict between receptive and aggressive drives. Peal (1968) offered clinical substantiation for this theory. After interviewing twenty-four patients who had been diagnosed as having a myocardial infarction, Peal noted that the process of receiving in these patients was very early associated with separation anxiety and accompanying feelings of weakness. These feelings frequently led to such specific defense patterns as massive avoidance, identification with the aggressor (particularly in instances of failure in the area of parental identification), and counterphobic mechanisms or overcompensatory reactions to feelings of inadequacy.

The initial attempt to identify personality patterns associated with coronary artery illness was that of Flanders Dunbar (1935), who set up a personality profile. The focal conflict of the coronary patient was identified as an attempt to surpass or subdue authority. A year later, Karl and William Menninger (1936) noted that coronary symptoms characteristically appear in a man who has a strong emotional attachment to his father and a very hostile attitude toward his mother. Both Dunbar and the Menningers emphasized the patient's total repression of the core conflict. The latter also noted that coronary symptoms are a reflection of very strong repressed aggressive tendencies. This impression was reaffirmed in the mid-1940s by Arlow (1945), who concluded that the coronary patient is a person who, out of fear rather than admiration, has made only a partial identification with the father. Arlow compared this fear of authority to that of phobic patients, the difference being that the latter admits his fear and develops mechanisms of flight and evasion, whereas the former denies this fear, transforms his anxiety into aggression, and develops a character deformation which predisposes him to coronary artery illness.

Bahnson and Wardwell (1962) picked up from this point some fifteen years later, since it was their belief that the research of the intervening years had veered away from the critical issue of parental identification and had, as a result, led only to greater ambiguity. On the basis of interviews with and self-administered tasks given to survivors of one myocardial infarction, Bahnson and Wardwell concluded that coronary patients, taken as a whole, had unresolved identification problems. They further concluded that the overall coronary group included two distinct types: the mother-oriented and the father-oriented. The mother-oriented were younger, passive-dependent people with strong succorant needs. They had lower ego strength, were more unstable with trends toward anxiety and depression, made greater use of regressive defenses, showed insufficient control of aggression, and were of lower socioeconomic status.

The father-oriented coronary patients, on the other hand, were older, more active and self-reliant, had strong compensatory sociocentric needs for achievement, had considerable control and ego strength, were of higher socioeconomic class, and made frequent use of compulsive and regressive defenses in an attempt to cling to social norms. Mother-oriented patients seem to comprise the majority of the clinical coronary group.

Franz Alexander (1950) decried the early attempts to establish a psychological profile or to isolate specific traits characteristic of the coronary patient. It was his contention that the emotional factors inherent in coronary artery illness are chronic, free-floating anxiety and repressed hostile impulses, but that the two are intertwined in a neurotic, vicious circle and that any attempt to be more specific would be futile.

These studies all point to the importance of intrapsychic factors in the development of a myocardial infarction. Another trend of research has been to study the role of "stress" as a factor precipitating coronary artery disease. Ostfeld et al. (1964), Lebovits et al. (1967), Syme and Reeder (1967), and Sales (1960) all have pointed to the importance of stress in the development of coronary artery illness. On the other hand, Mordkoff and Golas (1968) and Mordkoff and Parsons (1968) denied the importance of such factors. Hinkle and associates (1968) attempted to explore the relationship between occupational experience and coronary heart disease by conducting a five-year prospective survey of 270,000 men employed by the Bell Telephone System. Their findings indicate that men who attain the highest levels of management face no greater risk of coronary illness than the men who remain at lower levels. They suggest that the precursors for determinants of the risk of coronary artery illness are already established by the time the men reach adulthood and that subsequent experiences do little to alter these risks. Perhaps best known today is the work of Rosenman and Friedman (Friedman, 1964; Friedman and Rosenman, 1959; Friedman et al., 1960, 1964; Rosenman, 1967; Rosenman and Friedman, 1961, 1963; Rosenman et al., 1964, 1966), who have achieved a high degree of empirical specificity following years of investigation. They have identified as Type A the particular behavior pattern they find to be associated with coronary artery illness. Such persons are characterized as having an excessive sense of time urgency, striving for vocational deadlines, and having an enhanced competitive drive. People in whom this particular cluster of traits are not found are identified as Type B and show a relative immunity to the occurrence of clinical coronary illness. Later findings have led the authors to conclude that the Type A behavior pattern precedes rather than results from the illness.

It seems to me that confusion would mark any attempt to relate coronary artery illness to stress, since no objective measures of psychological stress exist. It is my contention that the subjective experience of stress occurs when a person is confronted with a situation which reenacts earlier unmastered traumatic life experiences. This means that it is difficult, if not impossible, to determine what is stress for a person unless one has access to that person's innermost thoughts, needs, and total life experiences.

In looking over the literature, one can easily see that, while the early studies offered great promise, we have as yet no clear understanding of the process by which psychodynamic patterns become translated into somatic responses; more specifically, cardiovascular function. The studies have, furthermore, tended to describe personality factors predisposing a person to the development of coronary artery illness, based on observations of people who have already suffered coronary damage. Such studies overlook the important personality changes which surely occur as a result of the traumatic experience itself. Cameron Hawley (1968) said, "No man can walk to the brink of death and not come back a different man." It certainly seems that such a life-threatening illness of sudden onset would produce massive intrapsychic changes. In no other illness is a person confronted with such a curious paradox—that he/she may die at any moment or may go on to recover full strength and vitality. It is an experience which challenges the patient's basic sense of trust in the environment and in his/her own personal integrity. Thus, the person's chances for survival, following the coronary, depend not only on the nature and extent of the coronary damage but also on the person's emotional response to the trauma and the meaning it has in terms of his/her own level of emotional maturity.

A very important determining factor is one's capacity to tolerate the regression to a state of dependency so necessary for recovery. This is quite comparable to the regression in the service of the ego which takes place in intensive psychotherapy and requires a similar stability of the internal organization. The coronary patient, however, in addition to tolerating a period of enforced immobility and regression to a state of dependency, must cope with the threat imposed by the physical damage and eventually make the necessary changes in his/her life situation. The ability to meet this enormous challenge depends on many factors, such as the person's capacity for trust, general orientation toward life (i.e., optimistic or pessimistic), ability to feel good about himself/herself even though regressed to a state of dependency, and sense of personal integrity even knowing that he/she has sustained damage to a vital bodily organ. These are all attributes developed in the earliest years of life.

An added challenge for the coronary patient in recent years is the ultramodern coronary care unit. This advance in medical science has resulted in the ultimate in technological care but at the price of dehumanizing the patient, who is frequently identified by the tracings of his electrocardiogram rather than by his given name. Perhaps symptomatic of our highly mechanistic society is that we have been able to develop elaborate engineering devices to monitor, stimulate, and even replace a damaged heart but have failed to pay attention to the human and emotional needs of the person who survives this experience. For some, the physical damage sustained may create an overwhelming threat to the person's sense of integrity and confidence in his own ability to achieve mastery over the environment. These are the patients cardiologists dread. If, however, the patient is fortunate enough to survive the initial period of shock and trauma, he then returns home to face the challenge of living with whatever meaning the experience has for him in terms of "where he was at" before the coronary damage occurred. The many ways of responding to this trauma depend on the person's level of maturity, both chronological and emotional. Certainly for some, the experience may lead to a reordering of priorities and, in turn, a more richly rewarding life. Studies have shown, however, that during the period of hospitalization, and immediately thereafter, the emotional impact is greater on older people, whereas the long-range adjustment is more difficult for younger people.

Miller (1969), observing patients on a coronary care unit, noted that some deny their illness, others use it as a basis for withdrawal of effort; some seem to give up and die, others seem to adjust reasonably well. Any life-threatening experience tends to have a disorganizing effect on people. How permanent the effect may be, again, depends on the stability of those people's internal organization before the experience, as well as the kinds of internal images they have constructed in infancy. By internal images, I refer to the fact that infants build up the expectation either that a "good mother" will feed, comfort, and protect them or that a "bad mother" will destroy them or at least allow others to do so. Their outlook on life becomes either optimistic or pessimistic. When stricken by a life-threatening illness in adulthood, then, people's potential for recovery depends on the kinds of internal images they have constructed, their orientation toward life, and their capacity for trust as well as the extent and location of the organic impairment.

One immediate response to the illness is anger. How could this happen to me? A guilt-ridden person may find answers to this question in his sense of inherent badness and the many sins he feels he has committed. If the occlusion or infarction serves as fulfillment for a need for punishment, then recovery may well depend upon whether partial or total sacrifice is the price demanded for expiation.

Another kind of response is a feeling of loss. The heart is a life-sustaining organ, and damage to this organ may not only severely threaten one's integrity as an individual but also one's potency as a vital human being. A period of mourning for the lost image of a well-functioning heart is to be expected, as this symbolically represents the person's feelings of being whole, intact, and functioning.

It has been found that about one out of every six cardiac patients fails to return to work because of psychological reasons even after being told by his physician that he is in good health. This represents an enormous waste of human potential above and beyond the 642,719 deaths currently occurring as a result of coronary artery illness each year.

In 1969, while on the staff of the Menninger Foundation, I was led, by a variety of personal and professional experiences, to suspect a close link between depression and coronary illness. A colleague of mine, Dr. Joseph Satten, also on the staff of the Menninger Foundation, and I obtained a small grant which allowed us to do some preliminary investigation in the area of the emotional correlates of coronary artery illness (Ginsparg and Satten, 1970). As we combed through the literature, we were impressed by the fact that all of the studies which involved in-depth psychological explorations were conducted after the infarct or occlusion. Feeling that significant personality changes must result from the physical assault itself, we decided to look at heart-attack victims prior to the illness. Our assumption was that the people most prone to develop a coronary occlusion or myocardial infarction in the first half century of their lives would be those who had failed to achieve a balance in the expression and inhibition of aggressive impulses and that these impulses, regardless of whether directed externally or internally, had become more than the organism could handle economically.

We recognized, of course, that people differ in the intensity of their anger, their structural capacities for handling anger, and the ability to tolerate angry feelings—all of which are probably determined by a particular combination of genetic, physiological, environmental, and psychological factors. We further assumed that people develop characteristic adaptational styles for the handling of anger, i.e., anger may be expressed behaviorally through acting out, through various symbolic mental representations as in emotional illness, or somatically as in physical illness. The reasons for the choice of style remain unclear. We have no adequate understanding of why one person handles his conflicts behaviorally and another, somatically. And, furthermore, given people who choose to go the somatic route with their conflicts, we still must clarify the reasons for the choice of system and choice of organ, i.e., why is the anger expressed through the cardiovascular system in one person, the cerebral-vascular system in another, the visceral, skeletal, or neuromuscular system in yet another? Surely organ vulnerability plays a part in the matter of choice, but it seems that psychodynamic predispositions also play a part.

The heart may become the "organ of choice" for the following reasons: (1) It is closely linked to the brain and responds automatically via the autonomic nervous system to both conscious and unconscious fear and anger. (2) As the organ which both provides and symbolizes the very essence of life itself, the heart may become the "organ of choice" in those conflicts which represent a "life and death" struggle, i.e., where the person's very survival is at stake because some set of circumstances has caused an upset in the balance between the life and death instincts. (3) In situations evoking intense rage, to which the heart responds with an accelerated cardiac rate and output, its oxygen requirement may transcend the capacity of the coronary circulation, a situation operationally similar to the events following strenuous physical exertion. While such instances seem superficially different from those cited under (2), in which the need for self-punishment is summoned, there is the suggestion that even here some shift in equilibrium has occurred so that previously adequate channels for the expression of anger no longer serve the person. (4) The heart may become the "organ of choice" for people who are identified with significant figures who have previously suffered from coronary artery disease.

It further seems that for the heart to become involved, the above factors must operate in such a way as to evoke the somatic equivalent of guilt even though the guilt as such may not be consciously experienced by the person. Indeed, it may be the very inability to tolerate the experience of guilt that causes it to be channeled into the body before it can be recognized. In other words, it seems that the coronary arteries are damaged primarily by anger which cannot be discharged, either because it is unrecognized—totally repressed; or it is partially recognized but the situation has such unconscious significance for the person that much anger remains undischarged; or it is recognized but the reality of the situation does not permit discharge. Under these circumstances, the anger is then deflected back upon the self, often as a type of somatic self-punishment. It further seems to me, as described earlier in this chapter, that once coronary artery damage has been sustained, the potential for survival in a person is affected by such factors as the depth and intensity of the self-destructive need. That is: Is the infarct itself sufficient retribution for some while total self-annihilation is required in others? To what extent are such factors as toleration of dependency needs and temporary immobilization, acceptance of bodily damage without resulting feelings of impotence, continued investment in future goals with the capacity for modification without loss of self-esteem, and intensity of guilt feelings, determining factors in the potential for survival following an infarct?

It is also my impression that much of the later postcoronary depression so frequently described in the literature was actually present in the precoronary state but masked by such factors as a flight of activity. The coronary patient is often described as having been "working himself to death" before the onset of the physical illness. Other signs of depression, such as overeating or even loss of appetite or excessive smoking, also are frequently noted before the illness. It is my opinion, however, that the depression was actually present before the infarct and that, at least in some cases, there is an "I want out" quality to the coronary occlusion. Furthermore, if these people are prone to handle anger somatically, and if the heart has become the "organ of choice," then they can be considered to be at high risk for the development of coronary artery illness. If such people then encounter a situation which brings on anger that they are unable either to discharge or to handle outside of the body and if, in turn, guilt or its equivalent is mobilized, they may deflect the excessive anger back upon the self as a form of somatic self-punishment. If the blood vessels are normal and the anger subsides, the result may be coronary artery spasm and anginal pain. If, however, there is an inherent weakness in the vascular system, or if the anger continues over an extended period of time, the possibility of a coronary thrombosis is greatly increased.

It was with this rationale that we developed a study to determine the nature of the self-destructive trends in coronary artery illness and to identify the processes through which the self-destructive impulses are channeled into the body rather than handled behaviorally as, for example, in suicide. Since we believed that significant personality changes must result from the physical assault itself, we thought it would be important to look at heart-attack victims prior to the physical illness, prior to the "walk to the brink of death" described by Cameron Hawley.

Since all Menninger Foundation patients receive both intensive and extensive diagnostic studies, we sent out a memorandum to all clinical staff members asking for the names of patients who had been evaluated and/or received psychiatric treatment and then sometime later developed some form of heart disease. We recognized that this sample would be skewed in that these patients had already been treated for an emotional illness; but we thought that if there was no clear link between coronary illness and any specific type of emotional disorder, then these patients' clinical diagnoses should be randomly distributed over the broad range of psychiatric categories. As the cases came in and the data were carefully analyzed, it became clear that there was no random distribution. In each case, the patient was found to be severely depressed, and in every chart, without exception, a caution regarding the possibility of suicide was stated somewhere in the diagnostic evaluation—if not in the psychiatric interview, then in the psychological test report or the social worker's report of the family evaluation. There was, furthermore, within the social history in each case some data which suggested that suicide might have been an unacceptable alternative to the person despite his feeling of hopelessness about his situation.

In some cases, there was a strong religious background. One man's father had committed suicide, and he had always vowed that he "would never do such a thing to his family."

One case which I had the opportunity to follow progressively from the time of occlusion had an unpredicted ending. The patient was a forty-eight-year-old man who had a history of previous psychiatric hospitalizations because of depression with suicidal ideation. He had been living at home with his family and employed when stricken with a massive infarction. When I interviewed the wife, the patient appeared to be making a good recovery, had been taken out of intensive care, and plans were being made for his return home. The family had all returned to their commitments, confident that the patient was out of danger and his recovery assured. His mood, as described by his wife, was "better than it had been in months." On a Sunday afternoon, two days after the wife had described this improvement in mood, as the family prepared to leave following a pleasant visit, the man startled his daughters by counseling them to study hard as they would "need a good education in this world." The girls then left and the man urged his wife to see to it that his daughters "hit the books," again because they would need an education. He advised his wife how to go about returning some storm windows he had purchased but had not used. The wife naturally became alarmed and asked her husband if anything was wrong. He insisted he was fine and asked her to leave so he could sleep. A short time later, the wife was called to return to the hospital. Her husband had been found dead lying in exactly the same position as when she had left him. The physiological signs both before death and in the autopsy afterward gave no explanation for the sudden death in this patient who appeared to be making a satisfactory recovery. To his family, however, he had communicated his anticipation of an imminent death and clearly bade them farewell. To his daughters, he suggested how they might best order their lives; to his wife he advised that the storm was almost over. The lifting of the patient's depression two days before his death is, furthermore, a common prodromal clue to suicide.

In another case, I was asked to perform a psychological autopsy on a middle-aged physician who had died from either an infarction or an overdose of barbiturates. Signs of both were present in the medical autopsy. A psychological autopsy was requested to determine the order of events, i.e., did the infarction occur in the course of a suicide attempt, or did the man recognize the symptoms of an infarction and, in a somewhat dazed state, misjudge the quantity of barbiturate administered? I must confess that after many hours of sifting through the data, it was still not possible to determine with certainty just what the sequence of events had been. A very telling point was the fact that the man made no attempt to use the telephone and call for help, something a man who really wanted to live might be expected to do before taking the drug. However, aside from the anguished queries of the family and an insurance company pressing for answers, it seems that the sequence of events was not of any real importance. The wish to die was clearly evident in this severely depressed man. In fact, his depression was the family's reason for wanting the psychological autopsy.

Two of the men in the sample had fathers who had committed suicide, and the patients had determined that no matter how bad things were, they would never do this to their families. Both men were admitted to a psychiatric hospital severely depressed, denying suicidal tendencies, but clearly reaching out for protection against such impulses, and both were regarded by the examining clinician as suicide risks. Both men were failing in their attempts to head family businesses and in their marriages, their wives threatening divorce if some change was not effected. Within three months after her husband's hospitalization, Mrs. A reduced the business deficit 25 percent. She resented the burdens placed upon her, however, and established an arbitrary deadline after which she would no longer run the business. The patient thereupon insisted on his release from the hospital by this date, but was persuaded by his hospital doctor to accept some delay. On the day preceding the deadline, Mr. A attended a movie in which the main character was in a situation remarkably like his own and at the end unsuccessfully attempted suicide. After the movie, Mr. A was described by fellow patients as being depressed and tearful and said he was not feeling well. He walked out onto the patio and collapsed. Death followed within minutes. The postmortem examination revealed a complete closure of the anterior branch of the coronary artery with no evidence of previous cardiac disease.

Mr. B was hospitalized for eleven months, during which time he showed little capacity for insight into his problems and engaged in considerable acting out in the hospital. He was discharged in remission for his depression, but with no real personality changes effected. Mr. B's business and marital difficulties continued, and he made periodic return visits to consult with his hospital doctor. Two of the visits, both occasioned by the departure of a child for college, were followed by coronary occlusions. Mr. B recovered, but when last heard from his difficulties had increased to the point where he had been asked to leave the family business. Both of these men had been described as having shown a lifting of their depression just before the onset of the cardiovascular symptoms, again a commonly recognized prodromal clue to suicide.

It is worthy of note that in the case of Mr. A, coronary attacks coincided with the attainment of greatly desired occupational goals. Similarly, Mr. B, a highly respected professional man, developed coronary symptoms when his predecessor died suddenly after a coronary attack. Here one can infer not only guilt but also identification with the displaced father surrogate.

The self-destructive theme is perhaps most clearly expressed in the following case: Mr. M was a member of a religious order. When he was eight years of age, his mother died of the flu she had contracted while nursing him. He was told by an aunt that he had killed his mother. Mr. M avoided girls throughout his adolescence and upon his graduation from high school, entered a monastery. While at a religious meeting, he met a woman he admired and with whom he then corresponded for eight years. During this time, he was having an affair with a nun who was summarily dismissed from the convent when one of his letters to her was intercepted. He then fled to the woman with whom he had been corresponding, and they were married. Within a few weeks of the marriage, Mrs. M required a radical mastectomy, perhaps convincing Mr. M that he would bring certain destruction to any woman who dared to love him and to any potential source of nurturance. He contacted the head of the religious order, who urged him to leave his wife and resume a life of religious service. Mr. M was torn between feelings of guilt and a need to obey the commanding father. The religious leader, at a loss about how to handle Mr. M, requested a psychiatric evaluation. During the final session of the evaluation, Mr. M told the psychiatrist that he felt his religious vows superseded any subsequent vows and that he would have to leave his wife but dreaded telling her. He was deeply troubled and concluded that he would hurt her least by waiting until she recovered from surgery and then leaving "on very short notice." Five weeks later, a tearful Mrs. M phoned to say that her husband had died suddenly of a coronary occlusion. Punishing to the very end, he had left behind notes indicating his intention to leave Mrs. M and to return to the religious order following her recovery.

Another interesting case became known to me when an article I had written (Ginsparg, 1973) on the psychological predisposition to coronary artery illness was published in a magazine which has a wide circulation among staff and former patients of the Menninger Foundation as well as others. A former hospital patient called long distance one day to say that he had not only just read the article but had gone over it carefully with both his psychiatrist and cardiologist while in bed recuperating from a massive myocardial infarction. He said the article was almost an exact replay of what had happened to him. He had been a hospitalized psychiatric patient some years previously and was now in outpatient treatment. On an afternoon three weeks earlier, he had seen his psychiatrist for his regularly scheduled appointment. He had told the latter he felt it all coming on again, i.e., he felt exactly as he had just before his earlier psychiatric hospitalization. The psychiatrist suggested that he try to hang in there a little longer until they could work it out. At three o'clock the following morning, he was stricken with a massive myocardial infarction.

This case dramatically emphasizes the close interplay between the psychological and the physiological predisposition to the illness. This patient knew something was about to give. With the strengthening of his personality that had resulted from psychiatric treatment, the "something" turned out to be the heart rather than the psychic functioning. The man said that during the immediate period of intensive care, his thoughts went back to the time when he was a patient in the psychiatric hospital and another patient, who had become a close friend of his, had made a suicide attempt. The patient had been taken to the local hospital, and the physician in charge of the section had returned some time later to tell the other patients that the man was out of danger, all vital processes had been stabilized, and he would make a good recovery. The hospital called an hour later to say that the man was dead. The coronary patient said, "I thought about him when I was admitted to intensive care, realized he had made a decision, and knew now I had the same decision to make for myself." He said the purpose of his call to me was to ask if I thought the patient had some element of control over the outcome of a coronary attack. I told him that he himself had demonstrated the importance of this control in the outcome of the illness, since he had in fact survived. The man said that there had been many factors involved in his decision, one of which was that he had not yet thanked his psychiatrist for all he had done for him. I asked him if he had done anything about this matter since the occlusion. The man replied, "I started a letter; it's pages long and I think I'm afraid to finish it, because once the letter is finished, I'll feel I can die."

A woman who had read the same article wrote to thank me for it, saying, "It fit me like a glove and was a help to me in trying to work out my own postcoronary problems. I had my fat ones! It's taken me two years plus and much reading trying to understand myself. I cannot see why the medical profession to a large extent continues to treat symptoms only, instead of digging deeper. Some of us are intelligent enough to realize that when all systems check out "go" and still we are miserable, that there has to be something more. . . . I've read and read, everything on retirement and aging and coronary and psychosomatic troubles, etc. etc. I'm beginning to catch on—but, why aren't patients considered rational and intelligent enough to be given help by their doctor other than pain killers, sleeping pills, antispasmodics, and tranquilizers? Really, I'm almost bitter about the whole thing. Again, thank you for your contribution. . . . I think it's the most. You are driving down the right road—It's so right. I know—I've been there and these horrible experiences are real but only when they sit on your own lap!"

Another case which might be cited is that of the United Mine Workers executive who a few years ago seemed to have suffered a stroke just before his arraignment on a charge of murder. It was only after his admission to the hospital that it became apparent that the stroke had been preceded by a suicide attempt.

And in a personal communication, a friend related that her elderly grandfather had awakened during the night, commented that he did not know why he was living as he was of no use to anyone, and a few hours later was found to have died in his sleep.

The common theme running through all of these cases is that death or disability served to remove the person from a situation he or she experienced as intolerable and to which he or she could find no other solution. All the psychiatric patients described above had requested psychiatric help, at least in part, because of suicidal ideation; but in each case, suicide had been an unacceptable alternative. The extent of psychiatric intervention had varied from an evaluation of several hours in one case, to 811 analytic hours in another. Each of these patients had been discharged from treatment as having received the maximum possible benefit, was in remission as far as the symptom of depression was concerned, but gave no indication of any significant characterological change. One possible hypothesis for the outcome is that as the ego was strengthened through psychotherapy, the self-destructive wish was deflected into the soma. Thus, in two of the cases a diagnostic evaluation had warned that treatment might arouse intense suicidal impulses. Instead, however, in one case the outcome was sudden coronary death following termination of treatment and resumption of a previous career; in the other, a prominent member of the community died suddenly of a coronary after setting a termination date for an analysis of several years. These men were presumably coping with feelings of loss and perhaps even guilt about their apparently successful goal attainments. Those who die suddenly after achieving a life goal or receiving a promotion usually are people who then feel that they have dared to succeed in their lifelong struggle to surpass the father.

These observations have important implications for the treatment of depressed patients. For if it is important to recognize that intrapsychic shifts may increase the risk of suicide in a patient, then it is equally important to acknowledge the possibility of death through physical illness when the unconscious death wishes are not confronted and properly resolved. The patients described here had characterological defects which remained unchanged in the course of treatment despite affective shifts and limited gains in object relationships. Furthermore, in those who survived the occlusion, there was a progressive decompensation of the ego to the point where the men were making only the most marginal adjustments and were being literally maintained by strong, albeit resentful, wives. Not only did the coronary not resolve the problem, but the postcoronary functioning was regressed and ineffectual.

This study also has important implications for the treatment of postcoronary patients. It has generally been left to the internist to deal with the patient's emotional response to his infarction. However, understanding and dealing with the intrapsychic factors which both lead to and result from an infarct requires the skill and expertise of an experienced mental health professional, who should be an integral part of the coronary care team. Ideally, programs of short-term crisis intervention should be built into the routine postcoronary care. Such programs could be established in the form of group therapy sessions for coronary patients and for spouses, who also suffer their own traumatic reactions. These reactions play an important part in the patient's recovery and in the later stability of the whole family. Almost every wife of a coronary patient can describe a deep-seated fear of waking up in the night beside a dead body. The focus of such crisis intervention should be on helping patients to accept that they have suffered damage to a vital bodily organ, to become aware of the psychological meaning this damage has for them, and to familiarize them with the reality factors of their illness (for example, the limitations that are necessary as opposed to those that are unnecessary). It is also important to explore the patients' current life situations, their priorities in life, their sources of satisfaction and dissatisfaction. Patients should be helped to identify the situations which create stress for them and to evaluate which of these situations can be eliminated from their lives and how they might better deal with those which cannot. In those instances where patients recognize a need to obtain a more intensive kind of treatment for themselves or their families, an appropriate referral may be made.

The reactions of many of our patients are not unlike those described by Modlin (1960) in the traumatic neuroses, where after the accident certain latent needs and conflicts come to the fore, for example, the wish to regress and be nurtured. In postcoronary patients, however, several typical patterns seem to develop. One pattern is depression, linked either to guilt and self-punishment or to the feeling of severe narcissistic injury. A second pattern is continued regression even after physiological recovery has occurred. This occurs in people who insist on being cared for and refuse to allow any demands to be made upon them even after they are physically recovered. A third pattern is overcompensatory or counterphobic. The person will deny feelings of narcissistic injury and his wish to regress, and instead becomes superhuman, attempting feats he would not have contemplated before the illness. The physician's advice to limit activities is largely ignored. A fourth pattern is the "reality-oriented" or "reality-confronting" attitude, in which the patient accepts his limitations realistically and is able to reorient his life. Some observers have noted that these people are "happier" after the coronary than before. This is probably the group in which the long-term survivors are to be found.

Anyone working with postcoronary patients must recognize that, as in all life-threatening illnesses, to confront death is to confront, in a very harsh and abrupt manner, the reality of one's own mortality, perhaps the greatest narcissistic injury of all. Those who have struggled since infancy with a fear of being overpowered by the destructive forces in the environment may experience this as the final defeat. The realization that one cannot control whether one is to live or to die may bring with it a feeling of total surrender. Suspicion and distrust then take over as the person is driven by an inner sense of impending doom, the source of which he cannot clearly identify. His relationships with others are further clouded by a feeling of envy for what they seem to possess that he does not; namely, prolonged life. He may then live in a manner which makes up in intensity what it lacks in extensity. In his perception of infinity as reduced to zero and tomorrow as belonging only to the world of others, he may be driven to live all of his tomorrows today and thereby depart in a self-fulfilling prophecy, for even supermen can live only so much at a time.

The basic thesis of this chapter has been that human survival is a psychophysiological process involving a peculiar balance between somatic vulnerability, maturity of ego development, and life experiences which symbolically reenact unmastered early infantile traumas—all of which combine to determine how many and what kind of tomorrows will constitute any given lifetime. In the words of

Sigmund Freud (1930/1961, p. 145), "The fateful question for the human species seems to me to be whether and to what extent their cultural development will succeed in mastering the disturbance of their communal life by the human instinct of aggression and self-destruction."

REFERENCES _____

Alexander, Franz. *Psychosomatic Medicine.* New York: Norton, 1950.

Arlow, Jacob A. Identification mechanisms in coronary occlusion. *Psychosomatic Medicine,* 7:195–209, 1945.

Bacon, Catherine L. Psychoanalytic observations on cardiac pain. *Psychoanalytic Quarterly,* 23:7–19, 1954.

Bahnson, C. B., and Wardwell, W. I. Parent constellation and psychosexual identification in male patients with myocardial infarction. *Psychological Reports,* 10:831–852, 1962.

Dassberg, H., Assall, M., and Dreyfuss, F. *Israel Annals of Psychiatry,* 2:117, 1964.

Dohrenwend, Bruce P. Toward the development of theoretical models. *Milbank Memorial Fund Quarterly,* 45:155–162, 1967.

Dunbar, F. *Emotions and Bodily Changes.* New York: Columbia University Press, 1935.

Engel, G. A life setting conducive to illness, the giving-up—given-up complex. *Annals of Internal Medicine,* 69:293–300, 1968.

Freud, S. Civilization and its discontents. *Standard Edition,* 21. London: Hogarth, 1961. (Originally published, 1930.)

Friedman, M. Behavior pattern and its pathogenetic role in clinical coronary artery disease. *Geriatrics,* 19:562–567, 1964.

Friedman, M., and Rosenman, R. Association of a specific overt behavior pattern with increases in blood cholesterol, blood clotting time, incidence of arcus senilis and clinical coronary artery disease. *Journal of the American Medical Association,* 169:1286, 1959.

Friedman, M., et al. Excretion of catecholamines, 17-ketosteroids, 17-hydroxycorticoids, and 5-hydroxyindole in men exhibiting a particular behavior pattern (A) associated with high incidence clinical coronary artery disease. *Journal of Clinical Investigation,* 39:758–764, 1960.

Friedman, M., et al. Serum lipids and conjunctival circulation after fat ingestion in men exhibiting type-A behavior pattern. *Circulation,* 29:874–886, 1964.

Ginsparg, Sylvia L. Psychogram or cardiogram: Which do you need? *Menninger Perspective,* 4(4), 1973. Published by the Menninger Foundation Office of Information.

Ginsparg, Sylvia L., and Satten, Joseph. Psychiatric aspects of rehabilitation in coronary artery illness. In *Proceedings, 78th Annual Convention, American Psychological Association,* 1970, pp. 707–708.

Hawley, Cameron. *The Hurricane Years.* Boston: Little, Brown, 1968.

Hinkle, L. E., Whitney, L., and Lehman, E. Occupation, education, and coronary heart disease. *Science,* 161:238–246, 1968.

Lebovits, B. Z., Shekelle, R., and Ostfeld, A. Prospective and retrospective psychological studies of coronary heart disease. *Psychosomatic Medicine,* 29:265–272, 1967.

Lieberman, M. A. Psychological correlates of impending death: Some preliminary observations. *Journal of Gerontology,* 20:2, 1965.

Menninger, Karl A., and Menninger, William C. Psychoanalytic observations in cardiac disorders. *American Heart Journal,* 11:10–21, 1936.

Miller, Paul R. Psychiatric observations of the coronary care unit. *Current Medical Dialogue,* 36:956–962, 1969.

Modlin, Herbert. The trauma in "traumatic neurosis." *Bulletin of the Menninger Clinic,* 24:49–56, 1960.

Mordkoff, A., and Golas, R. M. Coronary artery disease and response to the Rosenzweig picture-frustration study. *Journal of Abnormal Psychology,* 73:381–386, 1968.

Mordkoff, A., and Parsons, D. The coronary personality: A critique. *International Journal of Psychiatry,* 5:413–426, 1968.

Ostfeld, A. M., Lebovits, B., Shekelle, R., and Paul, O. A prospective study of the relationship between personality and coronary heart disease. *Journal of Chronic Diseases,* 17:265–276, 1964.

Paffenbarger, R. S., Jr. Chronic disease in former college students. *American Journal of Epidemiology,* 83:314–328, 1966.

Peal, S. Some psychological observations of patients with myocardial infarction: A pilot study. *Psychiatric Communications,* 10:1–20, 1968.

Reiser, M. F. Emotional aspects of cardiac disease. *American Journal of Psychiatry,* 107:781–785, 1950–1951.

Rosenman, R. Emotional factors in coronary heart disease. *Postgraduate Medicine,* 42:165–171, 1967.

Rosenman, R., and Friedman, M. Association of specific behavior pattern in women with blood and cardiovascular findings. *Circulation,* 24:1173–1184, 1961.

Rosenman, R., and Friedman, M. Behavior pattern, blood lipids, and coronary heart disease. *Journal of the American Medical Association,* 184:934–938, 1963.

Rosenman, R., et al. A predictive study of coronary heart disease. *Journal of the American Medical Association,* 189:15–22, 1964.

Rosenman, R., et al. The prediction of immunity to coronary heart disease. *Journal of the American Medical Association,* 198:1159–1162, 1966.

Sales, Stephen M. Organizational role as a risk factor in coronary disease. *Administrative Science Quarterly,* 14:325–336, 1960.

Schneider, Daniel. *Psychoanalysis of Heart Attack.* New York: Dial Press, 1967.

Syme, S. Leonard, and Reeder, Leo G., eds. Social stress and cardiovascular disease. *Milbank Memorial Fund Quarterly,* 45, Suppl., 175–180, 1967.

Weisman, A. D., and Hackett, T. P. Predilection to death. *Psychosomatic Medicine,* 23:232–255, 1961.

Wolf, Stewart. The end of the rope: The role of the brain in cardiac death. *Canadian Medical Association Journal,* 97:1022–1025, 1967.

PART THREE

DRUG ABUSE

9

DRUG ABUSE AS INDIRECT SELF-DESTRUCTIVE BEHAVIOR

CALVIN J. FREDERICK

DEFINITION AND CONCEPTUALIZATION

There is little doubt that drug abuse and self-destructive behavior are related problems in society today. The main question is the extent to which drug abuse may be a causal factor in precipitating self-destructive acts. The personal conflicts and tensions which give rise to such aberrant behavior may be expressed through different avenues. There are growing indications, however, that drug abuse itself can be a precipitator of self-destructive behavior. Deliberate drug overdoses demonstrate this convincingly, but less obvious indicators, such as feelings of haplessness and helplessness, signify a loss of hope and are a result of the addictive process.

Indirect self-destructive behavior (ISDB), by definition, is covert rather than overt or direct, with latent and subtle signs. The author views self-destructive behavior as on a continuum between self-assaultive on one end, and overt, unmistakable suicide on the other. The degree of personal awareness varies directly with the clarity of the behavioral act in the direction of suicide. Self-assaultive behavior is characterized by personal abuse of oneself, without total awareness of its life-threatening components. Anorexia nervosa and picking at a melanoma would constitute illustrations of self-assaultive behavior, assuming an absence of knowledge about the dangers of such phenomena. Self-destructive acts fall between the two ends of the continuum and suggest relatively more conscious understanding of one's behavior. It may be seen in people who possess a known physical problem but neglect proper health care. Specific instances are smoking after developing emphysema, overeating by cardiac patients, and neglect of medication in the presence of severe diabetes mellitus. Direct suicidal behavior involves any overt act with a relatively clear plan and intent to end one's life. Even though not so classified initially, self-assaultive and self-destructive acts can easily become suicidal.

Numerous psychological equivalents of suicide occur in everyday life without being recognized. In addition to the neglect of medical illnesses like those just cited, frequent reckless and inebriated driving and certain aspects of drug abuse can constitute suicidal behavior. Like such clinical syndromes as suicidal behavior and alcoholism, drug abuse and addiction are not unitary problems, and addicts and abusers do not compose a homogeneous population. At least four groups of persons engage in drug abuse and addiction: (1) those who are thrill-seekers and become addicted adventitiously; (2) those with various personality disorders; (3) rebellious youth; and (4) those who become addicted medically. It has not been fully determined, as yet, whether or not certain personality types become addicted to particular kinds of drugs. In the author's experience, rebellious young persons are more likely to use hallucinogenic drugs, whereas those less militant are inclined to use marihuana. Although additional data are needed to confirm this phenomenon, it has become increasingly apparent that addicts often ingest alcohol and then move into drug addiction, and vice versa. It is also now apparent that many persons become alcoholics as well as drug addicts at different ages of entry.

One of the difficult problems in today's society is that psychotropic drugs are prescribed medically in increasing numbers. About one-fifth of all prescriptions written in the last few years have been for psychotropic agents. Hypnotic drugs, which for our purposes will include amphetamines, stimulants, short-acting barbiturates, and glutethimides, are the most frequently used. Tranquilizers and antidepressives must be viewed separately for several reasons. First, the chemical and physiological reaction is not the same as in the other drugs noted. Second, no law prohibits the use of such drugs when medically prescribed. Third, there is no strong evidence to indicate the presence of physical addiction or habituation to them. Nevertheless, there is a serious problem with the use of all dangerous drugs, and it is generally agreed that no drug is entirely safe. Twenty-five percent of the United States population uses sedatives, stimulants, or tranquilizers, according to the 1975 White Paper on Drug Abuse. Many drug deaths from these substances are listed as accidental overdoses rather than suicides.

METHODS OF SUICIDE IN THE UNITED STATES _____

It might be helpful to look at the methods used in suicide over the past several decades to note how drugs have been used in direct suicide deaths (Table 1). Until the mid-twentieth century, breathing domestic coal gas was a frequent method of suicide. This was related to the use of coal for heat by most of the United States. After the introduction of natural gas into North American homes, the number of expirations from gas decreased dramatically, since natural gas is not poisonous if adequate oxygen is supplied with it. The dramatic decline in suicidal deaths from 1950 to 1960 no doubt reflects this changeover from coal to natural gas. In addition, deaths by hanging and strangulation decreased during the third quarter of this century, but the number of suicides from firearms and poison by other gases rose markedly. In the last twenty-five years, deaths from firearms and explosives have increased 28 percent, poison by other gases 61 percent, and solid and liquid substances (drug abuse) by 31 percent. Poison by domestic gas has decreased by 98 percent, whereas suicides from hanging and strangulation have declined by 36 percent. The noticeable rise in poisoning by gases other than the domestic type is due to motor vehicle exhaust intoxication, which accounts for 82 percent of self-inflicted deaths in this category.

The largest category of suicide fatalities in the United States involves *firearms and explosives.* The percentage of deaths from firearms has continued to rise, due in all likelihood to the easy access to guns in this country. When a gun is used, the chances of the suicidal act resulting in a fatality are much greater than when other methods are employed, such as poisons or cutting and piercing instruments. The probability of rescue in time to save a life is

TABLE 1 *Percent of Suicidal Deaths in the United States by Method in 1950, 1960, 1964, and 1975*

Method	1950	Percent 1960	1964	1975	25-year percent change
Solid and liquid substances	10.5	12.4	15.7	13.8	+31
Domestic gas	6.5	1.0	0.4	0.1	−98
Poisoning by other gases	6.2	9.4	10.8	10.0	+61
Hanging and strangulation	21.0	17.7	14.6	13.5	−36
Drowning	3.9	3.2	2.6	2.0	−49
Firearms and explosives	43.0	47.4	47.6	55.0	+28
Cutting and piercing	3.1	2.6	1.9	1.4	−59
Jumping	3.7	3.7	3.7	2.7	−27
Other and unspecified causes	2.1	2.7	2.7	1.5	−29

SOURCE: National Center for Health Statistics, Mortality Statistics Branch

increased with the use of less lethal means. In contrast to the United States, most European countries reveal low suicide rates by firearms. Suicide is committed in those countries principally by hanging or poison.

DRUG ADDICTION AS INDIRECT SELF-DESTRUCTION

In recent years, professionals have become more aware of the indirect or latent aspects of suicidal behavior. *Indirect suicide is rarely obvious to the unskilled observer or to the potential victim.* A variety of terms have been used to describe behavior of this nature, such as: psychological equivalents of suicide; hidden suicide; latent suicide; covert suicide; and indirect self-destruction. Although patterns may vary, as a rule, the following comprise the prominent characteristics of indirect suicide: (1) there is a lack of full awareness of the consequences; (2) the behavior is rationalized, intellectualized, or denied; (3) the onset is gradual, even though the death may appear to be precipitous; (4) open discussion seldom occurs, in contrast to obvious "cries for help" in direct suicide; (5) long suffering, martyrlike behavior often appears; (6) secondary gain is obtained by evoking sympathy and expressing hostility via the process; and (7) the death is often seen as accidental. Meerloo (1968) has spoken of hidden suicide in discussing some specific attitudes toward self-chosen death. Many people seem to move toward death without being fully aware that they are doing so. These incidents are never shown in the published statistics on suicide. In some parts of the world, people indicate a greater dread of life than a fear of death. Although life for the suicide attempter generally suggests a state of insecurity, death may hold the hope of eternal relief.

Hillman (1965) noted that Freud put death at the center of existence and observed that "all death is suicide," whether by an airplane crash, heart attack, or by an evident method called suicide. He commented further that "suicide is the urge for hasty transformation." There is little doubt that each suicide attempt suggests an experience approaching death. Hendin (1974) states that some young people present a bland front that conceals self-destructive impulses probably stemming from early painful relationships and anxiety related to their mothers. Many people who have been deprived of emotions early in life feel alive only when they experience some unusual thrill, become anxious, or feel pain. The life-and-death struggle seems to heighten the sensations and the feelings which some people need.

The interaction of youngsters with monsters, horror movies, books, etc., represents one dimension of the life-and-death struggle.

The thrill of being "scared to death" exemplifies this symbolically. The idea of being able to come to grips with one's innermost fears provides reassurance in the life-and-death struggle, even at an early age. The religious notion of being born again is another aspect of the same phenomenon. It helps to bear the anxiety associated with the reality of death. Religion provides a structure for dealing with the overwhelming anxiety of life in all its destructive aspects. On the other hand, fear of the unknown and resignation in the acceptance of death is a source of periodic turmoil in us all, as Shakespeare wrote so colorfully in his famous soliloquy in *Hamlet*.

Drugs can bring psychological as well as physical relief to people who are in mental anguish or bodily pain. Such relief leads to tension reduction and becomes automatically reinforcing, in keeping with one of the basic principles of learning theory. Any anxiety-reducing process is a strong reinforcement for the accompanying response. The probability of repeating such an act on subsequent occasions increases markedly thereafter. Thus, it is easy to see how drug addiction can be quickly learned. The relief which it offers initially becomes a way of "ending it all" on a temporary basis. In the psychoanalytic sense it is, to begin with, an offering of a portion of one's life, or body, as a symbolic payment in death for the value received from the drug. It stems from the old biblical notion that it is better to "cut off thy right arm rather than that thy whole body shall perish." Such an effective temporary sacrifice then makes it easier to give one's self up entirely to the anticipated effects of heavy drug use. One of the insidious aspects of the addictive process is that, initially, relief comes readily, but later a tolerance for drugs often develops, and increased dosages are required to bring relief. As drug abuse develops, it becomes easier and easier to ingest an overdose, either accidentally or "accidentally on purpose." Escape from stress into sleep brings a death equivalent temporarily, or an actual death permanently.

The dramatic increase, recently, in the use of the drug phencyclidine (PCP) warrants special mention. It became known through the drug subculture, initially in 1967, as the "PeaCe Pill" (PCP) or "peace pill," but a more commonly used term since the mid-70s has been "angel dust." It can be administered intravenously as well as in powder or pill form. It has become a new drug of choice because of its ready availability and the belief that it will bring about exotic effects similar to other psychedelic drugs like LSD, mescaline, and psilocybin. Without the user's knowledge, the drug is sometimes sold to him or her as a substitute for other drugs, but in many instances it is taken deliberately. In powder form, it is sniffed, and potentially lethal aspects have not deterred many users. During 1975, in the city of Detroit alone, PCP was reported as the most common drug found in emergency overdose management. Burns and Lerner (1976) note that the increasing availability of this "enigmatic psychoactive agent" is likely to expand its abuse and continue to challenge the medical community. Some of the first symptoms noted are alterations in body image, such as an elongation or floating away of arms and legs, and/or the contraction and extension of body size. These experiences resemble the psychedelic highs which the user often seeks. Unfortunately, the serious and potentially lethal side effects include high blood pressure, extreme temperature, seizures, coma, and cardiac arrest. Showalter and Thornton (1977) comment that the body-image distortions noted are often incorrectly interpreted as hallucinations by both patients and physicians. Instead, these symptoms are aspects of psychological impairment. Feelings of progressive depersonalization, isolation, and depression are likely to occur and last for hours. One of the most common presenting symptoms is severe anxiety. Along with disorganized thought, concrete thinking, mental blocking, and use of neologisms, increased dosages bring negativism, hostility, and apathy. The stage before coma is one of catalepsy, or "dissociative anesthesia," found in both humans and animals. Originally, phencyclidine was used to achieve this state during surgical procedures at both the human and infrahuman levels; but the drug was abandoned for administration to humans, and today it is legitimately available only for use by veterinarians.

There is general agreement among professionals and in the drug community alike that the potentially lethal aspects of phencyclidine are such that a massive educational campaign is needed to help prevent its broad dissemination and use. Those who still wish to take chances with the drug are indirectly suicidal and should be encouraged to obtain professional help. For further information, the reader is referred to Fauman et al. (1976), Lundberg et al. (1976), and Balster and Chait (1976).

Drug abuse may overlap with other types of indirect self-destruction associated with psychophysiological disorders, such as colitis, ulcers, and dysmenorrhea, since a heavy ingestion of drugs invariably takes its toll on gastric function and renal efficiency. Other physiological systems are affected, as well, including both the central and autonomic nervous systems. The side effects from chronic drug ingestion may result in such phenomena as nasal and lacrimal irritability, gastric distress, and constipation. The insidiousness of drug abuse is that the drug helps overcome the discomfort the person endures as a result of such side effects. A self-destructive quality can also be noted in the fact that the drug abuser is willing to undergo the secondary physical stresses of repeated drug abuse.

The phenomenon of suicidal contagion may spread through some high-risk members of the drug-abuse population, but there is no evidence to support it as a major contributor to the incidence of suicide. In some instances, publicity about the suicidal deaths of such well-known figures as Marilyn Monroe and Freddie Prinze has been thought to evoke a temporary increase in suicide, but this has not been related to drug abuse per se.

SELECTED RESEARCH RELATED TO DRUG ABUSE AND INDIRECT SELF-DESTRUCTION

Clinicians have long stated that, although behavior can be defined as suicidal only when an *intentional* act of self-destruction is performed, there are subintentioned deaths as well. In the last two decades research studies have begun to emerge which bear on this issue. Shneidman (1963) has proposed three essential orientations toward death in addition to the classical, basic categories of natural, accidental, suicidal, and homicidal. These are: subintentioned, intentioned, and unintentioned. It was his belief that subintentioned death comprised the vast majority of deaths. By definition, in the subintentioned death, the decedent plays some role, even though covert or unconscious, in hastening his or her own demise. Such behavior is obviously risk-taking, and shows a disregard for ordinary prudence in one's behavior. The behavior usually demonstrates narrowly focused judgment, which is indicated by the fact that such persons themselves facilitate, foster, or exacerbate their own deaths. Both research and clinical evidence suggest that addiction and drug abuse can be equivalent to suicide.

A number of key points warrant discussion regarding whether or not addiction is self-destructive. In the first place, one must accept the concept of subintentional death, and the view that much of the behavior leading to it may not be fully conscious. In the second place, it is unclear whether or not there are certain personalities which are suicidal and employ addiction as a form of self-destruction. Third, it must be demonstrated that addiction is followed by self-destruction. Once addiction has taken place, does it bring out or heighten self-destructive tendencies? While it appears that many addicts behave in self-destructive ways—such as deliberately taking bad doses of drugs, or becoming overdosed—more research is needed to answer these questions definitively.

Self-destructive behavior is not uncommon when lysergic acid diethylamide (LSD) is used. Incidents of actual death, the requirement of forcible restraint to prevent suicide, visual hallucinations of seeing oneself dead, and delusions of immunity to dangerous acts have all been reported. Robbins et al. (1969) have noted that many heroin drug abusers begin with tobacco and alcohol and then move to amphetamines, barbiturates, tranquilizers, and ultimately to illicit drugs. Such a sequence has frequently included marihuana, despite the contention that marihuana does not lead to heroin addiction.

In a research study performed in the District of Columbia and vicinity, Frederick et al. (1973) showed that many drug addicts had depressive personality traits and had attempted more suicides than might be expected in comparable age groups of nonaddicts. Moreover, this study demonstrated that: (1) addicts, in general, are more depressed than nonaddicts, particularly in younger age groups, whether on methadone or abstaining from it; (2) addicts are more self-destructive than nonaddicts; (3) addicts have more aberrant attitudes toward life and death than nonaddicts; (4) methadone appeared to act essentially as a palliative rather than as a cure; and (5) the problem of addiction is heightened among certain minority groups. Depression was found in 39 percent of the "attempt" population still on methadone, and rose to 60 percent in the group abstaining from methadone.

These findings underscored the presence of depression and were supported later by Weissman et al. (1976) in a study of lower-social-class males who were participating in a methadone maintenance program. They found approximately one-third of the subjects to be suffering from moderate to severe depression. The depressive symptoms were associated with a decrease in social functioning, an increase in stress in the preceding six-month period, and a history of alcohol abuse. It was emphasized that since the combination of depression and drug abuse creates a high risk for suicide, depressive symptoms require early detection and treatment. The treatment of most secondary depressions requires considerably more attention, particularly in the testing of psychotropic drugs in controlled medical trials.

Lester et al. (1976) obtained data on more than 200 suicide cases in Philadelphia in 1972, to discover additional correlates of choice of the method of suicide. Among the 25 variables used for comparison, 26 percent used coma-producing drugs, 26 percent died by hanging, 19 percent used firearms, 8 percent employed jumping as a method, and 6 percent died from drowning. The choice of method was differentially related to age, sex, race, marital status, and employment status. Moreover, suicides who used drugs had been psychiatrically hospitalized more often than those who employed hanging or firearms. Suicides using drugs or hanging had made more previous attempts and threats and had abused drugs more often than those using firearms. Both the psychological and demographic factors are useful for exploring this problem in greater depth.

Schuman and Polkowski (1975) studied sixty-two secondary school students in their classrooms over five weeks in an intensive drug-information program, looking for within-group changes in their perceptions. Peer pressure and "kicks" were cited as reasons for beginning the use of drugs, but peer pressure had relatively greater strength for girls than for boys. Boys and girls differed in reasons for stopping drug use. Peer-group and professional help was instrumental in the cessation of drug use for girls, while punishment was more effective for boys. In rating the relative dangers and pleasures of marihuana and heroin, most students did not discriminate effectively between the two drugs, although ratings of marihuana dangers decreased. Unexpectedly, responses concerning the health hazards of heroin did not increase. Thus, it may be inferred that in some instances, the potentially dangerous aspects of hard-core drugs may not be perceived accurately by many teenagers. This would lend support to the notion that there are, indeed, indirect aspects to self-destructive behavior in the sense that overdoses may be taken as a gamble, for "kicks," or as an attention-getting threat.

Data from the National Center for Health Statistics reveal the startling increase in suicides among younger age groups, between fifteen and twenty-five years of age over a period of twenty years, as shown in Figure 1. The overwhelming majority of overt deaths from drug addiction occurs among the younger age groups, but the indirect aspects of drug abuse as a form of self-destruction also seem much more apparent in the younger ages.

Suicide by overdose is not confined to the young, as shown by Benson and Brodie (1975), who cited the elderly as a high-risk population in both the United States and Great Britain. The older white male is a particularly high risk. Besides physical and mental illness, barbiturates and psychotherapeutic agents contribute to suicide. These drugs are often accessible to older persons for misuse. Suicidal acts are nearly always very serious among the elderly because of their physical states and psychological attitude. There are a few so-called suicidal gestures among the elderly. Because depression is common among older persons, the onset of declining income and prestige combined with a loss of mental and physical abilities make drug abuse and suicide easy routes to take for respite from their problems.

Overdosing with hard-core drugs as a method of suicide has now appeared with such frequency that addiction must be seriously con-

---

FIGURE 1 *Age-Specific Suicide Rates by Five-Year Age Groups: 1955, 1965, 1975*

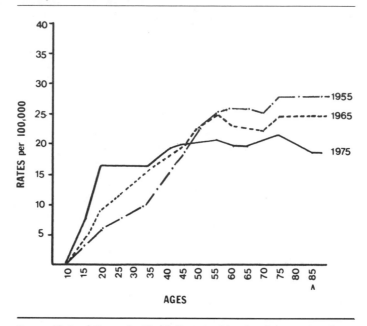

Source: National Center for Health Statistics, Mortality Statistics Branch.

---

sidered as a contributing factor to suicide. Braconnier and Olievenstein (1974) reported a study of thirty-five drug addicts, fifteen to twenty-four years of age, who made one or more suicide attempts. The subjects had all begun to abuse drugs between the ages of fifteen and twenty-one. Among the twenty-nine males and six females, in all of the families studied, one or both parents had taken psychotropic drugs or were alcoholics. A majority of the subjects used several drugs, hashish, LSD, barbiturates, solvents, amphetamines, and opiates being the most common. Six attempts were made under the actual influence of a drug, and four cases attempted suicide while using LSD. Thirty-one persons had made more than one attempt, and eight had made five or more. The most frequent methods used were ingestion of one or more medications or an overdose of heroin. In some instances, the consumption of alcohol was associated with drug ingestion.

Friedman et al. (1973) explored the relationship between drug overdose, depression, and suicide in 103 patients in a methadone maintenance clinic. A survey of these subjects disclosed that 33 had taken heroin overdoses. Reconstruction of the events leading to suicidal behavior indicated that most overdoses were covert or indirect suicide attempts. Thirty-eight percent of these covert attempts were related to incarceration, and 12 percent were accidents due to variability in street samples of the drug. Incarceration in jail should not be overlooked as a contributing factor in such instances.

A study by Jacobson and Tribe (1972) showed a suicide attempt rate of 112 per 100,000 population, and a female-male ratio of 2 : 1 in a predominantly urban sample. Among the 254 cases admitted to a psychiatric emergency unit, most patients were suffering from depression and had been admitted because of deliberate self-poisoning with barbiturates. It was thought that, psychodynamically, this was a cry for help in a dramatic attempt to draw attention to personal conflicts. This information is consonant with the clinical studies and experiences of the author (Frederick et al., 1973), Tobias (1972), and Weissman et al. (1976).

Some recent data gathered by Barton (1974) summarizes the essence of drug-related mortality in the United States. Vital certificates were used as source documents to analyze a sample of 5,138 drug-related deaths in 1963 and then to compare them with a sample of 9,920 drug-related deaths in 1971. The data revealed a 36 percent increase in deaths in which there was drug dependence, a 42 percent increase in deaths due to accidental poisoning, a 13 percent increase in deaths due to suicide by drugs, and a 36 percent increase in drug deaths listed as undetermined accident or suicide. It was emphasized that vital-statistics data are, in many instances, only estimates of the true cause of death, since the psychological factors are not usually explored in listing the mode of death.

The chronic use of either habit-forming medication or hard-core narcotics falls into the range of indirect suicide and self-assaultive behavior, whereas deliberate overdoses are direct suicidal acts.

TREATMENT IMPLICATIONS _____

Since depression has been convincingly demonstrated to be a prominent factor among the drug-abusing population, it is of paramount importance to treat the depression along with other components which contribute to personal conflicts. Aberrant attitudes toward life and death are significantly greater among addicts than nonaddicts; so, too, is a history of previous addictive behavior and being a member of a particular subcultural or age group. In an effort to find surcease from one's sorrows, the person is often drawn into interaction with others of similar age and socioeconomic background. Certainly, methadone treatment tends to help in the reduction of clinical depression as well as in attitudes toward violence, aggression, and morbidity. However, one must note that methadone merely ameliorates the onset of aberrant thoughts and conflicts.

Experienced clinicians working with severely depressed or suicidal patients are careful not to equate depression and suicide, since they often function separately. Admittedly, there is a continuing danger of suicide among severely depressed persons, but not every suicidal person is depressed, particularly in younger age groups. The clinician should be aware that suicidal adults and youth may each present a variety of psychiatric disorders, or even normal personalities, without any suitable diagnostic label. However, clinicians have been forced to view depression as more than mere repressed hostility. Many depressives show distressing obsessive-compulsive behaviors. They are chronic complainers with unreasonable expectations of themselves and others. Remaining dissatisfied, they are quick to criticize. They find it difficult to see themselves as blameworthy in interpersonal relations because their perpetual demands are virtually impossible to meet. By irritating others, depressives provoke negative responses. In their view, this further justifies their continued hatred and hostility. Their thought processes are rigid and resistant to traditional psychotherapy. Thus, a single therapeutic procedure is usually inadequate, which underscores the value of employing an eclectic program. The importance of clinical classifications should not be taken lightly, as the reader can see from Table 2.

Clinical information from a variety of sources in the author's ex-

TABLE 2   *Clinical Correlates of Suicidal Behavior*

Psychiatric Disorders	Adults	Youth
Depression	++	0
Schizophrenia	0	++
Neuroses (other than depression)	+	0
Paranoid state	++	0
Personality disorders	0	++
Alcoholism	++	++
Drug addiction	+	++
No nosology	++	++

++ = Strong relationship
+   = Moderate relationship
0   = Little or no relationship

perience has led to the compilation of the categories contained in Table 2. This compilation has proved of value in providing a backdrop against which clinicians can check their own impressions. It also serves to alert those working with suicidal, drug-addicted, and alcoholic persons especially, to the likelihood of self-destructive acts. Although useful in practice, the information must be regarded as tentative, since it has not yet been formulated upon the basis of thorough experimentation. The correlates represent firm clinical indicators but are not statistically exact. It should be noted that for our purpose here, depression is defined formally by the presence of disturbed vegetative signs such as insomnia, anorexia, apathy, withdrawal, and loss of sex drive. There is still a lack of agreement among professionals about the existence of true depression in younger age groups.

Owing to the problem of potential suicide, as well as the demanding and often cataclysmic aspects of the patient's behavior, many clinicians avoid taking such persons into psychotherapy. Most assuredly, therapists should have full confidence in themselves; otherwise they will be easily controlled by the drug user, or suicidal patient, and their efforts will prove ineffective and even harmful.

Group psychotherapy has been shown to be particularly effective by Frederick and Farberow (1970) and Billings et al. (1974), for a variety of reasons. Some of these are: (1) group support is provided by those suffering from similar problems; (2) it is more difficult to use the disorder to manipulate others, or dominate others, through excessive demands; (3) the base of transference relationships is broadened; (4) resistances are quickly identified and become ineffective; (5) practical issues in life are emphasized; and (6) individual goals and self-reliance phenomena are more easily fostered through solid competitive achievements. Group psychotherapy makes it more difficult for the individual to blame others for one's own dilemma and enhances the development of personal responsibility for deleterious behavior.

Tranquilizing agents, when carefully administered, can be very valuable in alleviating anxiety and assisting some disturbed persons to make use of their psychotherapy. In a like manner, methadone can facilitate availability to other forms of rehabilitation for the addict population. Methadone should be considered as merely one factor of a total treatment program, and one which needs to be carefully monitored. Drug addiction is a learned problem as well as a physiological disorder. The various features of learning theory as related to drug abuse and suicidal behavior have been delineated elsewhere by Frederick (1972) and Frederick and Resnik (1971). Comments emphasizing the importance of the psychological aspects of drug abuse have also been made by Goldstein (1972), Wikler (1965), and Jaffe (1970). Abstinence from methadone evokes a recurrence of depression and aberrant thoughts about violent death. The author has demonstrated that depressive symptoms and expressions of anxiety and resentment tend to be fewer in methadone users as compared with other addicts. The author (1972, 1973) found that more than twice as many hard-core drug users who were abstaining from methadone said they expected to die a violent death than a comparable group of users who were still on maintenance treatment. Problems with motivation and relearning new behaviors have been cited by Frederick and Resnik (1971) and Bratter (1973). The latter considers a reality-therapy approach as most effective in treating alienated, unmotivated drug-abusing adolescents. After patients are confronted with their self-destructive behavior, the clinician must become an advocate who forces behavior change by means of supportive direct intervention. It is apparent that methadone can be helpful as a palliative to bring about the positive adjustment in attitude which is necessary for rehabilitation. It is recommended that each addict be thoroughly examined with regard to personality structure, life-style, case history, and cultural milieu. Placement of the user in a familiar drug environment can cause a recurrence of the drug problem, since old associations return. The need for replacement drugs must be diminished at the same time that substitutes in living arrangements are initiated. Early crisis intervention, followed by focused psychotherapy, is helpful along with other components of the rehabilitation process. Even though one kind of behavior has been learned that is aberrant and deleterious, another can be learned as a substitute when needed. It is important to promote behavioral responses which are of value to the patient in order to offset strongly reinforced addictive life-styles. Otherwise the addict may well ask, in effect, "Why should I give up the pleasure which comes with addiction for something which is less gratifying?" The psychotherapeutic process must operate at the emotional level since logic will not suffice.

The self-reliance obtained through securing a new job and new friends often serves to build feelings of personal worth, independence, and self-confidence. This enables patients to relinquish the impulsive and dependent behavior patterns which have become an integral part of their personalities. The psychological growth process must be established in small increments, each success building upon previously reinforced responses to eliminate deleterious stimuli. The therapist should make sure that successes outnumber failures in assigning therapeutically valuable tasks to the patient for accomplishment. Nothing succeeds like success or adds to negative behavior like repeated failures.

The same reality-oriented, task-focused treatment should apply to any rehabilitation effort. Since the drug user may present a hapless quality as a result of numerous setbacks, small incremental gains are essential for achievement in breaking strongly reinforced destructive behavior patterns. These principles are necessary for growth in all treatment settings. The underlying problems must be undone while the drug user is being reconditioned to resist the tempting stimuli which he has used to diminish frustrations in the past. This reasoning is true for both inpatient and outpatient programs, including detoxification centers, methadone maintenance clinics, or settings of a therapeutic community type. Depending upon the nature of the problem, of course, one or more of these approaches to treatment might be employed at any given point.

In some instances, training projects designed to strengthen individual job performance skills can assist in building self-worth and serve as constructive additions to the therapeutic effort. Both the therapist and the user must continually remember that drug addiction is not essentially a biochemical disturbance, but principally a combined psychological and pharmacological problem. In essence, adjunctive reconditioning and pharmacological efforts must work hand in glove to help rehabilitate the addict and reduce the possibility of engaging in self-destructive acts, many of which can easily become life threatening. In the last analysis, the value of a human life is beyond measure.

REFERENCES _____

Balster, R. L., and Chait, L. D. The behavioral pharmacology of phencyclidine. *Clinical Toxicology*, 9:513–528, 1976.

Barton, W. I. Drug-related mortality in the United States, 1963–1971. *Drug Forum*, 4(1):79–89, 1974.

Benson, R. A., and Brodie, D. C. Suicide by overdoses of medicine among the aged. *Journal of the American Geriatrics Society*, 23:304–308, 1975.

Billings, J. H., Rosen, D. H., Asimas, C., and Motto, J. A. Observations on long-term group therapy with suicidal and depressed persons. *Life-Threatening Behavior*, 4:160–170, 1974.

Braconnier, A., and Olievenstein, C. Attempted suicide in actual drug addicts. *Revue de neuropsychiatrie infantile et d'hygiene mentale de l'enfance*, 22:677–693, 1974.

Bratter, T. E. Treating alienated, unmotivated, drug abusing adolescents. *American Journal of Psychotherapy*, 27:585–598, 1973.

Burns, R. S., and Lerner, S. E. Perspectives: Acute phencyclidine intoxication. *Clinical Toxicology*, 9:477–501, 1976.

Fauman, B., Aldinger, G., Fauman, M., and Rosen, P. Psychiatric sequelae of phencyclidine abuse. *Clinical Toxicology*, 9:529–538, 1976.

Frederick, C. J. Drug abuse as self-destructive behavior. *Drug Therapy*, 2:49–68, 1972.

Frederick, C. J., and Farberow, N. L. Group psychotherapy with suicidal persons: A comparison with standard group methods. *International Journal of Social Psychiatry*, 26:103, 1970.

Frederick, C. J., and Resnik, H. L. How suicidal behaviors are learned. *American Journal of Psychotherapy*, 25:37, 1971.

Frederick, C. J., Resnik, H. L., and Wittlin, B. J. Self-destructive aspects of hard core addiction. *Archives of General Psychiatry*, 28:579–585, 1973.

Friedman, R. C., Friedman, J. G., and Ramirez, T. The heroin overdose as a method of attempted suicide. *British Journal of Addiction*, 68:137–143, 1973.

Goldstein, A. Heroin addiction and role of methadone in its treatment. *Archives of General Psychiatry*, 26:291–297, 1972.

Hendin, H. Students on heroin. *Journal of Nervous and Mental Disease*, 158:240–255, 1974.

Hillman, J. *Suicide and the Soul*. New York: Harper and Row, 1965.

Jacobson, S., and Tribe, P. Deliberate self-injury (attempted suicide) in patients admitted to hospital in Mid-Sussex. *British Journal of Psychiatry*, 121:379–386, 1972.

Jaffe, J. H. Drug addiction and drug abuse. In L. S. Goodman and A. Gilman, eds., *The Pharmacological Basis of Therapeutics*, 4th ed. New York: Macmillan, 1970, pp. 276–312.

Lester, D., Beck, A. T., and Bruno, S. Correlates of choice of method for completed suicide. *Psychology*, 13:70–73, 1976.

Lundberg, G. D., Gupta, R. C., and Montgomery, S. H. Phencyclidine: Patterns seen in street drug analysis. *Clinical Toxicology*, 9:503–511, 1976.

Meerloo, J. A. Hidden suicide. In H. L. P. Resnik, ed., *Suicidal Behaviors: Diagnosis and Management*. Boston: Little, Brown, 1968, pp. 82–89.

Robbins, E., Gassner, S., Kayes, J., Wilkinson, R. H., and Murphy, G. E. The communication of suicidal intent: A study of 134 cases of successful (completed) suicides. In W. A. Rushing, ed., *Deviant Behavior and Social Process*. Chicago: Rand McNally, 1969, pp. 251–269.

Schuman, S. H., and Polkowski, J. Drug and risk perceptions of ninth-grade students: Sex differences and similarities. *Community Mental Health Journal*, 11:184–194, 1975.

Shneidman, E. S. Orientations toward death: A vital aspect of the study of lives. In R. W. White, ed., *The Study of Lives*. New York: Atherton, 1963.

Showalter, C. V., and Thornton, W. E. Clinical pharmacology of phencyclidine toxicity. *American Journal of Psychiatry*, 134:11, 1977.

Tobias, J. J. Overdosing and attempted suicide among youth in an affluent suburban community. *Police Journal*, 44:319–326, 1972.

Weissman, M. M., Slobetz, F., Prusoff, B., Mezritz, M., and Howard, P. Clinical depression among narcotic addicts maintained on methadone in the community. *American Journal of Psychiatry*, 133:1434–1438, 1976.

Wikler, A. Conditioning factors in opiate addiction and relapse. In D. M. Eilner and G. G. Kassebaum, eds., *Narcotics*. New York: McGraw-Hill, 1965, pp. 85–100.

10

COMPULSIVE ADDICTIVE BEHAVIOR
Drugs and Violence

J. THOMAS UNGERLEIDER

In this chapter, we will address the issue of the interaction of certain agents, called drugs, with people, resulting in a certain kind of behavior, namely, violence. We will focus on the drug-person-violence interaction as an indirect self-destructive behavior (ISDB) particularly toward the individual, but also toward the society in which he lives.

No drug itself invariably *causes* violence when consumed. There is a complicated reaction between the person who ingests, injects, or otherwise takes a drug and the resultant behavior. This reaction in large part is dependent on certain characteristics of the drug (dose, pharmacological effects, etc.) and of the person (body size, emotional maturity, etc.). It is also influenced by two other variables known as *set* and *setting*. The set is the attitude with which one approaches a drug experience, and the setting is the environment in which one takes the drug. We can say some drugs are associated with violence more often than other drugs, although violence is usually more a result of the circumstances in which the drug is taken than due to the effects of the drug itself.

The drugs which we will discuss are those that are often alleged to be associated with the behavioral abnormality called violence. Most of these are psychotropic drugs, chemicals which cause changes in both the psyche and in behavioral functions. It should be obvious, however, that there is a whole spectrum of other chemicals which can "cause" a wide variety of actions, some of them violent. For example, someone taking cortisone for a medical illness may have a psychotic reaction as a side effect and may become violent during that psychotic period. The violence may occur as a result of a delusional system or hallucinatory experience which directs the person to harm someone or correct an imagined grievance. Violent behavior may also result from a drug-induced acute anxiety or panic reaction. If not handled supportively, this panic may be interpreted as violence and responded to with counterviolence. (Law enforcement intervention, by arrest, for someone under the influence of a psychedelic drug provides the classic example of intervention-precipitated violence.) We also know that ingestion of a variety of substances can cause an organic brain syndrome with a delirious reaction and often violent-appearing, out-of-control behavior: for example, excessive amounts of antimotion sickness medications (Bonamine®, Marezine®, Dramamine®) or belladonna compounds (Jimson or "loco weed").

The psychotropic medications we will discuss are mostly considered drugs of abuse. Some drugs (e.g., marihuana) are illegal in certain states and cannot be used without the stigma of criminal behavior. Others can be legally *used* when medically prescribed, *misused* if taken incorrectly following medical prescription, or *abused* when obtained illegally and illicitly (i.e., amphetamines, barbiturates, tranquilizers). Others are both legal and encouraged—with devastating effects (i.e., alcohol).

The behavior we will be considering is self-destructive for a variety of reasons. The person involved with drugs and violence in many cases is brought into contact with the criminal justice system as a direct result of this behavior. He may eventually be jailed and/or acquire a criminal record. More immediately, his violent behavior may expose him to retaliation, perhaps including bodily harm. In addition, society takes a particularly dim view of violent behavior depending, of course, on its kind and intensity. Many view drug-taking as mental or physical illness; others view it as a moral defect—depending on the drug and the culture. Some consider the voluntariness of the drug-taking as but willful misbehavior. Strong feelings also exist in those whom the drug user contacts—be they the "significant other," general family, peers and/or those in the helping professions. Yet, many of those in society who are part of the professional mental health system recognize the cry-for-help aspect of some drug-taking with resultant self-destructive behavior, often via violence. Some law enforcement officials have estimated that nearly half of their drug-related arrests, especially for possession, are such cries for help, particularly on the part of young people who are unable to have their needs answered by family or responded to in schools.

Drug users are often people seeking external control; yet they have never had particularly warm receptions in hospital emergency rooms and notoriously do poorly in traditional outpatient therapeutic modalities because of the difficulties in verbal therapy when they are under the influence of chemical substances.

These people may seek controls for a variety of noncoping behaviors involving self-destructive acting-out patterns, particularly in adolescence, where a lack of frustration tolerance and goal-directed behavior is common. The warding off of anxiety, depression, or overt mental illness (psychosis), unsuccessful attempts to dampen emerging aggressive and sexual drives, striving to avoid the youthful dependence-independence conflicted strivings of becoming an adult, and attempts to deny lack of self-esteem are also frequently implicated.

Drug patterns include all ages and segments of society; reasons for use, of course, may vary tremendously, i.e., the ghetto despair versus the boredom of affluence. Only in some religions is the use of all such chemicals proscribed. Usage patterns also vary widely— some use drugs when alone, whereas others use them when in groups, i.e., secondary to peer pressure and for social group acceptance.

THE BEHAVIOR—GENERALLY _____

Symptoms of drug use vary depending on a number of factors, including route of administration and type and amount of drug. For example, use of needles for intravenous or other parenteral routes may cause local infections or generalized septicemia. Poor nutrition is often a concomitant of such drug use, and the possibility of overdose (OD) with anoxic brain damage or lethality as outcomes are the ultimate in self-destructive behavior. Accidental harm based on perceptual changes also may occur (lysergic acid diethylamide, LSD, is the best example) as can apparently irreversible memory defects (phencyclidine, PCP, is a good example). Severe psychomotor depression may result from some drugs (i.e., barbiturates) but elated states (from stimulants) can also occur. Time/dose factors and paradoxical (opposite) reactions are other possibilities.

We should remember that no two persons take drugs for identical reasons, and that the same person often takes drugs for different reasons at different times in his life.

Much of this behavior is conscious; some is not: Some people take drugs recreationally, for pleasure, or to satisfy curiosity, others to self-medicate and ward off negative feelings. The National Commission on Marihuana and Drug Abuse (1973) has described five types of drug use. These are: (1) experimental drug use—primarily among the young and motivated by curiosity; (2) recreational drug use—indulged in by most of us, for pleasure, with one drug or another; (3) situational or circumstantial drug use—taking drugs for specific events, for example, the stimulants to increase short-term study effectiveness or athletic performance; (4) intensified drug use—where drug use interferes with one's behavior and one's relationships at home, at work, and at play; and (5) compulsive drug use—where obtaining drugs ("copping," "scoring," and "shooting up") becomes the overriding preoccupation of daily life. Denial is a predominant defense mechanism, with little thought to risks involved or future consequences. A desire to relieve boredom or create a temporary exultant disequilibrium is frequently present.

Much risk-taking behavior is involved in the use of these chemical substances. Indeed, modern educational programs in schools increasingly take note of this as they focus on risk-taking behavior and the indirectly self-destructive aspects therein. Many young people use these drugs to "explore" their internal boundaries, much as the pioneers of old explored the west. In the process, they are contending, of course, with certain negative cultural taboos as well as with positive group identification processes. For example, there is an LSD taboo, although much of it arose over the mythologies of chromosome and brain damage. There is also a heroin taboo, and a needle taboo in our culture.

Along with the denial of possible future consequences, one sees very little "thought equals trial action" in the approach demonstrated by many of those who seriously abuse the drugs of which we speak. A variety of people who turn to drugs have previously been using coping mechanisms which involve the "doing defense," to ward off anxiety and depression. Some excellent athletes who sustain injuries and are unable to maintain this defense have resorted to the heavy use of chemicals. In other cases, the drug-taking may be purposive, to bring difficulties to the attention of parents and others. Use is often a group phenomenon; in some (not very effective) group therapy situations users compare kinds of drugs and boast of the numbers of "trips" they have taken. There is no one personality characteristic of the person who uses or abuses drugs. We do know that impairment of goal-directed behavior and diminished frustration tolerance results from drug-taking, but whether these results are due to the drug or to the interaction, both with the subculture and the criminal justice system, is difficult to assess. There is a direct relationship between drug-taking and overt self-destructive behavior, since an excess of some of these drugs causes death, particularly drugs like the barbiturates, alone or in combination with alcohol and opiates.

Terminology is important in discussing drug-taking; one should avoid use of the terms "narcotic" or "addiction," which connote negative but imprecise phenomena. The conception of "soft versus hard" drugs should also be avoided. The general route of administration is a relevant factor. Oral ingestion results in effects which continue for hours after the drug-taking ceases because of gastrointestinal absorption. However, with a drug that is smoked, like marihuana or phencyclidine (PCP), when the smoking stops, the delivery of the drug into the system stops at once. The pharmacological characteristics of the particular drug are also important. These depend upon the classification or kind of drug, the particular dose in which it is given, and whether or not the drug is taken alone or in combination with other drugs which may potentiate the effects. The primary drugs we will be considering are those that are alleged to be associated with violence. These include: (1) opiates (i.e., heroin); (2) stimulants (i.e., amphetamines, cocaine); (3) hallucinogens or psychedelics (i.e., LSD, marihuana); and (4) volatile solvents (i.e., glue). To illustrate the importance of *set* in the drug experience, young people who take excessive doses of short-acting barbiturates (i.e., secobarbital) may get, instead of sedation, a paradoxical excitation with an organic brain syndrome or delirium which can be associated with acts of violence. Even higher doses will result in stupor, coma, and eventual death. The lower or "usual" doses for those with a different set cause sedation and sleep. Drugs like alcohol and the barbiturates potentiate with each other and if the disinhibiting effects are those that are potentiated, more behavioral aberrations may result. The pharmacology of these drugs is also important when you consider that ingestion of a marked excess of alcohol, for example, results in less violence because of the stuporous effect and difficulty with psychomotor functioning. Effects over time are also important. Though some drugs like marihuana remain in body fat for seven to eight days, they are only active for several hours. Other drugs, more likely to induce tolerance, can cause more difficulties when discontinued. This is especially true of the barbiturates, alcohol, and some of the stimulants. Sudden cessation can be anywhere from uncomfortable, to life-threatening, to fatal.

THE PERSON _____

I have already described the types of drug use and some of the possible motivations of a person who takes these drugs. There is, of course, wide individual variation in response, as I have also noted. There are also cumulative effects from chronic use and the lessening effects due to tolerance. The personality of the user is important, but not helpful as a predictor of the kind of problems that a person will experience from a drug. Usually age is important in that there is less drug abuse as the person gets older except, perhaps, for heroin. The set and setting are extremely important. Initially, in fact, advice given in preparation for LSD experiences "to avoid bad trips" was: to be in a relaxed mental attitude (set), to be with a friend, babysitter, or guide, sitting on a comfortable thick carpet listening to Ravi Shankar's music and reading phrases from the Tibetan Book of the Dead (setting); but even these precautions did not prevent a variety of adverse reactions to that drug.

Expectation of what will occur is extremely important, however. In our early marihuana experiments at U.C.L.A., using only experienced adult males, we ran out of the initial batch of government-grown marihuana of good tetrahydrocannabinol (THC) potency, so we substituted tobacco cigarettes. Several of the subjects got the "best highs" ever from tobacco. Clearly, they were not being asked to smoke a drug and decide if it was marihuana or not but were really expecting the reinforcement of their previous good marihuana (experimental) experiences. Similarly, with our current cancer and marihuana antiemetic chemotherapy experiments, an older woman who had previously received Compazine® a number of times with her chemotherapy (as an antiemetic) entered the double-blind experiment and took drug X. She had a severe bout of muscle weakness, depression, and an inability to face impending death, which lasted about ten days. She referred to this as her "marihuana flashbacks" and became extremely upset from the experimental drug which she was sure was THC (marihuana). Of course, when the drug was decoded, it turned out to be Compazine that she had received and not THC at all.

THE (CRIMINAL JUSTICE) PROCESS _____

Violence is classified as criminal behavior in our society. Whether or not violence occurs during drug-taking depends on the drug/person interaction and the person/person interaction. Also of import are groups whose members want to assert their masculinity (machismo). Occasionally, we see also violence for secondary reasons, namely, to get money for drugs, although that (rare) phenomenon is excluded from the drug-violence considerations here. The particular drug of dependence that occasions the need for money is heroin, which rarely leads to violent types of behavior.

Likewise, violence during drug use may be precipitated by an external event. One well-known television series features an episode in which a youth was having a pleasant outdoor LSD reaction with visual illusions when the police came, read him his rights, announced that he was under arrest, and put his wrists in handcuffs. He went into a panic and tried to flee; the ensuing melee was then portrayed as drug-induced violence. During social-drinking situations violence may occur—when two friends are drunk they may get into a fight, and a crime of violence is committed between them. Under the rubric of person/drug interaction we must also consider changes over time in society, in drug costs, and in social responses. For example, bad trips from LSD were originally often reported. They are now seldom reported in medical facilities; yet widespread use of LSD continues. Does this mean that the users have "learned" to use the drug, and have few bad experiences, or that adverse experiences are now handled by other people who care for them far away from medical facilities?

The violent types of behavior are of different degrees, but include the following, on a scale of progression: (1) runaway, (2) disorderly conduct, (3) inciting to riot, (4) gang fighting, (5) assault and battery, and (6) homicide. On this continuum, violence varies from minimal to maximal. Within this general context, we can then perhaps observe the effects of specific drugs. The difficulties, however, in studying drug use and criminal behavior are many. Methods include: (1) self-disclosure, where lists of crimes by alleged drug users are analyzed by retrospective case study; (2) statistical study of alleged drug users for incidents of *detected* crimes—this can be compared with the criminal records of nonusers; (3) comparison of the drug users' rate of violence with that of other control groups; (4) comparison of users' rate of crime in the general population versus nonusers' rate of crime; (5) examination of case records of purported violence per drug user; and (6) laboratory experimental administration of drugs and observation of violent behavior in animals and/or humans. In this last case, the artificial experimental situation and difficulties in generalizing from one species to another are crucial. In all cases, methodological problems abound (Tinklenberg, 1973, 1975). All of the above methods provide only correlational relationships, at best, and do not differentiate use of a drug leading to criminal behavior (violence) from criminal behavior leading to drug use.

One obvious fact is that we are usually referring to *alleged* drug use, but violence also occurs without the criminal justice system being involved; and arrests differ from convictions. In only one study has the urine of arrestees been analyzed for drugs (Eckerman, 1971), but this, too, raises another set of problems. For example, for marihuana there is now a blood test which shows up metabolites, but since marihuana is stored in the body fat for seven to eight days, it will show up for days. Yet marihuana is only active for several hours. How, then, does one know how long ago the particular drug was ingested in relation to the self-destructive behavior or what its connection is with the alleged violent act? A special note should be made of this study by Eckerman, sponsored by the Bureau of Narcotics and Dangerous Drugs, in which drug use and crime were explored by studying 300 arrestees from each of six cities for a total of 1,800. In this study urine samples were taken and analyzed for a variety of drugs, including heroin, cocaine, methadone, amphetamines, and barbiturates. In addition, a personal interview including questions about other drug use was conducted. Sixty-eight percent of all arrestees had used a drug sometime in the past. However, when current use as indicated by urine sample results and questionnaire responses was studied, a greater concentration of arrest charges involving serious crimes was found among the nondrug users than among the drug users. Charges included criminal homicide, forcible rape, and aggravated assault. Drug users, however, were more heavily represented among those charged with property crime—with robbery, in particular, which is variously classified as either a person or a property crime. There was a clear and significant tendency, however, for heroin users, identified through urinalysis, to be charged with property crimes as opposed to crimes against the person. These results apply only to the six areas studied; nonetheless, analyzing these current arrest charges for drug users versus nondrug users, there was *no* indication that drug users were more often involved in crimes of violence. This was true for all drugs considered, by urinalysis and questionnaire, and included were tranquilizers, marihuana, psychedelics, and special substances like glue and ether.

The real questions, then, are: (1) do drug users experience increased aggressive tendencies; (2) is this translated into overt behavior; and (3) is this behavior violent or aggressive?

THE DRUG—SPECIFICALLY _____

MARIHUANA AND VIOLENCE

The relationship between the use of marihuana and violence was particularly studied by the National Commission on Marihuana and Drug Abuse (1972a). They reviewed the literature, which consisted of numerous unsupported and often emotional accusations about marihuana's contribution to violence. For example, "in at least two dozen comparatively recent cases of murder or degenerate sex attacks, marihuana proved to be a contributing cause" (Anslinger, 1937). Others denied these allegations or asserted that there was no evidence to support the thesis of an independent causal relationship (Indian Hemp Drugs Commission, 1894/1969). Others hypothesized that the drug could release inhibitions but not lead to aggressive behavior or crime (President's Commission, 1967). Additional evidence regarding the relationship of marihuana to violence can be found in laboratory experiments and in retrospective self-reports of ill effects purportedly experienced by marihuana users. Other clues, although not hard data, are gained by examination of criminal records of known marihuana users and recording the incidence of marihuana use among persons arrested or convicted of prior crimes. On balance, there is no evidence that marihuana heightens any aggressive tendencies or that its effects increase the likelihood of inciting the user to violence or crime (Canadian Government, 1970; National Commission on the Causes and Prevention of Violence, 1969). It is not that marihuana cannot be related to aggressive or violent behavior, but merely that the effects of the drug and the behaviors in question seem to operate independently. There are reports that marihuana decreases the inclination toward physical activity in contrast to the amphetamines and that in some studies it has been shown to induce timidity, fear, and passivity in the user. Experimental laboratory administration of marihuana to humans has resulted in feelings of relaxation and peacefulness. A college student questionnaire asked about marihuana and "losing control of my actions and doing antisocial things"; 22 percent said "rarely"; 77 percent, "never"; and 1 percent said "sometimes" (National Commission on Marihuana and Drug Abuse, 1972b, p. 427). In a survey prepared for the National Commission (1973), nearly all marihuana users denied that the effects of marihuana on them could be interpreted as violent in nature.

From the days of the Indian Hemp Commission, investigations of violence allegedly caused by hemp drugs have failed to produce reliable case histories to support this. Cases that do appear seem to involve predominantly panic (anxiety) reactions.

Others have compiled lists of violent crimes and tried to determine the portion of these offenses committed by cannabis (marihuana) users. Still others have sampled offenders rather than lists of offenses, identified the marihuana users in their samples, and reported the number of violent crimes that users perpetrated. And still others attempted to compare users' rates of violence with those of other populations consisting of nonusers. Results of all these studies indicate that some individuals who are identified as marihuana users do commit violent crimes, or have in the past, or go on to do so in the future, but the numbers are generally very small, both absolutely and relatively. Therefore, if there is any statistical (not causal) association at all, it is insignificant.

In summary, according to the National Commission (1972a), there is no reason to believe that marihuana use will "lead to the commission of aggressive or violent acts by the large majority of . . . individuals in the general population" (p. 73). Rather than inducing violent or aggressive behavior, marihuana was usually found to inhibit the expression of aggressive impulses. Only a small proportion of the marihuana users among any group of criminal delinquents known to the authorities and appearing in study samples have ever been arrested or convicted for such violent crimes as murder, forcible rape, aggravated assault, or armed robbery. When the unique experience of law enforcement and criminal justice communities was tapped by the National Commission, representative samples of prosecuting attorneys, judges, probation officers, and court clinicians were asked their opinion of the statement that "most aggressive acts or crimes of violence committed by persons who were known users of marihuana occurred when the offender was under the influence of marihuana" (1972a, p. 72). Three-fourths of the judges, the probation officers, and court clinicians indicated either that this statement was probably untrue or that they were unsure of its accuracy. Especially in contrast to the opiates, heavy marihuana users are not subject to the same degree of compulsion to obtain their drugs, a compulsion which may lead to property (not violent) crime.

ALCOHOL AND VIOLENCE

Controlled experiments after alcohol intake yield conflicting evidence. Most of the information which links alcohol to aggressive behavior comes from crime statistics and general observations. In one study, 60 percent of the offenders who committed violent homicide reported drinking before the crime (Wolfgang, 1958). Urine samples in another study, after commission of a felony, revealed the presence of alcohol in 82 percent of 163 persons charged with violent crimes (Shupe, 1964). Again, although alcohol may contribute to crime, it is not a causal factor. Available evidence does indicate that use of alcohol increases the probablility of violent crime for many people. The fact that many social drinkers find themselves less inhibited and even behaving "wildly" when they are drinking may lead one to think that some criminal behavior is directly related to drinking, but one can rarely say with certainty that a particular crime would not have occurred if the person had not been drinking. Besides homicide, aggravated assault is the type of crime most significantly associated with alcohol. On the other hand, alcohol seems to have only minimal involvement in robbery. We will not consider alcohol in automobile crashes as violent crime although violence is involved and these are criminal acts. An estimated one million traffic accidents and 35,000 fatalities due to alcohol occur in our country each year. Although alcohol abuse is a significant public health, safety, and welfare problem, and the most significant of all the abused drugs, for our purposes further elucidation of this topic is tangential. Alcohol-induced violence is related to dosage; very small amounts rarely predispose to aggression, and very large amounts result in stupor or coma. But the second stage of intoxication, that of paradoxical stimulation, is often associated with belligerence in word and deed in the drinker.

STIMULANTS AND VIOLENCE

AMPHETAMINES. The amphetamines are known to induce central nervous system stimulation. Route of administration and rapid buildup of tolerance are important here. A variety of usage patterns occur, including intermittent low-dose use, high-dose use, oral-sustained use, and repeated intravenous large-dose injections. The number of studies on amphetamine/crime relationships is small, but amphetamine abuse is apparently related to assaultive criminal behavior (Ellinwood, 1971; Connell, 1958). Study of arrests for criminal homicide, forcible rape, and assault showed a greater proportion of total arrests for current users of amphetamines than for current users of other classifications of drugs, with the exception of barbiturates. Clinical reports suggest that assaultive behavior can result directly from the pharmacological properties of the amphetamines or through paranoid reactions with hostility and occasional overt psychosis and delusions. There is a report of close association between amphetamine use and violent crime in the epidemic of amphetamine abuse that occurred in Japan in the mid-1950s. It was particularly striking because violent behavior is relatively rare among the Japanese. In addition, the incidence of this increase was markedly reduced when the market for amphetamines receded.

COCAINE. Cocaine's action is briefer than the amphetamines'; it is possible that use of large amounts of amphetamines results in violence more often than does use of cocaine. Cocaine has not been used very much until recently in this country, so there is not much data about cocaine and crime. Certainly its suspiciousness- and paranoia-inducing features suggest a link between cocaine psychosis and violence. However, despite the similarity between cocaine psychosis and violence, there is little reason to believe that cocaine users are involved in violent crime (Tinklenberg, 1973).

OPIATES AND VIOLENCE

The category of opiates includes opium, morphine, and their derivatives, plus their synthetic equivalents, codeine, heroin, methadone, and demerol. Because use of these drugs results in indifference to pain and satiation of all drives, i.e., hunger and sex, during their acute effects, the user is disinclined toward any type of assaultive action. Opiate dependence certainly is often related to an antisocial life-style, and robbery to support a habit has been well documented. Most known opiate-dependent persons have been de-linquent before they are identified as drug users, however. This fact supports the thesis that in general they have criminal predisposi-tions antedating their drug use, which then becomes a further ex-pression of these delinquent tendencies. There are, of course, many nondrug influences on the user's behavior, and there are no data directly comparing criminal proclivities of opiate users with those of the general population (Tinklenberg, 1973).

SEDATIVE-HYPNOTICS AND VIOLENCE

Barbiturates are general depressants of the central nervous sys-tem. The motor difficulties encountered with higher doses of bar-biturates tend to discline the user toward effective violence; there seems to be some evidence that more human aggression is con-trolled by barbiturates and tranquilizers than is evoked by them. However, there is a paradoxical excitation with increased irritability and a tendency toward violence which one can see clinically (Tinklenberg et al., 1974). In addition, barbiturates potentiate with alcohol; especially with the short-acting barbiturates, this potentia-tion may also be related to crime and violence. In some studies, barbiturates are most often implicated in arrests for criminal of-fenses, not all of which are violent offenses.

Nonbarbiturate sedative-hypnotics include Doriden®, Quaalude®, Placidyl®, and Noludar®. Few studies exist which link these drugs with crime, particularly violent crime. Illicit use (in large amounts) is not common except for Quaaludes® (Methaqualone). Misuse of these substances is so new that study of their relationship to crime is virtually nonexistent.

HALLUCINOGENS/PSYCHEDELICS AND VIOLENCE

LSD is the most powerful drug known to man—60,000 doses fit on the head of a pin. It is the prototype psychedelic drug. Set and setting are extremely important determinants of its effect. No test is available routinely for determining body-fluid levels of these drugs. Information is limited but suggests strongly that aggressive out-bursts rarely occur, although they may (rarely) be a part of a precipi-tated paranoid psychosis or panic reaction. Here especially the user's previous psychosocial history and his behavioral patterns are more important than the effect of the drug itself. The mechanism of action of psychedelics is poorly understood; the "flashback" data also remain ill-defined.

As far as violent crime is concerned, these psychedelic substances are seldom involved. In fact, they may reduce the inclination to such behavior.

A special type of hallucinogen, phencyclidine (PCP), has some unique qualities, including precipitation of an organic brain syndrome in some cases with possible associated abnormalities (Showalter et al., 1977).

TRANQUILIZERS AND VIOLENCE

The major tranquilizers (phenothiazines), which are used in psychiatry in the treatment of psychosis, are not linked to violent behavior. The minor tranquilizer class of drugs, including the benzodiazepines and meprobamate, has been studied very little, but they seem to be associated with reduction of assaultive tendencies because of their tranquilizing effects.

Minor tranquilizers are perceived by medical practitioners and other mental health professionals as helping to reduce, not contribute to, disruptive behavior (Matlins et al., nd).

SOLVENTS, RELATED SUBSTANCES, AND VIOLENCE

The solvents and related substances include glue, gasoline, kerosene, aerosol, and ether. The behavioral effects of these drugs are a general delirious impairment of brain function resulting in an organic brain syndrome, but there are few data about crime related to the effects of these drugs. Certainly, a delirious person may be assaultive, especially if it is unclear what he is experiencing perceptually. Glue and solvents are inhaled and delivered to the brain at a rapid rate. Sleepiness and stupor are quickly achieved, thus allowing less time for antisocial acts to occur, particularly as compared to alcohol intoxication (Cohen, 1973).

REFERENCES _____

Anslinger, H. J. Marijuana—An assassin of youth. *American Magazine*, July, 1937.

Canadian Government Commission of Inquiry. *Non-medical Use of Drugs.* Interim Report of the Commission. Ottawa, 1970.

Cohen, Sidney. Inhalant abuse. *Drug Abuse and Alcoholism Newsletter*, 1, Vista Hill Foundation, 1973.

Connell, P. H. *Amphetamine Psychosis.* London: Chapman & Hill, 1958.

Eckerman, William C. *Drug Usage and Arrest Charges, A Study of Drug Usage and Arrest Charges Among Arrestees in 6 Metropolitan Areas of the United States.* Research Report, Bureau of Narcotics and Dangerous Drugs, 1971.

Ellinwood, E. H. Assault and homicide—associated with amphetamine abuse. *American Journal of Psychiatry*, 127:1170–1175, 1971.

Indian Hemp Drugs Commission. Reprint by Thomas Jefferson Printing Company, Silver Springs, Md., 1969 Enterprises. (Originally published, 1894.)

Matlins, S., et al. Social impact of specified drugs. New York: Stuart Matlins Associates, Inc., unpublished.

National Commission on Marihuana and Drug Abuse. *Marihuana, A Signal of Misunderstanding.* First Report of the Commission. Washington, D.C.: U.S. Government Printing Office, 1972a. #20402.

National Commission on Marihuana and Drug Abuse. *Marihuana, A Signal of Misunderstanding.* Technical Papers of the First Report of the Commission, appendix, vol. 1: *Marihuana and Violence.* Washington, D.C.: U.S. Government Printing Office, 1972b. #20402.

National Commission on Marihuana and Drug Abuse. *Drug Use in America: Problem in Perspective.* Second Report of the Commission. Washington, D.C.: U.S. Government Printing Office, 1973. #5266-0003.

National Commission on the Causes and Prevention of Violence. *Drugs and Violence.* Staff Report. Washington, D.C.: U.S. Government Printing Office, 1969.

President's Commission on Law Enforcement and Administration of Justice. Task Force Report, Narcotics and Drug Abuse, Washington, D.C., 1967, p. 13.

Showalter, Craig V., et al. Clinical pharmacology of phencyclidine toxicity. *American Journal of Psychiatry,* 134:1234–1238, 1977.

Shupe, L. M. Alcohol and crime. *Journal of Criminal Law, Criminology and Police Science,* 44:661–664, 1964.

Tinklenberg, J. R. *Drugs and Crime.* Vol. 1, Part II, of the Technical Papers of the Second Report of the National Commission on Marihuana and Drug Abuse (*Drug Use in America: Problem in Perspective*). Washington, D.C.: U.S. Government Printing Office, 1973. #5266-0004.

Tinklenberg, J. R. Assessing the effects of drug use on antisocial behavior. *Annals of the American Academy of Political and Social Science,* 417:66–75, 1975.

Tinklenberg, J. R., et al. Drug intervention in criminal assaults by adolescents. *Archives of General Psychiatry,* 30:658–689, 1974.

Wolfgang, M. E. *Patterns in Criminal Homicide.* Philadelphia: University of Pennsylvania Press, 1958.

11

DRUG ABUSE AMONG ADOLESCENTS AND SELF-DESTRUCTIVE BEHAVIOR

REGINALD G. SMART

Much adolescent drug abuse suggests self-destructive activity. What clinicians frequently observe are affluent young people in the prime of life with all reasonable hopes of fulfilling their expectations; but their seat at life's feast displeases them somehow, and they resort to drugs in a strangely self-defeating or self-injuring manner. How common is this stereotype as opposed to others, such as that of the young ghetto dweller who drifts into drugs as a natural consequence of their high availability? Unfortunately such questions cannot be easily answered at present since little research has been directed at adolescent drug use concomitant with the whole range of self-destructive behaviors. There are numerous studies of drug abuse and overt suicide (attempted and completed), studies of depression and risk-taking among adolescent abusers, and some theoretical contributions to the etiology and treatment of adolescent drug abuse which assume self-destructive models. This review examines empirical evidence for a relationship between drug use and self-destructive behavior. Before examining such evidence, it is worth asking some questions. Major questions might include: (1) What is the nature and extent of all self-destructive behavior among adolescent drug abusers? (2) Which types of drug abuse are most likely to be associated with self-destructive behavior? (3) Does drug abuse lead to self-destructive behavior or vice versa? (4) What therapeutic treatment exists for self-destructive behavior among adolescent drug abusers?

Before searching for answers, thought should be given to certain conceptual and methodological problems surrounding the key terms "self-destructive behavior" and "drug abuse." Generally the terms "suicide" and "self-destructive behavior" have been applied

170

to such a variety of activities, behaviors, emotions, tendencies, and personality traits that they have little meaning outside a particular study. Such conceptual problems also apply to the term "drug abuse." To include both within the same analysis is to generate especially large problems in definition.

Although alcohol has been called "the most dangerous drug on earth" (Vista Hill Psychiatric Foundation, 1974) and is known to be associated with both suicide and self-destructive behavior, a consideration of alcohol and self-destructive behavior is beyond the scope of the present review.

CONCEPTUAL AND METHODOLOGICAL PROBLEMS_____

Conceptual problems are in part associated with theoretical approaches to both self-destructive behavior and drug abuse. The idea that suicide involves more than mere sudden self-inflicted death is historically associated with Menninger and his book *Man against Himself* (1938). He considers asceticism, alcoholism, and martyrdom as "chronic suicide," self-mutilations, malingering, and purposive accidents as "social suicide," and psychological factors in organic disease as "organic suicide." To some (Pokorny, 1974), if all such events are included as suicidal, "the word loses all useful meaning." Can they legitimately be included as self-destructive behavior? That depends upon one's definition of "self," be it the unique traits and behaviors of an individual (i.e., self-concept) or only the physical body. A psychological definition might encompass all types of self-defeating or self-punishing behaviors such as accidents, failure at school or in social relationships, problems at work, and the like. A physical definition generally would consider only suicide, suicide attempts, and self-mutilation (cutting, injuring) as self-destructive behavior.

Even if the least inclusive definition were used, with self-destructive behavior referring to bodily harm or death, conceptual problems remain. Many classifications of suicide (Pokorny, 1974) involve various degrees of seriousness and lethality in suicidelike behavior. For example, some (Stengel and Cook, 1958) include only definite, confirmed suicide where intent to die was obvious, considering cases of slight injury where there was no real danger to life as "threats or gestures." Others (Shneidman, 1966) include the categories "intentioned, subintentioned, unintentioned and contraintentioned," while still others (Dorpat and Boswell, 1963) classify suicidal behavior into suicidal gestures, ambivalent suicide attempt, serious suicide attempt, and completed suicide.

The same problems in suicide apply to the more inclusive term self-destructive behavior. It can be intentional or nonintentional, injurious physically or psychologically, fatal or nonfatal, serious or nonserious. When drug use is a contributing factor, there is the additional problem of determining whether drugs were used intentionally as a suicidal vehicle or whether drug use led to an unintentionally serious accident; e.g., a barbiturate overdose for someone who has been drinking very heavily beforehand could be accidental or intentional. An additional problem is in deciding whether the term "self-destructive" should be applied at all to suicide attempts or accidental completions which are entirely manipulative. Rather than suggesting an easy solution to all of these problems, this review considers a wide range of self-injuring, suicidal, and self-defeating behaviors as self-destructive, regardless of proved intent. In most of the research reviewed, the degree of the person's suicidal intent or planfulness was not known. It is suggested that the definitions used in individual research projects be accepted at face value, largely because issues of "seriousness" and "intent" are rarely reported.

A further problem is that those who attempt or complete suicide with drugs may not differ greatly from one another. The medical lethality of a suicide attempt with drugs does not relate very well to the person's intent to kill himself. This suggests that we need studies of suicide attempts as well as suicide completions. Lester and Beck (1975) rated the medical lethality of 145 suicides with drugs. A large number of characteristics related to the patient and his suicide, including drug and alcohol abuse, were unrelated to lethality. No generalizations could be made about suicide completers from this study, suggesting that people are ineffective at predicting their suicide success with drugs and that research should include a complete range of overdoses and near suicides as well as actual suicides, although the former are rarely reported.

There are also conceptual problems with the term "drug abuse." I have discussed some of these problems previously (Smart, 1974). Drug abuse has been defined as any use of an "illegal drug," "heavy" use, addiction or nonmedical use, i.e., use not in keeping with accepted medical practice. The preference here is that drug abuse refer to nonmedical use. This review essentially includes any use, however infrequent, of illicit drugs (and not including alcohol and tobacco) rather than only serious, chronic, heavy, or addictive use.

Methodological problems parallel the conceptual problems. It is rare for different investigators to use the same definitions or data-gathering tools for research. Another common problem is that the age of the population studied is not given in categories so that adolescents or young persons can be separately identified. If age categories are given they are frequently very broad, e.g., ages ten to twenty-four. Strict comparisons of results are therefore difficult and must be tentative.

Whitehead et al. (1973) noted that many studies of "self-injury" provide little indication of the real rate in the population. They gathered data on self-injury from a variety of sources in a medium-sized Canadian city, including interviews with self-injury cases in general hospitals, reports from psychiatric hospitals, social agencies and other health care agencies, statements by physicians, and reports by the county jail physician of self-injuries in jails. Typically, self-injury studies are much more selective and depend on only a few sources, usually hospitals alone or hospitals and physicians. These studies have produced estimates of self-injury between 40 per 100,000 and 220 per 100,000. The Whitehead study, however, produced an estimate of 730 per 100,000. Given the fairly low suicide rate in Canada, it is difficult to believe that the real rate of self-injury is three to four times as high as in the United States or Britain. A more likely explanation is that the larger the number of sources checked, the higher the reported rate of self-injury. Perhaps many studies miss a large proportion of self-injury cases because they survey only hospitals or physicians.

STUDIES OF SUICIDES AND SUICIDAL BEHAVIOR RELEVANT TO DRUG USE _____

Very few studies have directly attempted to assess the frequency of drug use or abuse among a sample of adolescents who attempt suicide or indulge in self-injury. No study has focused exclusively on adolescents, and most studies of suicide only mention drug use in passing if it contributed to the suicide.

A study by Hankoff and Einsidler (1976) is one of the few which provides information on drug use among those who attempt suicide. They studied 141 suicide attempters at a general hospital. Of the total, 23 percent were drug abusers, i.e., "habitually used hard or soft drugs for nontherapeutic reasons." One-third of the males but only one-quarter of the females were drug abusers. There was no difference between drug abusers and nonabusers in race or education. However, abusers were significantly younger than nonabusers; with a mean age of 24.8, some must have been adolescents. Drug abusers had made more previous suicide attempts and more in the follow-up period; more were also enrolled in treatment programs at the time of their suicide. Unfortunately, it is impossible in this study to determine the characteristics of adolescents separately from those of older suicide attempters.

A study by White (1974) of fifty consecutive poisoning admissions showed that the most common poisoning attempts occurred among lower-class girls who had taken barbiturates or aspirins, that neuroticism, family disturbances, and crises had often led to the suicide attempt, and that immigrants were overrepresented in the sample.

Some data on drug abuse among adolescent suicide attempters can be culled from general studies of whole populations. Studies of vital statistics (Barton, 1974) in the United States show an increase of 36 percent in deaths due to drug dependence between 1963 and 1971, a 42 percent increase in deaths due to accidental poisoning, and a 13 percent increase in deaths due to suicide by drugs. It has been recognized that about 30 percent of suicides in North America involve drug use and that both drug use and drug abuse are more common among young suicide attempters than among older suicide attempters (Lester and Beck, 1974).

Many observers have noted that barbiturates are most commonly used in suicides. For example, Holland et al. (1975) found that, in 385 suicides in New York, barbiturates were the most commonly used drug, often combined with alcohol. Studies done in Canada for the Le Dain Commission (1973) indicated that 8.5 percent of deaths attributed to suicide or self-injury involved barbiturates. However, most of these deaths involved persons over forty years of age. Fatalities due to overdose deaths in young persons on "trips" or taking barbiturates therapeutically were very rare.

The Le Dain Commission also reported deaths due to opiate narcotics by age. However, the Commission pointed out that such deaths are greatly underreported because toxicological analyses are not often a part of autopsies and physicians are reluctant or unable to report drug use as a cause of death. More than one-third of the acetylsalicylic acid-codeine deaths (the most common type) in Canada involved persons aged ten to twenty-five years. About half of the heroin and methadone cases were among young persons aged ten to twenty-four. The majority of cases investigated seem to involve other drugs. The precise cause of death in most narcotic overdose cases is unknown. Simple pharmacological overdose from heroin is apparently rare because the doses and concentrations taken are often not unusual. This also suggests that allergic reactions or shock are more important than suicidal or self-destructive impulses. However, problems arise in interpreting overdose or seemingly accidental deaths among drug addicts known to have made several earlier suicide attempts; it is difficult to interpret them as totally accidental.

A considerable problem exists in interpreting deaths from hallucinogens such as lysergic acid diethylamide (LSD). The lifetime frequency of suicide among LSD users is not known. However, the drug does produce delusions and hallucinations which could contribute to risk-taking and self-destructive behavior. Several LSD users have jumped from buildings, bridges, or trees apparently under the delusion that they could fly (Le Dain, 1973). Suicidal thoughts and attempts at self-mutilation under LSD have also been reported but are apparently rare.

Only one death has been attributed to cannabis use in Belgium (Heyndrickx et al., 1969). Cannabinoids were found in the body, and no other possible cause of death was apparent. Another case (Gourves et al., 1971) has been reported where suicide was attempted after the person had ingested a large dose of cannabis. The low toxicity of cannabis and the difficulties of ingesting and tolerating large amounts make it unlikely that successful suicide and cannabis use will often be associated.

The drugs most frequently associated with suicide among adolescents are probably the amphetamines, especially the injectable forms such as methamphetamine or "speed." The concept that "speed kills" developed soon after its use became popular in the late 1960s. The view was often expressed that speed users would live only months or sometimes a few years at the most. Indeed, many speed users came to know and like the designation "speed kills"; some consciously gave the impression that they were bent on a slow suicide and relished the thought. In some cases it probably represented an attention-getting activity as much as a deeply held conviction.

I remember a macabre interview I had in the early 1970s with two speed users who had come to the Addiction Research Foundation to sell their bodies for research purposes after their death. They expected to be dead shortly as "speed kills," although they were uncertain about how they might die.

Scientific investigations of amphetamine-related suicides and self-inflicted deaths are complex because amphetamines are difficult to detect in the blood. Since many speed users are young and lack evidence of long-term needle injections, investigations for drug use may not have been made in many suspicious deaths.

The Le Dain Commission found only 600 toxic or poisoning cases involving amphetamines in 1971. About half of them occurred in persons aged ten to twenty-four years. Only four deaths were ascribed to these drugs, two of which involved young people. This was at a time when the number of intravenous amphetamine users was estimated to be less than 7,500 persons.

More recently Kalant and Kalant (1976) reviewed data concerning amphetamine deaths in Ontario. Having access to published reports and to unpublished coroner's office reports for 1972 and 1973, they found very few deaths among patients receiving the drugs under medical supervision. Apparently only two of the forty-seven cases of death reported in the literature were suicides, and neither was an adolescent (i.e., under twenty-one years of age).

In general, little is known of the relationship between self-injury other than suicide or poisoning and drug use or abuse. Apparently no study has assessed the drug use of a large group of self-injury or self-mutilation cases seen in hospitals or clinics. Estimates of the association between the two phenomena depend very much upon investigations of suicidal or life-threatening behaviors.

ADOLESCENT DRUG USE IN GENERAL POPULATIONS: RELEVANCE TO SELF-DESTRUCTIVE BEHAVIOR

Most adolescent drug studies have been conducted with high school and college samples. Those for high school predominate by a factor of two or three to one, and virtually all samples include only adolescents (i.e., nineteen years and under). Unfortunately, few of these studies are even remotely concerned with suicidal or self-destructive behavior. Reviews of epidemiology in this area have been published by Mercer and Smart (1974) and Blumberg (1975). In general, these studies indicate that up to 80 percent of high school students drink alcohol and up to 50 percent have used cannabis in the past year. Use of hallucinogens such as LSD, methylene dioxyamphetamine (MDA), etc., usually involves less than 10 percent of students, and use of individual psychoactive drugs, less than 25 percent. About 19 percent of high school students in a Canadian study (Smart and Whitehead, 1974) had used some drug other than alcohol or tobacco in the past six months. Given the relatively high frequency of drug use and low frequency of suicide and self-destructive behavior, it is unlikely that the two are closely related in any direct causal way.

Another consideration is that most adolescents who use drugs other than alcohol and tobacco do so infrequently. The only drug which is typically used more than a few times per day by the average high school student is cannabis. It has a low level of toxicity, is rarely lethal, and has little known connection with suicide or self-destructive behavior. It has also been recognized (Mercer and Smart, 1974) that the vast majority of adolescent drug users (or abusers) were using drugs because "they were curious," "they wanted to try it," or "their friends were using it." Most planned or expected to use drugs only a few times for recreational or peer-acceptance reasons. This suggests that one should seek self-destructive explanations primarily among very heavy users or users of certain drugs or that one should examine personality factors (e.g., depression, poor self-concept, risk-taking tendencies) assumed to be the precursors of self-destructive behavior.

Reviews of personality factors associated with deviant drug use have been made by Braucht et al. (1973) and Sadava (1970). The literature in this area is very extensive and difficult to summarize. Much of it lacks a theoretical framework, and the characteristics of deviant drug use, such as depression, have been examined in only a few drug-use studies.

In his study of forty-one drug-abusing college students, Kuehn (1970) found "inexplicable depression" as well as a variety of other characteristics such as a tendency to be present-oriented, passivity in personal relationships, cognitive-schizoid difficulties, study difficulties not attributable to environmental problems, unrewarding sexual behavior, and use of repression, rationalization, intellectualization, and isolation as secondary defenses. Certainly this is a long list of correlates with only a passing reference to depression.

Studies by McAree et al. (1969) of college students found that users of marihuana only did not differ significantly from controls on the Minnesota Multiphasic Personality Inventory (MMPI). Multiple drug users showed primarily a schizoid rather than a depressed, suicidal pattern. Apparently none of the available studies has shown that the Depression Scale on the MMPI is especially elevated among college drug users in general. Of course, such studies are primarily of marihuana users whose use is rather infrequent and well-controlled. The MMPI Depression Scale contains items on suicidal ideation and self-destructive tendencies as well as on depression and sadness. Theoretically, it should help to identify cases with a high suicide or self-destructive potential.

One of the few studies of female drug users among college students examined their reactions to depression and risk-taking potential. The study by Rouse and Ewing (1973) of 184 female undergraduates was based on data from interviews and questionnaires; more marihuana users than nonusers reported a desire to be free of depression and unusual thoughts. Users also reported sleeplessness, violent dreams, involvement in accidents, consultations with psychiatrists in the past year, and willingness to take more risks than nonusers to achieve drug effects.

Sadava (1970) in his review of college students found nine sets of correlates or themes associated with drug use among college students, none of which was particularly associated with depression. These correlates were: (1) alienation and search for meaning; (2) disillusionment and rebellion; (3) need for stimulation; (4) self-definition; (5) interpersonal relationships; (6) escape from sexuality; (7) relief of anxiety and tension; (8) curiosity and novelty; and (9) hedonism.

STUDIES OF HEAVY DRUG-USING POPULATIONS: FACTORS ASSOCIATED WITH SUICIDE AND SELF-DESTRUCTIVE BEHAVIOR _____

Generally, the more dangerous forms of drug use are more likely to involve psychiatrically disturbed populations. High suicide rates and depression have been found among various types of drug addicts and multidrug users.

Most studies of suicide among drug abusers have been done with narcotic addicts. Narcotic addiction has often been seen as a "suicide equivalent" (Braconnier and Olievenstein, 1974). Indeed, much of the life of the narcotic addict seems a slow suicide or chronic self-mutilation. Addicts spend large amounts of time chasing drugs, hustling and earning money to pay for drugs. They often buy drugs of poor quality and are victimized in a variety of ways by pushers, police, and other drug users. Few of them use sterile injection procedures, and many experience physical signs of addiction such as withdrawal symptoms almost daily. Exhaustion from such a life-style is a reason often given for going off drugs or entering treatment.

Suicide rates among addicts in general are substantial, but the rate for adolescent addicts is difficult to determine as few studies are concerned with them exclusively. Of narcotic addicts at Lexington, Kentucky, 1 percent were said to have committed suicide with barbiturates between 1935 and 1966 (Braconnier and Olievenstein, 1974). Death rates among addicts have been estimated at about 1 percent per year with approximately half of them poisoning, overdoses, or clear suicides. The possibility that overdoses represent subintentional suicides in addicts exists but cannot be substantiated.

Friedman et al. (1973) explored the relationship between overdose, depression, and suicide in patients at a methadone clinic. About one-third had taken heroin overdoses in their lives and *most* were covert suicides. Only 12 percent of the overdoses were related to drug variability, and 38 percent were related to incarceration. Unfortunately data on adolescents are not separately given.

An interesting psychodynamic study by Hendin (1974) examined heroin abuse among a small group of students. In this study twenty students were examined in detail, using psychoanalytic interviewing techniques and psychological tests. Short-term therapy was given when possible. Of the twenty students, seven were addicted and most took other drugs as well as heroin. The students were all males and from either affluent, middle-class backgrounds or from ghettos. "Passivity and surface blandness" were seen as cloaks for self-destructive and destructive impulses. Heroin had self-destructive implications even for students who were not addicted to it. Several of the case histories indicated that heroin use itself was indulged in almost as a substitute for self-destruction. How typical these cases are is of course difficult to say, as all were in treatment.

Whether depression and tendencies toward self-destruction are typical of young multidrug users in general is debatable. A study by Studer (1974) of young drug-abusing patients (ages fourteen to twenty-five), alcoholics, and college students on the Szondi Test indicated that drug abusers had a greater need for self-destruction. Bron (1976) also studied sixty-six juvenile drug users and found that death fantasies and suicidal thoughts were accompanied by increasing drug consumption.

Gendreau and Gendreau (1971) attempted to supply a sophisticated answer to the question of personality differences between addicts and nonaddicts. They compared MMPI results for an addict and a nonaddict group carefully matched for age, IQ, socioeconomic background, criminal experience, and opportunity for drug use. They found no difference on the twelve scales of the MMPI, including Depression. Few studies take the care to develop such control groups.

Other studies present conflicting data about the role of depression in all types of drug users. Salzman et al. (1972) studied sixteen drug continuers and sixteen discontinuers with a variety of psychological tests. The main drug used was marihuana. They found no elevation in the MMPI Depression Scale; however, drug continuers did show more signs of risk-taking on the items (Choice Dilemmas) involving possible loss of life or bodily injury.

Two studies of heavy drug users (Smart and Jones, 1970; Cox and Smart, 1972) examined users who were not in treatment. The study of LSD users (Smart and Jones, 1970) involved 100 illicit or street users not in treatment and 46 nonuser controls. On the standard MMPI plus several special scales, LSD users and nonusers did not differ in depression. The majority of abnormal scales for LSD users suggested psychopathy or schizophrenia with a few psychoneurotic patterns. The special scales indicated more alienation and lower ego strength among users than among nonusers. However, the study as a whole does not suggest greater depression or suicidal tendencies among LSD users than among nonusers.

In addition, the study by Cox and Smart (1972), which examined seventy-five speed users gathered from nontreatment sources, revealed somewhat similar results. The predominant MMPI pattern suggested psychosis, with some users showing signs of conduct disorder. Depression scores did not stand out for the group as a whole, although they were higher for moderate or heavy users and snorters than for casual users. It should be noted that suicide among speed users is an important risk during the withdrawal phase (Le Dain, 1973).

Kalant and Kalant (1976) found only twenty-six deaths among amphetamine users in Ontario, most of which were not clearly suicide. The population of users was estimated to be about 1,500 at that time; hence the rate of suicide among amphetamine users is very low, far lower than that for alcoholics. However, it would be of interest to have longitudinal or cohort studies of suicide conducted among all types of young drug abusers.

With regard to drug use other than opiates and speed, data about suicidal and self-destructive tendencies are very incomplete. There are apparently no long-term studies of any nonnarcotic drug-using populations which would allow an assignment of lifetime suicide risks. Such studies would be extremely useful since all that is available at present are point-prevalence studies or retrospective studies based on self-report of clinical populations.

There are two studies of suicide among persons given LSD in medical settings (Le Dain, 1973), but most would not have been adolescents. In general these studies indicated that few serious long-term problems occurred with LSD. A few suicides were reported in one study, but it is unclear whether the rate is higher than in other psychiatric populations not given LSD.

A highly controversial paper by Kolansky and Moore (1971) described psychological disturbances among young people who were "moderate to heavy cannabis" users. Among the disturbances seen were psychosis, anxiety, paranoia as well as depression, and suicide attempts. This paper has been criticized because the disturbances are, with little justification, attributed to cannabis use itself. It should be noted, however, that this study is typical of much research in the field in that it is based on clinical judgments of persons seeking treatment.

TREATMENT IMPLICATIONS _____

Because self-destructive behavior occurs so frequently among young drug abusers seeking treatment, its modification has often been an aim of psychotherapeutic efforts. A number of interesting therapeutic approaches have been described for adolescents, most of them with little empirical assessment such as pre- and postevaluations or comparisons with untreated control groups. It might be noted here that drug abuse is cited as the most frequent problem seen by college counselors (Varakas, 1974), but suicide is the least frequently seen problem.

An important question about some types of treatment is whether they actually increase suicide risks for drug abusers. Weissman et al. (1976) studied 106 young, lower-class males in a methadone maintenance program in New York City. Using standard rating scales, they found that about one-third of these patients were moderately to severely depressed. Depressive symptoms were associated with a decrease in social functioning, an increase in personal stress, and a past history of alcohol abuse. On the other hand, Dole (1972) reported successful methadone detoxification for 22,000 heroin addicts in jail. He reported that both violence and suicide were reduced and that the program was a starting point for other community-based treatments.

Several studies have been made of residential treatment for adolescent drug abusers. Gold and Coghlan (1975) examined changes in locus of control and self-esteem among fifty-three adolescent abusers (primarily heroin) who had six months of residential treatment. They found increased belief in internal control and higher self-esteem for both males and females. Females who left without authorization and engaged in self-destructive acts were considered to be more externally controlled and to have lower self-esteem. It should also be noted that no untreated control group was used and that only those who completed the program were studied, thus increasing the probability of finding positive results for the program.

A much less positive report was made of a therapeutic community by Brook and Whitehead (1973). They began a program for adolescent speed users who were primarily multidrug users. Almost all had had previous treatment, criminal records, frequent changes of residence, and had made at least one suicide attempt before admission. About 85 percent left before completing the twelve-month program; 50 percent left within the first two weeks. Follow-up studies indicated little difference between those who completed treatment and those who did not. The authors concluded that therapeutic communities were not a preferred treatment for drug abusers and that little evidence exists for their high reputation.

Several theoretical and clinical papers have described treatment for adolescents, essentially with little outcome data. For example, Bratter (1973) described his experiences in working with seventy-five alienated, unmotivated drug-abusing adolescents from affluent homes. These adolescents came from well-educated and cultivated families; they were, however, oriented toward pursuing wealth or social prominence. There was a lack of communication between parents and children. Bratter viewed drug abuse as a self-destructive activity in itself and used a confronting reality therapy, which involved establishing a therapeutic alliance, then forcing behavioral change in very direct ways (e.g., writing confronting letters, taking an advocacy role with great strictness) and promoting growth and development. This approach took two-and-a-half years on the average, with about two sessions per week. Of the seventy-five treated, forty-five were employed or in school; nineteen were seen as failures in that they were still addicted, or in therapeutic communities or methadone programs, or in jail. The outcomes for eleven adolescents were not known, since they moved away. Only one had died, and it was not stated whether this was a suicide or not.

Reese (1974) has also described a "forced treatment" program for adolescent drug abusers. Those admitted were fifty-four adolescents, aged sixteen and seventeen, who were multidrug users and who had low self-concepts, symptoms of depression and suicidal gestures, school and social problems, and frequent arrests. The goals of the thirty-day involuntary program were to "gain control over their self-destructive behavior" and to begin a process of self-help using family and other treatment resources. Treatment included daily "rap" sessions, group psychotherapy, family therapy, and behavioral controls. After a varied follow-up period, thirty-eight of the forty-eight adolescents were said to be "doing well"; however, most had been in long-term treatment programs, group homes, or mental hospitals. Only seventeen were at home and doing well. Suicides were not mentioned, although it was noted that one adolescent was shot by a policeman.

An unusual case history of a suicidal girl, treated with a variety of methods, has been reported by Schmideberg (1974). She was addicted to phenobarbital and had made six serious suicide attempts. A program of therapy was developed wherein she lived in an apartment with a nurse companion and saw Schmideberg daily. The patient has married and after twenty years is leading a happy life.

SUMMARY AND CONCLUSIONS _____

Given the research available to date, the following conclusions can be drawn:

1. Conceptual and methodological problems are considerable for both the terms "self-destructive behavior" and "drug abuse." These problems make the analysis and interpretation of research about self-destructive behavior in adolescent drug users very difficult.

2. The extent of self-destructive behavior found in any population depends upon the number of sources used; the larger the number of sources, the greater the frequency of cases found.

3. No study has examined the total range of possible self-destructive behaviors among adolescent drug abusers. The majority of studies has been concerned with suicide (attempted or successful) or with personality attributes supposedly associated with self-destructive behavior, such as low self-esteem, risk-taking, and depression.

4. Perhaps as many as 23 percent of suicide attempts seen at general hospitals occur among drug abusers.

5. Although barbiturates are the most commonly used drugs in suicide attempts, very few of these suicides involve adolescents.

6. In some studies about one-third of the ASA-codeine deaths and half of the heroin deaths involve young people (under twenty-five). Most of these are not clear suicides but are overdoses. Clinical studies of heavy users suggest, however, that a majority of so-called "overdoses" are intentional suicides. Real overdoses due to drug variability are apparently unusual.

7. Suicides attributable to drugs frequently used by adolescents, such as solvents, hallucinogens, and cannabis, are apparently rare.

8. The best case for a connection between intentional self-destruction and adolescent drug use can perhaps be made for speed. This drug was believed by users to lead to a slow death and at least some seem to enjoy the possibility. However, reported suicides from amphetamines among adolescents are rare.

9. Suicide rates among heroin addicts in general are known to be high, but these rates for adolescents are not known directly.

10. Studies of general populations indicate that most adolescent drug users use drugs infrequently and for reasons of curiosity and experimentation. It is unlikely that self-destructive tendencies would be prominent in their motivation for use.

11. Studies of heavy drug users (e.g., speed users) are somewhat inconsistent in showing that unusual depression is associated with drug use. However, studies of drug users of many types who are seeking treatment do indicate that depression and self-destructive tendencies are prominent. The possibility exists that these factors initiate treatment or are selective factors employed by treatment agencies.

12. Studies of many types of treatment for adolescent addicts emphasize the role of self-destructive factors and the need to re-

duce their importance. Evaluation studies of treatment are typically positive in their assessment of outcomes, but few have included untreated control groups. Further work on treatment for self-destructive adolescent drug users is certainly required.

REFERENCES _____

Barton, W. I. Drug-related mortality in the United States, 1963–1971. *Drug Forum*, 4:79–89, 1974.

Blumberg, H. Surveys of drug use among young people. *International Journal of the Addictions*, 10:699–720, 1975.

Braconnier, A., and Olievenstein, C. Suicidal drug addicts. *Perspectives Psychiatriques*, 3:183–189, 1974.

Bratter, T. E. Treating alienated, unmotivated, drug abusing adolescents. *American Journal of Psychotherapy*, 27:585–598, 1973.

Braucht, G. N., et al. Deviant drug use in adolescence: A review of psychological correlates. *Psychological Bulletin*, 79:92–106, 1973.

Bron, B. Drug abuse and suicidal tendencies. *Schweizer Archiv für Neurologie, Neurochirurgie und Psychiatrie*, 118:73–94, 1976.

Brook, R. C., and Whitehead, P. C. "414." A therapeutic community for the treatment of adolescent amphetamine abusers. *Corrective and Social Psychiatry*, 19:10–19, 1973.

Cox, C., and Smart, R. G. Social and psychological aspects of speed use: A study of types of speed users in Toronto. *International Journal of the Addictions*, 7:201–217, 1972.

Dole, V. P. Detoxification of sick addicts in prison. *Journal of the American Medical Association*, 220:366–369, 1972.

Dorpat, T., and Boswell, J. An evaluation of suicidal intent in suicide attempts. *Comprehensive Psychiatry*, 4:117–125, 1963.

Friedman, R. C., et al. The heroin overdose as a method of attempted suicide. *British Journal of Addiction*, 68:137–143, 1973.

Gendreau, P., and Gendreau, L. P. Research design and narcotic addiction proneness. *Canadian Psychiatric Association Journal*, 16:265–267, 1971.

Gold, S. R., and Coghlan, A. J. Locus of control and self-esteem among adolescent drug abusers: Effects of residential treatment. *Drug Forum*, 5:185–191, 1975.

Gourves, J., et al. Coma dû au cannabis sativa: Un cas. *La Presse medicale*, 79:1389–1390, 1971.

Hankoff, L. D., and Einsidler, B. Drug abuse among suicide attempters. *International Journal of Offender Therapy and Comparative Criminology*, 20:26–32, 1976.

Hendin, H. Students on heroin. *Journal of Nervous and Mental Disease*, 158:240–255, 1974.

Heyndrickx, A., Scheiris, C., and Schepene, P. Toxicological study of a fatal intoxication by man due to cannabis smoking. *Journal de pharmacie de Belgique*, 24:371–376, 1969.

Holland, J., et al. Drugs ingested in suicide attempts and fatal outcome. *New York State Journal of Medicine*, 75:2343–2349, 1975.

Kalant, O. J., and Kalant, H. Death in amphetamine users: Causes and estimates of mortality. In R. J. Gibbins, et al., eds., *Research Advances in Alcohol and Drug Problems*, vol. 3. New York: Wiley, 1976.

Kolansky, H., and Moore, W. T. Effects of marihuana on adolescents and young adults. *Journal of the American Medical Association*, 216:486–492, 1971.

Kuehn, J. L. Student drug user and his family. *Journal of College Student Personnel*, 11:404–413, 1970.

Le Dain, G. *Final Report of the Commission of Inquiry into the Non-Medical Use of Drugs*. Ottawa: Information Canada, 1973.

Lester, D., and Beck, A. T. Age differences in patterns of attempted suicide. *Journal of Death and Dying*, 5:317–322, 1974.

Lester, D., and Beck, A. T. Attempted suicide correlates of increasing medical lethality. *Psychological Reports*, 37:1236–1238, 1975.

McAree, C. P., Steffenhagen, R. A., and Zheutlin, L. S. Personality factors in college drug users. *International Journal of Social Psychiatry*, 15:102–106, 1969.

Menninger, K. *Man against Himself*. New York: Harcourt, Brace, 1938.

Mercer, W., and Smart, R. G. The epidemiology of psychoactive and hallucinogenic drug use. In R. J. Gibbins, et al., eds., *Research Advances in Alcohol and Drug Problems*, vol. 1. New York: Wiley, 1974.

Pokorny, A. D. A scheme for classifying suicidal behaviors. In A. T. Beck, et al., eds., *The Prediction of Suicide*. Bowie, Md.: Charles Press, 1974.

Reese, C. C. Forced treatment of the adolescent. *American Journal of Occupational Therapy*, 28:540–544, 1974.

Rouse, B. A., and Ewing, J. A. Marihuana and other drug use by women college students: Associated risk-taking and coping activities. *American Journal of Psychiatry*, 130:486–491, 1973.

Sadava, S. W. College student drug use: A social-psychological study. Doctoral dissertation, University of Colorado. University Microfilms, N070–23749, 1970.

Salzman, C., Lieff, J., Kochansky, G. E., and Shader, R. I. The psychology of hallucinogenic drug discontinuers. *American Journal of Psychiatry*, 129:755–761, 1972.

Schmideberg, M. Treatment of an acting-out suicidal girl addicted to phenobarbital. *International Journal of Offender Therapy and Comparative Criminology,* 18:196–197, 1974.

Shneidman, E. S. Orientation toward death: A vital aspect of the study of lives. *International Journal of Psychiatry,* 2:167–200, 1966.

Smart, R. G. Addiction, dependency, abuse or use: Which are we studying with epidemiology? In E. Josephson and E. Carroll, eds., *Drug Use: Epidemiological and Sociological Approaches.* Washington, D.C.: Hemisphere, 1974.

Smart, R. G., and Jones, D. Illicit LSD users: Their personality characteristics and psychopathology. *Journal of Abnormal Psychology,* 75:286–292, 1970.

Smart, R. G., and Whitehead, W. The uses of an epidemiology of drug use: The Canadian scene. *International Journal of the Addictions,* 9:373–388, 1974.

Stengel, E., and Cook, N. *Attempted Suicide.* New York: Basic Books, 1958.

Studer, F. Drugs and Szondi Test: A comparative study of drug addicts and alcoholics. *Annales Medico–Psychologiques,* 2:435–440, 1974.

Varakas, K. M. Ethical behavior of community college counselors. *Journal of College Student Personnel,* 15:101–104, 1974.

Vista Hill Psychiatric Foundation. Drug X: The most dangerous drug on earth. *Drug Abuse and Alcoholism Newsletter,* 2:1–4, 1974.

Weissman, M. M., et al. Clinical depression among narcotic addicts maintained on methadone in the community. *American Journal of Psychiatry,* 133:1434–1438, 1976.

White, H. C. Self-poisoning in adolescents. *British Journal of Psychiatry,* 124:24–35, 1974.

Whitehead, P. C., Johnston, F. G., and Ferrence, R. Measuring the incidence of self-injury: Some methodological and design considerations. *American Journal of Orthopsychiatry,* 43:142–148, 1973.

12

THE PARTICIPATORY ASPECTS OF INDIRECT SELF-DESTRUCTIVE BEHAVIOR
The Addict Family as a Model

M. DUNCAN STANTON AND SANDRA B. COLEMAN

In this chapter, indirect self-destructive behavior (ISDB) will be considered from a perspective which differs somewhat from the usual approaches. Rather than regarding ISDB as it pertains to the individual, we will address it within its interpersonal/familial systems context. The basic unit, then, will be the system of significant others, including their interactions. This is not to deny the validity of interpretations based on the individual, but only to propose that predictive and heuristic advances can also be achieved at the interpersonal level.

More specifically, we will try to explicate the process whereby ISDB can be adaptive, functional, noble, sacrificial, and understandable when viewed within its interpersonal context. The vehicle we will use is that of drug addiction, primarily heroin. However, we hope that the particular line of thinking to be followed can also be applied to other forms of ISDB.

FAMILY THEORY

Before proceeding directly to a discussion of ISDB within the drug-abuser's family, it seems appropriate to acquaint the reader with an overview of some aspects of family theory, especially as many of the theoretical formulations are discontinuous with conventional views of people and their problems. Familiarity with this material should be helpful in understanding the role of drugs in the family.

The concepts below have been developed by people working in

the family field over the last twenty to twenty-five years. Although a single, comprehensive, universally embraced theory of family functioning has not yet been developed, these core concepts have gained widespread acceptance (Steinglass, 1976).

THE FAMILY AS A SYSTEM

Rather than being simply a collection of persons, the family is a functional system. The members are interdependent, and actions by one (or more) of them affect the others. For example, illness or sudden success in one member influences the rest. Individuals within the family represent subsystems within the primary organizational unit, as do coalitions within it, such as parents versus children, or father and son versus mother and daughter. In most families the interactions between subsystems will be changing regularly, depending on particular circumstances. For instance, a disagreement about whether to watch a football game or a tennis match on television might crystallize a male versus female subsystem conflict within a family. Another topic could result in a realignment of other subsystems, such as those of father-daughter versus mother-son. Further, to be assessed accurately, the family system must be viewed as more than the sum of its parts, i.e., more than just the people within it, and as equaling both the members *and* their interactions. Thus a particular behavior by a member, such as a symptom, must be regarded in the light of how the other members of a family are contributing to it or making it possible, and also how the behavior is in turn affecting these other members.

FAMILY HOMEOSTASIS

The family has a sense of balance and stability. When disruptions occur in the balance, such as the death of a member, built-in mechanisms take hold in order to compensate and return to stability. In the case of a death, other members may assume the duties and roles of the deceased. For example, an oldest son, or the last son living in the home, may assume male head-of-household roles on death of the father. Another kind of imbalance could occur when a child starts school and the family has to readjust to a new situation in which this child will not be home all day with a parent (usually the mother). However, if the need for the original homeostatic condition is too great, pressure will bear on the child to stay at home, leading perhaps to a school phobia. Thus homeostasis can have either adaptive or maladaptive consequences.

An aspect of homeostasis is the feedback loop. This refers to regulatory, usually repetitive, patterns of behavior which families manifest. An example might be when parents and a child are driving in a car together. Spouse A is driving and spouse B is in a hurry to get to their destination (and conveys this before the trip). A accelerates through a yellow light, B grabs the dashboard handle and criticizes A, who retorts and steps on the gas. B protests more loudly, A shouts back, and the child, C, starts crying. At this point the argument stops while B attends to C and A slows down. Thus C's behavior becomes one element in a feedback process which serves to restore homeostasis. Chances are that such a pattern has occurred before and will recur in the future. All families show such patterns, albeit in positive ways, too, such as in a round of joking or showing affection.

THE "IDENTIFIED PATIENT" OR "SCAPEGOAT"

From a family viewpoint, difficulties or symptoms in one member are part of a total family process in which that member is labeled as the problem. In the above example, the child might be seen as the problem for "crying too much." The child then becomes the scapegoat, or the "identified patient" if taken to a facility for treatment. However, a more realistic assessment might portray the identified patient as the member expressing a disturbance existing in the entire family. He may be protecting or stabilizing the family. Nonetheless, this should not be misconstrued as a "poor, mistreated child" syndrome, because the child contributes to the process. In the above example, if the pattern had occurred many times before, the child might have erupted into crying as soon as the family entered the car, even though no feelings of animosity had existed between the parents at the outset of this particular trip.

BEHAVIORAL CONTEXT

It is important to know the conditions leading up to and surrounding a particular behavior. In the above example, the context of the child's crying included not only the three family members, but also the car, the pressure to get somewhere on time, and the lateness in getting started. In addition, it might be important to know where they were going and if undue pressure to be punctual came from that source. In any case, simply knowing that the child cries, without knowing the context, leaves us with an incomplete understanding of the event.

FAMILY BOUNDARIES

"Family boundaries" separate the family from outside influences and also divide family subsystems. They can be too rigid or too permeable. For instance, a parent-child subsystem which is too close and interdependent may have a permeable boundary within itself and a rigid boundary between it and other family subsystems. Further, a family with rigid external boundaries sees the outside world as threatening and may resist all influences from external systems such as the school or neighborhood.

INTERGENERATIONAL COALITIONS

When problems occur in a family member, such as a child, one should first look for struggles between family coalitions which cut across generational lines. An example is when one parent and a child are overtly or covertly pitted against the other parent and another child. Since the usual family coalitions in our society break down between generations—parents forming one coalition and children another—overstrong intergenerational coalitions are usually sources of difficulty. Sometimes they take the form of parents not talking directly to each other but instead communicating through a child. This puts the child in the awkward position of resolving split loyalties. He is used as a tool in the conflict. It also can give him undue power in the system, which he can exploit to get his way or become unruly. Most parents prevent this by uniting to form their own generational coalition, but if they cannot do this, he may play them off against each other. Different interpretations have been given as to why this occurs (e.g., perhaps one parent is not given permission by grandparents to maintain a satisfactory marital relationship), but whatever the explanation, the process is well recognized in families with one or more "problem" members.

FAMILY ROLE SELECTION

Family members are assigned particular roles within their families, often before they are born. The roles depend on such variables as birth order, sex, energy level, and what is happening in the family at birth. A child born during a period of parental bereavement will have different experiences from those of a child born at a time of joy or financial success. In extreme cases a child may be "assigned" to one parent as belonging to him or her, while the other parent may "adopt" a later child. Sometimes a parent or parents "buy" freedom from their own parents by giving away a child to this older couple to raise. The role of "black sheep" is often assigned to one member in each generation of a family, as is the role of the "responsible" or "parentified" child. Reilly (1976) notes that naming is important, as children are sometimes raised in the role of the person, usually a relative, after whom they are named; he also has observed that drug addicts are sometimes named after relatives who had an addiction problem. To believe, then, that the environment for all children in a family is the same is to make a grave miscalculation. Family members are *not* treated identically, although less dysfunctional or disturbed families will allow offspring more role flexibility. This point is important in the drug and alcohol area because it speaks to the question of why all siblings don't take drugs with equal frequency, especially if all of them have equal opportunity to observe the drug-taking patterns of their parents. "Modeling" parents' behavior is only a partial explanation for drug-taking behavior.

FAMILY LIFE CYCLE

Most families encounter similar stages as they progress through life, such as birth of first child, child first attending school, children leaving home, death of a parent or spouse, etc. These are crisis points, which, although sometimes tough to get through, are usually weathered without inordinate difficulty. On the other hand, symptomatic families develop problems because they are not able to adjust to the transition. They become "stuck" at a particular point. Like a broken record, they repetitively go through the process without advancing beyond it. An example is the family of the youthful schizophrenic who will not let him leave but keeps him in a role of incompetence—even when he palpably demonstrates his capabilities (Haley, 1973).

THE NOBLE SYMPTOM-BEARER

As can be inferred from the above, the symptomatic member in a family can in many ways be viewed as a sacrificial person. He gives up his reputation and well-being in the service of the family (Boszormenyi-Nagy and Spark, 1973). He may protect them from the intrusion of outside "helpers" by drawing attention to himself and his problem. Trying to cope with his troubles may be a rallying point which brings the family together; in some families he is almost the only person who can unite the system, and if his problem disappears the family becomes fragmented. Of course he also perpetuates the problem sometimes, even in the face of growth or improvement in other members; he may try to get them to "hark back" to the old homeostatic condition. This view of the symptomatic member is a radically new one to most people and is sometimes hard to believe. Perhaps one has to observe it occurring to be convinced. One may have to see, for example, how a son can temper his success and not realize his potential so as not to make his uneducated father appear to be the least competent family member. Perhaps one has to observe an "identified patient" child burst out with symptoms at the point where his parents begin to move toward divorce, thus reuniting them around helping him and postponing the separation. Whatever the case, this is a process which does occur in many families, and acknowledging it can help in the understanding of why symptoms occur as they do.

ADDICTION AND THE FAMILY _____

The indirect self-destructive aspects of drug addiction have been elaborated on elsewhere in this volume. The dangers of overdose and contact with unlawful elements in society, the significance of the "failure to succeed," etc., have been adequately described and will not be repeated here. Our goal is to focus on some of the essential facets of the addictive process itself and the interpersonal context within which it occurs. For the most part our discussion will deal with narcotics addiction, especially heroin, although many of the points probably pertain to other forms of compulsive drug use as well.

The structural and dynamic elements which typify the majority of addict families have been discussed in several literature reviews (Harbin and Maziar, 1975; Klagsbrun and Davis, 1977; Seldin, 1972; Stanton, 1979). In an attempt to identify predominant patterns shown by these families, Stanton (1979) has determined that the following conclusions typically apply: (1) one parent, usually of the opposite sex, is engaged in an overinvolved, indulgent, overpermissive relationship with the drug abuser; (2) the other, same-sex parent competes with the abuser and is negative, inconsistent, uninvolved, or absent; (3) in a disproportionate number of families one parent—usually the father—is absent from the home due to death or separation before the abuser's sixteenth birthday; (4) the incidence of parental drug abuse or alcoholism, especially among fathers, is much greater than the norm.

Other trends have also emerged from the literature. Concerning the addict's marriage and the family of procreation, the relationship appears to be a direct reenactment of the relationship between the addict and opposite-sex parent. It is a repetition of the family of origin, with similar roles and interaction patterns. Perhaps more salient, however, is the fact that male addicts are less likely to marry than nonaddict males, and among those addicts who do marry, the rate of multiple marriages is above average for both sexes. There is also increasing evidence that the majority of addicts are very closely tied into their families of origin. They either reside with parent(s) or live close by and maintain regular contact. All of this seems to tie into a failure by the family of origin to release the addict to become an individuated, autonomous person. Even when he or she attempts flight into marriage from the family, there is subtle or overt encouragement for the marriage to fail and for the addict to return home to the family.

SEPARATION ISSUES

A commonly described dilemma for the addict family is that of separation. An early study focusing on the developmental role of symbiosis or separation-individuation among addicts was conducted by Attardo (1965). A scaled comparison of mothers of drug addicts, schizophrenics, and normal adolescents revealed that the symbiotic needs of addicts' mothers were higher than those of either of the other two groups. This became more pronounced during the time when the addicts were eleven to sixteen years of age. Similarly, one of the authors (S.B.C.) is currently studying an assortment of variables among thirty heroin addicts. Data are derived from therapists' questionnaires and weekly therapy progress notes taken from five months of treatment. Preliminary findings from both sources show a marked difference in the periods of childhood and adolescence described as the "worst" and "best" period of life. Of the four developmental age periods, the years from birth to five and from six to twelve were consistently considered "best," and the "worst" periods those from sixteen to nineteen and from twenty on.

The point at which separation conflicts most often surface appears to be adolescence, when the major task is to separate from one's family. The onset of heavy drug use is most likely to be tied to the time when the young person is developing close outside relationships with peers and the possibility of leaving the family becomes imminent. These families show so much fear of separation that they cannot allow autonomy readily, especially to the offspring who becomes addicted. If the addict takes steps to become independent and competent, the parents develop symptoms, a crisis occurs in the family, or the parents themselves start to separate (Stanton et al, 1979). Thus, it is difficult for a drug-using youngster to negotiate his way out of the family. Because the adolescent is needed by the family, he cannot traverse this stage readily and gets "stuck" in a chronic, repetitive pattern of leaving and returning, succeeding and failing, which revolves around his individuation and growing up. Drugs become the vehicle through which the process is manifested, for when he is on drugs he is incompetent and when off he is more dependent. Viewed in this way, the cyclic process of addiction makes sense as a homeostatic phenomenon. Among other things, addiction helps to keep the family together.

Related to difficulties in leaving home are those surrounding marriage by the addict. As mentioned above, marital relationships are often tentative and close ties to the family of origin are generally maintained. Again, this seems to tie into a failure by the parental system to release the addict to become an individuated, autonomous person who can cultivate close outside relationships.

In addition to separation anxiety related to these described individuation conflicts, Stanton et al. (1978) note that other events, such as changes in parental employment, can exacerbate separation fears within the family. Again, the lack of the father's presence in the home is a significant consideration. Finally, the frequency of drug and alcohol use among the parents can be interpreted as one mechanism which these families use for dealing with separation.

DEATH ISSUES

There is evidence that issues surrounding death are an important facet of the means by which the addictive process is both generated and maintained. Whether symbolic or real, death appears to be an integral part of functioning for these families.

DEATH AMONG ADDICTS. A number of authors have documented the high death rates and low life expectancies among drug addicts (Ferguson et al., 1974; Frederick et al., 1973; O'Donnell, 1964, 1969; Vaillant, 1966a). Among abstinent addicts, Frederick et al. (1973) also found that most of them expect to die through violent means. This has been corroborated from the other side by Haberman and Baden (1978), whose data show that 58 percent of all sudden deaths in New York City occurred among people with a drug or alcohol problem. Further, Whipple (1973) found that drug users tended to view death-related words as more active, positive, and potent than did nonusers. Gertler et al. (1973) determined that addicts were more likely to express a wish for death than either psychiatric patients or hospital staff, and suggested that the addicts' life-style reflects an unusual degree of involvement with death, accounting for increased anxiety associated with death issues. On this point Alan Glass (personal communication, 1976) quotes a group of heroin addicts with whom he worked as saying, in a searching and emotional session, that "we are trying to come as close to death as we can without actually going through with it."

SUICIDE. It seems fair to conclude, as Frederick (1972), Stanton (1977), and others have done, that the high addict death rate is more than a result of living in dangerous environments and is to a great extent—if not primarily—a suicidal phenomenon. This idea dates at least from 1938, when Menninger likened addiction to "chronic suicide," and it gained support from a study by Pescor and Surgeon (1940) of suicidal behavior among addicts. Others have also suggested that drugs are an alternative to or an equivalent of suicide

(Cantor, 1968; Litman et al., 1972) or that the addict is trying to tell his family and society how close they have brought him to it (Winick, 1963).

THE ADDICT FAMILY AND SUICIDE. Related to the above, not only does drug-taking in a family member serve a family homeostatic function and assist in quelling separation fears, it also has a direct self-destructive component. Stanton (1977) has made a case for the family basis of the addict's suicidal behavior. This is not just "depression" or despondence over a "worthless" life but is an active family process wherein the addict acts out a death wish which is also entertained for him by all or most of the other members. It is often quite explicit, with members stating openly that they would rather see the addict dead than lost to friends, spouse, or outsiders. He becomes a savior or martyr who is sacrificed in noble manner through responding to the family's suicidal conspiracy. In some ways it resembles the "psychic homicide" described by Meerloo (1959, 1962), in which a suicidal person acts out the command of someone with whom he identifies; however, Meerloo's concept is essentially dyadic, and does not encompass the concept of a total family system.

Corroboration of this process also comes from other contexts. Rosenbaum and Richman (1972), in a study of forty cases in which suicide was attempted by drug overdose, noted that (1) the family often "expected" the suicide, (2) the suicide was frequently an imitation of an earlier, similar act by a parent or older sibling, and (3) other family members participated directly in the suicidal act. Murphy et al. (1969) found that survivors of suicide by a loved one constitute a high-risk group for committing suicide themselves. Cain and Fast (1972), in a study of children who were survivors of a parental suicide, found that many identified strongly with the deceased parents' impulses, and subsequently maintained a deep conviction that they would die in the same way. Finally, Rudestam (1977), using the "psychological autopsy" method to study responses to suicide in the family, determined that the remaining, postsuicide family relationships may actually have been strengthened. All of this points to the importance of viewing the suicidal facet of addiction as a sacrificial, reciprocal phenomenon rooted in the family.

DEATH AND THE ADDICT FAMILY. One of the more striking patterns that has been identified in addict families is the high incidence of early loss of one or both parents by the drug-abusing member; often this is due to death (Ellinwood et al., 1966; Harbin and Maziar, 1975; Klagsbrun and Davis, 1977; Oltman and Friedman, 1967; Rosenberg, 1971; Vaillant, 1966b). An association between initial drug use and death of a parent or another significant person, such as a peer, has been noted by Miller (1974). In a study of the histories of twenty-five addict families, Coleman (1975) found that 72 percent had experienced at least one traumatic, untimely, or unexpected death. Further, Blum et al. (1972) determined that in high drug "risk" families a greater frequency of deaths had occurred among grandfathers of addicts when the fathers were young.

It is our experience that death issues are part of the "hidden agenda" of these families. Often they will introduce death or bereavement into treatment, whether or not these were on the mind of the therapist (Coleman and Stanton, 1978; Stanton, 1977). Such issues were found to be a dominant, repetitive topic of discussion by Coleman (1978a, 1978b), in a content analysis of two years of progress notes from group therapy with siblings of addicts. Finally, Reilly (1976) has noted that death and mourning problems have invariably had to be dealt with in his work with families of addicts. The connection between this tendency and the high rates of family death and loss seems apparent.

A MODEL OF ISDB AND ADDICTION _____

In this section we will try to pull together the earlier discussion and present a two-part model. The first concerns the etiological aspects of this behavior and has been presented more fully in an earlier paper (Coleman and Stanton, 1978). The second deals with the homeostatic, nonlinear features of the process and its related structural components.

ETIOLOGICAL ASPECTS

What seems to be significant is that the addict family's inability to allow individuation of the drug-using member (with its attendant fear of separation) derives from unresolved and premature deaths experienced by one or both parents. The parents are still undergoing a sort of mourning process, are perhaps still feeling "adrift," and have become "stuck" at a particular stage in the family developmental process (Noone and Reddig, 1976). They have not worked through or outgrown the loss. Partly as a result of this, the addict is selected as a "revenant" of the decedents (usually a grandparent or grandparents) so that the need to keep him close is paramount (Reilly, 1976). In fact, his parents may not even be able to discipline him for fear that he will reject them and leave. Consequently, his entry into adolescence and the threat of eventual loss that this implies bring about a reawakening of the original loss experience. It is not surprising, then, that panic ensues.

If possible loss of the drug-abusing member becomes such a prob-lcm, why, as implied earlier, does the family conspire to bring about his possible demise? At first glance these two ideas seem contradictory. However, there seems to be an important distinction in these families between loss of the addict to outsiders versus loss through death; the second alternative appears to be the more acceptable of the two. It is almost the only allowable separation (Stanton et al., 1979). We believe that a major reason for this is that the family, particularly the parents, uses the addict for reenactment of previously experienced deaths of significant others. Through this process he *becomes* the deceased member. In this way they can once again participate vicariously in the event in hopes of mastering it. They have not learned other, more appropriate vehicles for mourning. Coleman (1975) examined family roles, communications, and interactions as they pertained to symbolic representations of death; she distinguished three death-related phases within the addiction process, i.e., the imminence of death, the funeral, and the resurrection. Thus, the addiction becomes analogous to a slow dying process. It is also an extreme example of the way in which all families vest a dying member with special status and view him as a symbolic representation of deceased ancestors (Kastenbaum and Aisenberg, 1972). It is no wonder his demise is viewed as sacrificial and noble.

Addiction, then, can be seen as part of a *death-related continuum.* Different self-destructive behaviors rest at various points along it according to their severity. From this viewpoint, the distinction between ISDB and more direct actions may be more apparent than real. These two facets may differ more in a quantitative than a qualitative sense. In fact, such a dichotomy may even be misleading if taken too literally. Addiction is a way of traveling along the continuum without necessarily reaching the end point, i.e., of responding to the wishes of significant others without total surrender. It can serve as a means for at least partially fulfilling the family "death wish" while avoiding complete demise.

A HOMEOSTATIC MODEL

The previous discussion addresses some of the possible reasons for the development of addiction in a family member. It is based on a linear model in which a causal chain of events occurs, e.g., premature loss by parent of grandparent leads to the fear of separation by parent(s), thence to dependence on offspring, then to fear of loss of offspring, consequent disallowance of autonomy, emergent drug use by offspring, etc. It does not take into account the complex set of feedback mechanisms involved in the drug-taking process and the repetitive cycles that evolve. It tends to "blame" parents or even the whole family rather than recognizing that all are involved in a sequence of behaviors. If behavior X by one family member is followed by behavior Y of another, which is then succeeded by Z performed by a third and subsequently followed by a return to X—a cyclic pattern—who is to say that the person who did X is more to blame or is more responsible than the one who performed Z? Early in the chapter we gave the example of a family driving together in a car in which the behavioral sequence involved contributions by all three members. In the addict family a sequence has been identified in which the parents of the addict start to argue and begin to talk about separation; the addict gets "dirty" (uses drugs) or acts out in some other self-destructive way; the parents shift attention to him and stop discussing separation; if he later gets "clean" (drug free) or makes some other individuating move, they will start to fight again (Stanton et al., 1979). To paraphrase Haley (1973, 1976) and Hoffman (1976), the sequence, not just the drug-taking, serves some kind of change-resistant, or homeostatic, function. Moreover, this kind of sequence does not represent causality in the usual sense but is a cycle. Each person's behavior is influenced by the behavior of the other person, and influences their behaviors in turn. This is the sort of nonlinear model which has been described by Minuchin et al. (1975) and others. It is a way of conceptualizing what is happening within the interpersonal system *at the present time.*

INTERVENTION

We have used the above model with some success in dictating modes of intervention in the family addictive process (Stanton, 1978; Stanton et al., 1978). This involves identification of the sequence and therapeutically intruding at crucial points to alter and redirect it (Stanton and Todd, 1978). It is our experience that if the family pattern evolves to the point where the addict actually dies, the sequence is only momentarily halted, and a new triad is eventually formed with another child or grandchild. As mentioned earlier, this is the way the family repetitively preserves its mourning process.

We have recently described some of the clinical techniques developed to deal with the unresolved issues of death (Coleman and Stanton, 1978). Our paper includes a transcript from an intense therapy session in which the mother of two teenage addicts "revisited" the scene of her mother's deathbed, an episode which had taken place some twenty-five years before. In treatment, the sequence of repeatedly reenacting the death scene was changed, along with the context in which it was performed, i.e., the husband and therapist were present. Thus, the pattern of ineffective mourning was altered and new elements were introduced into the cycle.

This is an example of how restructuring and the entry of new transactional sequences can have a beneficial effect.

IMPLICATIONS FOR OTHER FORMS OF ISDB

Although our discussion thus far has focused on the interpersonal/familial aspects of one form of ISDB—drug addiction—the conceptualizations presented are hardly limited to this subgroup. Many other types of ISDB may also have participatory features and involve significant others. Such phenomena as role selection, intergenerational coalitions, acts of martyrdom, and repetitive, homeostatic patterns, in addition, may apply to them. In some, the parallels to drug addiction are clear. For instance, alcoholism is almost directly comparable (Davis et al., 1974; Steinglass, 1976). Further, Alexander and Parsons (1973) have shown how delinquency can be seen as a family process which can be altered effectively through changing the family system pattern. Considering schizophrenia—a disorder with many ISDB aspects—Searles (1961) identified fear of death as one of its major adaptive or defensive functions. Ten years later Welldon (1971) dramatically described the identified schizophrenic patient as symbolizing a deceased family member. Paul and Grosser (1965) also reported that families with an emotionally disturbed member have difficulty in dealing with previous losses, resulting in resistant symbiotic family relationships.

One area in which the interpersonal/familial systems approach might be fruitful is in the study of physical disease and its psychosomatic components, especially in the light of the work of Lewis et al. (1976) on psychological health in family systems. When they looked for longitudinal differences in physical illness, these researchers found a correlation between the family's ability to discuss death in a personal way (as it applied to either the nuclear or extended family) and the number of "well" versus "sick" days among their members. In their study, the types of illness were largely psychosomatic and included references to ulcerative colitis, duodenal ulcer, asthma, etc. Further, a particularly important family systems approach to physical disease is Grolnick's (1972) literature review, which suggests that many psychosomatic illnesses are associated with some of the rigid structural components described in our discussion of the patterns found in addict families. Thus it is appropriate to ask, for example, whether exacerbations of cardiac conditions are predictable from knowing a family behavioral cycle. Or, like many psychosomatic disorders such as anorexia (Minuchin et al., 1975), is hyperobesity predicted on a nonlinear, cyclic process?

Other forms of ISDB merit exploration from an interpersonal

systems and family homeostatic viewpoint. For instance, does the dying process that hemodialysis patients face compare with the deathlike pattern that addict families engage in? As with the aforementioned example of a family driving together, are traffic accidents partly contingent on family feedback loops? In what way is gambling behavior a dependent variable within a repetitive interpersonal cycle? These are all legitimate questions for future investigation.

One final note. We believe the kinds of models which have been used in describing and predicting ISDB have, for the most part, been too limited. Often they rest on "personality," "type," or "trait" concepts which are static and do not take into account (1) cross-generational variables, (2) the impact of interpersonal systems, and (3) the vacillations and patterns that emerge when ongoing behavior is examined. We hope that the field can move toward theoretical models which are more dynamic, time based, and responsive to interactional patterns and sequences.

REFERENCES _____

Alexander, J., and Parsons, B. Short-term behavioral intervention with delinquent families: Impact on family process and recidivism. *Journal of Abnormal Psychology*, 81:219–255, 1973.

Attardo, N. Psychodynamic factors in the mother-child relationship in adolescent drug addiction: A comparison of mothers of schizophrenics and mothers of normal adolescent sons. *Psychotherapy and Psychosomatics*, 13:249–255, 1965.

Blum, R., et al. *Horatio Alger's Children.* San Francisco: Jossey-Bass, 1972.

Boszormenyi-Nagy, I., and Spark, G. M. *Invisible Loyalties.* New York: Harper and Row, 1973.

Cain, A. C., and Fast, I. Children's reaction to parental suicide: Distortions of guilt, communication and identification. In A. C. Cain, ed., *Survivors of Suicide.* Springfield, Ill.: Thomas, 1972.

Cantor, J. Alcoholism as a suicidal equivalent. In *Proceedings of Fourth International Conference for Suicide Prevention.* Los Angeles: Delman, 1968.

Coleman, S. B. *Death—the Facilitator of Family Integration.* Paper presented to the American Psychological Association, Chicago, September, 1975.

Coleman, S. B. Sib group therapy: A prevention program for siblings from drug addict programs. *International Journal of the Addictions,* 13:115–127, 1978a.

Coleman, S. B. Siblings in session. In E. Kaufman and P. Kaufmann, eds., *From Enmeshed Enemy to Ally: The Family Treatment of Drug and Alcohol Abusers.* New York: Gardner, 1978b.

Coleman, S. B., and Stanton, M. D. The role of death in the addict family. *Journal of Marriage and Family Counseling,* 4:79–91, 1978.

Davis, D. I., Berenson, D., Steinglass, P., and Davis, S. The adaptive consequences of drinking. *Psychiatry,* 37:209–215, 1974.

Ellinwood, E. H., Smith, W. G., and Vaillant, G. E. Narcotic addiction in males and females: A comparison. *International Journal of the Addictions,* 1:33–45, 1966.

Ferguson, P., Lennox, T., and Lettieri, D. J. *Drugs and Death: The Nonmedical Use of Drugs Related to All Modes of Death.* Rockville, Md.: National Institute on Drug Abuse, 1974. (DHEW Pub. No. ADM 75188)

Frederick, C. J. Drug abuse as self-destructive behavior. *Drug Therapy,* 2:49–68, 1972.

Frederick, C. J., Resnik, H. L. P., and Wittlin, B. J. Self-destructive aspects of hard core addiction. *Archives of General Psychiatry,* 28:579–585, 1973.

Gertler, R., Ferneau, E., and Raynes, A. Attitudes toward death and dying on a drug addiction unit. *International Journal of the Addictions,* 8:265–272, 1973.

Grolnick, L. A family perspective of psychosomatic factors in illness: A review of the literature. *Family Process,* 11:457–486, 1972.

Haberman, P. W., and Baden, M. M. *Alcohol, Other Drugs and Violent Death.* New York: Oxford University Press, 1978.

Haley, J. *Uncommon Therapy.* New York: Norton, 1973.

Haley, J. *Problem-Solving Therapy.* San Francisco: Jossey-Bass, 1976.

Harbin, H. T., and Maziar, H. M. The families of drug abusers: A literature review. *Family Process,* 14:411–431, 1975.

Hoffman, L. Breaking the homeostatic cycle. In P. Guerin, ed., *Family Therapy: Theory and Practice.* New York: Gardner, 1976.

Kastenbaum, R., and Aisenberg, P. *The Psychology of Death.* New York: Springer, 1972.

Klagsbrun, M., and Davis, D. I. Substance abuse and family interaction. *Family Process,* 16:149–173, 1977.

Lewis, J. M., Beavers, W. K., Gossett, J. L., and Phillips, V. A. *No Single Thread: Psychological Health in Family Systems.* New York: Brunner/Mazel, 1976.

Litman, R. E., Shaffer, M., and Peck, M. L. Suicidal behavior and methadone treatment. In *Proceedings of the 4th National Conference on Methadone Treatment.* New York: National Association for the Prevention of Addiction to Narcotics (NAPAN), 1972.

Meerloo, J. A. M. Suicide, menticide and psychic homicide. *Archives of Neurology and Psychiatry,* 81:360–362, 1959.

Meerloo, J. A. M. *Suicide and Mass Suicide.* New York: Grune and Stratton, 1962.

Menninger, K. *Man against Himself.* New York: Harcourt, Brace, 1938.

Miller, D. *Adolescence: Psychology, Psychopathology, and Psychotherapy.* New York: Aronson, 1974.

Minuchin, S., Baker, L., Rosman, B. L., Liebman, R., Milman, L., and Todd, T. C. A conceptual model of psychosomatic illness in children. *Archives of General Psychiatry,* 32:1031–1038, 1975.

Murphy, G. E., Wetzel, R. D., Swallow, C. S., and McClure, J. N. Who calls the suicide prevention center? *American Journal of Psychiatry,* 126:314–324, 1969.

Noone, R. J., and Reddig, R. L. Case studies in family treatment of drug abuse. *Family Process,* 15:325–332, 1976.

O'Donnell, J. A. A follow-up of narcotic addicts. *American Journal of Orthopsychiatry,* 34:948–954, 1964.

O'Donnell, J. A. *Narcotic Addicts in Kentucky.* Washington, D.C.: U.S. Government Printing Office, 1969.

Oltman, J.E., and Friedman, S. Parental deprivation in psychiatric conditions, III. In personality disorders and other conditions. *Diseases of the Nervous System,* 28:298–303, 1967.

Paul, N. L., and Grosser, G. H. Operational mourning and its role in conjoint marital therapy. *Community Mental Health Journal,* 1:339–345, 1965.

Pescor, M. J., and Surgeon P. A. Suicide among hospitalized drug addicts. *Journal of Nervous and Mental Disease,* 91:287–305, 1940.

Reilly, D. M. Family factors in the etiology and treatment of youthful drug abuse. *Family Therapy,* 2:149–171, 1976.

Rosenbaum, M., and Richman, J. Family dynamics and drug overdoses. *Life-Threatening Behavior,* 2:19–25, 1972.

Rosenberg, C. M. The young addict and his family. *British Journal of Psychiatry,* 118:469–470, 1971.

Rudestam, K. E. Physical and psychological responses to suicide in the family. *Journal of Consulting and Clinical Psychology,* 45:162–170, 1977.

Searles, H. F. Schizophrenia and the inevitability of death. *Psychiatric Quarterly,* 35:631–664, 1961.

Seldin, Nathan E. The family of the addict: A review of the literature. *International Journal of the Addictions,* 7:97–107, 1972.

Stanton, M. D. The addict as savior: Heroin, death, and the family. *Family Process,* 16:191–197, 1977.

Stanton, M. D. Some outcome results and aspects of structural family therapy with drug addicts. In D. Smith, et al., eds., *A Multicultural View of Drug Abuse: The Selected Proceedings of the National Drug Abuse Conference, 1977.* Cambridge, Mass.: Schenkman, 1978, pp. 378–388.

Stanton, M. D. Drugs and the family. *Marriage and Family Review,* 2:1–10, 1979.

Stanton, M. D., and Todd, T. C. Structural family therapy with heroin addicts. In E. Kaufman and P. Kaufmann, eds., *From Enmeshed Enemy to Ally: The Family Therapy of Drug and Alcohol Abusers.* New York: Gardner, 1978.

Stanton, M. D., Todd, T. C., and associates. *The Family Therapy of Drug Addiction.* New York: Gardner, 1978.

Stanton, M. D., Todd, T. C., Heard, D. B., Kischner, S., Kleiman, J. I., Mowatt, D. T., Riley, P., Scott, S. M., and Van Deusen, J. M. Heroin addiction as a phenomenon: A new conceptual model. Manuscript, 1979.

Steinglass, P. Family therapy in alcoholism. In B. Kissin and H. Begleiter, *The Biology of Alcoholism,* vol. V. New York: Plenum, 1976.

Vaillant, G. E. A 12-year follow-up of New York narcotic addicts, II. The natural history of a chronic disease. *New England Medical Journal,* 275:1282–1288, 1966a.

Vaillant, G. E. A 12-year follow-up of New York narcotic addicts, III. Some social and psychiatric characteristics. *Archives of General Psychiatry,* 15:599–609, 1966b.

Welldon, R. M. C. The "shadow of death" and its implications in four families, each with a hospitalized schizophrenic member. *Family Process,* 10:281–302, 1971.

Whipple, C. I. Meaning of Death in Drug Users. Paper presented to the Midwestern Psychological Association, Chicago, May 10–12, 1973.

Winick, C. Some psychological factors in addiction. In D. Wakefield, ed., *The Addict.* Greenwich, Conn.: Fawcett, 1963.

PART FOUR

ALCOHOL ABUSE, HYPEROBESITY, AND CIGARETTE SMOKING

13

ALCOHOLISM AS INDIRECT SELF-DESTRUCTIVE BEHAVIOR

JOHN C. CONNELLY

The self-destructive consequences of alcoholism are all too evident. The alcoholic person frequently has serious health problems such as cirrhosis, pancreatitis, and central nervous system dysfunction. He or she is more likely than others to be involved in fatal accidents such as car wrecks, fires in the home, and drownings, according to a U.S. Department of Health, Education, and Welfare report (1974). In addition, the alcoholic is a high risk for suicide (Palola et al., 1962; Rushing, 1968). Overall life expectancy of the alcoholic person is approximately twelve years less than the general life expectancy (American Medical Association, 1977). Even beyond the realm of physical destructiveness, alcoholism leads to deleterious consequences for the person in terms of broken interpersonal relationships and impaired vocational performance.

Should the self-destructiveness of alcoholism be considered as direct or indirect? This may seem like an academic question, but it highlights a number of important considerations. Direct self-destructive behavior, such as suicide or self-mutilation, is usually associated with signs and symptoms of depression (e.g., sleep disorder, fatigability, decreased libido, inability to concentrate or see alternatives, feelings of worthlessness, hopelessness, and helplessness). Direct self-destructive behavior is often in reaction to immediate stress; it is an attempt to alleviate intolerable pain. It can be thought of as a gamble for many between life and death, the decision being left up to chance. Even if the goal of the self-destructive act is not death, some degree of suicidal intent is generally acknowledged.

In indirect self-destructive behavior (ISDB), on the other hand, self-destructive intent is not nearly as evident and, in fact, is frequently denied. ISDB is not readily associated with signs and symptoms of depression, and often the mood of the person seems light and controlled. It is not apparently associated with an immediate precipitating stress. A strong need for gratification is generally present without conscious consideration for others or for longer-term consequences.

According to these criteria, alcoholism, with its characteristic pattern of denial, low frustration tolerance, need for immediate gratification, and self-centeredness, qualifies as an indirect self-destructive condition; nevertheless, alcoholism can also greatly overlap with direct self-destructive behavior (DSDB) as seen in the frequent association of the condition with depression, with feelings of hopelessness, and with high risk-taking behavior.

In this chapter, the relationship between alcoholism and self-destructive behavior, both direct and indirect, will be explored. Background material on alcoholism will be presented, followed by a discussion of pertinent literature regarding alcoholism and self-destructive behavior. Case examples will be used to illustrate certain types of self-destructive behavior including their dynamics. The chapter will conclude with a brief discussion of treatment implications.

THE NATURE OF ALCOHOLISM _____

Alcoholism in the United States has long been recognized as a major health problem. The National Institute of Alcohol Abuse and Alcoholism estimates that of the 70 percent of the adult population that drink, approximately 10 percent have serious problems with alcohol. The ravages of this illness are seen not only in the broken lives and disrupted families of the alcoholic, but also in the staggering annual cost to the nation. Estimates are that alcoholism costs the nation more than twenty-five billion dollars a year—arising mainly from absenteeism, lost production, motor vehicle accidents, and medical expenses (U.S. Department of Health, Education, and Welfare, 1974).

Alcoholism can be defined in many ways, depending on the perspective of the writer. In the American Medical Association's recently released manual on alcoholism, the following general definition is offered: "Alcoholism is an illness characterized by significant impairment that is directly associated with persistent and excessive use of alcohol. Impairment may involve physiological, psychological or social dysfunction" (American Medical Association, 1977). A key concept in this definition is that drinking continues despite the development of problems directly related to the drinking. Preoccupation with alcohol and loss of control over its consumption are characteristic of the illness.

There is no known single cause of alcoholism: psychological, sociological, physiological, and possible genetic factors all play a role. Alcoholics cannot be recognized by personality type; psychotic patients may become alcoholic as may neurotic and borderline patients, and even people with seemingly well-integrated personalities. It is true, however, that because of alcohol's ability to reduce tension and pain, to provide oral gratification, to temporarily "dissolve" a harsh conscience, and to give a greater sense of relatedness, persons who are impulsive and alienated from others, with low frustration tolerance and a punitive superego, are particularly vulnerable to this illness.

There is no biochemical test to diagnose alcoholism, although considerable work is going on in this area. Some researchers do postulate a constitutional predisposition to alcoholism in certain people. Goodwin (1971), for example, in his studies on adoptees raised apart from their biological parents, finds that the incidence of alcoholism in subjects with one biological alcoholic parent is significantly greater than for those with no alcoholic biological parent.

People with alcohol problems can be classified according to the severity of addiction or the type of addictive process. Knight (1937), for example, described alcoholics as essential and reactive, a distinction which is still useful today. The essential alcoholic is that person who has never really been able to drink in a controlled manner. From the first drink he has tended to have problems with the use of alcohol, and these problems have become manifest at an early age. The essential alcoholic's personality structure is characterized by a borderline personality organization (Hartocollis, unpublished manuscript). The reactive alcoholic, on the other hand, is a person whose alcoholism develops later in life, after years of more or less controlled drinking. People with this pattern frequently have achieved more than the essential alcoholic in terms of life goals and have more highly integrated personality structures. The slide into alcoholism often begins as a reaction to a change in life circumstance, such as loss of a loved one, change in job, or change in state of health. The reactive group is the larger one, and the transition from controlled drinking to alcoholism may be a rapid or a gradual process. Jellinek (1962) has documented in a lucid and detailed way the various stages in this process. Particularly in the early stages of the disease, the adaptive qualities of alcohol use can still be seen, as for example its capacity to bring about relaxation and induce a sense of well-being. Once the "crucial" stage (in Jellinek's terminology) is reached, with beginning loss of control, alcoholism tends to become self-perpetuating in an increasingly destructive spiral. In most cases, outside intervention is needed to break this self-perpetuating, destructive progression. Helpful intervention may be in the form of involvement in Alcoholics Anonymous (AA), participation in an inpatient or outpatient alcoholism treatment program, pastoral counseling, etc. Some alcoholics respond quickly, without experiencing a great deal of disruption in their lives; others only after repeated failures, at the expense of family, friends, and jobs; still others never recover, but continue to pursue relentlessly a very destructive course, which eventually leads to premature death.

ALCOHOLISM AND SUICIDE

An association between alcoholism and overt self-destructive behavior is well documented. In studies of suicide attempts and successful suicides, a high incidence of alcoholism has been repeatedly noted. Palola et al. (1962), studying all the attempted suicides during a four-month period at King County Hospital in Washington, found that 23 percent of attempted suicides and 31.4 percent of completed suicides involved alcoholics. Dahlgren (1945), in his large study on suicide and attempted suicide in Sweden, found that 30 percent of those who attempted or completed suicide were alcoholics.

In studies of alcoholic patients, the incidence of attempted or completed suicide is even more striking. Rushing (1968) found that 25 to 30 percent of the alcoholics he studied had attempted suicide. In a study of AA members, Palola et al. (1962) found a similar incidence of attempted suicide. Beck et al. (1976), on the basis of a review of the literature, state that between 7 and 21 percent of alcoholics eventually die by suicide. Norvig and Nielsen (1956), in a five-year follow-up study of 221 treated alcoholics in Denmark, found that 7 percent committed suicide. Kessel and Grossman (1961) report that 8 percent of their alcoholic population in Scotland eventually committed suicide, and they comment that this is 75 times higher than expected for the general population.

Frankel et al. (1976) discuss three major theoretical frameworks that might be used to explain the relationship between drinking and self-injury. Their first postulate is that alcoholism facilitates suicidal behavior; the second, that alcoholism is a form of chronic suicidal behavior; and the third, that alcoholism and suicide are effects of the same underlying cause.

Briefly stated, the common-cause theory holds that the association of alcoholism and suicide is based on the presence of common underlying factors such as social disintegration, similar personality types, and depression. Although there is not much hard evidence supporting this theory, in a general sense it has plausibility since suicidal behavior and alcoholism can be conceptualized as attempts to cope with intense intrapsychic pain, and depression is frequently the underlying affect in both. The second theoretical framework, namely that alcoholism is a form of chronic suicide, has the most relevance to this chapter and will be discussed in a separate section.

The third framework states that alcoholism facilitates suicidal behavior. Ringel and Rotter (1957) have identified three types of alcoholic suicide attempters, all of whom would fall within this general framework. In type one, alcohol intoxication facilitates the suicidal impulse. Such a hypothesis intuitively makes sense, since it is generally believed that people with suicidal thoughts are more prone to act on them under the influence of alcohol. When Frankel et al. (1976) attempted to document this hypothesis, however, they were unable to demonstrate a consistent relationship. More specifically, the pharmacological effects of alcohol were not found consistently to facilitate suicidal impulses, and although alcohol did seem to increase a person's willingness to take risks, these risks were not associated with patterns of self-injury.

The second type of alcoholic suicide attempter identified by Ringel and Rotter (1957) is one in which intoxication catalyzes an angry abreaction associated with much interpersonal conflict and motor hyperactivity. An example of this type is the person who, while intoxicated, has an angry argument with his or her spouse and impulsively makes a suicide attempt. Mayfield and Montgomery (1972), in their study of twenty-six alcoholic suicide attempters, identified about one-third who fit this pattern. Such patients seldom sustain serious injury, and the suicide attempt generally takes place at the beginning of the drinking bout. Mayfield and Montgomery's study also supported Ringel and Rotter's conceptualization of another type of alcoholic suicide attempter, in whom the suicide attempt is at the end of a long drunk, and related to feelings of grief, remorse, and, in general, depression. This last group, the largest, is the one in which most serious suicide attempts occur. Other investigators also have noted that prolonged intoxication may be a crucial factor in suicide. Tamerin and Mendelson (1969), for example, have observed the development of severe depression after two weeks of experimental intoxication.

A severe depressive syndrome could have at least two explanations. It can be understood in terms of Bibring's (1953) formulation of depression as a basic reaction to situations of narcissistic frustration that the ego appears powerless to prevent. In the alcoholic's case, the narcissistic frustration could be brought about by uncontrollable drinking and unwanted, bizarre behavior while intoxicated. The depressive syndrome can also be understood in terms of the effects of chronic alcohol intoxication on central nervous system catecholamine metabolism. Evidence is appearing that alcohol has an effect on central nervous system catecholamines (Grote et al., 1974), but the current state of knowledge permits only speculation about the possibility of depletion of norepinephrine and dopamine with resultant depression.

The sociological perspective adds another dimension to the understanding of the association between alcohol and suicide. In a study by Murphy and Robbins (1967), the characteristic that distinguished alcoholic suicide attempters from other suicide attempters was the presence of a significant loss in the six weeks preceding the suicide attempt. The loss was usually of a significant person, but it could also be loss of a job or something similar in importance. Rushing (1968) postulated that alcoholics are likely to commit suicide when the deterioration of their social relationships reaches a critical point. Beck et al. (1976) add that when the typical depression in the alcoholic is accompanied by loss of hope, a suicide attempt is likely. Other characteristics of the suicidal alcoholic are noted by Ritson (1968) and include the following: older age; last sibship position; positive attachment to mother and resentment toward father; previous suicide attempts; and highly self-critical attitude.

To recapitulate:

1. Alcoholism has clear self-destructive consequences for the person afflicted with it.
2. Approximately 10 percent of alcoholics eventually commit suicide, and an additional 25 percent attempt suicide.
3. Alcoholism potentially contributes to this overt self-destructive behavior in various ways, as by facilitating latent suicidal impulses, catalyzing angry abreaction resulting in suicide attempts, and promoting the development of severe depression either from psychological mechanisms or physiological ones.
4. Characteristics of alcoholics at high risk for suicide include: recent loss, depression with hopelessness, social isolation, older age, highly self-critical attitude, last sibship position, and history of previous suicide attempts.
5. The self-destructive consequences of alcoholism for the approximately 65 percent of alcoholics who do not attempt or complete suicide must be considered as indirect self-destructiveness since no overt self-destructive act is involved and no conscious self-destructive intent is present.

ALCOHOLISM AND INDIRECT SELF-DESTRUCTIVE BEHAVIOR

Alcoholism is viewed by many as a disease similar to diabetes or cancer. Along with the disease concept, there is a tendency to discredit psychological explanations of alcoholic behavior; nevertheless, an association between alcoholism and indirect self-destructive behavior is quite compatible with the view of alcoholism as a disease of complex nature. If the person who is diabetic denies his illness, refuses to seek proper treatment, and only haphazardly follows his physician's recommendations, then it is obvious that his illness has a self-destructive component. Such denial, refusal to seek treatment, and resistance to following treatment recommendations are characteristic of the alcoholic who still drinks. To be sure, there are alcoholics (see case 1) who become alarmed at the first sign of deterioration of health or the development of other problems related to alcohol and seek help quickly. In such people there is little evidence of a significant self-destructive component in their alcoholism.

The indirect self-destructiveness of alcoholism can have its origin in one of two very different sources: in frustrated infantile needs and in the alcoholic process itself. Karl Menninger remains the most eloquent spokesman for the former position.

In his book *Man against Himself,* Menninger (1938) develops Freud's idea of a life instinct or primary creative instinct and a death instinct or primary destructive instinct. These so-called instincts would be analogous to the forces of anabolism and catabolism in biology. Menninger believes that as the person matures these forces or drives become modified, fused to varying degrees, and invested in external objects. In certain circumstances, the life and death drives tend to revert back on the person of origin, the self. If, according to Menninger, one's destructive impulses are not neutralized properly, suicide may occur; if the destructive drive is partially neutralized, various forms of chronic partial self-destruction may be the result. Although many psychiatrists would not accept the concept of the death instinct as such, the idea of aggressive drives and libidinal drives in interaction is generally well accepted.

Menninger further reasons that, alcohol addiction being one form of chronic self-destruction, it has an adaptive function in that it spares the person from immediate suicide. As he puts it, "Alcohol addiction . . . can be considered a form of self-destruction used to avert a greater self-destruction, deriving from elements of aggressiveness, excited by thwarting ungratified (infantile) eroticism, and the feeling of the need for punishment from the sense of guilt related to the aggressiveness" (p. 161). Alcoholism allows for some expression of aggressiveness and at the same time permits gratification of infantile oral needs, but at the price of indirect self-destructiveness. Palola et al. (1962) view alcoholism as a defense against total self-destruction, but a defense that becomes increasingly eroded with age. They believe that when hope disappears through lack of opportunity to reach life goals, destructive drives previously subordinated by other drives become unbound, and may be released against the self in the form of total self-destruction.

In a way quite distinct from the one just described, the alcoholic process itself can generate and perpetuate the pressure for ISDB and, eventually, suicide. Initially, alcohol gratifies needs, relaxes tension, and sedates; but as the alcoholic process develops, there is characteristically an erosion of health, a deterioration of performance and interpersonal relations, broken promises, lying, hurting, etc. All these failures inflame an already punitive superego and result in intensification of feelings of worthlessness, badness, guilt, and remorse. Such feelings demand recompense, and one readily available way is through the self-inflicted punishment of alcoholism. And so the cycle goes. The alcoholic person tries to break the cycle, but as he more often than not finds himself unable to do so his feelings of guilt and worthlessness increase, further contributing to self-destructive patterns, including resistance to help. In distinction to the self-destructiveness related to frustrated infantile needs, if the vicious circle of self-destructiveness related to the alcoholic process can be broken and abstinence achieved, other manifestations of self-destructive behavior might not be expected to develop. In both instances the ISDB can be conceptualized as the person's active attempt somehow to come to terms with an intolerable situation without the ultimate step of suicide. The distinction is important, as it relates to different treatment needs in the two instances. Some examples may be helpful in clarifying the relationship between self-destructive behavior in its various forms and alcoholism.

CASE 1

Mr. B, an insurance company executive in his fifties, had successfully held the same job for about ten years and had been a social drinker for almost twenty years. Even though he liked his job, it provided him with little challenge, and he was becoming bored and mildly depressed. In order to deal with his boredom and to relax, he began drinking excessively, and over the period of two years he started to experience a number of physical problems, conflicts at home around his drinking, and increasing depression. After an episode of bizarre behavior presumably related to his alcohol use, he became frightened and entered a treatment program. He was rapidly able to become involved in AA, his thinking cleared, and his relationships improved. After treatment was ended he made some changes in his life-style, reset his priorities, and was able to resume and maintain a stable level of functioning without alcohol.

In this case, there is little evidence of a significant self-destructive component. When serious problems began to develop, Mr. B became alarmed, sought help, and was able to make a sustained recovery.

CASE 2

Mrs. R is a sixty-nine-year-old woman with a history of stable functioning throughout her life, including the raising of two physician sons. After her husband died when she was sixty-five she became depressed and began drinking excessively for the first time in her life. She developed an organic brain syndrome, followed by deterioration of her health and overall functioning. The changes were so striking that the family rapidly confronted her. Following this confrontation, she voluntarily entered an alcoholism treatment program. When her thinking cleared, she was helped to come to terms more appropriately with the loss of her husband, and her depression began to lift. She was then able to resume an active, well-functioning life without alcohol.

In this example, the self-destructiveness was clearly related to loss of a significant relationship. With the recognition not only of the alcohol problem, but also of the depression related to the loss, appropriate treatment could be instituted, and the patient was able to return to her previous level of functioning.

CASE 3

Mrs. N was a woman with a long-standing neurotic character style manifested by a chronic sense of guilt, constant self-denial, and an ongoing experience of personal suffering. At the same time she was a sensitive, giving person with a basically stable life pattern. She did virtually no drinking until after the tragic death of her twelve-year-old son when she was thirty-three; she thereupon became extremely distraught, depressed, and self-blaming. She made a suicide attempt, though not a serious one, and thereafter embarked on a severely destructive drinking pattern, which continued for several years and then abruptly stopped. She was resistant to treatment during this time and was able to say in retrospect that the destructive drinking was all that stood between her and suicide.

In this example, a relatively stable life adjustment included a compensated form of indirect self-destructive masochistic behavior. The person was able to function well and competently, but only at the cost of constant self-denial and the experience of suffering. With the change in circumstances brought about by the death of a son, this stable balance was disrupted and an additional form of ISDB appeared—alcoholism. For several years the abuse of alcohol was necessary as a buffer against an overt suicide act. In this case the neurotic need for some form of indirect self-destructive behavior was related to an early life situation in which, as the only child, the patient was adored by her father, whom she saw as warm and giving, while she experienced her mother as cold and distant. The father was tragically murdered when the patient was four and in the midst of her Oedipal fantasies. These childhood experiences left painful scars that she was to live with for the rest of her life, but which until the death of her son were contained within a fairly stable life-style.

CASE 4

Mr. M is a forty-two-year-old, separated man working for a Ph.D. in education, who has had a serious progressive drinking problem for at least eight years, recalcitrant to any attempt at treatment. Mr. M has been through excellent programs with the same results—several months of sobriety, then heavy drinking again. Even before alcoholism became a problem, Mr. M experienced difficulty in his work and family situation, since he was always championing unpopular causes. Numerous recommendations had been made to him for AA, psychotherapy, and marital therapy, but he always had reasons not to follow through on the recommendations. After recovery from each serious drinking bout, including one involving delirium tremens, Mr. M always emerged feeling extremely optimistic. Those working with him, however, experienced their own optimism and concern as continually dashed and consequently felt increasingly frustrated, angry, and discouraged.

A review of this man's background showed that he had been raised in a very strict family, in which the father was the local school principal. The patient had been a very obedient child until high school, and then in various ways, never direct, he began to rebel; he found reason to go to a college that his father didn't recommend; he began to smoke and drink surreptitiously. He insisted that all of this was done with a clear conscience. The closer he came to attaining a Ph.D. degree, which his father never had, the more overt was his self-destructive behavior, not only with drinking but also with risk-taking, which resulted in many accidents. This was a case of a very malignant form of ISDB; the patient could not accept help because he could not afford to give up his alcoholism, as it was based on powerful but unconscious self-destructive impulses.

CASE 5

Mr. S, a forty-two-year-old accountant with a wife and three children, had been a heavy drinker for many years. In the eight years before treatment, there had been a gradual erosion of his performance on the job, culminating in several inappropriate episodes at work when drunk. His marriage had also deteriorated to the point where his wife was seriously considering divorce. Despite repeated cautions about drinking too much, he continued until he was finally forced into treatment involuntarily. After a stormy early course with much negativism, Mr. S became invested in treatment and felt more hopeful about the future. Since discharge from treatment he has maintained sobriety with the help of AA, his problems seem to be resolving, and there is no new evidence of self-destructive behavior.

This case illustrates the powerful self-destructive influence that the alcoholic process itself can exert on a person. Treatment finally had to be forced on the person because at that point he had lost hope that he could change and, in fact, he did not feel that he deserved a better kind of existence. With the breaking of this self-destructive cycle, he became more hopeful, more able to invest in others, and has maintained sobriety with no other manifestations of ISDB.

TREATMENT IMPLICATIONS _____

The attitude toward treatment of the alcoholic person has changed significantly in the past twenty years from one of avoidance and frustration to one of guarded optimism. Alcoholism treatment programs have multiplied, and most of these programs have certain features in common. There is emphasis on group therapy techniques, AA participation, and Al-Anon participation for the family. The cornerstone of treatment is helping the person discover that he or she can live without alcohol by relying on outside help—"a power greater than oneself," in AA terms.

Still, recovery rates for alcoholism leave much to be desired, in part because not enough attention is paid to individual differences and individual treatment needs. The identification of individual differences in the alcoholic person's self-destructive behavior has clear treatment implications. The alcoholic who has suffered a significant loss in the past month or two, and who is expressing feelings of hopelessness, represents a high risk for suicide and should be treated accordingly. Also at risk for direct suicidal behavior is the alcoholic person in his fifties or sixties who has been on a drinking spree for at least two weeks and has alienated himself from most sources of interpersonal support.

For the alcoholic whose ISDB is sustained by the alcoholic process itself, the usual alcoholism treatment with an emphasis on AA may well be enough, because once the self-perpetuating cycle of alcoholism is broken and hope is renewed, there is no internal pressure to continue the self-destructive behavior. On the other hand, the alcoholic person whose ISDB is being sustained not only by the alcoholic process itself but also by internal pressures relating to early childhood frustration and conflicts, represents an entirely different case. In such a case, the internal need for self-destructive behavior persists even after the alcoholism cycle is broken and, therefore, he or she needs additional treatment.

Although there are no pathognomonic characteristics of alcoholics with this type of ISDB, certain findings should raise the index of suspicion. The patient's history, for example, can provide very pertinent information. If there are indications of other types of ISDB such as serious accidents, multiple surgery or physical complaints of a questionable nature, and increased risk-taking behavior, to mention a few, then a strong underlying self-destructive component should be suspected. A history of a highly conflictual relationship with one or both parents and a lifelong experience of guilt with no real sense of joy may be taken as presumptive evidence of unresolved internal conflict, which can find expression in ISDB. Paradoxically, those patients with a more deep-seated self-destructive component to their alcoholism often show much promise early in treatment, only to dash the treaters' hopes later on. Psychiatric treatment focusing specifically on the self-destructiveness is needed to prevent relapse or the emergence of a new form of self-destructive behavior. Such additional treatment may vary from intensive long-term psychotherapy aimed at the resolution of internal conflicts, to brief psychotherapy aimed at reestablishing a previously stable equilibrium.

REFERENCES ————————————————————————

American Medical Association. *Manual on Alcoholism.* Chicago: AMA Publication, 1977.

Beck, A., Weissman, A., and Kovacs, M. Alcoholism, hopelessness and suicidal behavior. *Journal of Studies on Alcohol,* 37:66–67, 1976.

Bibring, E. The mechanism of depression. In P. Greenacre, ed., *Affective Disorders: Psychoanalytic Contributions to Their Study.* New York: International Universities Press, 1953.

Dahlgren, K. G. *On Suicide and Attempted Suicide.* Lund, Sweden, 1945.

Frankel, B., Ferrence, R., Johnson, F., and Whitehead, P. Drinking and self-injury: Toward untangling the dynamics. *British Journal of Addiction,* 71:299–306, 1976.

Goodwin, D. Is alcoholism hereditary? *Archives of General Psychiatry,* 25:545–549, 1971.

Grote, S. S., Moses, S. G., Robins, E., et al. Study of selected catecholamine metabolizing enzymes: A comparison of depressive suicide and alcoholic suicide with controls. *Journal of Neurochemistry,* 23:791–802, 1974.

Hartocollis, P. Alcoholism, A borderline disorder. Unpublished manuscript.

Jellinek, E. M. Phases of alcohol addiction. In D. Pittman, and C. Snyder, eds. *Society, Culture and Drinking Patterns.* New York: Wiley, 1962.

Kessel, W., and Grossman, G. Suicide in alcoholism. *British Medical Journal,* 2:1671–1672, 1961.

Knight, R. The dynamics and treatment of chronic alcohol addiction. *Bulletin of the Menninger Clinic,* 1:233–250, 1937.

Mayfield, D., and Montgomery, D. Alcoholism, alcohol intoxication and suicide attempts. *Archives of General Psychiatry,* 27:349–353, 1972.

Menninger, K. *Man against Himself.* New York: Harcourt, Brace, 1938.

Murphy, C., and Robbins, E. Social factors in suicide. *Journal of the American Medical Association,* 199:81–86, 1967.

Norvig, J., and Nielsen, B. A follow-up study of 221 alcohol addicts in Denmark. *Quarterly Journal of Studies on Alcohol,* 17:633–642, 1956.

Palola, E., Dorpat, T., and Larson, W. Alcoholism and suicidal behavior. In D. Pittman, and E. Snyder, eds. *Society, Culture and Drinking Patterns.* New York: Wiley, 1962.

Ringel, E., and Rotter, H. Zum problem des selbstmordeversuches in Rousch. *Wein Zeitschrift für Nervenheilkunst,* 13:406–416, 1957.

Ritson, E. Suicide amongst alcoholics. *British Journal of Medical Psychology,* 41:235–242, 1968.

Rushing, W. Alcoholism and suicide rates by status set and occupation. *Quarterly Journal of Studies in Alcohol,* 29:399–412, 1968.

Tamerin, J., and Mendelson, J. The psychodynamics of chronic alcoholism: Observations of alcoholics during the process of drinking. *American Journal of Psychiatry,* 125:886–899, 1969.

U. S. Department of Health, Education, and Welfare. *Alcohol and Health,* Second Special Report to the U. S. Congress, Washington, D. C.: DHEW Publication, 1974.

14

ALCOHOL ABUSE AMONG WOMEN AS INDIRECT SELF-DESTRUCTIVE BEHAVIOR

MARCELLINE M. BURNS

W omen with alcohol problems? Most of us would prefer not to think about wives, daughters, mothers, and sisters who drink too much. As one writer has expressed it, we do not want to believe that the hands which rock the cradle are shaky hands. Unfortunately, it appears that the problem of alcohol abuse among women has reached such proportions currently that the traditional, idealized views of women as nondrinkers suffer seriously in the face of reality.

Alcohol abuse and alcoholism are, for many people, "red flag" words. Not only are they associated with a wide range of meaning, they may also evoke emotionally charged responses, particularly in people who have had direct and painful association with alcohol abusers. This ambiguity and emotion serve to obscure the nature of the problem; thus it is essential to open a discussion of alcohol abuse among women by first defining the behavior. What are alcohol-use practices which earn the label "alcohol abuse"? Note that it is a *severely* pejorative term in its application to women.

A number of satisfactory definitions appear in the literature. Selection of one of these versus introduction of still another reduces to a personal, arbitrary decision. Hence, borrowing liberally from Lindbeck (1972), "alcohol abuse among women" is used here to mean the repetitive use of alcohol by a woman in a manner and to an extent which causes her physical, emotional, social, or vocational harm.

Ethanol is a toxic substance, and when it is ingested in large quantities the damaging consequences for physiological functioning are severe. Prolonged heavy use may impair the liver and other organs irreparably. When drinking produces a blood alcohol content exceeding 0.40 to 0.50 percent, coma and death ensue. Nonetheless, alcohol is a legal substance which is readily available to adults, including an indeterminate number of people who ultimately use it in direct suicide attempts. The overdose, often in combination with other drugs, and the traffic accident which was not truly accidental, are perhaps the most common occurrences of this kind.

Direct suicide with alcohol, in this sense, is overtly, aggressively destructive, and in some cases traumatic life events and extreme despair are identifiable as the sources of motivation for the attempt. It is visible behavior toward which therapeutic efforts sometimes can be directed, albeit often with little apparent effect. In contrast, a woman (or a man) who is indirectly destroying selfhood with alcohol is more subtle in the exercise of destructive tendencies. For example, public drinking may be held well within socially acceptable limits, and further, the person may appear on the surface to be stable and integrated.

It once was a widely held impression that female alcoholics were degraded and immoral people, but it has become obvious that such a view is not tenable. They are actually a highly diverse population, reflecting the full range of personal characteristics. Whatever the particular individual personality, circumstance, or life-style, the behavioral dynamics are certain to be complex in a woman whose alcohol use constitutes indirect self-destructive behavior (ISDB). Of major importance is that what may be a most significant source among women of the motivation toward self-destruction has gone largely unrecognized.

THE LITERATURE

Examination of the alcohol literature from the perspective of ISDB produces support, primarily from clinical data, for the view that alcohol abuse by women is self-destructive. However, the literature is seriously lacking in investigations of the phenomenon. Relatively few studies have focused specifically on alcohol use among women. Further, in this writer's opinion, investigators generally have missed the mark in their conceptualizations of the source of the destructive tendencies.

Incidence and prevalence data appear for the most part in the context of larger population studies. In *American Drinking Practices* (Cahalan et al., 1969) the tabled data show about 40 percent of women up to age fifty to be abstainers or infrequent drinkers. Approximately 45 percent are shown to be light or moderate drinkers, and 15 percent are classified as heavy drinkers. Past age fifty, a marked decline in drinking was apparent in this sample of 1,569 women. Note that these estimates are based on a survey conducted more than a decade ago; it is probable that important changes in drinking practices have occurred during the seventies. Unfortunately, we do not yet have adequate data to document the nature and extent of those changes among women.

Knupfer (1964) reported data from the California *Drinking Practices Study* which showed fewer women than men to be heavy drinkers. She found intense disapproval of drunkenness by women, with both male and female respondents expressing the attitude that heavy drinking does not fit the woman's proper role.

Knupfer and Room (1964), reporting on 1962 data from San Francisco, found a cumulative effect of age, sex, and socioeconomic status, with those who were least likely to drink heavily characterized as underprivileged nonparticipants in American society; note that the underprivileged were specifically identified as the old, the poor, and *women.*

Alcohol studies typically have focused on use patterns among men. In 1975, the California Office of Alcoholism, referring to studies of women, pointed out that "many do not include empirical data or are based on clinical rather than population studies. Generalizations are made about increased drinking, but data are lacking." In the same year, the Research Task Force of the National Institute of Mental Health identified alcohol use and abuse by women as an area of needed research.

Two decades ago Lisansky (1957) pointed to the neglect of research in the area of sex differences in psychopathology:

> . . . there is an implicit assumption in much of the literature of psychopathology that any particular psychological disorder is much the same among women as among men, that etiology, psychodynamics and symptom patterns are probably alike for both sexes. This may be a valid assumption but we do not know. [p. 588]

Ten years later Curlee (1967) reviewed the literature and concluded that, in general, society has been reluctant to consider and treat the woman alcoholic. Although still another decade has elapsed, the current literature does not demonstrate any major change in research or treatment priorities.

Estimates of the actual numbers of women who are involved with detrimental alcohol use vary widely, depending on the source of the data and the particular population. Private physicians have estimated that among their patients the ratio of male to female alcoholics is 3:1. In police custody, the ratio of men to women alcohol abusers is believed to be 11:1. There are various other estimates as well as a consensus that many women remain undetected and untreated. In terms of the total population figures (estimated by the National Council on Alcoholism as 80 million who drink, 6.5 million who are alcoholic), a very conservative estimate in 1977 is approximately one million women who have serious problems with alcohol and whose drinking can be characterized as heavy and thus as self-destructive. Although it is true that the seventies have been a decade of rapid change, with some easing of restrictions on women, for the vast majority such a strong social taboo on heavy drinking continues that it is unlikely that the behavior is not, at some level, quite purposefully destructive.

> Women are supposed to be, and in fact are, more conservative, or more conventional in matters relating to propriety, to morals and to general freedom of activity than are men. This is undoubtedly related to the harshness of social judgments in cases of role infringement. [Clark, 1964, p. 4]

Compared to men, the woman who drinks heavily is considered to be exhibiting the greater pathology. The rationale is that since she is subject to such great disapproval and scorn, her extreme drinking surely must have developed in response to severe emotional disturbance. As Knupfer (1964) expressed it, "the woman alcoholic has been exposed, shunned and pitied as a role breaker through the whole long process of getting to be an alcoholic." Winokur and Clayton (1968) reported that male alcoholics tend to be sociopathic, but that alcoholism in females is usually a primary affective disorder. Women alcoholics are characterized as depressed, suicidal, and delusional. Rathod and Thomson (1971) described the alcoholic woman's experience as encompassing far more deprivation and emotional trauma than men, their current state being more depressed and suicidal. Lisansky (1957) viewed the female alcohol abuser as a woman who is poorly adjusted to her social milieu and who, therefore, drinks to excess. Hirsch (1962) pointed out that the social consequences of drinking are greater for women than men, more frequently leading to rejection by friends and associates. Even so, women drink to insensibility more often than men. Curlee (1967) vividly described the pathology of alcohol abuse for women as a vicious circle:

> . . . the home is the biosocial core for the woman far more than for the man; her drinking is likely to cause difficulties at this vital core from the very beginning, thus undermining the basis of the woman's identification and sense of value. The drinking, therefore, is doubly destructive; it not only is destructive of the

> self-image in the same ways as for men; but it also destroys the most fundamental source of the woman's self-esteem. [pp. 17–18]

Overall, the literature on women and alcohol exhibits a striking "sameness"—not unexpectedly, as there is only a very limited body of information. As Belfer et al. (1971) pointed out, the alcoholic woman is a large unknown quantity in terms of her numbers, psychological characteristics, and drinking patterns.

Unfortunately, in the absence of empirical data, both the myth and trivia have appeared. In illustration, it is reported to be the opinion of some physicians that women drink to relieve the fear associated with competitive social situations. It is also reported that women are more hostile, angry, unhappy, self-centered, withdrawn, depressed, emotional, lonely, and nervous, and are not as likable as men alcoholics! Even if these negative descriptors were accurate, one has to question whether they make any contribution toward conceptualizing issues or advancing methodologically sound study of the behavior.

To attribute pathological drinking, as one investigator does, to menstrual tension is not only misleading, it is demeaning. Although there may be, within the whole constellation of contributing variables, a causal relationship between various aspects of sexuality and reproductive function and alcohol use, it is unlikely that significant numbers of women are acting out self-destructive tendencies due primarily to menstrual tension.

Much of the literature compares the woman who drinks to the man who drinks, and therein lies a substantial reason for the sameness, the lack of insight, and the frequent failure to understand the behavior. As Sherfy (1955) points out, "the major disorders in sexuality resulting from vicissitudes in the complex feminine development in our culture so color the personality that the clinical picture in the woman appears quite different from that of the man." A woman abuses alcohol *as a woman.* Her experience does not simply mirror the male experience, nor will it fit a model of alcohol use which is based on the drinking patterns and practices of men. Rather, the motivation for and dynamics of alcohol use by women will be elucidated through examination of the behavior *within the context of womanhood.*

It is worthy of note that the extant literature about women is curiously composed, with deficiencies which are probably attributable to the male-female comparison base. Only recently has the fetal alcohol syndrome been identified as an area for high-priority research. Moreover, it will be agreed that women usually believe and are frequently reminded that the role of mother is vitally important.

That being the case, it is strange indeed that the impact of alcohol abuse on the mother-child relationship has merited no attention.

In reviewing the respective literatures, one is struck by the apparent commonality of personal characteristics which have been attributed by investigators to both the suicide and the female alcoholic abuser. The examples which follow are illustrative only and almost certainly are not exhaustive, but they suffice to pose some significant questions. For example, are alcoholism and suicide for some people simply different potential positions on a continuum of maladaptive responses? Perhaps the alcoholic woman demonstrates a distorted attempt at survival, protecting herself with her alcoholism from the more immediate destruction by suicide.

Characteristics of Suicide Victims	*Characteristics of Female Alcoholics*
Parental absence during childhood	Emotional trauma in childhood (loss of parent)
Marital disharmony	Problems in interpersonal relations (marriage, family); disorganized life
Disorganized life	
Bad relationship with key individual	Lack of self-discipline
Emotionally isolated	Immature
Women were depressed; men suffered personality disorder	Poor emotional adjustment
	Depressed
	Primary affective disorder in females (sociopathic or other personality disorder in males)

ALCOHOL ABUSE AS ISDB _____

Farberow (1967) characterized suicide as the person's own rejection of society and self, and the woman alcoholic clearly has established these benchmarks of destruction. Not only is she numbing and obliterating her "self" with alcohol, it is reasonable to conclude, in view of the climate of disapproval of drinking by females, that she is also dramatically demonstrating her rejection of society. It is, of course, noteworthy that there is a high rate of both attempted and accomplished suicides among alcoholic women. Sadly, there are thousands upon thousands more women who are just as certainly set on a course of destruction but who do not come to public attention and whose ISDB goes unrecognized and untreated.

"Drinking" is pervasive in this society, occurring in virtually all population strata. Socioeconomic, educational, ethnic, or age boundaries do not separate drinkers and nondrinkers, although certain religious affiliations may do so. Actually, a surprisingly small number of groups proscribe alcohol use as a condition of membership, although many individuals do so out of personal choice.

Given that female alcohol abusers mirror the diversity of the larger population of alcohol users, the task of examining their ISDB is formidable. *Why* do women drink in ways which are destructive? Is it reasonable to expect that there may be common denominator(s) in their life histories or current circumstances? If we reject the unsupported clinical impressions, the negative comparisons with men, and the trivial conjecture, and if methodologically sound studies are going to be undertaken, a first essential task is to develop alternate hypotheses.

Returning again to the literature, there appears to be only one characteristic which is attributed by a majority of investigators to alcohol-abusing women. The woman who drinks too much is believed to be suffering from an affective disorder. According to Schuckit (1972), "Alcoholism in women occurs frequently secondary to an affective illness and is accompanied by more suicidal behavior than seen in males." Winokur and Clayton (1968) found females to be more often depressed. Hart (1974) cited the emotional difficulties which characterize the typical female alcoholic. Rathod and Thomson (1971) found more women with depressive illness and suicidal thoughts. Mann (1973) believes that a deep, underlying depression is present in most women alcoholics and that they may use alcohol to mask the depression.

These investigators, and others as well, agree that the woman who misuses alcohol is depressed. It is thought provoking that men who drink too much are so described less often. Perhaps this is a clue which merits examination. Women's excessive drinking is related to depression. To what, then, is the depression related? The following section develops one hypothesis in response to these and related questions. It is seriously offered and, like any hypothesis, may or may not find support over the long term. More important, it will, I hope, generate thought and study, and alternate hypotheses.

A HYPOTHESIS _____

Alcohol abuse by women as a self-destructive behavior is related to the role *of women*

The woman's role is often a limiting, second-class role. A social and economic system, and interpersonal relationships within that system which restrict the development of the full self, tend to develop instead the characteristics of despair, dependency, helplessness, hopelessness, passivity, and rage. These, in turn, for some women serve to initiate and sustain the addictive, destructive use of alcohol. This view is poignantly expressed by a woman speaking from her experiences as both provider and consumer of health services:

> . . . I know more and more women are resorting to alcohol and drugs in a desperation born of trying to cope with and adjust to our incomplete everyday lives.
> I know the deadly guilt, anxiety, and stress that is frequently borne by women in the wife and mother role. I know the pretense women try desperately to maintain about the joys of motherhood, the joys of sex, the joys of nurturing others, and the joys of self-denial and service. [MacLennon, 1976, p. 35]

In the same collection of papers there appears a description of a woman alcoholic, and again the writer notes the frustrations of a restricted role:

> Typically, this woman is between 35 and 45 years of age. While her children were growing she did not take the time, or perhaps did not have the time, to involve herself in community activities. Nor did she work towards her personal growth and identity. Now she no longer feels needed or worthwhile. . . . she sinks into hopelessness and helplessness. The veneer of respectability dissipates and she becomes the overt chronic alcoholic. [MacLennon, 1976, pp. 46–47]

In a study of sixty-nine women alcoholics, Wood and Duffy (1966) found that none were "happy drunks." Rather, they were women for whom alcohol released rage and reduced anxiety, helping her feel like the woman she wanted to be. Belfer et al. (1971) believe the concept of role confusion is particularly significant in view of what appears to be an increase in serious drinking by *young* women.

We will return later to the literature in discussing this view of the relationship of role and alcohol use. First, it is important to consider the possible impact of the women's movement.

There is currently a considerable amount of rhetoric about the changing role of women, changes which can be expected to affect alcohol use patterns. It is relevant that Mary Mann, founder of the National Council on Alcoholism, believes that the business or professional woman, i.e., a woman whose role has moved away from the traditional female role, will present the same picture of alcoholism as a man. If women and their roles in society change, it is realistic to anticipate that their use of alcohol and the related problems will change.

As yet, however, for most women there is far more rhetoric about change than real change. The evidence of status quo is apparent in *all* socioeconomic indices. One unfortunate result of the rhetoric, as well as of the actual changes, has been confusion. A woman who hears constantly about her changing role and new opportunities must now cope with a sense of failure because *she* is still limited and restricted. She does not feel as if she has achieved liberation, in either the best or the worst sense of that word. Most women continue to be defined in terms of their relationships to men, and only rarely do they achieve the selfhood, the autonomy, and the confidence from which to claim personal recognition and achievement. As Clara Synigal, the director of a halfway house for women put it, "I find that women have an identity problem, and that's what we work on most here. The women here don't know who they are. In the past, they've always been somebody's wife, girlfriend, sexual partner, mother—they're always part of somebody else's whole" (Sandmaier, 1977).

Looking through the eyes of a woman, speaking from a woman's experience, with a woman's view of the typical division of labor and responsibility, opportunities and status, the "sameness" of the literature begins slowly to dissipate as the data coalesce into possibilities for insight and meaning.

Pollmer (1955) attributes drinking by women to an exceptionally high degree of anxiety, the origin of which is unknown and about which she can do nothing. Kinsey (1968) also reported that women alcoholics value alcohol for its ability to relieve anxiety. Isn't it possible that the nonspecific anxiety, from which women seek relief, is a chronic existential anxiety, and that it is intensified for women by the limits and restrictions under which they live? It is not surprising that women are anxious, nor that they seek relief. Intense anxiety is painful and debilitating, and it can be predicted that some proportion of those who experience it will seek the temporary euphoria and numbness readily available from alcohol. Repetitive compulsive escape from pain or guilt via alcohol is, of course, the essence of a developing dependency and abuse.

Contrary to popular arguments against the feminists' position, the current normative role for women (in particular, the urban American woman) is not entirely a time-honored, traditional role which evolved naturally from reproductive and child-care functions. Quite the opposite: in agrarian societies of earlier eras women were valued as responsible, economically necessary, and vital partners. Contrast the potential for satisfaction from that meaningful role—which admittedly often required very hard labor—with the stereotypical modern woman who has no function of importance beyond parenting and homemaking. Although the rewards associated with childbearing and family life may be many, the role of motherhood is demanding of time and energies for relatively few years. The commonly cited "empty nest" syndrome has the potential to provoke crises for women who are totally child-centered and have no other meaningful activity (Curlee, 1969). It is not at all remarkable that physicians believe their alcohol-abusing female patients are attempting to escape the boredom of too much leisure, a dull and monotonous life.

Clearly, substance abuse is one of a wide variety of behaviors, some positive and enriching, some negative and destructive, in which women engage to offset boredom and emptiness. At the outset alcohol may be, especially for women with few resources, the coping mechanism, the buffer, which renders trauma and pain bearable, the salve to dull harsh reality. So used and so needed, it is by definition destructive of the life experience, perhaps ultimately of life itself.

The meager or negative self-esteem which characterizes women who have turned to alcohol begins to be explicable. Where there is little opportunity for growth and achievement, there also is little opportunity for self-affirmation and a sustained sense of personal worth. It is highly pertinent that in a study of women alcoholics (Hart, 1974) the women claimed that they did *not* drink in response to crisis, as frequently reported, with such events as divorce, menopause, hysterectomy, abortion, miscarriage, desertion, and death being cited as precipitating events. Rather, the women attributed their drinking to an effort to improve their own self-image. Note, too, that a primary goal of the self-help organization, Women for Sobriety, is to enable the women to develop self-esteem as the first step toward responsible and competent living without alcohol.

Although it is apparent that a moralistic view of women who drink as being "loose" and promiscuous is inappropriate, the association of excessive alcohol use with sexual dysfunction continues to appear in various guises. Wilsnack (1973a, 1973b) postulated that the alcoholic woman is drinking to feel more womanly because she experiences chronic doubt about her adequacy as a woman. Parker (1972) cited defective and incongruent femininity. Schuckit (1973) claims that the common view of the woman alcoholic as someone who experiences intense sexual pleasure is invalid: "The fact is that few women alcoholics report sexual satisfaction. The tenor of their lives centers on boredom, unhappiness and restlessness, with a sexual adjustment of parallel quality." The argument most frequently expressed in the literature is that the woman feels insecure in her feminine role and tries via alcohol to bolster her confidence in her own womanliness. Almost certainly there is some validity in this view, but there is a risk of attributing too much to it, thereby creating a blindness to the larger issue.

The hypothesis here is that although insecurity in the feminine role may contribute to the misuse of alcohol, it is dissatisfaction *with* the feminine role, as it is constituted in modern, urban society, which is of major significance for many women. Though it is difficult indeed to cope with a fragile sense of feminine adequacy, the more fundamental problem is to develop and sustain a sense of adequacy as a human being, and women must do so within a system that fosters their passivity and dependency and severely limits opportunities for full development. Both men and women, as individuals, must confront restriction. Women, as women, are further limited by a circumscribed role. It is suggested that *for some women* this leads to feelings of helplessness and hopelessness, which in turn produce the deep depression that may finally lead to alcohol abuse.

The social definition of man's and woman's places in the world *is* changing. The changes are slow but inevitable, and this fact provides an opportunity to examine social processes and social pathology. It is vitally important to examine women's use of alcohol not only in comparison to that of men but as a socially significant behavior which may relate to and evolve with their changing role.

REFERENCES _____

Belfer, M. L., Shader, R. I., Carrol, M., and Harmatz, J. S. Alcoholism in women. *Archives of General Psychiatry*, 25:540–544, 1971.

Cahalan, D., Cisin, I. H., and Crossley, H. M. *American Drinking Practices.* New Haven, Conn.: College and University Press, 1969.

Clark, W. Sex roles and alcohol beverage usage. *Drinking Practices Study.* State of California, Department of Public Health, 1964.

Curlee, J. Women alcoholics. *Federal Probation*, 32(1):16–20, 1967.

Curlee, J. Alcoholism and the "empty nest." *Bulletin of the Menninger Clinic*, 33:165–171, 1969.

Farberow, N. Crisis, disaster, and suicide: Theory and therapy. In E. S. Shneidman, ed., *Essays in Self-Destruction.* New York: Aronson, 1967.

Hart, L. Attitudes among a group of female alcoholics toward alcoholism. *British Journal of Addiction*, 69:311–314, 1974.

Hirsch, J. Women and alcoholism. In W. C. Bier, ed., *Alcoholism and Narcotics.* New York: Fordham University Press, 1962.

Kinsey, B. A. Psychological factors in alcoholic women from a state hospital sample. *American Journal of Psychiatry*, 124:1463–1466, 1968.

Knupfer, G. Female drinking patterns. In *Selected Papers Presented at the Fifteenth Annual Meeting of the North American Association of Alcoholism Programs*. Washington D. C.: NAAAP, 1964, pp. 140–160.

Knupfer, G., and Room, R. Age, sex, and social class as factors in amount of drinking in a metropolitan community. *Social Problems*, 12:224–240, 1964.

Lindbeck, V. L. The woman alcoholic: A review of literature. *International Journal of Addiction*, 7:567–580, 1972.

Lisansky, E. S. Alcoholism in women: Social and psychosocial concomitants. *Quarterly Journal of Studies on Alcohol*, 18:588–623, 1957.

MacLennon, A., ed. *Women: Their Use of Alcohol and Other Legal Drugs*. Toronto: Addiction Research Foundation of Ontario, 1976.

Mann, M. Another view of women alcoholics. *Proceedings, First Annual Alcoholism Conference of the National Institute of Alcohol Abuse and Alcoholism*. HEW Publication No. (NIH) 74-675, 1973.

Parker, F. B. Sex-role adjustment in women alcoholics. *Quarterly Journal of Studies on Alcohol*, 33:647–657, 1972.

Pollmer, E. *Alcoholic Personalities*. New York: Exposition Press, 1955.

Rathod, N. H., and Thomson, I. C. Women alcoholics: A clinical study. *Quarterly Journal of Studies on Alcohol*, 32:942–952, 1971.

Sandmaier, M. Women helping women: Opening the door to treatment. *Alcohol Health and Research World*, 2(1):17–23, 1977.

Schuckit, M. The alcoholic woman: A literature review. *Psychiatry in Medicine*, 3(1):37–43, 1972.

Schuckit, M. Depression and alcoholism in women. *Proceedings, First Annual Conference of the National Institute of Alcohol Abuse and Alcoholism*. HEW Publication No. (NIH) 74-675, 1973.

Sherfy, M. J. Psychopathology and character structure in chronic alcoholism. In O. Diethelm, ed., *Etiology of Chronic Alcoholism*. Springfield, Ill.: Thomas, 1955.

Wilsnack, S. C. Femininity by the bottle. *Psychology Today*, 6(11):39–102, 1973a.

Wilsnack, S. C. The needs of the female drinker: Dependency, power, or what? *Proceedings, First Annual Alcoholism Conference of the National Institute of Alcohol Abuse and Alcoholism*. HEW Publication No. (NIH) 74-675, 1973b.

Winokur, G., and Clayton, P. J. Family history studies, IV: Comparison of male and female alcoholics. *Quarterly Journal of Studies on Alcohol*, 29:885–891, 1968.

Wood, H. P., and Duffy, E. L. Psychological factors in alcoholic women. *American Journal of Psychiatry*, 123:341–345, 1966.

15

HYPEROBESITY AS INDIRECT SELF-DESTRUCTIVE BEHAVIOR

CHRISTOPHER V. ROWLAND, JR.

Attempting a scientific definition of hyperobesity would be somewhat like attempting a scientific definition of sexual promiscuity. How much is too much, with whom, for whom, and where, would be broad generalizations indeed. Kilograms, actuarial statistics, and skin-caliper measurements can be useful and interesting in a general sense, like frequency and type of sexual activity, but do not help us much in a medical definition of disease in a given person. A Sumo wrestler who was unable to attain 300 pounds could be as much out of a job as a fashion model who could not remain at 100 pounds. Similarly, a diabetic person could be under excellent control at 150 pounds, but out of control at 20 pounds lighter, or heavier, with abrupt dietary changes.

Yet given an individual person, placed and understood in the context of his times, society, cultural background, occupation, family and friends, and his own idea of himself, it is relatively easy for another person, medically trained or not, to say that so-and-so is obese or, worse yet, hyperobese. In fact, the person has usually long ago made the painful diagnosis for himself.

There are rare cases of hyperobesity secondary to thyroid or other endocrine defects that can be fairly readily diagnosed and treated. There are probably also many more metabolic gut-absorption and lipid-storage disturbances than are currently definable by biochemical measurements. Whatever these disturbances may eventually turn out to be, the great majority of hyperobese people remain the victims of too great calorie intake and too little calorie expenditure. In a sense, one is in the same position that Freud was in seventy years ago, when the hope of discovering the biological substrate of mental illness was a promise and not a reality, and the clinician is left working in a more personal, psychological way with the patient.

Overeating and inactivity, then, are certainly the twin cor-
nerstones of hyperobesity, and are addictive and interrelated in a
profound and self-destructive way. Not that the hyperobese person
intends pain and suffering for himself in any direct way; in fact, to
the contrary, he tends to seek reduction of tension and avoidance of
conflict and physical discomfort. The fairly obvious damaging
effects on body and person are secondary: cardiovascular disease,
diabetes mellitus, back and joint problems, hypertension, job
discrimination, social and sexual limitations, fatigue, respiratory
distress, and an endless list of other woes.

Hilde Bruch was probably one of the first workers in the area of
eating disorders to point out the adaptive nature of overeating and
obesity, in her study of New York families during the late 1930's, a
time when immigration and economic depression put enormous
strains on family structure:

> There is also a great need to appease anxiety and tension, and
> food may gain inordinate importance. To many mothers, the
> offering of food is their way of expressing their affection and
> devotion and of appeasing their anxiety and guilt about the
> child. The child seems to increase his demands as his needs for
> gratification and security in other areas remain unfulfilled.
> [Bruch and Touraine, 1940, p. 204]

The primitive but totally basic value of food on the table and fat
babies to families that had been through starvation and massacre
can become an enormous external, then internalized, force. The
familial behavior was surely addictive in that it was compulsively
performed at least thrice per day, and the aim was to preserve, not
destroy, the self. It might be noted here that the person with an
eating disorder faces unique problems, not shared by those with
other addictions. Whether he overeats or addictively starves
(anorexia nervosa) (Rowland, 1968, 1970), he must still face the
feared and loved stimulus on a regular basis. In contrast, the alcohol, drug, or skydiving addict can totally abstain, and use such de-
fences as repression, denial, and isolation to control behavior. Such
daily contact with the addictive stimulus has special implications
for treatment programs. Alcoholics Anonymous can usefully encourage drinkers to live without alcohol, but hyperobese people
must live within their addiction.

The "conceptual confusion" (Bruch, 1961) found in this group of
patients adds further to the dilemma. They have great difficulty in
perceiving, sorting out, and appropriately responding to internal
stimuli. For instance, the urge to be with another person might be

confused with the urge to eat with another person. An example from my own practice is a fifty-six-year-old man whose massive obesity began at age six, following a prolonged period of hospitalization and separation from his family for a severe burn. The hospital staff had learned to "silence" his loneliness and pain with snacks—and he continued to do this for himself over the next fifty years. In the course of a long period of psychotherapy, he was able to appreciate that what he felt in the late evening was a return to his childhood anxiety and pain—added to a fairly lonely adult life. He then began to separate these feelings from physical hunger and to gratify them more appropriately.

A second aspect of this man's case is of interest here—his markedly reduced physical activity. In spite of his 400-pound frame, he could easily slip into the waiting room and seat himself without my hearing him from the office. He could slide into, or out of, a chair with no wasted motion, and exhibited minimal bodily movement during the hour. He especially loved to be quiet and to think or read, and recalled with special fondness evenings spent studying in the library during law school. His childhood in a tough Irish neighborhood was remarkably free of physical conflict and athletic competition, and his wartime service sounded quite peaceful.

In discussing the problem of anxiety, Freud (1926/1959, pp. 88–89) in fact linked in his own mind these two activities in relation to symptom formation and inhibition:

(b) The function of nutrition is most frequently disturbed by a disinclination to eat, brought about by a withdrawal of libido. An increase in the desire to eat is also a not uncommon thing. The compulsion to eat is attributed to a fear of starving; but this is a subject which has been but little studied. The symptom of vomiting is known to us as a hysterical defence against eating. Refusal to eat owing to anxiety is a concomitant of psychotic states (delusions of being poisoned).

(c) In some neurotic conditions locomotion is inhibited by a disinclination to walk or a weakness in walking. In hysteria there will be a paralysis of the motor apparatus, or this one special function of the apparatus will be abolished (abasia). Especially characteristic are the increased difficulties that appear in locomotion owing to the introduction of certain stipulations whose non-observance results in anxiety (phobia).

Both eating and physical activity can be conceived of as "autonomous ego functions" as described by Hartman, Kris, and Loewenstein (1946). Both, when functioning at their most mature level, are adaptive, preservative, and gratifying to the individual and species. However, when they are invaded from below by raw instinctual pressures or distorted from above by neurotic superego guilt, maladaptive identifications, or primitive idealizations, or by a sudden increase of force from the external world, these ego functions lose their normal usefulness. To use Freud's model for regression—an army in retreat—these two ego functions fall backwards, become disorganized, and begin to lose contact with headquarters. A declining blood sugar level no longer signals the cerebral cortex to initiate a search for food; a nice day no longer causes a search for the tennis racquet. This regressive perceptual disorganization allows other signals of instinctual need to be picked up and responded to inappropriately. Urges for sexual closeness, emotional intimacy, sleep, intellectual activity, privacy, expression of rage or anger, etc., pour in and are not sorted out. "Cue eating" as described by Schachter (1968) is a good example of this problem. The person responds not to physiological hunger but to the presence of roast beef sandwiches, the time on the clock, the appearance of food, the smell of food, even the images evoked by reading a menu.

The problem of ego regression is one encountered in other areas of psychopathology and, in fact, is part of everyday life. A given person can perform a certain task considerably better at 9 A.M. than at 6 P.M., when the forces of fatigue, hunger, boredom, sleepiness, etc., make him yearn for more immediate gratification. The global and persistent regression found in chronic schizophrenia, and certain character neuroses, tends to leave the person at the mercy of encroaching external forces and unable to assert himself in his own behalf. Freud (1918/1955), and Blum (1974) pointed out the Wolf Man's near total dependence on other people, even to the point of requiring an assistant to dress him. More dramatic ego regression and reversal can be seen in traumatic neuroses, postoperative pyschosis, etc.

The matter of symptom choice is complicated beyond understanding, but Hilde Bruch's (1957, 1973) concept of coercive parenting is clinically useful in understanding obesity. She describes two styles of child rearing; in the healthier one, there is a relaxed, empathetic parent (usually the mother) who is able to perceive, process, and respond to the infant's needs appropriately. There is also an infant who is able to transmit need signals of sufficient strength to be picked up by the parent. For example, it is a clinical question whether autistic children can evoke maternal response. In the happy situation where mother and child mesh, the mother can encourage the child to appreciate and act on his own needs in a maturing and independent direction. This begins with the earliest feeding interaction and extends through late adolescence. The smoothness of this path depends on many factors, including an "average expectable" environment, paternal and sibling relationships, state of health, losses through death or separation, and so on.

In the adult with an eating disorder, a somewhat coercive and rigid experience with his parents is a frequently encountered piece of history. He had enough to eat when and at what time someone else said so, wore what someone else wanted, and went to bed when it was convenient. Household rules are important in these families, and there seems to have been too little "give" to allow the child an opportunity to work out his own way.

The result tends to be a person who is "field dependent" (Rowland, 1972), who is too other-directed, who responds too strongly to signals from other people and things. And it is here that indirect self-destructiveness makes its mark. If left to their own devices, people seem to have some sense of what is best for them, a sort of ego adaptiveness. Under the aegis of "causes," however, incredibly destructive situations can arise. The Spanish Inquisition, Nazi Germany, the Vietnamese War are examples of rampant patriotism on a national scale. Fierce family loyalty by a victimized member can perpetuate his own illness, as can rigid adherence to his own superego or ego ideals. Various kinds of risk-taking or thrill-seeking (Balint, 1959) behavior can also be understood in this way: a person who jumps motorcycles over cars could be seeking prestige, money, relief of guilt feelings, etc., all of which are placed ahead of his own physical intactness. He does not want to break a leg, but this may be a reasonable price to pay to keep his self-esteem intact. Violent crime, asceticism, martyrdom, and gambling could be viewed in a similar way. So could the anorexia nervosa patient who, maintaining herself at a just-viable weight, literally puts her life on the line for the sake of her independence (Blitzer et al., 1961).

What, then, can one say about the treatment of people with hyperobesity? Stunkard (1957; Stunkard and McLaren-Hume, 1959), Bruch (1973), and many others have attested to the futility of simple diet-and-exercise programs for patients with a true eating disorder. Nor do these patients easily lend themselves to classical psychoanalytic treatment, particularly in the early stages of therapy. There is too great a need for emotional contact with the other person, for some direct assistance in sorting out feelings, and for avoiding the deeper regression associated with analysis. The method and manner of treatment must also mesh with an assessment of the patient's overall diagnostic picture. Quite psychologically healthy people can be quite obese—where the obesity is more in keeping with familial identification, culture, occupation, etc. Here a more analytic mode of analysis itself may be appropriate. If a concurrent or underlying schizophrenia is present (Federn, 1947), treatment must proceed more gingerly, and adjunctive measures, including antipsychotic medication, may be useful. In this group, what is practical and wanted by the patient—including no treatment—must receive heightened consideration.

One can use Elizabeth Zetzel's (1970) model of therapeutic outcome in considering this group of people. Just as no one is entirely freed of anxiety or depression by analytic treatment, so no one with an eating disorder is finally "cured." However, an increased capacity to experience, differentiate, and bear painful affect and to use insight constructively can make an enormous difference in a person's life. The ego is freed to function in a more self-preservative, self-interested fashion, which can include reduction to a more reasonable weight level.

Here, perhaps, two case histories can serve as working models. Although neither patient was massively obese, and thus both were possibly less difficult to treat, the basic psychodynamics are there and are fairly easy to follow. The first patient, a fifty-two-year-old French Protestant professor of mathematics, was self-referred via his surgeon for consultation about weight loss. He had had a myocardial infarction fifteen years previously, and a grafting of an aortic aneurysm three years previously. His physicians and the patient all agreed that careful diet control, weight loss (from 250 pounds), and an adhered-to exercise program would be most helpful to him. He had become depressed six months before the infarction, during which time his wife's carcinoma was reaching a terminal phase and he was led to abandon long-held career ambitions. This situation clearly brought back a drawn-out, painful childhood situation; his mother died suddenly when he was six, leaving him in the care of an indifferent and sometimes cruel father and various begrudging relatives. His next period of security came in late adolescence when he was an infantryman in World War II. Here he was seen as competent, was fed regularly and copiously, and for the first time knew what the rules were. After the war his large food intake and suddenly reduced physical activity shot his weight from a lean 180 pounds to 250 pounds, where it more or less remained. Since his mother's death, he had responded to an often demanding and often cruel environment by trying to be "good."

Being good as a child was most tangibly rewarded in school, where he was an excellent student and was praised by his teachers. However, intellectual achievement was not a value of his family and peers and served to further his isolation. He was known as "four eyes" among his schoolmates, and as "nigger lips" at home. Although he is now a tall, rather distinguished-looking and attractive man, he matured late (about seventeen years) and was, in fact, the smallest male in his class. His body image throughout much of his adult life was that of a scrawny, ugly, preadolescent boy who was weak and unathletic.

Increasingly, in college and graduate school, he was rewarded for academic attainment, and this trend continued in his work life. He produced well, was promoted, had children, had very little time for himself, and looked forward to a major position in his firm. At this point the position was available, but it necessitated a move across the country—away from his wife's physician, whom they both erroneously believed was keeping her alive. He did not make the move, had the infarction, was passed over for promotion, and his wife died anyway. His long-standing depression ensued, with his weight remaining at 250 pounds in spite of efforts to reduce it. A disastrous remarriage to a paranoid woman came next, a divorce, and several liaisons with women in which he played a decidedly masochistic role. He seemed to respond to women as he did to food; if she was there, he must have her, even if the outcome was to his own detriment. He had even had a similar experience in a previous period of psychotherapy. The therapist was of some help to him initially, in getting him out of his second marriage, but then clearly lost interest in him, becoming bored and distracted, even reading office mail during therapy sessions. Here again the patient felt lucky that anyone would even half-heartedly listen to him, and continued long after he should have stopped.

In my experience with him, he proved to be an interesting and engaging (albeit depressed) person, who made fairly rapid progress during a year and a half of weekly visits. His long-standing depression cleared fairly abruptly after about a year, after which he was able to get on top of his diet and lose 60 pounds. He ended his relationship with a semialcoholic woman who was causing him considerable financial and physical grief and began seeing a woman whom he considered more his equal and with whom he could really have fun. His job became much more interesting to him for the first time in fifteen years, and he began pulling his personal affairs together. I think it is important to note here that this weight loss and other gains came not from an act of will (of which he has always had an abundance), but from an increased capacity to perceive and act on his own inner promptings in a constructive way.

The second case is that of a thirty-year-old woman who came for analysis because of depression. The pervasive, but not paralyzing, depresssion had occurred in the context of the disintegration of her marriage of five years. She had an eating disorder that went back to childhood, characterized by weight increases of twenty to fifty pounds, followed by periods of strenuous dieting, regaining the weight, more dieting, etc. Whether starting a new diet or breaking an old one, weight and diet had become such a frustrating obsession with her that she sounded more like an anorexia nervosa patient— but without the cachexia.

She was a physician herself and had married another physician during medical school. When they first met, he had seemed to her to be a retiring, gentle person with a small-boy wistfulness about him that greatly appealed to her. In spite of her own enormous work schedule, she immediately began to mother him, and by the third year of marriage he had blossomed into a genuine narcissist. After completing his own training, he began openly to have affairs, worked on only a part-time basis, and behaved in a remarkably passive, critical way at home. During the second year of analysis, as she became more assertive, he left the marriage to become a sort of itinerant guru.

Her own father (also a physician) had created a notably deprived family setting in the midst of plenty. His father had died in his early forties of a myocardial infarction, and the patient's father became obsessed with the fear that he himself would "die young" while in his early twenties. Accordingly, he placed himself, his rather passive wife, and all the children on a strict low-cholesterol diet and kept the family rigidly controlled, weight-conscious, and fearful. His tyranny extended to all areas of family life, including money, strict dress codes, school performance, etc. However, males were treated differently; the father could indulge in boats and gem collections, and the son could smoke pot and have girls in his room. For the girls, promised reward could be forgotten; for example, the patient was given a sports car at graduation, but it was an old one that wouldn't run. The patient's mother had experienced considerable maternal deprivation herself and turned to her husband for mothering. She was unable to give much emotional support to the patient and was too loyal to her husband to attempt to block his eccentric behavior toward the daughters.

Treating herself with forbidden foods came to be both a way of mothering herself and of rebelling against her father. He seemed to be most interested in her when she received good grades in school or accomplished projects at home, and her life became an endless stream of accomplishments from the first grade onward. Since her father's interest was a sometime thing, she learned to reward herself with food in return for overworking. A secondary gain in becoming fat was that he would at least be interested enough to harass her for that, and give her rewards for losing weight (so many dollars per pound, maybe). This struggle became internalized and continued pretty much unchanged after she left home for college. Her many successes in the outside world did little to change her own poor opinion of herself, and she continued to meet and master all challenges with total disregard of the price she was paying.

The patient had been raised to believe that marriage was "forever" and that it was primarily the woman's job to make it work. Her husband had, on paper, all the prerequisites, and she took the failure of the marriage as her own fault, feeling that she had totally failed in her father's eyes. A good deal of the analysis was focused on what she actually felt, saw, and experienced in specific situations. Her loyalty to people was overwhelming, and she could distort fairly malicious behavior into something she could understand or accept. Dreams, parapraxes, food binges, or periods of bleak despair tended to follow such situations and indicated her real sense of outrage. As the analysis moved along, she began to make less masochistic choices in relationships and to demand more of a quid pro quo for services rendered. Her obsession with weight and food intake was not much focused on until late in the analysis (about the end of the third year) and began to lessen after she became more aware of other feelings. She could then talk fairly comfortably about such matters, but still maintained a fairly high weight at the end of the analysis. Her depression had long since cleared, and she was generally moving in a more self-assertive, independent direction. The patient returned a year later for a brief period of psychotherapy related to new directions in her work life. During the year, she had lost forty pounds, and she looked remarkably different.

In summary, both patients presented an eating disorder intertwined with symptomatic clinical depression, set in a background of masochistic and obsessional character trends. They represent a middle range of patients with eating disorders, showing neither the more schizophrenic illness found in some nor the symptomatic neurosis in a fairly healthy character structure found in others. Both patients were able to move from a masochistic, indirectly self-destructive position—in terms of both their obesity and their general life-style—toward a stronger, more adaptive mode. They became less vulnerable to regression and childhood pressures and better able to react to current realities.

Some further comments can be made at this juncture, in terms of Farberow's concept of indirect self-destructive behavior (ISDB) as opposed to more direct self-destructive behavior (DSDB). The three patients presented in this chapter were distinctly nonsuicidal and relatively unaware of self-destructive trends in themselves at the initial consultation. They were aware of depressive episodes and affect, but tended to use activity and denial to ward off depression and the return to awareness of painful childhood memories. As treatment progressed, the patients tended to feel worse, were more aware of painful, internal conflict, and were more horrified at where their behavior led them. A vignette from another patient will illustrate this point. This man was massively obese, lived in a fifteenth-floor apartment, and for some years had enjoyed eating dinner while looking at his splendid view of the city. During the second year of psychotherapy, he began to have dreams of killing himself in his car and then an unequivocal impulse to hurl himself from his dining-room window. In a sense, his ISDB was converted to DSDB, as there was a stripping away of denial and projection and a heightened awareness of internal conflict.

REFERENCES _____

Balint, M. *Thrills and Regression*. London: Hogarth, 1959.

Blitzer, J. N., Rollins, N., and Blackwell, A. Children who starve themselves—anorexia nervosa. *Psychosomatic Medicine*, 23:368–383, 1961.

Blum, H. P. The borderline childhood of the Wolf Man. *Journal of the American Psychoanalytic Association*, 22:721–743, 1974.

Bruch, H. *The Importance of Overweight* [1st ed.] New York: Norton, 1957.

Bruch, H. Conceptual confusion in eating disorders. *Journal of Nervous and Mental Disease*, 133:46–54, 1961.

Bruch, H. *Eating Disorders: Obesity, Anorexia Nervosa, and the Person Within*. New York: Basic Books, 1973.

Bruch, H., and Touraine, G. Obesity in childhood, V: The family frame of obese children. *Psychosomatic Medicine*, 2:141–206, 1940.

Federn, P. Principles of psychotherapy in latent schizophrenia. *American Journal of Psychotherapy*, 2:129–144, 1947.

Freud, S. From the history of an infantile neurosis. *Standard Edition*, 17. London: Hogarth, 1955. (Originally published, 1918.)

Freud, S. Inhibitions, symptoms and anxiety. *Standard Edition*, 20. London: Hogarth, 1959. (Originally published, 1926.)

Hartmann, H., Kris, E., and Loewenstein, R. M. Comments on the formation of psychic structure. *The Psychoanalytic Study of the Child*, 2:11–38, 1946.

Rowland, C. V., Jr. Psychotherapy of six hyperobese adults during total starvation. *Archives of General Psychiatry*, 18:541, 1968.

Rowland, C. V., Jr., ed. Anorexia nervosa: A survey of the literature and review of 30 cases. *International Psychiatric Clinics*, 7:37–137, 1970.

Rowland, C. V., Jr. Diagnosis and treatment of anorexic states. *Postgraduate Medicine*, 51:159–162, 1972.

Schachter, S. Obesity and eating. *Science*, 161:751–756, 1968.

Stunkard, A. J. The dieting depression. *American Journal of Medicine*, 23:77, 1957.

Stunkard, A. J., and McLaren-Hume, M. The results of treatment for obesity: A review of the literature and report of a series. *Archives of Internal Medicine*, 103:79, 1959.

Zetzel, E. R. Anxiety and the capacity to bear it. In *The Capacity for Emotional Growth*. New York: International Universities Press, 1970, pp. 35–52.

16

CIGARETTE SMOKING AS INDIRECT SELF-DESTRUCTIVE BEHAVIOR

EDWARD LICHTENSTEIN AND DOUGLAS A. BERNSTEIN

The aim of this paper is to consider the degree to which cigarette smoking can be construed as indirect self-destructive behavior (ISDB). Our inquiry and analysis must be speculative since ISDB is a relatively new, not clearly defined construct for which adequate measurement procedures have yet to be developed. There are no direct tests of the relationship between ISDB and cigarette smoking, but there are relevant conceptual dimensions, and a good deal of data bear indirectly on the question. We shall begin by describing some of the parameters and characteristics of cigarette smoking in the United States today, after which we will attempt to clarify the meaning of ISDB and offer some alternative conceptions. This material will provide the basis for our analysis of the relationship between ISDB and cigarette smoking.

PARAMETERS OF CIGARETTE SMOKING

About 40 percent of the adult American population regularly smoke cigarettes (U.S. Public Health Service, 1976). Nearly all smokers take up the habit in adolescence and most continue to smoke for the rest of their lives (Russell, 1971). Overall, cigarette use is more prevalent among adult men than adult women (39 percent versus 29 percent, USPHS, 1977), but in recent years the proportion of males who smoke has been dropping while smoking among females, especially those in their teens, has been on the rise (USPHS, 1976). The portability and pervasiveness of cigarettes in our society allows smoking to occur almost anywhere and, except where expressly prohibited by law (as in most theaters) or custom (as in most places of worship), it seems to take place everywhere. Of all the behaviors considered in this volume, cigarette smoking is engaged in by the most people and occurs in the largest number of situations. Although more adults use alcohol than cigarettes, the number of alcohol *abusers*, though certainly and tragically large, is far smaller than the number of tobacco abusers. Moderate use of alcohol (social drinking) does not adversely affect the body, but the moderate or "social" smoking (at least ten to twenty cigarettes a day) engaged in by the vast majority of consumers does have health consequences.

Medical evidence concerning the deleterious health consequences of habitual cigarette smoking has been accumulating since the early 1960s (Department of Health, Education, and Welfare, 1976). Today, cigarette smoking is firmly established as the primary cause of lung cancer. Coronary heart disease is the most important single cause of excess mortality among cigarette smokers. And, compared to nonsmokers, cigarette smokers have an increased incidence of respiratory diseases (such as emphysema), the major causes of both permanent and temporary disability in the United States. There is suggestive evidence linking smoking to several other diseases, and it also appears to influence the outcome of pregnancy (DHEW, 1976).

It is also apparent that the risk of developing many serious diseases is reduced by the cessation of smoking (Schumann, 1971; DHEW, 1976). These data, as well as figures concerning work days missed and the possible effects of smoking on unborn children, have led the World Health Organization (1975) to conclude that smoking-related diseases are the major cause of disability and premature death in developed countries and that the control of smoking could do more to prolong life and improve health than any other single action in the whole field of preventive medicine.

Although the overwhelming majority of the scientific and medical communities would agree with these conclusions, dissenting views encourage some smokers to believe that the adverse effects of their habit have not been conclusively demonstrated. The contradictory statements sometimes made by various scientists, medical authorities, and tobacco industry representatives, together with the fact that *most* tobacco users (though at greatly elevated risk) will not actually suffer from serious diseases, combine to create in many smokers the view that cigarettes are risky in a probabilistic sense, the odds being similar to those associated with driving a car. This view is reflected in society's, and the federal government's, clearly ambivalent attitude toward cigarette smoking. On the one hand, the government insists that cigarette manufacturers print a health warning on every cigarette pack and funds a good deal of research intended to explicate the causes, consequences, prevention, and cessation of smoking. For every dollar spent in this way, however, the same government pours many more into subsidies for tobacco growers.

Concern over the effects of "passive smoking" on nonsmokers who must inhale smokers' sidestream and expired smoke in inadequately ventilated places has highlighted another dimension of societal ambivalence toward cigarettes. The desire to protect pregnant women, persons with chronic respiratory or cardiovascular diseases, and anyone else who simply prefers not to endure oxygen deprivation and local irritation of the eyes or nasal mucosa, has prompted the appearance of "no smoking" ordinances which cover an increasing number of locales. In addition, establishment of "no smoking" areas within restaurants and other places is becoming commonplace. Civil libertarians remind us, however, that it is possible to go too far in this direction. In spite of the danger smokers pose (mainly to themselves), it is argued that they must not be treated in a discriminatory fashion and that their rights, as well as those of nonsmokers, must be kept in mind. Nevertheless, the increasing intolerance of smokers by people and ordinances has created a source of friction in families, social gatherings, work groups, and even random interactions among strangers in public places.

PHASES OF THE HABIT: INITIATION, MAINTENANCE, CESSATION

In discussing the cigarette-smoking habit, three phases must be considered. These are initiation, maintenance, and cessation (if the latter occurs). Both research and theory suggest that different social, psychological, and physiological processes are involved at each stage (Dunn, 1973), and these distinctions must be considered in analyzing the possible role of ISDB in smoking.

As noted above, most people learn to smoke relatively early in life, usually before they are twenty. Initiation of smoking behavior is largely a function of psychosocial factors such as curiosity or wishes to experiment, rebel, conform to peer values, and appear more "grown-up." Once a young person gets past the initial clumsiness and unpleasantness of smoking and develops some skill in controlling inhalation, physiological factors become a powerful supplementary factor in maintaining the habit. Nicotine has been shown to be a potent reinforcer in both animals and humans, and there is much converging evidence to support the conclustion that it serves as a primary or unlearned reinforcer of smoking (Russell, 1976). Each drag of the cigarette is thus rewarded by another dose of nicotine. Recent studies have clearly demonstrated that smokers regulate both the number of cigarettes and the puff rate in order to control nicotine dosage and will not smoke nicotineless cigarettes (Russell, 1976). Nicotine is delivered to the brain more efficiently through inhalation of tobacco smoke than through oral ingestion or even direct injection. This may account, in part at least, for the failure of nicotine-bearing chewing gum to provide an adequate substitute for smoking (Russell et al., 1976).

Cessation of smoking, like its initiation, seems to be largely a function of psychosocial variables. Concerns about health, the appearance of physical symptoms, the cost of cigarettes, social pressure, discomfort over dependence, and the wish to provide a good model for children or others may all motivate attempts to stop smoking (Danaher and Lichtenstein, 1978). Survey data indicate that 71 percent of smokers acknowledge the general relationship between smoking and disease and that about half of those verbalize a wish to stop smoking (Gallup Opinion Index, 1974). Yet most of them continue to smoke, and would-be quitters are usually unsuccessful. Among those who participate in organized smoking cessation programs, only about 20 percent remain abstinent for at least one year (Bernstein, 1969; Bernstein and McAlister, 1976; Bernstein and Glasgow, in press; Hunt and Bespalec, 1974; Lichtenstein and Danaher, 1976). Scant information is available on the outcome for those who try to quit on their own, but there is little reason to believe that they are more successful.

INTRANSIGENCE OF CIGARETTE SMOKING

Why is it so difficult to stop smoking? One possible reason is that smoking represents a form of ISDB whose motivation is too strong and firmly rooted to be overcome by conscious "willpower" or superficial attempts at behavior change. The dependency-producing, unlearned effect of nicotine is a second major factor in the tenacity of the cigarette habit, as already noted.

A third consideration is that smoking is possible under such a wide variety of circumstances and that a number of *learned* reinforcers serve to maintain the habit. Numerous stimulus situations (a cup of coffee, a beer, a cocktail, the end of a meal) in which smoking occurs repeatedly become signals which lead to the experience of an urge or desire to smoke whenever they are encountered. In this way, smoking may become cued and/or reinforced by such things as: the oral, manual, and respiratory manipulations involved in lighting, handling, and puffing a cigarette; the pleasure and relaxation associated with drinking alcohol, finishing a good meal, or having a cup of coffee; the perceived diminution of unpleasant affects (e.g., anxiety, tension, boredom, or fatigue). For some smokers, the combination of primary and learned reinforcers may produce a dependency such that going without a cigarette is highly unpleasant. For them smoking may be further reinforced by the reduction of actual or anticipated "withdrawal symptoms."

Given a sufficiently broad learning history, the same smoker may reach for a cigarette when in relaxed and enjoyable situations, when bored, tense, or upset, or in need of a "lift." No other substance can provide so many kinds of reinforcement, is so readily and cheaply available, and can be used in so many different settings.

Another significant factor in the tenacity of the smoking habit may be the sheer number of learning trials involved. A person smoking 20 cigarettes a day consumes about 7,300 cigarettes a year, and each of these provides an occasion for experiencing one or more of the reinforcers we have described. It is important to note, of course, that not all cigarettes are enjoyable, as smokers with sore throats or respiratory infections or those who light more than their usual number on a given day will testify. It is therefore not unreasonable to suggest that smokers experience reinforcement on a partial schedule, the effect of which undoubtedly contributes to the resistance of their habit to extinction or suppression. Finally, the encouragement and modeling of smoking provided by certain segments of society is another potent anticessation force. The behavior of other smokers as well as advertising by cigarette companies provide constant reminders to continue (or initiate) smoking.

A major implication of this analysis is that the initiation, maintenance, and intransigence of cigarette smoking can be readily understood without resorting to ISDB as an explanatory construct: adolescents' social experimentation and risk-taking activities (e.g., tobacco, alcohol, sex, psychoactive drugs) are most plausibly viewed as a function of rebelliousness, peer pressure, and striving to emulate valued models, as noted above. The sheer frequency and ubiquitousness of smoking undermines the hypothesis that all smoking is influenced by ISDB, unless one assumes that ISDB is that prevalent or frequent. We do not. There are immediate, powerful physiological and psychological cues and rewards for maintaining smoking, whereas its negative consequences are distant in time and probabilistic in nature.

The challenge for ISDB theorists is to demonstrate that the construct can illuminate or explicate aspects of the development, maintenance, and modification of smoking behavior in ways which are more logical and parsimonious than those already available.

INDIRECT SELF-DESTRUCTIVE BEHAVIOR: WHAT IS IT AND HOW DO WE KNOW IT'S THERE? _____

As Litman suggests in his chapter, self-destructive behavior may be temporary or crisis-engendered (direct), or a chronic, habitual pattern of behavior bound up with the person's identity or usual functioning (indirect). When it does reflect self-destructive tendencies, cigarette smoking clearly appears to be of the latter sort. Farberow (1977) has described another dimension of ISDB: the degree of subjectively perceived riskiness of the behavior. Smokers vary considerably in their perception of riskiness, depending on their beliefs about health consequences and their physical condition.

Labeling self-destructive behavior as "indirect" implies that the underlying intent or consequences may be unknown to the actor or not acknowledged openly to him/herself or others. It is important, therefore, to consider the issue of how one objectively determines that the harmful nature of a behavior is or is not known to, or acknowledged by, the actor (Farberow, 1977). It is true, for example, that some smokers are probably uninformed about the harmful or risky implications of their smoking (Fishbein, 1977); but if one chooses to assume that such unawareness is defensive or otherwise motivated (and thus perhaps indicative of ISDB), one should make that assumption, and the bases for it, quite explicit.

It is important also to distinguish between knowledge that smoking may, *in a probabilistic sense*, be self-destructive and that smoking clearly *is* hastening one's own death. Asymptomatic smokers are taking risks with the odds clearly in their favor. They are in a position similar to that of the person who does not wear a seat belt or engages in sport parachuting: "Somebody who does what I do will experience negative consequences, but chances are it won't be me." In such cases, ISDB appears, at best, to be a value-laden and superfluous label for otherwise explainable observed behavior.

Consider, on the other hand, the person who has emphysema, diagnosed heart disease, or chronic obstructive pulmonary symptoms and who continues to smoke. From anyone's point of view, it is virtually certain that for such a person smoking is self-destructive. The degree of certainty varies with the specific condition (e.g., it is somewhat less for coronary disease than for emphysema), but clearly people with symptoms cannot use the rationalizations or other defenses that the asymptomatic smoker still has available. If ISDB has relevance for smoking, it appears to be strongest in these cases.

One final conceptual issue must be considered. Do we define behavior as self-destructive on the basis of the act itself or must we have some independent evidence of a suicidal or self-destructive urge? Suppose, for example, a man is seen falling from the Golden Gate Bridge. Is this sufficient evidence of suicide? Probably not. One would want additional information about suicidal talk, despondency, drug use, social isolation, or personal misfortune. Murder would also have to be ruled out. We should apply a similar kind of logic to the "diagnosis" of ISDB. If we do not, the risk of circular reasoning is obvious: "Smoker X is engaging in indirect self-destructive behavior." "How do we know he has self-destructive tendencies?" "Because he smokes." The long struggle to break free of a similar cycle in the conceptualization of "mental illness" (e.g., Ullman and Krasner, 1975) has made many clinicians wary of this kind of thinking.

RELATION OF ISDB
TO CIGARETTE SMOKING _____

Our analysis of ISDB accords it the status of a plausible rival hypothesis which must compete with other explanations of smoking behavior. Since the onset and continuation of cigarette smoking are assuredly multidetermined, we can easily entertain several "causes" for each, but the plausibility of any one explanation and the weight assigned to it (in terms of variance accounted for) must be judged with respect to the particular circumstances involved. This orientation requires us to consider information that supports *and* contradicts an ISDB hypothesis, with respect to both smoking in general and individual cases.

To do this, we must search for evidence of a general association between cigarette smoking and other risk-taking or ISD behavior. At the individual level, one must look for clinical or objective evidence of self-destructive tendencies other than cigarette smoking itself. If an emphysemic or Buerger's disease patient says that "it doesn't matter what the hell I do, I've had it anyway," we can accept this as a bit of evidence consistent with the postulation of self-destructive tendencies. But suppose an emphysemic person clearly verbalizes his/her knowledge of the relationship between smoking and the speed with which he/she will succumb to the disease and tries unsuccessfully to stop smoking. Should we say that smoking in this case represents ISDB and invoke covert or unconscious mechanisms, or is it more sensible to suggest that the reinforcing and dependence-producing properties of cigarette smoking accounted for the failure of the person to quit?

Obviously, the ISDB explanation is less parsimonious and more inferential, but might still be useful if it could suggest successful intervention strategies for this (or any other) type of smoker. We suggest that specification of the implications of the ISDB hypothesis for antismoking treatment be given high priority by its proponents. Evaluation of the resulting smoking-modification procedures with persons thought to be engaging in ISDB would provide an excellent arena for examining various aspects of the ISDB hypothesis itself. If ISDB concepts have relevance to particular smokers and to the modification of their smoking behavior, the evidence will be clearly visible against the bleak backdrop of overwhelmingly negative long-term results generated by virtually all other approaches currently available. We turn, therefore, to a consideration of cognitive factors in quitting smoking.

COGNITIVE MECHANISMS IN SMOKING AND QUITTING _____

A cognitive analysis of the decision to keep smoking or attempt to quit is compatible with our social-learning approach. Cognitive analyses of smoking decisions converge on three basic components or beliefs that must be present if a person is seriously to attempt cessation (Lichtenstein and Danaher, 1978). First, the smoker must believe in a personal susceptibility to health risk because of smoking. Second, the smoker must believe that some available action can reduce or eliminate the risk. Third, the smoker must believe that he/she is capable of taking or succeeding in the necessary action.

There is good reason to believe that many smokers do not perceive personal susceptibility. Fishbein (1977) has extensively researched the literature on smoker awareness and beliefs about health risk. He describes three levels of belief:

1. *Awareness.* A person may believe that "the Surgeon General has determined that cigarette smoking is dangerous to health."
2. *General acceptance.* A person may believe that "cigarette smoking is dangerous to health."
3. *Personalized acceptance.* A person may believe that "my cigarette smoking is dangerous to my health."

Fishbein (1977) concludes that there is little data about Level 1 beliefs, but available evidence indicates that many smokers are not well informed at Level 2: "Almost 50% of all current smokers have still not fully accepted [at Level 2] the general, undifferentiated proposition that smoking cigarettes is dangerous to health" (Fishbein, 1977, p. 2). He concludes that there is even less acceptance of linkages between smoking and specific health consequences such as heart disease or emphysema. Although not much is known about personalized acceptance (Level 3), Fishbein notes that it usually (and logically) lags behind general acceptance.

An implication of this reasoning is that there should be good evidence that the smoker acknowledges personal susceptibility before the ISDB construct can be invoked. Even then, ISDB may not always be the best explanation of failure to quit. If the patient (1) believes that it is too late to change, that the damage has been done, (2) is ignorant of the benefits of quitting even after a serious illness has been diagnosed, or (3) despairs of actually quitting (usually on the basis of personal failure), continued smoking could hardly be called ISDB. Careful explanations by a physician or other medical authority and/or the construction of a personalized program of quitting assistance may be enough to bring about abstinence in some cases.

As noted, it is with respect to the patient with a smoking-related illness who understands the benefits of quitting and the implications of continuing to smoke, but chooses to do the latter, that the ISDB construct seems to have most relevance. A crucial question here is whether such persons remain smokers because the strength of their habit makes quitting nearly impossible or because they do not want to quit, a fact which may reflect self-destructive tendencies. This question is not easily answered. Some kind of independent evidence for ISDB tendencies is required. Such evidence may be sought in the patient's case history or in current behavior samples. Prior serious accidents, suicide attempts, verbalizations of despair and hopelessness, the presence of financial, family, or occupational problems and stressors, as well as other "classic" indicators of depression and predictors of suicide, can be assessed. Somewhat more subtle behaviors, such as missing required examinations or treatments, or noncompliance with a medical regimen (e.g., not taking medication, deviation from a prescribed risk-reducing diet), should not be overlooked.

Convergence of two or more indicators of ISDB would strengthen confidence in the utility of the construct for smokers of this type. Farberow and Nehemkis (in press) described such convergence in a group of Buerger's disease patients. Because the patients exhibited several ISDB behaviors, invoking the construct was a plausible step. The search for additional convergent evidence would be facilitated, in turn, by refinement of the ISDB construct such that verbal, behavioral, and physiological indicators were more precisely specified. Since the usefulness of ISDB rests on its construct validity, a theoretical network within which to test it is sorely needed. Until such a network is constructed, ISDB will provide a high-inference method for describing or labeling certain behaviors, but its explanatory or predictive value will remain undetermined.

REFERENCES

Bernstein, D. A. The modification of smoking behavior: An evaluative review. *Psychological Bulletin*, 71:418–440, 1969.

Bernstein, D. A., and Glasgow, R. E. The modification of smoking behavior. In O. F. Pomerleau and J. P. Brady, eds., *Behavioral Medicine: Theory and Practice*. Baltimore, Md.: Williams and Wilkins, in press.

Bernstein, D. A., and McAlister, A. The modification of smoking behavior: Progress and problems. *Addictive Behaviors*, 1:89–102, 1976.

Danaher, B. G., and Lichtenstein, E. *How to Become an Ex-Smoker*. Englewood Cliffs, N.J.: Prentice-Hall, 1978.

Department of Health, Education, and Welfare, Public Health Service. *The Health Consequences of Smoking: A Reference Edition*. Atlanta: Center for Disease Control, 1976.

Dunn, W. L., Jr. Experimental methods and conceptual models as applied to the study of motivation in cigarette smoking. In W. L. Dunn, Jr., *Smoking Behavior: Motives and Incentives*. Washington, D.C.: Winston, 1973.

Farberow, N. L. Response to the distinguished contributions award: Suicide: Doesn't everybody? *The Clinical Psychologist*, 31:16–17, 1977.

Farberow, N. L., and Nehemkis, A. M. Indirect self-destructive behavior in patients with Buerger's disease. *Journal of Personality Assessment*, in press.

Fishbein, M. Consumer beliefs and behavior with respect to cigarette smoking: A critical analysis of the public literature. A report prepared for the Federal Trade Commission, Appendix A, 1977.

Gallup Opinion Index. *Public Puffs On after Ten Years of Warnings*. Report #108, 1974.

Hunt, W. A., and Bespalec, D. A. An evaluation of current methods of modifying smoking behavior. *Journal of Clinical Psychology*, 30:431–438, 1974

Lichtenstein, E., and Danaher, B. G. Modification of smoking behavior: A critical analysis of theory, research, and practice. In M. Hersen et al., eds., *Progress in Behavior Modification*, vol. 3. New York: Academic, 1976, pp. 70–132.

Lichtenstein, E., and Danaher, B. G. What can the physician do to assist the patient to stop smoking? In R. E. Brashear and M. L. Rhodes, eds.,

Chronic Obstructive Lung Disease: Clinical Treatment and Management. St. Louis: Mosby, 1978.

Russell, M. A. H. Cigarette smoking: Natural history of dependence disorder. *British Journal of Medical Psychology.* 44:1–16, 1971.

Russell, M. A. H. Tobacco smoking and nicotine dependence. In R. J. Gibbons, et al., eds., *Research Advances in Alcohol and Drug Problems,* vol. 3. New York: Wiley, 1976, pp. 1–47.

Russell, M. A. H., Wilson, C., Feyerabend, C., and Cole, P. V. Effect of nicotine chewing gum on smoking behavior and as an aid to cigarette withdrawal. *British Medical Journal,* 2:391–395, 1976.

Schumann, L. M. The benefits of cessation of smoking. *Chest,* 59:421–427, 1971.

Ullmann, L. P., and Krasner, L. *A Psychological Approach to Abnormal Behavior.* Englewood Cliffs, N.J.: Prentice-Hall, 1975.

U.S. Public Health Service, Center for Disease Control. *Morbidity and Mortality Weekly Report,* 26(19), 1977.

U.S. Public Health Service. *Adult Use of Tobacco, 1975.* Washington, D.C.: U.S. Government Printing Office, 1976.

World Health Organization. *Smoking and Its Effects on Health: Report of WHO Expert Committee.* Geneva, Switzerland, 1975.

PART FIVE

SELF-MUTILATION, AUTO ACCIDENTS, AND GAMBLING

17

SELF-MUTILATION AS INDIRECT SELF-DESTRUCTIVE BEHAVIOR
"Nothing to Get So Cut Up About . . ."

MICHAEL A. SIMPSON

This time I slashed up my wrist. I crushed a burnt-out light bulb and saved the pieces of glass. But razor blades are better. I cut parallel lines across my arm, avoiding the old scars. I watched myself cutting, not feeling a thing, as if it wasn't really my own arm. My head was full of images of blood and the glass glittered and gleamed. The blood creeping stickily across my skin felt good and real. The blood is me. The cuts are neater than my handwriting. They're not too deep—just deep enough. I'm in control, in an odd way, just when I'd been getting out of control. I'm really alive again, when I'd been feeling so dead. I told them I flushed all the glass down the toilet. I lied. I've got the best bits hidden away. For next time."

DEFINITION

Though rarely described in standard textbooks of psychiatry or psychology (never adequately described) and absent from the sociological literature, self-mutilation is common human behavior (Simpson, 1976). We may define it simply as behavior producing physical injury to the person's own body, regardless of apparent or putative intent. It may involve removing, destroying, maiming, disfiguring, or impairing the appearance or function of some body part or parts.

Such behavior, some of which we must clearly distinguish from the common variety we shall discuss as a form of indirect self-destructive behavior, may be seen in widely differing circumstances. In this chapter we will not discuss in detail either mutilations regarded as culturally unremarkable or trivial (biting of fingernails, cutting hair and nails, or piercing ear-lobes for earrings), or mutilations which are culturally accepted as decorative social conventions (such as scarifications and tattooing) or as part of shared public ritual (in initiations, warfare ceremonies, and genital circumcision, subincision, or introcision) (Montagu, 1946; Battacharyya, 1968; Schechter, 1962). High incidences of self-injurious behavior are reported among subnormal, autistic, schizophrenic, or brain-damaged children and adults (Dehissavoy, 1961; Frankel and Simmons, 1976; Green, 1967, 1968; Shodell and Reiter, 1968)—especially in the form of scratching, biting, or head-banging. A common fault in psychological reviews of the topic, such as those by Bachman (1972) and Carr (1977), has been to draw conclusions based almost entirely on behavioral studies of psychotic or retarded persons—conclusions which cannot and should not be assumed to generalize to the rest of the population. Accordingly, we will consider such studies only where they seem relevant to the more common and general situation.

We should also recognize as largely separate categories two varieties of distinctly direct self-destructive behavior. There are those who cut with highly lethal intent, the "course cutters," as Pao (1969) called them, who seem more likely to be male, older, suffering from a psychotic depression, and to cut once, deeply, and with significant risk to life (Phillips and Muzaffer, 1961; Barter et al., 1968). There are also the overtly schizophrenic who for compelling delusory reasons produce what are often bizarre self-mutilations.

SELF-MUTILATION—THE TYPICAL PROBLEM

The situation in which an emotionally disturbed person cuts himself is very well known in clinical practice. Such acts—often of wrist-slashing, as described in the introductory paragraph—are usually classified as suicide attempts but rarely distinguished appropriately from other varieties of suicidal behavior. Yet although the act may seem overtly self-destructive, the process and motivation are far more complex than is usually recognized. Wrist-cutting is a supremely economical technique whereby a delicate dermal injury can serve multiple psychological functions in the cutter, while stirring up an inordinate amount of attention from others whose outrage and alarm is usually out of all proportion to the scale of the event. Such self-mutilators are almost inevitably very badly handled by the doctors and nurses they encounter. They arouse a strong sense of hopelessness and hostility among such professionals, whose ambivalence may be dramatic as they vacillate between regarding the patient as of high risk and high lethality (and to be curbed and restricted by all means) and as indulging in highly manipulative and frivolous acting out. Typical staff responses usually only encourage further self-mutilation; and indeed, such self-injurious behavior, not uncommon among the community at large, may be far safer and more easily resolved when health professionals are not involved at all.

INCIDENCE

Self-mutilation is seen in emergency rooms, general and psychiatric wards of hospitals, and in general practice; and there are many incidents which are never seen by anyone but the cutter. Studies of incidence are not very satisfactory. Phillips and Muzaffer (1961) described an incidence of 4.3 percent in a group of psychiatric inpatients. Barter et al. (1968), studying suicide attempts in hospitalized adolescents, found that self-inflicted injury accounted for 37.8 percent of attempts, cutting being equally used, proportionately, by boys and girls. Ballinger (1971) found that 3.4 percent of a group of general psychiatric patients (3 percent males and 4 percent females) had injured themselves in the course of a month.

Weissman (1975), surveying all suicide attempters seen at a major medical center, found that 11.7 percent had cut their wrists. This study, which dealt with patients coming to or brought to the emergency room or admitted to the hospital following a self-inflicted cut, is likely to have sampled more serious and suicidally intended cuts than would be found among persons cutting during an admission or those cutting at home and not seeking hospital assistance. This may explain why Weissman, unlike many others, found little difference between cutters and other suicide attempters.

Many cases of self-mutilation are not reported or recorded at all. The wounds are often easily cared for by the patient without help, or may be treated by doctors as accidental, nonintentional, simple lacerations. The true incidence is certainly underestimated in the studies cited so far. Whitehead and his associates (Whitehead et al., 1972, 1973; Johnson et al., 1973, 1975), in an unusually thorough study collating many sources of information within a defined community in Canada, estimated an incidence of self-injury (including suicide, self-poisoning, and self-mutilation) of 730 per 100,000 population annually—a far higher figure than earlier estimates, which varied from 40 to 220 per 100,000 annually. Many cases had not been seen in hospitals. They found a high incidence of previous self-injury (60 percent) among such patients, though their physicians were aware of only 20 percent of such episodes, and only 46 percent of the patients themselves initially reported such previous events. They also found (Johnson et al., 1975) that males who had cut themselves were three times as likely to cut on subsequent self-injuries. It appears that wrist cutters are about as likely to have a history of previous attempts as any other suicide attempter (Weissman, 1975; Clendenin and Murphy, 1971; Simpson, 1975).

High incidences of self-mutilation are seen among prisoners (Reiger, 1971; Panton, 1962; Danto, 1973). In prison, self-cutting is, along with hanging, the favored means of attempting suicide (Beigel and Russel, 1972). This is not simply due to the relative un-availability of other methods, it is also a technique to manipulate one's way into better conditions in the prison hospital or special unit by using the grammar of suicide, in self-mutilatory self-defense to escape severe physical ill-treatment, or as a sort of celebration of humiliation when there is nothing left to attack but oneself. Virkku-nen (1976) compared cutters in prison to noncutters with a similar antisocial personality disorder. He found the cutters more prone to repeated outbursts of rage or fighting, drug abuse and other vari-eties of self-destructive behavior, and tattooing. The cutters seemed to feel especially oppressed by the restricted environment and relative absence of stimuli.

THE TYPICAL CUTTER _____

The stereotype of the cutter, described in many papers, is a young, single woman. Two major studies (Weissman, 1975; Clen-denin and Murphy, 1971) have found them to be no younger, or more likely to be female, than other suicide attempters. Most clinical studies have been based on hospitalized psychiatric patients, and in these groups females have clearly outnumbered males (Pao, 1969; Rosenthal et al., 1972; Nelson and Grunebaum, 1971; Graff and Mallin, 1967; Novotny, 1972). Green (1968) found more girls than boys among his self-mutilating schizophrenic children. Fabian et al. (1973), in a study of self-injury in a psychiatric hospital, may pro-vide some indirect evidence. Women were responsible for 60 per-cent of all cases of self-injury: 72 percent of his category I (superfi-cial attempts, 63 percent of which were by laceration); 77 percent of category II (more serious attempts, 53 percent of which were lacera-tions); and only 30 percent of category III (potentially lethal at-tempts, only 23 percent of which were by cutting).

Clendenin and Murphy (1971), who looked at a population of suicide attempts known to the police, found 11.5 percent were by self-cutting, and that the wrist cutters, compared to the others, were younger, more often single, and more often male (40 percent com-

pared to 28 percent). But in overall numbers, women cutters pre-
dominated 1.5 to 1.

The cutter may have worked in a paramedical or related field
(Grunebaum and Klerman, 1967; Goldwyn et al., 1967). In
McEvedy's series (1963) five out of thirteen, and in Simpson's series
(1975) ten out of twenty-four, were nurses, medical secretaries, or
had strong medical interests or connections. Waldenberg (1972)
found that significantly more cutters had a history of problems at
school and trouble with the police.

The self-mutilator is quite readily recognized and labeled by patients and staff (Crabtree, 1967) and may cling to his deviant identity, having no other as effective. Friedman et al. (1972) described
them as characteristically having "low self-esteem, excessive self-
criticism and intense guilt, and fierce self-denigration," which he
regarded as due to "the presence of a severe, relentless, primitive
superego." They tend to act out against rules and restrictions, often
so as to involve others in the event, and abscond from the hospital or
discharge themselves against medical advice (nine out of twenty-
four in one series absconded repeatedly) (Simpson, 1975).

While cutters seem to be most commonly seen and described in
their teens and twenties, such behavior can occur at almost any age.
In the Gardners' series (1975), the age of their patients ranged from
18 to 56 years, though the mean was 28.8, and the age at their first
cut ranged from 9 to 56 years (with a mean of 23.9).

Novotny (1972) regarded them as having narcissistic infantile
personalities with masochistic features. Many speak of hating their
own bodies, and may have fantasies of bodily mutilation. One wrote
to me: "I had a dream once. I dreamt that a boil on my inner leg
broke open and that an enormous hole was there. I looked in it and
saw the bone, a light beige color, and all the muscle tissue in braid
like walls around the bone. I woke up simply delighted. So *that's*
how it looks!" Another wrote about her cutting in a handwriting that
regressed grossly from neat adult script to infantile scrawl, ending:
"Sometimes I want to cut off my breasts. They've got to be the
ugliest things I've ever seen. And sew up vagina. I'll never use it
anyway. And it STINKS."

DIAGNOSES

That these patients are disturbed and disturbing is very widely
agreed. There isn't much agreement beyond that. A confusing host
of diagnoses have been proposed, most of which fail to help us to
understand the patients or comprehend or manage their problems.
The choice of diagnosis seems to depend both on the physicians'
favored diagnostic "set" and on whichever aspect of the patient they

happen to encounter. The "acting-out" behavior, the theatrical and ritual components of the drama, and the fragments of seductive transference suggest hysteria to some (Grunebaum and Klerman, 1967), psychopathy to others. The incomprehensibility of some of the behavior, the primitive aggressive and sexual fantasies, the withdrawal and depersonalization, lead others to a diagnosis of schizophrenia.

The symptomatology is variable, too. Rosenthal et al. (1972) found that twenty-three of their twenty-four cutters listed depression as their main symptom; sixteen complained of chronic feelings of emptiness rarely mentioned by their controls. In Simpson's study of twenty-four cutters (1975), nine complained of depression as their first or second most serious symptom, twenty-one complained of emptiness and eighteen of tension. What seems most typical, as Grunebaum and Klerman emphasized (1967), is rapidly fluctuating mood swings, from depression to optimism. But these are not prolonged into classical depression, hypomania, or manic-depressive illness, and do not usually respond well to antidepressant medication or to phenothiazine or other tranquilizers. The mood may vary rapidly in the course of a single day. Eleven out of twenty-four cutters in Simpson's study (1975) showed such instability of mood. Other features may include ingestion of sharp objects, self-burning with cigarettes, and breaking windows or furniture. They may go "in and out of psychosis in a split second" (Pao, 1969), showing, at times, perceptual distortions, tenuously formulated and varying delusional systems, and other primary-process experiences. At other times they will be found to be quite free of psychotic features.

Asch (1971) regarded the main problem as a primitive form of depression, anhedonia (Glauber, 1949); Clanon (1965) suggested the term "psychoschizopathic"; and Siomopoulos (1974) classified self-mutilation as an impulse neurosis like kleptomania and pyromania. Schizophrenia and especially borderline states (Mack, 1975) have been favored diagnoses in various published series (Rosenthal et al., 1972; Nelson and Grunebaum, 1971; Graff and Mallin, 1967). Of all the available diagnoses in common use, the borderline syndrome is the most appropriate and most useful (Simpson, 1977).

Self-mutilators show a variety of features suggestive of borderline states (Grinker et al., 1968; Gunderson and Singer, 1975; Kernberg, 1967), including precarious maintenance of object cathexis, episodic anxiety bordering on panic, poor control of impulses with little regard for pain or other possible consequences, and intense but varying affect.

OTHER CHARACTERISTICS OF
SELF-MUTILATORS _____

DRUG AND ALCOHOL ABUSE

Nearly 50 percent of the mutilators in the series described by Simpson (1975), Rosenthal et al. (1972), Novotny (1972), and Waldenberg (1972) used alcohol and drugs in excess, and others have also described the association (Pao, 1969, Graff and Mallin, 1967; Grunebaum and Klerman, 1967). Alcohol is the drug most commonly abused by cutters. Johnson et al. (1975) found that 58 percent of males and 37 percent of females had had at least one drink during the six hours preceding self-injury; many had consumed six or more drinks. The Gardners (1975) did not find a significant difference between cutters and controls in drug or alcohol abuse; but they specifically excluded everyone who had mutilated while affected by alcohol or drugs, which certainly biased their findings. Asch (1971) and Simpson (1976) have commented that hallucinogens are often particularly disturbing and anxiety-provoking for the self-mutilator, by blurring further the already tenuous distinction between self and object which such people experience. Amphetamines are more popular and are described as amplifying sensation and stimulating body awareness.

DYSOREXIA

Substantial dysorectic symptoms may be quite common among self-mutilators, and acts of cutting may be associated in time with binge eating or its associated vomiting. Several investigators have briefly mentioned the association (Novotny, 1972; McEvedy, 1963; Waldenberg, 1972; Asch, 1971; Siomopoulos, 1974). In Simpson's series (1975), 75 percent reported dysorectic symptoms; and in the study by Rosenthal et al. (1972), fifteen out of twenty-four described either compulsive overeating, severe anorexia, or episodes of both, and seven had frequent nausea. Malcove (1933) proposed that there is a relationship between physical mutilation and learning to eat. From the Japanese experience, Y. Nogami (personal communication, 1974) has described binge eating in patients similar to the typical cutter, and 28 percent of his patients had cut themselves. N. Shinosaka (personal communication, 1974) has described similar mutilations in anorexia nervosa. Anorexia nervosa and self-mutilation may have some similar origins, in regard to disturbances of the experience of body image, self-directed aggression, and indirect self-destructive behavior.

SEXUAL IDENTITY AND BEHAVIOR

Self-mutilators show sexual identity problems. In Simpson's series (1975) 66 percent showed substantial disturbance of sexual identification, and 25 percent were at some time actively homosexual or disturbed by homosexual impulses. Pao (1969) emphasized the repugnance his female cutters showed toward their female sexuality and described the male cutters as "pretty boys"; Asch (1971) similarly described effeminacy in male self-mutilators. On psychological tests both sexes showed uncertainty about sexual identity. Rosenthal et al. (1972) found 65 percent of female cutters exhibited greater identification with father than mother (as compared with 25 percent of the control group) and they also differed clearly on the Draw-A-Person Test. The Gardners (1975) found a significantly higher incidence of psychosexual disorder among the mutilators than among the controls, remarking that "as a group they were more likely to be frigid or actively lesbian."

This all-or-nothing quality of the mutilator's sexual behavior may be relatively common. Their promiscuity has been commented on by numerous investigators (Pao, 1969; Simpson, 1975; Graff and Mallin, 1967; Waldenberg, 1972; Asch, 1971), while the absence of sexual experience in others is also clear (Simpson, 1975; Graff and Mallin, 1967).

Rosenthal et al. (1972) have implied a relationship between cutting and menstruation. They reported that 65 percent of their female self-mutilators had a negative, unhappy, disgusted, or frightened reaction to menarche, unlike the control group. Almost half of their mutilators had always had irregular menstrual periods and frequent amenorrhoea, and those with the more abnormal menstrual patterns were more frequent cutters.

It is not clear whether menstruation has any more direct relationship with self-mutilation, which usually does not begin until a year or two after menarche (Pao, 1969). The Rosenthal study (1972) suggested that more than 60 percent of acts of self-mutilation occurred during menstruation, 30 percent in the two days preceding menstruation and 30 percent in the last two days of the period or the first postmenstrual day. Although Crabtree (1967) also described an increased incidence of mutilation during menstruation, and Bettelheim (1962), in his fine study of symbolic wounds, described a girl who cut herself only during menstruation, other studies have found no relation between mutilation and menstruation (Waldenberg, 1972; McEvedy, 1963).

There have been several recent reports of self-mutilation of the female genitalia (French and Nelson, 1972; Goldfield and Glick, 1970; Simpson, 1973; Standage et al., 1974); it has even been suggested that the clinical features of such cases may comprise a discrete syndrome, which Goldney and Simpson (1975) have proposed that we call the "Caenis syndrome."

OTHER PERSONALITY MEASURES

The Gardners (1975) used the Middlesex Hospital Questionnaire (Crown and Crisp, 1966), which measures six common groups of symptoms and traits—Anxiety, Obsessional, Depression, Phobia, Somatic, and Hysteria—and the forty-question section of the Tavistock Inventory (Sandler, 1954) relating to obsessive and compulsive traits. The self-mutilators, as compared with control psychiatric patients, scored insignificantly higher on measures of obsessionality. This may be compared to the findings of McKerracher et al. (1968), who also used the Middlesex Hospital Questionnaire and found that self-mutilators scored significantly higher on obsessional, phobic, and somatic items; the obsessional symptoms provided the best discrimination between subjects and controls. This is intriguing, as McKerracher's patients were a very different sample of mutilators, being criminal subnormal and psychopathic patients in the special hospital at Rampton.

VERBALIZATION

Self-mutilators seem to have difficulty in verbalizing emotions, especially anger, though they may be able to express themselves effectively on other matters. In Simpson's series (1975), 66 percent showed significant difficulties in verbalization, and an improved facility in verbal emotional expression was associated with clinical improvement and cessation of cutting. Graff and Mallin (1967) suggested that their patients had a reduced ability to give and receive verbal communication as a result of early maternal deprivation, often showing behavioral disturbances during the preverbal stages of childhood and later a difficulty in effectively conveying their wants and in accurately understanding what was said to them. They considered that this made the usual verbal psychotherapy unlikely to be helpful, and suggested a special effort to help the patient use words rather than more primitive gestures. Grunebaum and Klerman (1967) also emphasized that the cutter "often does not or cannot verbalize the extent of her tension," adding that "the ability to communicate discomfort is a critical variable in determining whether a slash will occur."

In a study of schizophrenic children, Shodell and Reiter (1968) postulated that the ability to verbalize would help the children to use language instead of physical action to release frustration and tension, and indeed they found that verbal children were significantly less likely to mutilate themselves than nonverbal children.

BACKGROUND AND FAMILY RELATIONSHIPS

Many researchers have described the unsatisfactory nature of the childhood and background of the self-mutilator. Lester (1970, 1972) has stated that suicides typically have had childhood experiences of complete parental deprivation due to divorce or death, whereas self-mutilators more often have experienced partial loss through emotional distancing and inconsistent maternal warmth. In Waldenberg's study (1972), significantly more cutters than controls came from broken homes and had cold and distant mothers. Graff and Mallin (1967) found the typical cutter to have a "cold, domineering mother and a withdrawn, passive father." Grunebaum and Klerman (1967) made similar observations, also commenting that the father was unable to set limits, that the mother commonly acted out herself though setting high standards for the patient, and that open display of aggression was common among the parents. Their patients' conceptions had often been illegitimate or the cause of their parents' marriages; they had frequently been placed in foster homes and felt unwanted and rejected by both parents. Bach-y-Rita (1974), who studied violent prisoners who cut themselves, stressed how commonly they had suffered marked early environmental deprivation, violent families, and cruel parents. Mason and Sponholz (1963), in a study of rhesus monkeys reared in isolation, found a correlation between isolation in childhood and self-mutilating behavior.

Rosenthal et al. (1972) found that 60 percent of their self-mutilating patients had been hospitalized for surgery or serious illness or had had lacerations needing multiple stitches before the age of five, often before eighteen months of age. (None of the control group had a similar history.) Friedman et al. (1972) found a constant underlying fear of abandonment; Pao (1969) and Kafka (1969) found screen memories of early experiences of being abandoned and a lack of maternal handling during infancy; Novotny (1972), Asch (1971), Siomopoulos (1974), Waldenberg (1972), and Vereecken (1965) have made similar observations. R. M. Dorn (personal communication, 1974) has pointed out the similarity between the dreams of some mutilators and those of children who have been abused in childhood.

CHARACTERISTIC FEATURES OF SELF-MUTILATION ————————————————

LETHALITY

It is widely agreed that the act of self-cutting is usually of low lethality (Pao, 1969; Simpson, 1975; Rosenthal et al., 1972; Graff and Mallin, 1967; Novotny, 1972; Grunebaum and Klerman, 1967;

Goldwyn et al., 1967; Asch, 1971; Siomopoulos, 1974; Lester, 1970; Rinzler and Shapiro, 1968). Weissman (1975) found that persons who cut their wrists were rated as having significantly less potential risk to life than other suicide attempters. The Gardners (1975) found that only nine of their twenty-two subjects even mentioned suicide when giving reasons for their behavior, and that they gave this explanation perfunctorily and later made it clear that they were not aiming at self-destruction. Many self-mutilators very specifically deny direct suicidal intent, offering other clear motivations, described below.

THE CUTS

The typical self-mutilator makes multiple delicate, superficial incisions which may heal without noticeable scarring or may leave an intricate network of dozens of fine or coarse scars. It is uncommon for them to cut only once. Bach-y-Rita (1974) found, on average, 93 scars per patient (range 3 to 150), and in Rosenthal's series (1972) half the patients had cut more than 5 times and three totaled more than 200 episodes of cutting. The Gardners (1975) found the number of cuts per subject ranged from 2 to "well over 100." Wrist-cutting is the classic variety, though they may cut right up the forearms, face, breasts, abdomen, or legs. The act of cutting is almost always performed in private—in twenty-one out of twenty-two cases in one series (Gardner and Gardner, 1975).

Cuts vary in depth from superficial scratches to deep lacerations, though drawing blood is usually required. Favored implements are razor blades or glass from broken glasses, mirrors, windows, or light bulbs. Other techniques may be used, such as burning with cigarettes, dermatitis artefacta, and tattooing.

PRECIPITANTS

Among the motives proposed by such authors as Offer and Barglow (1960) to explain self-mutilation have been the desire to gain attention, the need to be loved and cared for, attempts to control aggression, tension reduction, and attempts to gain prestige in the social group in the ward. Such elements do seem to play a part in the dynamics of self-mutilation, but they are insufficient to account for it. Why should one choose to cut one's wrist to gain love or prestige?

The most frequent precipitants of an episode of self-mutilation are an impasse in interpersonal relations or the loss or threat of loss of or abandonment by a significant other (Novotny, 1972; Grunebaum and Klerman, 1967; Goldwyn et al., 1967; Friedman et al., 1972)—such as being jilted by boyfriend or girlfriend, or arguments with parents. Rosenthal et al. (1972) found cutting related to staff absences and departures, over half of the cuts occurring on

Friday or Saturday, with another peak incidence in the afternoon the residents attended an outside clinic, away from the wards. They found cutting commonest in two periods—half occurring between 10 A.M. and 2 P.M., and the other half between 4 P.M. and 8 P.M. In contrast to these findings concerning inpatients, Johnson et al. (1975) found most cases of self-injury arrived at the emergency room during late night or early morning hours; only 29 percent of males and 32 percent of females presented themselves during the normal 9 A.M. to 5 P.M. professional working day. No day of the week was especially favored, but significantly more females were seen on weekends.

Cuts may occur when active planning for discharge begins or in relation to arguments with the staff, thwarted wishes and refused requests, badly handled transference reactions, or the doctors' departure for vacation or rotation in the course of residency training. Watson (1970), using the Repertory Grid Technique to study the motives of one mutilating patient, found her cutting was consistently associated with the constructs "feeling depressed, feeling angry, thinking people were unfriendly, wanting to talk to someone and being unable to, and having the same thoughts for a long time." Another precipitant patients mention with some regularity is the frustration of experiencing strong emotions one cannot express in words or to any understanding hearer.

Epidemics may occur within hospitals and similar institutions where new and vulnerable patients can learn cutting behavior, and it is encouraged by such typical and common staff responses describing behavior as "fragmented and diffuse, with widespread confusion, guilt, heated arguments, and breakdowns in communication." The staff become alarmed and amplify the patient's fears. Although wrist-slashing is a private ritual with primarily internal motivations, patients may soon discover and begin to value the rewards of secondary gain. A degree of competition may arise between patients, the patient with the most cuts or stitches earning the distinction of being the most awful or the most unhappy. Though the initial cut may be secret, patients often, as Simpson wrote (1976), "manage to flaunt the wound or their bandage like a newly-engaged girl wearing her diamond ring for the first time."

Simpson (1975, 1976) has described an epidemic in a general hospital psychiatric ward which ultimately involved twelve patients and two nurses, and Matthews (1968) has described an epidemic in an adolescent unit.

THE PROCESS OF CUTTING

There is a striking degree of similarity between the many descriptions of the act of self-mutilation in the literature (Simpson, 1975,

1976; Pao, 1969; Graff and Mallin, 1967; Grunebaum and Klerman, 1967; Waldenberg, 1972; Friedman et al., 1972; Siomopoulos, 1974; Kafka, 1969; Gero and Rubinfine, 1955; Burnham and Giovacchini, 1969). In response to the varying precipitants, the person experiences anger, depression, frustration, rejection, abandonment, and especially tension, which predominates. Tension may rise over the course of a day, and the idea of cutting may occur. Planning the occasion, or remembering where the blade has been hidden, may be somewhat comforting. Increasingly there is "a feeling that something is going to happen," or that "I have to do something. I'm going to cut" (Bach-y-Rita, 1974). The patient usually seeks solitude if not already alone, for the act is an intensely private ritual. As the increasing tension or rage at the frustrating object becomes overwhelming, there is transition into a state of depersonalization which is described as "unreal," "empty," "numb," "floating—as if I had no inside"; "you feel a lot, but then you don't feel anything" (Rosenthal et al., 1972). The person becomes totally self-engrossed, withdrawn, and uninterested in the surroundings or other people.

Blank (1954) has described depersonalization as "an emergency defense against the threatened eruption into consciousness of a massive complex of feelings of deprivation, rage, and anxiety." But, as Miller and Bashkin (1974) have pointed out, for it to function as a usable defense, a dependable means of ending the depersonalized stage is needed. Self-mutilation fulfills that function. The flat, dead, dissociated state is not bearable for long. Suddenly they cut. They may claim not to be fully aware of the act of cutting, saying, for example, with some surprise: "I find that I've cut myself." Yet clearly they exercise some control, for the extent and depth of their wounds are usually limited and the site seems more often chosen than random. Some comment that they stop cutting when they have had "enough blood," or simply "enough."

Self-mutilation does not, then, constitute an act of suicide or direct self-destructive behavior. It is in many ways an act of antisuicide (Simpson, 1976), for the cutting is used as a direct, reliable, and rapidly effective way of coming back to life from the dead, unreal, preceding state. Self-mutilation in this context almost amounts to self-therapy, achieving swift reintegration, repersonalization, and ending a very unpleasant sequence. Grunebaum and Klerman (1967) have called wrist-slashing a "self-prescribed treatment that does not involve verbalizing feelings in psychotherapy." It produces great relief. One cutter wrote: "I feel well, I laugh and sing while I cut myself, unless I am too engrossed in watching the blood or examining what's inside."

Some patients explicitly describe the process as like sexual intercourse or masturbation (Waldenberg, 1972; Friedman et al., 1972;

Burnham and Giovacchini, 1969), when the rising tension is followed by relief and pleasure of orgasmic quality, leading to calm and peaceful relaxation or even sleep. As G. Daskalogrigorakis (personal communication, 1976) has written: "Blood-letting in the evening lets me sleep."

BLOOD

Blood has a special significance for the self-mutilator and plays an essential part in the process of reintegration: the sight and feel of blood is important; and sometimes seeing the gaping wound and "seeing what's inside." Rosenthal et al. (1972) have suggested that among the meanings of the cutting are: "I bleed: therefore I am alive" or "I do have insides: I can see them."

Blood serves as a transitional object (Simpson, 1977), a "potential security blanket capable of giving warmth and comforting environment . . . carved within oneself" (Kafka, 1969). Functioning as a significant transitional boundary experience, it enables the patient to recathect the depersonalized body image and ego boundaries, clarifying the sense of real boundaries between inside and outside, self and not-self.

Kahne (1967) has remarked on the persistence of transitional phenomena into adult life, and Modell (1963) attributed the etiology of such borderline personalities to a "developmental disorder of character that leads to an arrest of object relationships at the stage of the transitional object." Fintzy (1971) has asked: "Do borderline patients ever give up their transitional objects, or do they retain them in a disguised way?" Such covert retention of a special use of transitional objects is, as we shall see, relevant to the developmental origins of the state. Blood provides a permanently available, efficiently stored, and readily released source of warm and brilliant envelopment. Gero and Rubinfine's patient (1955) described a pleasure in the sensation "of opening up, of creating a gap, and the sweet feeling of blood flowing out." Kafka's patient (1969) spoke of "the exquisite border experience of sharply 'becoming alive'" when the blood flowed "like a voluptuous bath, a sensation of pleasant warmth which, as it spread over the hills and valleys of my body, moulds its contour and sculpts its form." Others have recorded the spontaneous expression of fascination with and enjoyment of blood (Pao, 1969; Rosenthal et al., 1972; Offer and Barglow, 1960); "I had to see blood, I wanted to see blood come out" (Conn, 1932), and "incredibly exciting, incredibly beautiful . . . it makes me feel very happy."

In one case (Burnham and Giovacchini, 1969) the patient experienced blood as "warm, comforting and maternal" and likened it to the feeling of freshly voided urine when she wet the bed as a child.

It is interesting to note that whereas the usual transitional objects of early childhood have the tactile qualities of body surfaces (of the child and mother), these patients seem to prefer transitional objects with the liquid, warm, and enveloping qualities of amniotic fluid.

Color shock may be a component of the process. Some of Asch's patients mentioned experiencing their surroundings as becoming drained of color before they cut: "There was too much white, white nurses, white doctors, white sheets, white walls. It was such a relief to cut and see the red blood appear."

These phenomena may also be related to the behavior of the "needle freaks" (Levine, 1974), drug addicts who become dependent on the use of the needle, may use sexual imagery to describe penetration by the needle, and may describe "booting" (drawing their own blood in and out of the needle) as being like masturbation (Howard and Borges, 1971).

Some of the patients of Goldwyn et al. (1967) considered that the flowing blood "drained something bad from them," and Simpson's case (1973) of female genital self-mutilation felt "something evil and tense within her, leaking away." It is one's own, fresh, flowing blood that is specifically sought—there is much less or no interest in stale or clotted blood, in menstrual blood, or in other people's blood.

Let us consider two final descriptions of the fascination of blood by different patients. P. Richardson (personal communication, 1973; cited in Simpson, 1976) has described the experience with poetic sensuality: "The real thing that excites most is to see my blood, the pleasure of it coming, crawling and dribbling over your flesh—you know that it's really you coming out. Deep rich red, the color, the velvety warmness. Sometimes I give myself a nosebleed just to feel my nose being warmed, invaded by liquid rubies or a vintage claret—it moves slow like the birth of a child or like wearing an Afghan coat on a cold day . . . " (p. 299). A young woman wrote to me in a letter smeared with her blood: "I don't really waste my blood any more. I used to smear it all about or just watch it drip. When I sleep—I like to suck on it. But usually now I bottle it. I must have nearly a million plastic pill bottles with it in! It eventually dries up—but I am working on a solution to that. I tried painting with it, but I couldn't get enough blood without having someone take notice. I did try to ask my doctor to extract a few cups or so from me. But he would not. People are funny sometimes."

PAIN

Typically, pain is not felt when the cutting takes place, and many investigators have noted this fact (Pao, 1969; Rosenthal et al., 1972; Graff and Mallin, 1967; Goldwyn et al., 1967; Asch, 1971; Bach-y-

Rita, 1974). The patient may feel no pain while inflicting severe lacerations, cutting tendons (Grunebaum and Klerman, 1967), lacerating the vagina and cervix (Simpson and Anstee, 1974; Gerstle et al., 1957), or even removing both testicles (Lowy and Kolivakis, 1971) or a prolapsed uterus (Vedrinne et al., 1969) without anesthetic. It is often possible to suture the wounds without using an anesthetic.

Only two out of twenty-four of Simpson's patients (1975) felt pain when cutting, only two of twenty-one studied by Novotny (1972), and just 28 percent of McKerracher et al.'s subjects (1968). Though the pain can return soon afterwards, it may be absent for hours or even a couple of days. When pain is felt, it also helps to mediate the return to reality: "To feel is reassuring that one is alive, even if that feeling is pain" (Burnham and Giovacchini, 1969).

FUTURITY

Repeated episodes of depersonalization and recurrent crises produce a significantly discontinuous experience of existence and self in such people, whose ego boundaries are porous at best. Some describe a sense in which the self-inflicted cuts and their resultant scars are a visible, concrete, constant reminder that they have lived, and suffered, and continued living. In Miller and Bashkin's phrase (1974): "He preserves in the flesh . . . the history of events he could not integrate into the fabric of his personality." Later, when the patient has improved, he may want the scars to be magically removed by plastic surgery, closing the dermal diary, somehow erasing the experiences they had recorded.

FOLLOW-UP AND OUTCOME

The lack of any really adequate follow-up studies is very striking. It seems that unexpected improvements may follow after the patient is transferred to a more old-fashioned, custodial institution, perhaps because setting limits is easier, and especially because there is less intense staff involvement with the patients (Grunebaum and Klerman, 1967; Watson, 1970). Nelson and Grunebaum (1971) have published the only follow-up study, having managed to follow nineteen self-mutilators for five to six years after initial admission. Ten were regarded as well or improved (with regard to criteria of social adjustment and decreased psychiatric symptoms). Four showed no significant change in quality of adjustment or symptoms; they continued to mutilate themselves and require frequent hospital admissions. Two committed suicide.

THE DYNAMICS OF
SELF-MUTILATION—EXPLANATIONS
AND THEORIES _____

The first notable major conceptualization of the motivations of self-mutilators was produced by Karl Menninger (1938). He described three components to the suicidal impulse: the wish to kill, the wish to be killed, and the wish to die (or, in other versions, a wish to hurt others, a wish to be punished, and a wish to escape from an unbearable situation). Self-mutilation can be seen as satisfying a need to hurt and to be hurt. The aggression may be both active and passive, directed against an introjected object. Such an act also "atones or propitiates by sacrifice for the aggressive acts and wishes of the past, and it also provides an anticipatory protection as if to forestall future punishment and permit further indulgences by the advance payment of a penalty." Menninger regarded self-mutilation as a type of indirect and incomplete self-destructive behavior which allowed one to live while gratifying irresistable urges, by concentrating the suicidal impulse on part of the self as a substitute for the whole—*focal suicide*. He also saw self-mutilation as representing the "surrender or repudiation of the active masculine role," and considered self-castration as the prototype, with the part of body which gets damaged being "an unconscious representative of the genital."

Self-mutilation is an "intense intrapersonal act in the context of a tense interpersonal situation" (Simpson, 1976).

Others (Simpson, 1975) have thought that self-mutilation represents an attempt to counteract, by a physical act performed by and against the self, an overwhelming situation. This is related to the concept of identification with the aggressor (A. Freud, 1946) and to the observation that people in helpless and overwhelmingly passive situations may identify with their aggressor and act out against themselves, the victim.

The sexual significance of cutting has been explored by several writers. Deutsch (1944) saw the act, in women, as a way of "solving the menstrual conflict." Menstrual irregularities and conflicts and even amenorrhoea are not uncommon in such women. But where it is impossible to eliminate bleeding, she suggests they produce vicarious menstruation, with displacement and referral of the bleeding to a part of the body away from the genitals, rendering the bleeding more readily visible and explicable. Asch (1971) also proposed a form of displaced genital bleeding, pointing out that self-cutting is rare before menarche and commenting that "the relief in seeing the gaping, open wound may be part of the recreation, through an identification with the aggressor, of some conception of menstruation, as a helplessly and passively experienced genital mutilation" (p. 613). Rado (1933) referred to self-cutting as the "choice of the lesser evil," a symbolic castration that avoids real castration.

Vereecken (1965) emphasized the patients' poor id control and the failure to regulate autoeroticism and autoaggression; he also thought the mutilation was a masturbation equivalent. Siomopoulos (1974) also saw the repeated self-cutting as distorted autoerotic activity, "opening up symbolically on [the] skin multiple little genitals . . . which become available for all sorts of autoerotic manipulations."

Though the Gardners (1975) have found habitual cutters to be significantly obsessional on psychological tests, Siomopoulos (1974) has stated that whereas the obsessive-compulsive patient experiences his impulses as ego-alien, the cutter finds his behavior (even if unavoidable and unwelcome) to be ego-syntonic.

Graff and Mallin (1967) considered that the cut attacked and punished the introjected rejecting mother, preverbally expressed the hate, sought to elicit caring responses from others, and gave relieving self-stimulation. Friedman et al. (1972) expressed similar views.

Hoffer (1950) postulated a "pain barrier" mechanism which normally protects the infant from its own destructive impulses and proposed that self-mutilation was due to a defect in this mechanism. Stengel (1965) pointed out a discrepancy, in subnormal patients, between reactions to self-inflicted and extraneous noxious stimuli, suggesting that "self-inflicted pain is experienced differently from pain the cause of which is outside the body."

Declich (1956) saw self-mutilation as expressing an altered sense of corporality, leading to "a rejection of the part of the body which the individual no longer recognizes as part of himself and which he really wishes to remove."

Kafka (1969) has emphasized that such patients use their body as a transitional object. Their preoccupation is with the unfinished business of establishing their body image and with problems of limits—of the body itself, of their own power and competence and their aggression and capacity for feeling and suffering. They seek achievement of a unitary self, contained within the limiting membrane of the skin, with an inside and outside, and a reliable distinction between self and not-self. Kafka wrote of "the perpetual human task of keeping inner and outer reality separate yet interrelated."

Just as one of the primary biochemical tasks of the developing fetus is to establish a reliable immunological distinction between self and not-self, so must the developing child achieve a similar psychological distinction. Masterson (1972) has argued cogently that the borderline patient may represent an arrest of ego development during the separation-individuation phase (six to thirty-six months) as described by Margaret Mahler (1965), perhaps in the rapprochement subphase.

Sigmund Freud (1923/1961) described the ego as ultimately derived from bodily sensations, chiefly those from the surface of the body, and remarked: "Pain, too, seems to play a part." Anna Freud (1972) has suggested that the experience of being the victim of aggression developmentally precedes the defensive outward turning of the aggression toward an object. The concept of victim, and the ability to direct aggression outward (to escape from self-aggression), are learned on the child's own body surface in the course of an appropriate aggressive dialogue between mother and child.

Orgel (1974) has also argued that the reactions of the earliest libidinal object to the child's aggression plays a role in the developing distinction between self and not-self; that as the child responds to the mother's libidinal cathexis of his body with a narcissistic cathexis of his own, the setting up of the normal pain barrier can occur. Interference with this process could be expected to result in a relative deficiency of the pain barrier and of the development of a normal body image and bodily cathexis, as well as an inability to externalize primitive aggression or to use more usual or mature defenses to deal with situations of threat.

Perhaps these patients experience a lack of the normal aggressive dialogue the "good-enough mother" must provide as she mediates the child's successful progress from pleasure to reality principle. They often seem, like Orgel's patient, to be trying in later life to provoke retaliatory anger from significant others, to seek appropriate counteraggressive contact. This may also help to explain their great difficulty in coping with highly permissive and unstructured inpatient settings, repeatedly recorded in the literature.

Frances and Gale (1975) have described a case of congenital indifference to pain, with severely impaired body image and self-boundaries, who used head-banging as a source of highly cathected proprioceptive sensory experience to strengthen those tenuous boundaries. Lacking the Cartesian confidence of "I think, therefore I am," they work on the principle of "I feel, therefore I am," or "I suffer, therefore I am." Dabrowski (1937) wrote of a boy who mutilated himself by dropping boiling water on his hand, explaining that "only this can bring me back the feeling of myself!"

Studies of the nature of depersonalization fit the self-mutilator's experiences, too. Waltzer (1968) considered it to represent for the ego an unstable compromise between ambivalent feelings and thoughts of wanting to live and wanting to die; a dissociated state in which the person "acts as both participator and observer" and "responds as though his behavior were being carried out by another person." He also agrees that though depersonalization is entered to avoid painful affect and anxiety, it can also of itself precipitate "severe and overwhelming panic secondary to the sensations of unreality and fragmentation."

Yap (1970) has studied self-mutilation from an existential point of view and has similarly seen it in the context of needing to affirm the reality of self in the presence of a core of existential doubt, a crippled *Dasein*.

Carr (1977) has reviewed other major hypotheses, such as those viewing self-mutilation as a learned operant, maintained by positive social reinforcement or by the termination of an aversive stimulus (negative reinforcement); or as a means of providing sensory stimulation; or as the product of aberrant physiological processes. This is a useful review, although limited by his failure to appreciate differences between self-injurious behavior in subnormal children and in adults. Simpson (1976) has discussed other organic hypotheses.

MANAGEMENT

There seems to be a good deal of self-mutilation as a private ritual in which health professionals do not get involved. But one point is universally agreed—self-mutilation arising within clinical treatment facilities is very difficult to manage (Simpson, 1976).

Many problems arise from staff responses to it. Pao (1969) avers that it can evoke castration anxiety in the staff. They are also alarmed by its unpredictability, the rapidity of the regression, the self-engrossed object-unrelated state, the primitive aggression. Staff attitudes are often deeply stirred by a slash, and fluctuate between rage, guilt, resentment, shame, sympathy, understanding, frustration, and an urge to retaliate. Staff uncertainty amplifies the patient's fears. There are often fierce quarrels within the staff about how best to manage the patient who becomes a "special patient" with all the risks Burnham (1966) and Main (1957) describe as attending that status. Strauss et al. (1964) discuss how such patients challenge the usual team approach. Staff vary between rejecting the patient, wanting to ignore her "manipulation" and "attention-seeking," and taking the risk seriously and wanting to impose very strict limits. The therapist may be forced into an adversary position with colleagues, having to take the patient's part in all confrontations.

Most of the literature on self-mutilation is unhelpful (Grunebaum and Klerman, 1967) in managing such patients, though the literature on treatment of the borderline syndrome—such as the papers by Friedman (1969, 1975) and Adler (1973) and the book of Masterson

(1972)—is far more useful. Psychotherapy is fraught with difficulties but can produce very rewarding results. Patients may need to become aware of the nature of their emotional interactions with others and the disturbing effects they have on people; they need to learn how to like themselves, to learn to feel more competent and to have more satisfying relationships. They will need to learn alternative ways of coping with their problems, and this may include behavioral techniques (Loomis and Horsley, 1974) and autogenous relaxation training.

CONCLUSIONS

We can see that self-mutilation is a relatively common and highly complex form of human behavior that is very often not directly suicidal in intent or in effect, engaged in without conscious intent to die (and indeed often as a means of mediating a return to life from a feeling of deadness). It has long-term, cumulative, serious, harmful effects—physical, psychological, and social. Although it may seem to be more overtly self-injurious than other varieties of indirect self-destructive behavior, it shares many features with them, rather than with direct self-destructive behavior. It is similar in its dynamics and coping mechanisms and in its management problems. Our growing understanding of the nature and motivations of such acts is beginning to allow us the luxury of rationally planning the management of these most disturbing problems.

REFERENCES

Adler, G. Hospital treatment of borderline patients. *American Journal of Psychiatry*, 130:32–35, 1973.

Asch, S. S. Wrist-scratching as a symptom of anhedonia: A predepressive state. *Psychoanalytic Quarterly*, 40:603–617, 1971.

Bachman, J. A. Self-injurious behavior: A behavioral analysis. *Journal of Abnormal Psychology*, 80:211–224, 1972.

Bach-y-Rita, G. Habitual violence and self-mutilation. *American Journal of Psychiatry*, 131:1018–1020, 1974.

Ballinger, B. R. Minor self-injury. *British Journal of Psychiatry*, 115:535–538, 1971.

Barter, J. R., Swaback, D. O., and Todd, D. Adolescent suicide attempts: A follow-up study of hospitalized patients. *Archives of General Psychiatry*, 19:523–527, 1968.

Battacharyya, N. N. Indian puberty rites. *Indian Studies Past and Present*. Calcutta, 1968.

Beigel, A., and Russel, H. E. Suicidal behavior in jail—prognostic considerations. *Hospital and Community Psychiatry*, 23:361–363, 1972.

Bettelheim, B. *Symbolic Wounds*. New York: Collier, 1962.

Blank, H. R. Depression, hypomania, and depersonalization. *Psychoanalytic Quarterly*, 22:20–37, 1954.

Burnham, D. L. The special-problem patient: Victim or agent of splitting. *Psychiatry*, 29:105–122, 1966.

Burnham, D. L., and Giovacchini, P. L. Symposium on impulsive self-mutilation: Discussion. *British Journal of Medical Psychology*, 42:223–229, 1969.

Carr, E. G. The motivation of self-injurious behavior: A review of some hypotheses. *Psychological Bulletin*, 84:800–816, 1977.

Clanon, T. L. Persecutory feelings and self-mutilation in prisoners. *Corrective Psychiatry/Journal of Social Therapy*, 11:96–102, 1965.

Clendenin, W. W., and Murphy, G. E. Wrist cutting: New epidemiological findings. *Archives of General Psychiatry*, 25:465–469, 1971.

Conn, J. H. A case of marked self-mutilation presenting as a dorsal root syndrome. *Journal of Nervous and Mental Disease*, 75:251–262, 1932.

Crabtree, L. H. A psychotherapeutic encounter with a self-mutilating patient. *Psychiatry*, 30:91–100, 1967.

Crown, S., and Crisp, A. H. A short clinical diagnostic self-rating scale for psychoneurotic patients. *British Journal of Psychiatry*, 112:917–923, 1966.

Dabrowski, C. Psychological bases of self-mutilation. *Genetics and Psychology Monographs*, 19:1–104, 1937.

Danto, B. L., ed. *Jail House Blues*. Orchard Lake, Mich.: Epic, 1973.

Declich, M. Some considerations on the problem of self-mutilation. *Rassegna Studia Psychiatrica*, 45:603–621, 1956.

Dehissavoy, V. Head-banging in early childhood: A study of incidence. *Journal of Pediatrics*, 58:803–805, 1961.

Deutsch, H. *The Psychology of Women*, vol. 1. New York: Grune and Stratton, 1944.

Fabian, J. J., Maloney, M. P., and Ward, M. P. Self-destructive and suicidal behaviors in a neuropsychiatric inpatient facility. *American Journal of Psychiatry*, 130:1383–1385, 1973.

Fintzy, R. T. Vicissitudes of the transitional object in a borderline child. *International Journal of Psycho-Analysis*, 52:107–114, 1971.

Frances, A., and Gale, L. The proprioceptive body image in self-object differentiation. *Psychiatric Quarterly*, 44:107–126, 1975.

Frankel, F., and Simmons, J. Q. Self-injurious behavior in schizophrenic and retarded children. *American Journal of Mental Deficiency*, 80:512–522, 1976.

French, A. P., and Nelson, H. L. Genital self-mutilation in women. *Archives of General Psychiatry*, 27:618–620, 1972.

Freud, A. *The Ego and the Mechanisms of Defence*. New York: International Universities Press, 1946.

Freud, A. Comments on aggression. *International Journal of Psycho-Analysis*, 53:163–171, 1972.

Freud, S. The ego and the id. *Standard Edition*, 19. London: Hogarth, 1961. (Originally published, 1923.)

Friedman, H. J. Some problems of inpatient management with borderline patients. *American Journal of Psychiatry*, 126:299–304, 1969.

Friedman, H. J. Psychotherapy of borderline patients: The influence of theory on technique. *American Journal of Psychiatry*, 132:1048–1052, 1975.

Friedman, M., Glasser, M., Laufer, E., Laufer, M., and Wohl, M. Attempted suicide and self-mutilation in adolescence: Some observations from a psychoanalytic research project. *International Journal of Psycho-Analysis*, 53:179–183, 1972.

Gardner, A. R., and Gardner, A. J. Self-mutilation, obsessionality and narcissism. *British Journal of Psychiatry*, 127:127–132, 1975.

Gero, G., and Rubinfine, D. On obsessive thoughts. *Journal of the American Psychoanalytic Association*, 3:222–243, 1955.

Gerstle, M. L., Guttmacher, A. F., and Brown, F. A case of recurrent malingered placenta praevia. *Mount Sinai Journal of Medicine* (New York), 24:641–646, 1957.

Glauber, J. P. Observations on a primary form of anhedonia. *Psychoanalytic Quarterly*, 18:67–78, 1949.

Goldfield, M. D., and Glick, I. D. Self-mutilation of the female genitalia: A case report. *Diseases of the Nervous System*, 31:843–845, 1970.

Goldney, R. D., and Simpson, I. G. Female genital self-mutilation, dysorexia, and the hysterical personality: The Caenis syndrome. *Canadian Psychiatric Association Journal*, 20:435–441, 1975.

Goldwyn, R. M., Cahill, J. L., and Grunebaum, H. U. Self-inflicted injury to the wrist. *Plastic and Reconstructive Surgery*, 39:583–589, 1967.

Graff, H., and Mallin, R. The syndrome of the wrist-cutter. *American Journal of Psychiatry*, 124:36–41, 1967.

Green, A. H. Self-mutilation in schizophrenic children. *Archives of General Psychiatry*, 17:234–244, 1967.

Green, A. H. Self-destructive behavior in physically abused schizophrenic children. *Archives of General Psychiatry*, 19:171–179, 1968.

Grinker, R. R., Werble, B., and Drye, R. *The Borderline Syndrome: A Behavioral Study of Ego Functions*. New York: Basic Books, 1968.

Grunebaum, H. U., and Klerman, C. L. Wrist-slashing. *American Journal of Psychiatry*, 124:527–534, 1967.

Gunderson, J. G., and Singer, M. T. Defining borderline patients: An overview. *American Journal of Psychiatry*, 132:1–10, 1975.

Hoffer, W. Oral aggressiveness and ego development. *International Journal of Psycho-Analysis*, 31:45, 1950.

Howard, J., and Borges, P. Needle sharing in the Haight: Some social and psychological functions. *Journal of Psychedelic Drugs*, 4:71–80, 1971.

Johnson, F. G., Ferrence, R. G., and Whitehead, P. C. Self-injury: Identification and intervention. *Canadian Psychiatric Association Journal*, 18:101–105, 1973.

Johnson, F. G., Frankel, B. G., Ferrence, R. G., et al. Self-injury in Canada: A prospective study. *Canadian Journal of Public Health*, 66:307–316, 1975.

Kafka, J. S. The body as transitional object—a psychoanalytic study of a self-mutilating patient. *British Journal of Medical Psychology*, 42:207–212, 1969.

Kahne, M. J. On the persistence of transitional phenomena into adult life. *International Journal of Psycho-Analysis*, 48:247–258, 1967.

Kernberg, O. F. Borderline personality organization. *Journal of the American Psychoanalytic Association*, 15:641–685, 1967.

Lester, D. Attempts to predict suicidal risk using psychological tests. *Psychological Bulletin*, 74:1–17, 1970.

Lester, D. Self-mutilating behavior. *Psychological Bulletin*, 2:119–128, 1972.

Levine, D. G. "Needle freaks": Compulsive self-injection by drug users. *American Journal of Psychiatry*, 131:297–300, 1974.

Loomis, M. E., and Horsley, J. A. *Interpersonal Change: A Behavioral Approach to Nursing Practice*. New York: McGraw-Hill, 1974.

Lowy, F. H., and Kolivakis, T. L. Autocastration by a male transsexual. *Canadian Psychiatric Association Journal*, 16:399–405, 1971.

McEvedy, C. Self-inflicted injuries. Doctoral dissertation, University of London, 1963.

Mack, J. E., ed. *Borderline States in Psychiatry*. New York: Grune and Stratton, 1975.

McKerracher, D. W., Loughnane, T., and Watson, R. A. Self-mutilation in female psychopaths. *British Journal of Psychiatry*, 114:829–832, 1968.

Mahler, M. S. On the significance of the normal separation–individuation phase: With reference to research in symbiotic child psychosis. In M.

Schur, ed., *Drives, Affects, Behavior,* vol. 2. New York: International Universities Press, 1965.

Main, T. F. The ailment. *British Journal of Medical Psychology,* 30:129–145, 1957.

Malcove, L. Bodily mutilation and learning to eat. *Psychoanalytic Quarterly,* 2:557–561, 1933.

Mason, W. A., and Sponholz, R. R. Behavior of rhesus monkeys reared in isolation. *Journal of Psychiatric Research,* 1:299–306, 1963.

Masterson, J. F. *Treatment of the Borderline Adolescent: A Developmental Approach.* New York: Wiley, 1972.

Matthews, P. C. Epidemic self-injury in an adolescent unit. *International Journal of Social Psychiatry,* 14:125–133, 1968.

Menninger, K. *Man against Himself.* New York: Harcourt, Brace, 1938.

Miller, F., and Bashkin, E. A. Depersonalization and self-mutilation. *Psychoanalytic Quarterly,* 43:638–649, 1974.

Modell, A. H. Primitive object-relationships and the predisposition to schizophrenia. *International Journal of Psycho-Analysis,* 44:282–292, 1963.

Montagu, M. F. A. Ritual mutilation among primitive people. *CIBA Symposia,* 8:421–436, 1946.

Nelson, S. H., and Grunebaum, H. A follow-up study of wrist-slashers. *American Journal of Psychiatry,* 128:1345–1349, 1971.

Novotny, P. Self-cutting. *Bulletin of the Menninger Clinic,* 36:505–514, 1972.

Offer, D., and Barglow, P. Adolescent and young adult self-mutilation incidents in a general psychiatric hospital. *Archives of General Psychiatry,* 3:194–204, 1960.

Orgel, S. Fusion with the victim and suicide. *International Journal of Psycho-Analysis,* 55:531–538, 1974.

Panton, J. H. The identification of predispositional factors in self-mutilation with a state prison population. *Journal of Clinical Psychology,* 18:63–67, 1962.

Pao, Ping-nie. The syndrome of delicate self-cutting. *British Journal of Medical Psychology,* 42:195–206, 1969.

Phillips, R. H., and Muzaffer, A. Some aspects of self-mutilation in the general population of a large psychiatric hospital. *Psychiatric Quarterly,* 35:421–423, 1961.

Rado, S. Fear of castration in women. *Psychoanalytic Quarterly,* 2:425–475, 1933.

Reiger, W. Suicide attempts in a federal prison. *Archives of General Psychiatry,* 25:465–469, 1971.

Rinzler, C., and Shapiro, D. Wrist-cutting and suicide. *Mount Sinai Journal of Medicine* (New York), 35:485–488, 1968.

Rosenthal, R. J., Rinzler, C., Wallsh, R., and Klausner, E. Wrist-cutting as a syndrome: The meaning of a gesture. *American Journal of Psychiatry*, 129:1363–1368, 1972.

Sandler, J. Studies in psychopathology using a self-assessment inventory. I. The development and construction of the inventory. *British Journal of Medical Psychology*, 27:142–152, 1954.

Schechter, D. C. Breast mutilation in the Amazons. *Surgery*, 51:554–560, 1962.

Shodell, M. J., and Reiter, H. H. Self-mutilative behavior in verbal and nonverbal schizophrenic children. *Archives of General Psychiatry*, 19:453–455, 1968.

Simpson, M. A. Female genital self-mutilation. *Archives of General Psychiatry*, 29:808–810, 1973.

Simpson, M. A. The phenomenology of self-mutilation in a general hospital setting. *Canadian Psychiatric Association Journal*, 20:424–434, 1975.

Simpson, M. A. Self-mutilation and suicide. In E. S. Shneidman, ed., *Suicidology: Contemporary Developments*. New York: Grune and Stratton, 1976, pp. 281–315.

Simpson, M. A. Self-mutilation and the borderline-syndrome. *Dynamische Psychiatrie/Dynamic Psychiatry*, 42:42–48, 1977.

Simpson, M. A., and Anstee, B. H. Female genital self-mutilation as a cause of vaginal bleeding. *Postgraduate Medical Journal*, 50:308–309, 1974.

Siomopoulos, V. Repeated self-cutting: An impulse neurosis. *American Journal of Psychotherapy*, 28:85–94, 1974.

Standage, K. F., Moore, J. A., and Cole, M. G. Self-mutilation of the genitalia by a female schizophrenic. *Canadian Psychiatric Association Journal*, 19:17–20, 1974.

Stengel, E. Pain and the psychiatrist. *British Journal of Psychiatry*, 111:795–802, 1965.

Strauss, A., Shatzman, L., Bucher, R., et al. *Psychiatric Ideologies and Institutions*. Glencoe, Ill.: Free Press, 1964, pp. 317–329.

Vedrinne, J., Moine, C., and Guillemin, G. Voluntary genital mutilation in women. *Médecine Legale et Dommage Corporel*, 2:156–157, 1969.

Vereecken, J. L. Recidiverende automutilatie. *Nederlandse Tijdschrift voor Geneeskunde*, 109:2280–2284, 1965.

Virkkunen, M. Self-mutilation in antisocial personality disorder. *Acta Psychiatrica Scandinavica*, 54:347–352, 1976.

Waldenberg, S. S. A. Wrist-cutting—A psychiatric injury. M. Phil. dissertation, London University, 1972.

Waltzer, H. Depersonalization and self-destruction. *American Journal of Psychiatry*, 125:399–401, 1968.

Watson, J. P. The relationship between a self-mutilating patient and her doctor. *Psychotherapy and Psychosomatics*, 18:67–73, 1970.

Weissman, M. M. Wrist cutting. *Archives of General Psychiatry*, 32:1166–1171, 1975.

Whitehead, P. C., Ferrence, R. G., and Johnson, F. G. Physicians' reports of self-injury cases among their patients not seen in hospital. *Life-Threatening Behavior*, 2:137–146, 1972.

Whitehead, P. C., Johnson, F. G., and Ferrence, R. G. Measuring the incidence of self-injury: Some methodological and design considerations. *American Journal of Orthopsychiatry*, 43:142–148, 1973.

Yap, K. B. *Automutilatie*. Holland: Van Loghum Slaterus, Deventer, 1970.

18

THE ACCIDENT PROCESS AND DRUNKEN DRIVING AS INDIRECT SELF-DESTRUCTIVE ACTIVITY

MELVIN L. SELZER

I t is admittedly not easy to depict a traffic accident as an *indirect* form of self-destructive behavior. Indeed, it is probably the most direct self-destructive behavior dealt with in this volume. Nevertheless, there is considerable evidence that most behaviors culminating in traffic accidents are essentially the product of unconscious (or subintentional) mental activity.

Traffic accidents are obviously the final outcome of behaviors that are not only complex but quite often reflective of such nonpsychological phenomena as road conditions, traffic flow, and adverse weather. Nevertheless, most traffic accidents are not random phenomena, and some 90 percent can be attributed to driver acts of commission or omission (McFarland and Moore, 1957). An earlier belief in a simple "accident-proneness" model (Greenwood and Woods, 1919) has long since been displaced by detailed studies of various accident-related phenomena.

There is general agreement that certain personality factors influence driving habits in a predictable way and are ultimately related to traffic accidents. Conger (1961) and Conger et al. (1957) compared low- and high-accident drivers and found the high-accident group displayed significantly more impulsivity, aggressive behavior, low tolerance for tension, dependency, and extremes of both egocentricity and unreflectiveness. The group also had poorer reality testing and greater emotional instability.

In a now classic study, Tillman and Hobbs (1949) examined high- and low-accident-rate taxi drivers. The psychological findings were similar to those reported later by Conger. They also found their high-accident group demonstrated a high incidence of past and current social stress and social maladjustment reflected by truancy during school years, frequent job changes, frequent arrests, and so forth.

In a study of fifteen men who died of self-inflicted gunshot wounds and fifteen men who died in auto accidents, two-thirds of those killed in accidents had recently moved into positions of increased responsibility or were contemplating doing so (Tabachnick et al., 1966). In addition, twelve of the fifteen drivers had a recent history of "emotional upset" after being criticized or slighted. The psychopathology common to the driver group included aggressiveness, depressive tendencies, distant or loose relationships with others, immaturity, exhibitionistic tendencies, and the "overuse of alcohol" (probably a euphemism for drinking problems).

McMurray (1970) used an entirely different method to correlate life-change stress with accidents. He used driver records to demonstrate that the accident rate of persons undergoing divorce doubled during the six months immediately before and after the divorce.

Using only measures of social maladjustment such as a broken home, truancy, poor employment records, marital discord, and repeated contacts with social service or public health agencies, McFarland and Moseley (1954) were able to classify truck drivers as accident-free or accident repeaters with an accuracy of 85 percent.

Although there can be no question that occasional drivers can and do make conscious and overt attempts to commit suicide by means of a motor vehicle, these appear to be relatively infrequent events when compared to the mass of serious and fatal accidents which occur annually in the United States. Is it possible that depression and suicidal proclivities that are less than conscious could result in higher accident frequencies? In an effort to shed some light on this question, Selzer and Payne (1962) classified sixty psychiatric patients according to whether or not they had previously seriously considered committing suicide or had made an actual suicide attempt. The thirty-three men thereby classified as suicidal were responsible for 89 automobile accidents for a mean of 2.7 per person. The twenty-seven nonsuicidal men accounted for 36 accidents for a mean of 1.3 accidents per person. Nevertheless—and this is an important point—all but one of the accidents in the study were regarded by the subjects as completely fortuitous!

The accident process offers the self-destructive person a unique way out because he can end his life without consciously confronting himself with his suicidal intent. The automobile lends itself to this process because of the frequency of its use and the very real hazards of driving.

Studies which indicate that risky driving behavior is not present throughout a driver's entire lifetime have complicated the attempt to identify high-risk drivers. Indeed, there is evidence that the frequency of accident involvement shifts during different periods of people's lives (Cresswell and Grogatt, 1963; Schuster and Guilford, 1964).

LIFE EVENTS AND ACCIDENTS

A number of studies have appeared in the last three decades linking illness of all descriptions to stress and/or life changes. One of the earliest of these studies appeared in 1951 and would have us believe that most physical illness is related to specific interpersonal crises in the lives of those who become ill (Hinkle et al., 1957). The study involved 3,000 men in three different populations during a two-year period of their adult lives. Those with the greatest number of illnesses and highest degree of disability experienced illnesses of many etiologies involving different body systems. The most remarkable finding of the study was that the episodes of sickness usually appeared in clusters and were not distributed randomly throughout a lifetime. The investigators concluded that the factors which affected the susceptibility of subjects to illness did not exert a constant influence over time. Nor were there any predictable periods of life when illness clusters appeared. In general, the clusters of illness appeared to be periods of demonstrable conflict with parents or spouse, threats to social position, loss of significant emotional supports, or excessive demands created by the illness or evasive behavior of family or close associates.

In a related but different approach, Rahe et al. (1964) studied patients suffering from a variety of diseases and compared them with healthy controls. The most salient finding was that the ill group experienced marked changes in their personal and economic status during the two-year period preceding the onset of their illness. The reported "life changes" were events such as loss of close friends or relatives, severe financial hardship, and changes in family constellations. In this and subsequent studies, Holmes and Rahe (1967) did not try to define and measure stress directly. Rather, they chose to measure life events (i.e., divorce, job change, etc.) which implied a need for psychological adjustment and perhaps, therefore, also implied stress. A life-change unit score was assigned to each type of event, reflecting a group assessment of the magnitude of readjustment to that event. Thus the impact of life change for individuals in a given unit of time was determined by the sum of the life-change units in the period of time under investigation.

Using these quantitative assessments of life change versus severity of illness, the investigators demonstrated that the greater the degree of total change in a subject's life during the previous year, the higher the risk of subsequent illness and the greater the likelihood of severe rather than minor illness (Rahe et al., 1966; Rahe, 1969; Rahe et al., 1971). Other studies recorded higher than average accumulations of life changes preceding the onset of myocardial infarction, sudden cardiac death, and depression (Theorell and Rahe, 1971; Rahe and Paasidivi, 1971; Rahe and Link, 1971; Paykel et al., 1969).

The study of depression by Paykel et al. (1969) is of particular importance because it provides a potential link between earlier studies that related personality factors such as depression to accidents, and the possibility that life changes may trigger the accident process by potentiating the effect of personality factors. In that study, a group of clinically depressed patients admitted to a mental hospital was compared with a healthy control group. During the prior six months the depressed patients had experienced far more inimical events. If most depressions of clinical magnitude are indeed preceded by life changes, then depression itself, which in many studies is found to be correlated with accidents, may be regarded as a secondary or intermediary factor in accident causation. Perhaps other personality factors implicated in traffic accidents may prove to be in part a function of life changes.

If, indeed, phenomena as multietiological as a broad range of human illnesses are related to life changes, a significant causal link may exist between life events and accidents (which are usually a direct result of human behavior), particularly if we accept the hypothesis that up to 90 percent of traffic accidents result from driver factors (McFarland and Moore, 1957).

A life-change–stress–accident sequence may in part explain certain accident phenomena for which existing explanations remain unpersuasive. Among these are the high accident rates of the very young and the very old. Late adolescent and young adult drivers are obviously undergoing many life changes. It is clearly a trying period for many. It encompasses such significant events as graduation from or leaving school, choice of life vocation, search for a job, and getting married.

The high accident rate of the elderly is a more intricate problem. Obviously, a physical decline of vision, hearing, and overall responsiveness occurs. The incidence of impairing illness and of drug-taking for those illnesses is generally greater. However, some studies suggest that the elderly driver learns to compensate for many of his deficiencies and limitations of which he is more aware than are younger drivers (McFarland and Moore, 1957; Kent and Novotny,

1961). In addition, an aged person is usually confronted with a number of life changes that may be less than welcome: involuntary retirement, income shrinkage, loss of significant others, and so forth. Adjustments to life changes might well contribute to the increased susceptibility of the elderly to traffic accidents.

In an effort to determine if life events of the type discussed above are indeed significantly correlated with accidents, Selzer and Vinokur (1974) studied the accident records of 532 male drivers. These revealed that life changes and the subsequent subjective stress induced by the changes are more closely correlated with accidents than are the demographic, personality, and social maladjustment variables that had previously been the focus of accident studies.

One cannot complete a discussion of antecedent events and accidents without mentioning a still little understood aspect of the accident process. This is the degree of stress that may occur *immediately* before the accident. One investigation of ninety-six drivers who caused a fatal accident found that 19 percent had become acutely upset by events during the few hours immediately before the accident (Selzer, 1969). (This was a minimal figure, as in most instances the driver responsible had not survived the accident, and his preaccident activities could not be determined.) Not surprisingly, most of the acutely upsetting events preceding the accident were quarrels with members of the opposite sex.

THE ROLE OF ALCOHOL_____

The relationship between vehicular accidents and excessive alcohol intake predates the automobile. Not surprisingly, the problem has burgeoned with the rise in both discretionary income and automobile ownership. The scope of the drunk-driving problem in the United States, though long suspected (Selzer, 1961), has only recently been fully appreciated, as a result of roadside surveys. A carefully randomized nationwide survey of motorists stopped between 6 P.M. and 3 A.M. on Friday and Saturday nights revealed 5 percent had a blood alcohol concentration of 0.10 percent or higher (Wolfe, 1974). In effect, this finding reveals there are literally millions of drunk drivers on our roads and highways on these nights. In another assessment of the magnitude of the problem, Borkenstein (1972) estimated that there would be 4 million drunk driving violations per year in a city of 1 million people. The numbers are of epidemic, if not pandemic, proportions. What harm, then, is done by drunk drivers? Some 50 percent of serious and fatal accidents involve drivers who have been drinking excessively. They are responsible for approximately 30,000 deaths and a fearsome toll of serious and crippling injuries annually. Since an overwhelming ma-

TABLE 1 Demographic Data

	Means		
	Group A (N = 294)	Group D (N = 306)	Group L (N = 253)
Age	33.2	37.3	35.1
Education (years)	11.5	11.4	13.6
Income ($/year)	10,500	10,400	12,500
Race (%)			
White	81	86	83
Black	13	9	14
Other	6	5	3

jority of persons arrested for drunk driving are alcoholics (Popham, 1956; Selzer et al., 1967; Yoder and Moore, 1973), the drunk driver is essentially a substance abuser.

In an effort to define more sharply the drunk-driving population in psychosocial terms, I and my associates undertook two surveys of groups of men arrested for drunk driving (group D) and compared them with alcoholics (group A) and a control group (group L) (Selzer and Vinokur, 1975; Selzer et al., 1977; Selzer and Barton, 1977). Women were excluded because of their very low representation in drunk-driving groups. As will be seen, the drunk-driving group resembled the alcoholic group in many ways, fell between the alcoholic and control groups in other variables, and occasionally resembled the control drivers.

The demographic data for the groups are shown in Table 1.

Table 2 reveals that the alcohol group acknowledged virtually as many episodes of drunk driving in the previous twelve months as did group D.

As seen in Tables 3 and 4, there are differences between the groups on the perceived safety of driving after drinking and on their self-reports of the effects alcohol had on their driving. The alcoholics, and to some degree the drunken drivers, felt they were more

TABLE 2 Number of Times Have Driven after Drinking More than Four Drinks in the Past Twelve Months

Means			t Scores		
Group D	Group A	Group L	D-A	A-L	D-L
4.89	4.47	1.89	1.59	9.74*	11.69*

* p < .0001

TABLE 3   Perceived Safety of Drinking after Driving

	Means			t Scores		
	Group D	Group A	Group L	D-A	A-L	D-L
No. of drinks can have and still drive well?	3.39	4.00	2.96	5.62**	8.78**	3.81**
Can you drive home safely after drinking heavily?[1]	3.00	3.17	2.74	1.42	3.31*	2.09

[1] Range = 1–5; 1 = never, 5 = always
  * $p < .01$
** $p < .0001$

capable of driving safely after drinking large amounts than did group L. Is it possible that this is an accurate self-assessment? Did groups A and D have a greater tolerance for alcohol than group L and were they thus better able to drive after drinking heavily? Table 4 indicates otherwise. The respondents were asked what effect drinking had on their driving, and marked a 5-point scale ranging from "Never" to "Almost always" for the series of items shown. Compared to the control group, group A said drinking made them both more relaxed and more careless, made them take more chances and drive faster, and in general made them drive "differently." The drunk drivers said they were more relaxed, more careless, took more chances, and drove faster than did group L. Thus the alcoholics and

TABLE 4   Perceived Effects of Alcohol Consumption on Driving

	Means			t Scores		
Item[1]	Group D	Group A	Group L	D-A	A-L	D-L
Drive more carelessly	2.41	2.60	2.01	1.95	5.48***	3.85**
Tend to speed	2.05	2.06	1.72	0.16	3.65**	3.65**
Drive differently, but don't know in what way	2.33	2.74	2.11	4.17***	5.83***	2.12
Drive in a more relaxed manner	2.66	2.80	2.18	1.30	5.52***	4.51***
Take more chances	1.99	2.24	1.59	2.88*	6.72***	4.26***

[1] Range = 1–5; 1 = never, 5 = always
    * $p < .01$
  ** $p < .001$
*** $p < .0001$

TABLE 5   Percentage of Respondents Who Have Been Arrested for
Drunken Driving

Group D	Group A	Group L	χ^2	df	Sig.
96%	56%	2%	484.1	2	.0001

the drunk drivers appear to be wrong in their belief that they can
drive safely after several drinks. The apparent discrepancy between
expressed confidence and self-reported effects could make them
even more of a threat on the highways.

The respondents were asked about arrests for drunken driving
(Tables 5 and 6). One of the most striking findings was that over half
of the alcoholics had been arrested for drunken driving. Furthermore, the mean number of drunken-driving arrests for group D was
1.54, indicating that many of these men had been arrested more
than once for this offense. In fact, 39 percent of group D and 28
percent of group A had been arrested more than once for drunken
driving.

STRESS

As one parameter of stress in the three groups, subjects were
asked how frequently they had problems with wives, children, parents, or in-laws which made them angry, worried, or irritated. The
six frequency options ranged from "Several times a week" to "Once
a year or less." Responses were combined as "family problems" and
appear in Table 7.

Subjects also indicated the degree of distress caused by these
family problems on a 5-point scale ranging from "Extremely disturbing" to "Not disturbing at all" (family problem distress).

As expected, alcoholics and drunk drivers had more family problems than the controls (Table 7). The alcoholics clearly had more
family problems (M = 9.11) than the control group (M = 7.65). The
difference in means between group D (M = 8.43) and the control
group approached .01 significance (p = 0.0162). However, the alco-

TABLE 6   Average Number of Arrests for Drunken Driving

Means			t Scores		
Group D (N = 306)	Group A (N = 288)	Group L (N = 269)	D-A	A-L	D-L
1.54	1.07	.03	5.68*	12.36*	18.55*

*$p < .0001$

TABLE 7   Family and Job Problems

	Means			t Scores		
	Group D	Group A	Group L	D-A	A-L	D-L
Family problem frequency (items = 3; range = 0–18)	8.43	9.11	7.65	1.87	4.15***	2.41
Family problem distress (items = 3; range = 0–15)	8.13	7.99	6.52	0.29	3.37**	3.23*
Job problem frequency (items = 2; range = 0–12	6.08	7.04	6.23	3.75**	3.01*	0.60
Job problem distress (items = 2; range = 0–10)	5.29	5.51	4.87	1.02	2.95*	1.92

* p < .01
** p < .001
*** p < .0001

holics (M = 7.99) and drunk drivers (M = 8.13) were statistically similar for "family problem distress," with both more troubled than the control group (M = 6.52).

Similar questions and response scales were used for respondents' job situations (Table 7). The "job problem frequency" cluster included "How often do you find yourself tense while at your job, having no time to relax for a while?" and "How often do you have problems with your bosses, subordinates, or co-workers that make you seriously irritated, angry, or aggravated?" The "job problem distress" category included two items: how serious and disturbing the respondent considered his job problems to be, and how much distress was experienced from problems with bosses, subordinates, or co-workers. The job stress data revealed no differences between groups D and L; group A acknowledged significantly more job problems.

PERSONALITY FACTORS _____

SELF-ESTEEM

The survey included a self-esteem scale (Rosenberg, 1965), on which respondents were asked to agree or disagree with seven statements, including: "I am able to do things as well as most people"; "On the whole, I am satisfied with myself"; "I feel that I have a number of good qualities." Table 8 shows that the drunk

TABLE 8 Personality Factors

	Means			t Scores		
	Group D	Group A	Group L	D-A	A-L	D-L
Self-esteem (items = 7; range = 0–7)	6.07	5.16	6.34	8.85***	11.03***	2.79*
Self-control (items = 10; range = 0–10)	6.23	4.90	7.02	7.48***	11.34***	4.54***
Responsibility (items = 10; range = 0–10)	5.84	6.19	6.79	2.09	3.41**	5.82***
Paranoid thinking trends (items = 7; range = 0–7)	2.12	2.81	1.83	5.16***	7.07***	2.32
Depression (items = 12; range = 0–24)	12.33	16.69	10.43	8.35***	11.45***	3.75**
Aggression: Buss-Durkee (items =5; range = 0–5)	2.44	2.64	1.83	1.68	6.07***	4.75***
Aggression: fighting/throwing (items = 2; range = 0–5)	1.11	1.33	0.48	1.64	6.04***	4.83***

* $p < .01$
** $p < .001$
*** $p < .0001$

drivers had lower self-esteem than the control group but more than the alcoholic drivers.

SELF-CONTROL

The degree of control over one's impulses was another variable thought to be a likely discriminator among the groups. Obviously, alcoholics cannot control their drinking, and drunk drivers are unable to control circumstances that lead them to drive in a potentially dangerous manner.

Ten self-control items from the California Psychological Inventory (Gough, 1960) were used. Subjects were asked to agree or disagree with such statements as: "I get excited very easily"; "I often act on the spur of the moment without stopping to think"; "I often lose my temper"; "I must admit I often try to get my own way regardless of what others may want."

The data revealed that the drunk drivers had less self-control than the control group but more than the alcoholics (Table 8).

RESPONSIBILITY

A potentially important psychological variable in assessing drunk drivers is the degree of responsibility they feel toward others. Responsibility in this survey refers to a person's appreciation of the need to participate in and live by the rules of a community. The responsibility scale consisted of ten items from the California Psychological Inventory (Gough, 1960). Subjects were asked whether they agreed with such statements as: "A person who doesn't vote is not a good citizen"; "If I get too much change in a store, I always give it back"; "It's no use worrying my head about public affairs; I can't do anything about them anyway." The drunk drivers (M = 5.84) and alcoholics (M = 6.19) were similar to each other in scoring lower on expressed levels of responsibility than the control group (M = 6.79), who were significantly more responsible (Table 8).

PARANOID THINKING

To determine the presence of paranoid thinking trends, five items from the Buss-Durkee Inventory (Buss and Durkee, 1957) were used for an index of paranoid thinking. Subjects agreed or disagreed with such statements as: "I know that people tend to talk about me behind my back," and "I usually wonder what hidden reason another person may have for doing something nice for me." In addition, two other items were included in the scale: "I often feel that someone holds a grudge against me," and "There are a number of people who seem to be jealous of me." Drunk drivers (M = 2.12) and the control group (M = 1.83) were similar on this variable, and both groups were much less paranoid than the alcoholics (M = 2.81) (Table 8).

DEPRESSION

A modified version of the Short Zung Self Rating Depression Scale was used, consisting of twelve questions which are related to affect ("blue"; "crying") or elicit symptoms associated with depression ("I get tired for no reason"; ". . . trouble sleeping"; etc.) (Zung, 1965). Respondents checked how frequently they experienced these feelings on a 5-point scale ranging from "Never" to "Always." The drunk drivers (M = 12.33) were more depressed than the control group (M = 10.43) but less so than the alcoholics (M = 16.69) (Table 8).

AGGRESSION

It was hypothesized that groups A and D would be more aggressive than the control group because of their impulse-control difficulties. The study included five items from the Buss-Durkee Aggression Inventory (Buss and Durkee, 1957). Subjects were asked to agree or disagree with five statements reflecting aggressive and irritable feelings, such as: "If someone hits me first, I let him have it," and "If somebody annoys me, I am apt to tell him what I think of him." Table 8 shows that the drunk drivers and the alcoholics were similar to each other on this variable and that both had more aggressive qualities than the control group.

In addition to the Buss-Durkee items, two other items were included: "How often during the past year have you been involved in a fist fight?" and "How often during the past year did you become so angry that you threw or broke things?" Subjects were asked to indicate how often this had occurred on a 5-point scale ranging from "Never" to "Four times or more." The drunk drivers (M = 1.11) and the alcoholics (M = 1.33) were much more violent than the control group (M = 0.48) (Table 8).

DISCUSSION _____

One salient, though not unexpected, finding in this study was that over 68 percent of the men arrested for drunk driving were alcoholics. Similar data have been reported for decades. It is worth reemphasis here because of continued official resistance to the knowledge that most drunk drivers are alcoholics.

What additional factors were present in the drunk-driver population that could contribute to their drunken-driving conduct? When compared to the control group, the drunk drivers were more aggressive, more depressed, had lower self-esteem, were less responsible, and had less self-control. Factors such as low responsibility and impaired self-control imply a quality of impulsivity that may explain the difficulty in finding solutions to the drunken-driving problem.

The data indicate that most drunk drivers—whether or not they are alcoholics—usually have distinctive psychosocial and drinking problems. Most would undoubtedly benefit from rehabilitative programs. One problem in establishing rehabilitation programs for them is that drunken driving is not a definable illness—it is an event that must first occur before any curative effort can be mobilized.

Another almost paralyzing deterrent is the sheer number of drunk drivers and how very few can be apprehended. Indeed, there is reason to believe that apprehension and conviction of drunk drivers, as now implemented, is a waste of time, not only in terms of those apprehended (Buss and Durkee, 1957) but because of the myriad undeterred drunk drivers not apprehended at all.

Although the overall problem cannot be modified given our present enforcement system, the case-finding importance of drunken-driving arrests should not be overlooked. Many alcoholics are now successfully treated following a drunken-driving arrest. Had these drivers not been arrested, their treatment would not have taken place for many more self-destructive years.

What can be done to reduce the high incidence of drunken driving? Methods to deter drivers before they become drunk are essential. Attempts to educate or appeal directly to the driving public have not been particularly successful; neither have stringent penalties, particularly the long-overrated Swedish approach (Ross, 1975). Is there anything in the data provided in this paper that could lead to a meaningful approach to the not yet apprehended drunk driver? Unfortunately, the data discourage any idea of a direct approach to the drivers themselves. Most are alcoholics, and I am not aware of any public relations method for successfully coping with that syndrome. Furthermore, the forms of psychosocial impairment found in many of both the alcoholic and nonalcoholic drunk drivers make it unlikely that they would respond to "prearrest" educational programs.

Given the relative futility of arrest and our belief that drunk drivers are impervious to appeals, what is left? Judicious curtailment or manipulation of alcohol sales will have to be considered, although this will undoubtedly raise howls of anguish from predictable sources and evoke pained silence from others. The protests will come from those who profit commercially from the production of alcoholic beverages and from their advertising beneficiaries. The silence will come from government officials and legislators fearful of tax losses, irate voters, or both.

A reduction of alcohol consumption may be attempted in three ways: banning all advertising, manipulating the hours during which alcoholic beverages can be sold, and increasing taxation.

The least painful approach for the general public would be a complete and total ban of all alcohol advertising, regardless of media or type of beverage. Given the appalling consequences of alcoholism and drunken driving, a ban on advertising would be a small price to pay for an overall reduction in total alcohol consumption. Others have posited that only through a reduction in total alcohol consumption can society anticipate any real drop in alcoholism rates. This reasoning can obviously be extended to the drunk-driving syndrome. Unfortunately, there is no certainty that a total ban on alcohol advertising would reduce consumption, but one suspects that it would. Comparisons with the elimination of cigarette advertising from United States television are not valid. When that ban took effect, other forms of advertising ballooned.

Manipulation of the hours when alcoholic beverages can be sold may well be the most feasible way of controlling drunken driving and its related mishaps. Since these episodes are essentially night-time phenomena, experimentation with halting package sales at 3 P.M. or earlier and all liquor sales at 10 or 11 P.M. would be in order. It could be argued that one could still buy as much liquor as possible early in the day. True enough, but such purchases require planning and prudence, attributes that are obviously not common in drunk-driving populations—and particularly absent during the hours before their arrests.

Increased taxation of alcoholic beverages is a proved method of reducing sales and hence consumption. However, it penalizes all drinkers indiscriminately and probably should be considered as a last resort, if at all.

REFERENCES _____

Borkenstein, R. F. A proposal for increasing the effectiveness of ASAP enforcement programs. Mimeographed. Bloomington, Ind.: Indiana University, 1972.

Buss, A. H., and Durkee, A. An inventory for assessing different kinds of hostility. *Journal of Consulting and Clinical Psychology,* 21:343–349, 1957.

Conger, J. J. Research trends in traffic safety. *Traffic Safety Research Review,* 5:30–32, 1961.

Conger, J. J., Gaskill, H. S., Glad, D. D., Rainey, R. V., Sawrey, W. L., and Turrell, E. S. Personal and interpersonal factors in motor vehicle accidents. *American Journal of Psychiatry,* 113:1069–1074, 1957.

Cresswell, W. L., and Grogatt, P. *The Causation of Bus Driver Accidents: An Epidemiological Study.* London: Oxford University Press, 1963.

Gough, H. *Manual for the California Psychological Inventory, rev. ed.* Palo Alto, Calif.: Consulting Psychologists Press, 1960.

Greenwood, M., and Woods, H. M. *Preliminary Report on Special Tests.* Sacramento: California Department of Motor Vehicles, 1919.

Hinkle, L. E., et al. Studies in human ecology. *American Journal of Psychiatry,* 114:212–220, 1957.

Holmes, T. H., and Rahe, R. H. The social readjustment rating scale. *Journal of Psychosomatic Research,* 11:213–218, 1967.

Kent, D. P., and Novotny, G. B. Age and automotive accidents. *Geriatrics,* 16:271–277, 1961.

McFarland, R. A., and Moore, R. C. Human factors in highway safety: A review and evaluation. *Journal of Medicine,* 256:792–798, 1957.

McFarland, R. A., and Moseley, A. L. *Human Factors in Highway Transport Safety.* Cambridge, Mass.: Harvard School of Public Health, 1954.

McMurray, L. Emotional stress on driving performance: The effect of divorce. *Behavior Research in Highway Safety,* 1:100–114, 1970.

Paykel, E. S., et al. Life events and depression. *Archives of General Psychiatry,* 21:753–760, 1969.

Popham, R. E. Alcoholism and traffic accidents. *Quarterly Journal of Studies in Alcohol,* 17:225–232, 1956.

Rahe, R. H. Life crisis and health change. In R. A. Philip and J. S. Winterborn, eds., *Psychotropic Drug Response: Advances in Prediction.* Springfield, Ill.: Thomas, 1969.

Rahe, R. H., Gunderson, E. K., and Arthur, R. J. Demographic and Psychosocial factors in acute illness reporting. *Journal of Chronic Disease,* 23:245–255, 1971.

Rahe, R. H., and Link, E. Psychosocial factors and sudden cardiac death: A pilot study. *Journal of Psychosomatic Research,* 15:19–24, 1971.

Rahe, R. H., McKean, J. D., and Arthur, R. J. A longitudinal study of lifechange and illness patterns. *Journal of Psychosomatic Research,* 10:355–366, 1966.

Rahe, R. H., Meyer, M., Smith, M., Kjaer, G., and Holmes, T. H. Social stress and illness onset. *Journal of Psychosomatic Research,* 8:35–44, 1964.

Rahe, R. H., and Paasidivi, J. Psychosocial factors and myocardial infarction: II. An outpatient study in Sweden. *Journal of Psychosomatic Research,* 15:33–39, 1971.

Rosenberg, M. *Society and the Adolescent Self-Image.* Princeton, N.J.: Princeton University Press, 1965.

Ross, H. The Scandinavian myth: Effectiveness of drinking-and-driving legislation in Sweden and Norway. *Journal of Legal Studies,* 4:285–295, 1975.

Schuster, D. H., and Guilford, J. D. The psychometric prediction of problem drivers. *Human Factors,* 6:393–421, 1964.

Selzer, M. L. Personality versus intoxication as crucial factor in accidents caused by alcoholic drivers. *Journal of Nervous and Mental Disease,* 132:298–303, 1961.

Selzer, M. L. Alcoholism, mental illness, and stress in 96 drivers causing fatal accidents. *Behavioral Science,* 14:1–10, 1969.

Selzer, M. L., and Barton, E. The drunken driver: A psychosocial study: II. *Drug and Alcohol Dependence*, 2:239–253, 1977.

Selzer, M. L., and Payne, C. E. Automobile accidents, suicide, and unconscious motivation. *American Psychiatry*, 119:237–240, 1962.

Selzer, M. L., Payne, C. E., Kelly, W., and Gifford, J. Alcoholism, mental illness and the drunk driver. *American Journal of Psychiatry*, 120:311–326, 1967.

Selzer, M. L., and Vinokur, A. Life events, subjective stress, and traffic accidents. *American Journal of Psychiatry*, 131:903–906, 1974.

Selzer, M. L., and Vinokur, A. Driving and psychosocial characteristics of drunk drivers. In *Proceedings, 19th Annual Conference of The American Association for Automotive Medicine*. San Diego, Calif., 1975, pp. 244–252.

Selzer, M. L., Vinokur, A., and Wilson, T. A psychosocial comparison of drunk drivers and alcoholics. *Journal of Studies in Alcohol*, 38:1294–1312, 1977.

Tabachnick, N., Litman, R. E., Osman, M., Jones, W. L., Cohn, J., Casper, A., and Moffat, J. Comparative psychiatric study of accidental and suicidal death. *Archives of General Psychiatry*, 14:60–68, 1966.

Theorell, T., and Rahe, R. H. Psychosocial factors and myocardial infarction: I. An inpatient study in Sweden. *Journal of Psychosomatic Research*, 15:25–31, 1971.

Tillman, W. A., and Hobbs, G. E. The accident-prone automobile driver: A study of psychiatric and social background. *American Journal of Psychiatry*, 106:321–331, 1949.

Wolfe, A. C. 1973 U.S. national roadside breath testing survey: Procedures and results. (Report No. UM-HSRI-AL-74-4.) Ann Arbor, Mich.: University of Michigan Highway Safety Research Institute, 1974.

Yoder, R. D., and Moore, R. A. Characteristics of convicted drunken drivers. *Quarterly Journal of Studies in Alcohol*, 34:927–936, 1973.

Zung, W. A self-rating depression scale. *Archives of General Psychiatry*, 12:63–70, 1965.

19

GAMBLING
An Existential-Humanistic Interpretation

IGOR KUSYSZYN

G ambling has been defined as the willingness to risk something in the hope of a gain. Studies of personality factors related to risk-taking suggest there is a general tendency in people either to approach or to avoid risk-taking situations (Knowles et al., 1973). Risk-taking has also been seen as an activity which is in and of itself rewarding (Von Neumann and Morgenstern, 1947). While some studies have shown some people to prefer risk to gain (Goodnow, 1955; Cohen, 1972), the preference for risk has also been interpreted as a need to reach an optimum level of physiological arousal (Berlyne, 1960).

The thesis of this chapter is that gambling is a functional activity in that it provides a convenient means of satisfying two basic human needs. Through gambling, the gambler may *confirm his existence* and *affirm his worth.* He both confirms his existence and affirms his worth *by having an effect* (real or imagined) in his gambling environment. By having an effect, or coming close to having an effect, he becomes cognitively, emotionally, and physically aroused; this arousal confirms his existence. And by having this effect he also feels good about himself. This "good" feeling helps to affirm his worth, especially when his gambling effectiveness (expertise) is recognized by others.

The motives for *self-destructive* forms of gambling are similar, i.e., the confirmation of existence and affirmation of worth. The self-destructive gambler confirms his existence through the arousal of painful emotions and negative, self-depreciating cognitions (i.e., "I'm no good"). In the case of the self-depreciating cognitions, the gambler affirms his *lack of worth* over and over again. I believe, however, that the purpose of his gambling is the *striving* for a confirmation of worth and that he gets a glimpse of his worth on the few occasions that he wins (has an effect on his gambling environment). In terms of reinforcement theory, it is this positive partial reinforcement that maintains the gambling behavior. The self-destructive gambler's motives, therefore, are to confirm his existence (through pain) and to search for his worth through continuous gambling.

Seven existential concepts are related to the motives of the confirmation of existence and the affirmation of worth: autonomy, freedom, desire, choice, action, responsibility, and identity. According to Jean-Paul Sartre, a man is the sum of his actions. A man self-actualizes or achieves his sense of *identity* (selfhood) through his *actions* (trying to have an effect on his environment) and by taking *responsibility* for those actions. (Conversely, when responsibility for one's actions is denied, the "becoming" of the self is also automatically denied.) From the time of birth (possibly earlier) all organisms have a strong natural need to grow. In humans this growth takes the form of a continuous process of self-discovery through never-ending series of actions. The organism becomes emotionally aware very early in life that among the most pleasant kinds of self-discovery are those which result from *autonomous* action. Our feeling is most profound when we ourselves have caused (are responsible for) the feeling.[1] In turn, in order for the action to be autonomous, we need absolute *freedom* to act. Absolute freedom can be attained only by taking absolute responsibility for one's actions. By taking absolute responsibility for one's actions one becomes the sole creator of one's essence, one's self, one's *identity*. One also becomes a free spirit.

Central to the idea of action is the idea of *choice*. It is in the process of independently choosing a course of action that the act of authentically creating the self occurs. The nature of the choice is determined by our present incomplete, always-seeking-for-fulfillment psychosociobiological self. That is, we *desire* one choice rather than another according to our biological (including genetic), psychological (experiential), and social history. The biological drives toward self-expression are the most authentic. The psychological and social drives are more at the mercy of the influence of others through the process of socialization (conditioning). Stress on socialization early in life dampens the natural desire for self-expression and leads to inauthentic (unhealthy) choices later in life. Conversely, a supporting social environment fosters an open per-

---

[1] This need to be a cause is termed "effectance motivation"—we have a need to have an effect on our environment. Conversely, by affecting our environment we are affected by the feedback we cause. Much research evidence supports the existence of effectance motivation (see White, 1959; Kusyszyn, 1977).

son, a person with the courage of self-expression and the willingness to suffer to achieve a valued state of being in relation to other men's expectations and his own.

What has all this to do with the gambler? How do gamblers confirm their existence and affirm their worth? To set the scene for the exposition of the thesis, we must first place gambling in the arena of play. Gambling is, more than anything else, *adult play*. After all, gamblers are referred to as players who play games, play cards, play dice, play the horses, play the stock market, and so on. Gamblers do not gamble for the purpose of winning money, because 99 percent of them lose yet continue to gamble (Jacoby, 1963). They gamble in order to play. When gambling is taken as a play activity, its relationship to the existential concepts becomes readily apparent.

The gambler (player) exhibits a *freedom* of *choice* in that he *independently* (of his own free will) chooses the game he most *desires*. He also chooses the manner of his participation in the game (according to his psychosociobiological history). His style of participation is an expression of his present self, and his participatory *actions* are a search for his true self or *identity*. That the gambler takes *responsibility* for the outcome (wins and losses) which his actions produce is axiomatic. He takes responsibility through the staking of his hard-earned money. The staking of the money commits him to and involves him (cognitively and emotionally) in the activity. The gambler has under complete personal control the degree of his commitment to the game. He has the freedom to alter his degree of commitment at any time. For example, he can raise or lower the size of his bet; he can quit any time. (It's only a game.) The freedom for self-regulation of involvement provides for self-expression and self-stimulation. These (together with the responsibility already taken for the actions) lead to "peak" experiences, to the confirmation of existence and the affirmation of worth. The reason why a person chooses gambling over any other activity to express his existential needs is that he has been exposed to gambling as an activity during childhood, engaged in by parents, relatives, and/or peers. The activity, therefore, was always seen as legitimate and acceptable within his subculture. Gambling was also selected because the person really believed he had the skills to participate successfully. These included such skills as problem solving, information processing, arithmetic ability, etc. These were skills which could be used in gambling and thus served to actualize the self. The "peak experiences" and feeling of self-worth which resulted served as strong reinforcers.

An amusing example of how gambling provides for the experiencing of worth comes from Zola (1963). Zola was observing a group of horse-race bettors. He writes, "One regular revealed the meaning of being a winner when amid the talk and praise of his selection, he yelled, 'What do you think I am, a nobody?' "

It is through the free, independent self-regulation of action that the gambler confirms his existence. The gambler proves to himself over and over again that he is alive by speeding up his heart rate and increasing his muscle tension and by becoming emotionally aroused either positively with hope, excitement, and euphoria, or negatively with anxiety, disappointment, sorrow, and regret. He further confirms his existence and affirms his worth by eliciting, with his actions, cognitive-emotional states involving the self. He elicits feelings of pride, courage, and esteem. He also confirms his existence through the arousal of other-directed emotions such as anger, hostility, and aggression. The gambler replaces Descartes's dictum "I think, therefore I am" with "I *feel*, therefore I am."

Lem Banker, a professional sports bettor, said the following about watching a televised football game he had bet on: "You live and die a dozen times on a Sunday afternoon. It's a three-hour mystical experience." Dostoevsky (1866/1972), in *The Gambler*, writes: "I had got this at the risk of more than life. I dared to run the risk and now I am a man again."

A British horseplayer being interviewed by a social scientist said the following: "You ask me why I gamble and I tell you, it's the thrill. I know the game is crooked and I haven't a chance, but when I put my money on a horse and hear its name on the speaker, my heart stands still. I know I am alive" (Newman, 1972, p. 206).

It seems to me that all forms of play, not just gambling, are media for existential growth. It is tragic that we do not play more in life.

HEALTHY AND PATHOLOGICAL GAMBLING: WHERE DOES SELF-DESTRUCTIVE GAMBLING FIT? _____

A classification scheme portraying sixteen varieties of healthy and pathological gambling is presented in a attempt to provide a framework within which "self-destructive" gambling may more clearly reveal itself. The entire framework is composed of combinations of only four variables: (1) *money*, (2) *time*, (3) *other people*, and (4) *the gambler*. The four factors are depicted as relatively independent: (1) a lot of money is either won or lost (relative to the total amount available);[2] (2) a lot of time or only a little time is devoted to gambling; (3) other people are either interfered with or are not interfered

---

[2] Large, not small, amounts of money are meant here. In *social* gambling only small amounts are either won or lost. For this reason social gambling is omitted from the present framework. It should be stated for the record, however, that social gambling is the most common form of gambling in real life, encompassing approximately 99 percent of all gambling.

with (family, friends, society); and (4) the gambler perceives himself as healthy or he perceives himself as sick (self-concept).

In terms of the present scheme the frame outlining the *professional gambler* is the one in which a lot of money is won, a lot of time is devoted to gambling, other people are not affected negatively, and the gambler feels good about himself (see type 1). One common type of "compulsive" gambler is depicted as a person who loses a lot of money, spends a lot of time gambling, interferes with the lives of others, and feels bad about it all (see type 12). All sixteen forms of gambling are depicted in Table 1.

The present framework employs combinations of variables based purely on logic. Because of its logical base the framework is all-inclusive and forces the serious scholar to consider all sixteen possible forms of gambling. Although some of the healthy forms may be distasteful to or even repressed by a clinician, selective perception is not given the chance to operate within the present model. Because objectivity is forced on the reader, certain philosophical, ethical, social, and scientific questions pertaining to gambling automatically arise and beg to be answered. Several such questions are raised below, accompanying the descriptions of certain gambling types.

THE EIGHT WINNING TYPES

TYPE 1. Wins a lot of money. Spends a lot of time gambling. Feels good about his gambling. Does not affect other people negatively. This is the happy professional. He is not sick. In Maslow's (1970) terms, he may be self-actualizing. His gambling behavior is self-instructive (not self-destructive) in that it plays a major role in his psychological growth.

TYPE 2. Wins a lot of money. Spends a lot of time gambling. Feels bad about his gambling. Does not affect other people negatively. This is the unhappy professional. Is he "compulsive"? No, because he has the skill and control to win a lot of money. This type is similar to Bergler's (1957) "success-hunter"—the gambler who has both a conscious and an unconscious desire to win, not lose. Is he sick? Probably. How is he sick? We do not know. There may be some self-destructive tendencies, but they are not directly related to his gambling; they may stem from something else entirely. All we can say with confidence is that his gambling behavior is not as self-actualizing as it could be.

TYPE 3. Wins a lot of money. Spends a lot of time gambling. Feels good about his gambling. Affects other people negatively. This is the happy professional among nonsupportive people. His

---

TABLE 1 *A Model of Sixteen Gambling Types*

Winners	*Losers*
1. *The professional gambler* Wins a lot of money Spends a lot of time Feels good Others not affected	9. *The happy sportsman* Loses a lot of money Spends a lot of time Feels good Others not affected
2. *The unhappy professional* Wins a lot of money Spends a lot of time Feels bad Others not affected	10. *The unhappy sportsman* Loses a lot of money Spends a lot of time Feels bad Others not affected
3. *The bothersome professional* Wins a lot of money Spends a lot of time Feels good Affects others negatively	11. *The happy habitual* Loses a lot of money Spends a lot of time Feels good Affects others negatively
4. *The bothersome unhappy professional* Wins a lot of money Spends a lot of time Feels bad Affects others negatively	12. *The classical "compulsive" gambler* Loses a lot of money Spends a lot of time Feels bad Affects others negatively
5. *The happy lottery winner* Wins a lot of money Spends very little time Feels good Others not affected	13. *The happy binge player* Loses a lot of money Spends very little time Feels good Others not affected
6. *The unhappy lottery winner* Wins a lot of money Spends very little time Feels bad Others not affected	14. *The unhappy binge player* Loses a lot of money Spends very little time Feels bad Others not affected
7. *The bothersome lottery winner* Wins a lot of money Spends very little time Feels good Affects others negatively	15. *The bothersome binge player* Loses a lot of money Spends very little time Feels good Affects others negatively
8. *The bothersome unhappy lottery winner* Wins a lot of money Spends very little time Feels bad Affects others negatively	16. *The acute "compulsive?"* Loses a lot of money Spends very little time Feels bad Affects others negatively

friends and family disapprove. Is he sick? No. Is he "compulsive"? No. Yet "help" may be forced upon him. He may even be ostracized if he does not conform to the others' wishes. What should he do? Can he remain authentic? How? It might even be considered self-destructive for this gambler to *terminate* his gambling. He is faced with an existential crisis. What happens depends on the nature of his relationships with his family and friends.

TYPE 4. Wins a lot of money. Spends a lot of time gambling. Feels bad about his gambling. Affects others negatively. This is the unhappy professional among disapproving friends. Is he sick? Probably. Is he "compulsive"? No. Does he need help? Yes. Will he get help? Most likely because of the others' reactions. Is his gambling self-destructive? Yes, because it is not self-actualizing. He experiences, instead, depression, hostility, anxiety, and low self-esteem.

TYPE 5. Wins a lot of money. Spends very little time gambling. Feels good about his gambling. Does not affect other people negatively. This is the happy lottery winner among understanding friends. Obviously not sick.

TYPE 6. Wins a lot of money. Spends very little time gambling. Feels bad about his gambling. Does not affect other people negatively. This is the unhappy lottery winner among understanding friends. Why is he unhappy? Is he sick? How?

TYPE 7. Wins a lot of money. Spends very little time gambling. Feels good about his gambling. Affects others negatively. This is the happy lottery winner among nonsupportive friends. Who is "sick" here?

TYPE 8. Wins a lot of money. Spends very little time gambling. Feels bad about his gambling. Affects others negatively. This is the unhappy lottery winner who bothers other people. Is he sick? Probably. In which ways is he sick? This category probably contains a small number.

THE EIGHT TYPES OF LOSERS

TYPE 9. Loses a lot of money. Spends a lot of time gambling. Feels good about his gambling. Does not affect other people negatively. This is the millionaire playboy who loves to gamble. Is he sick? We don't know. Should he receive clinical help? That is an ethical question.

TYPE 10. Loses a lot of money. Spends a lot of time gambling. Feels bad about his gambling. Does not affect other people. This is the sad loser who is alone in the world. This is a strongly self-destructive type, but unfortunately he does not bother others because there is no one who cares. He is probably compulsive and sick in other ways as well. How will help reach him?

TYPE 11. Loses a lot of money. Spends a lot of time gambling. Feels good about his gambling. Affects others negatively. This is the happy loser who bothers other people. This is probably the most common type of habitual gambler. In terms of self-concept, he does not see himself as being compulsive. He sees his gambling as a positive activity which adds pleasure and meaning to his life. In Glasser's (1976) terms, this is a *positive addiction* for the gambler. Is this man sick? Society may say he is; he may say he is not. His behavior may or may not be self-destructive at the present time. He may bring destruction upon himself in time by losing his disapproving "friends." On the other hand he may find new approving friends. If he is wealthy enough to afford his losses, he will be happy and continue to self-actualize among his new friends.

TYPE 12. Loses a lot of money. Spends a lot of time gambling. Feels bad about his gambling. Affects other people negatively. This is the sad loser who makes other people's lives miserable. This is the most common type of gambler to come to the attention of treatment agents and institutions. This is the classical "compulsive" gambler about whom so much has been written. Regrettably, this single type, out of at least sixteen possible types, is the *only* type that exists for most clinicians, laymen, newspaper reporters, and Hollywood film producers. This sad state of affairs offers an instructive comment on the values of society. Thanks to the media, this rare type (the frequency of this type is about one in a thousand persons who gamble) is in the eyes of the world the most common type. I believe it is the responsibility of every social scientist who writes about gambling to correct the imbalance.

TYPE 13. Loses a lot of money. Spends very little time gambling. Feels good about his gambling. Does not affect other people. This type and the three types which follow are rare because it is difficult to lose a lot of money in a short span of time. However, Type 13 is found among wealthy gamblers who go on occasional junkets to Las Vegas and among wealthy gamblers who have high credit ratings with their bookmakers during the football, baseball, and basketball seasons. Well-to-do business men and famous movie stars regularly lose hundreds of thousands of dollars in these quick and painless ways. Are they sick? Are they self-destructive or does gambling simply provide a temporary respite from a complicated existence?

TYPE 14. Loses a lot of money. Spends very little time gambling. Feels bad about his gambling. Does not affect other people negatively. This is the unhappy binge player who is without friends. Is he compulsive? Not in the usual way. His behavior becomes self-destructive when he loses control from time to time and acts out impulsively.

TYPE 15. Loses a lot of money. Spends very little time gambling. Feels good about his gambling. Affects other people negatively. This is the happy, wealthy binge player who can afford to lose a lot of money but finds it bothers other people. Is he self-destructive? He can become so if he loses his fortune, or his friends, or both.

TYPE 16. Loses a lot of money. Spends very little time gambling. Feels bad about his gambling. Affects other people negatively. This is the unhappy binge player who bothers other people. He is sometimes found in the stock market. He sometimes commits suicide. He is obviously self-destructive.

THE ISDB TYPE OF GAMBLER —————————————

From the point of view of society, the types who come closest to being either directly or indirectly self-destructive (ISD) are the acute compulsive, or the unhappy binge player who bothers other people (type 16); the classical compulsive gambler, or the sad loser who makes other people's lives miserable (type 12); and the unhappy sportsman, or the sad loser who is alone in the world (type 10). The other types who might be partly indirectly self-destructive are the unhappy binge player who is without friends (type 14); the bothersome unhappy professional who is among disapproving friends (type 4); and the unhappy professional (type 2). In each instance the gambling is self-destructive, for it is not self-actualizing. Instead, the activity is characterized by denial, impulsivity, hostility, and anxiety.

In general the ISD-type gambler is one who engages in *excessive* behaviors. Besides taking monetary risks, he also takes social, physical, and moral risks. He may eat to excess, drink to excess, play to excess, spend to excess, etc. The excessive behaviors are part of his hyperactive, impulsive style. The ISD gambler will more often be found in Gamblers Anonymous groups and in psychiatric care, where he is seen as compulsive or pathological. He is sometimes a professional gambler; he is never just a social gambler.

The ISD gambler, in his excesses, engages in unchecked fantasies. He dreams of winning great amounts of money, which will then buy him anything he desires—cars, status, power, friends, even a reputation as a philanthropist. Money is thus seen as a tool, necessary only for solving problems and affirming self-worth. Money has little value in itself. Unfortunately, this attitude affects his relationships in his family, for his fantasies include getting them everything they need with his imagined winnings. He is blind to their needs for affection; self-worth is proved only by winning.

IMPLICATIONS OF THE
SIXTEEN-TYPES MODEL _____

Marshall McLuhan and others before him have demonstrated how imperfect language is for describing reality. McLuhan accuses us of "label-libel." Once we have labeled a piece of reality, we tend to focus our attention on the implications of the label rather than on the actual piece of reality. Label-libel impedes scientific progress. In medicine and in psychology the careless labeling of pathologies can have perilous consequences for treatment. For these reasons it is important to recognize that the problem of defining pathological gambling is multifaceted. If a definition is to approach veridicality, it must include references to nonpsychological as well as psychological factors.

The present writer's bias is that the gambler's self-percept should be the factor which determines whether his gambling is labeled pathological or healthy. However, a completely objective approach to defining gambling must contain at least six attributes: self-concept, professionals' (clinicians) perceptions, nonprofessionals' perceptions, time spent in gambling, amount of money involved, and whether money is being won or lost.

This multifaceted approach to gambling types has myriad implications. At *the level of the individual,* the model suggests that one can be healthy although a loser and that one can be unhealthy although a winner. These two possibilities may appear paradoxical, even to professionals, in our materialistic, achievement-oriented culture. An open-minded stance is required if we are to understand all the possibilities (see Newman, 1975).

At the family level the model underlines the importance of the attitudes of the family members toward the gambler. Their attitudes can significantly contribute to whether his gambling is labeled healthy or pathological. The degree of their concern will also determine how soon the gambler receives treatment (whether he needs it or not).

This brings us to *the level of the treatment agent or agency.* If one subscribes to the present model, one must face the possibility of confronting a healthy, self-actualizing gambler who is being pushed into treatment by unsympathetic relatives. The clinician's values are forced to the surface. To what degree should he intervene? To whom is he responsible? Who will benefit from his actions? Who may suffer? Who will take the responsibility for the consequences of his actions? These are existential questions. There are no ready answers. As long as the model continues to raise such questions, it will be proving its worth by contributing to our thinking about both pathological and nonpathological gambling.

REFERENCES _____

Bergler, E. *The Psychology of Gambling*. New York: Hill and Wang, 1957.

Berlyne, D. E. *Conflict, Arousal, and Curiosity*. New York: McGraw-Hill, 1960.

Cohen, J. The nature of gambling. In I. Kusyszyn, ed., *Studies in the Psychology of Gambling*. Toronto: York University, 1972.

Dostoevsky, F. *The Gambler and The Diary of Polina Suslova*. Chicago: University of Chicago Press, 1972. (Originally published, 1866.)

Glasser, W. *Positive Addiction*. New York: Harper and Row, 1976.

Goodnow, J. J. Determinants of choice distribution in two-choice situations. *American Journal of Psychology*, 68:106–116, 1955.

Jacoby, O. *Oswald Jacoby on Gambling*. New York: Hart, 1963.

Knowles, E. S., Cutter, S. G., Walsh, D. H., and Casey, N. Risk-taking as a personality trait. *Social Behavior and Personality*, 1:123–136, 1973.

Kusyszyn, I. How gambling saved me from a misspent sabbatical. *Journal of Humanistic Psychology*, 17:19–34, 1977.

Maslow, A. H. *Motivation and Personality*, 2nd ed. New York: Harper and Row, 1970.

Newman, O. *Gambling: Hazard and Reward*. London: Athlone, 1972.

Newman, O. The ideology of social problems: Gambling, a case study. *Canadian Review of Sociology and Anthropology*, 12(4, Part 2), 1975.

Von Neumann, J., and Morgenstern, O. *Theory of Games and Economic Behavior*. Princeton, N. J.: Princeton University Press, 1947.

White, R. W. Motivation reconsidered: The concept of competence. *Psychological Review*, 66:297–333, 1959.

Zola, I. K. Observations on gambling in a lower-class setting. *Social Problems*, 10:353–361, 1963. (Also in R. D. Herman, ed., *Gambling*. New York: Harper and Row, 1967.)

PART SIX

CRIMINAL ACTIVITY AND DEVIANCE

20

SELF-DESTRUCTIVENESS AMONG OFFENDERS

HANS TOCH

On the face of it, it is inviting to view crime—which by definition is *punishable*—as activity that reliably ignores or defies the offender's long-term self-interest. This assumption is presupposed in the slogan "Crime does not pay," which holds true for some offenses but not for others and, within offense categories, applies with different force to different offenders.

On the average—to the misfortune of society and of our search for self-destructive perspectives—crime *does* pay. *Most* crime has no untoward punishment consequences, and if the average offender "played the odds" he could find no reason for interrupting his predatory or criminal career.[1] An offender might be self-destructive in other respects—he might steal, for example, to support an unfaithful wife—but he would not be *self-destructively criminal*.

The presumption of self-destructiveness may seem most attractive when it is applied to imprisoned offenders. Here we may consider particularly (1) prison veterans, who belong to the 70 percent or 80 percent who have been convicted before (and who are not to be confused with the 30 percent who will be convicted again), and (2) individual offenders, such as the average murderer, who have committed highly visible acts that carry a high probability of apprehension. There are also offense categories in which individual acts are not risky, but in which chronicity increases visibility and raises the probability of apprehension. Some such categories involve high-risk criminal careers, such as check forgery; others involve pathological or compulsive patterns, such as those of the recidivistic sex offender.

---

[1] For documentation of this point see clearance rates in the FBI's Uniform Crime Reports for the United States (any years). In considering these rates, remember that they exclude criminal victimization that is unreported to the police. Such victimization covers an unknown number of incidents, which is estimated (from victimization surveys) to be appreciable. Some offenses, such as rolling married clients of ladies of the night, have almost no chance of being reported, according to victimization surveyors.

A particularly inviting case for self-destructiveness could be made in relation to persons who seem to "arrange to be reimprisoned." While such behavior patterns are hard to validate, relevant case studies highlight self-generated increases in risk, such as that of the burglar who remains on the scene as police sirens approach, or of the check artist who records his address on the checks he cashes. Paradoxically, conduct which leads to imprisonment can be constructive under specifiable conditions. Prison is an environment that contains strictures and deprivations, but it is also a multiservice agency supplying housing, food, clothing, medical and dental care, educational and other opportunities. Some people who are unable to negotiate the complex challenges of the outside world may cheerfully pay the price prison exacts for the simplified existence it provides. Such a contingency may be pitiful, but it is hardly self-destructively motivated.

This example is of general interest in the issues that it raises for us. There are obviously contingencies an "outside observer" regards as unambiguously undesirable, as sufficiently painful to be avoided at all costs. The person *in* the situation, however, may have a different perspective. For one, the undesirability of certain contingencies is *relative,* and the observer may see hypothetical options that the subject does not. Jumping into a frying pan is self-destructive, but the jumper may see his alternative as the fire; the "deep blue sea" can clearly be refreshing when the "devil" lurks at one's back. Drug trafficking may thus be risky, but it may be a welcome alternative to unskilled labor or unemployment; prison may look less ominous when it is viewed from a slum street corner than from an ivy-covered study.

To make this point is not to resolve a question, but to pose it. We risk defining self-destructiveness out of existence if we accept each person's assessment of his available options at face value. A drug addict, for instance, would appear non-self-destructive if we accepted his premise that he faces a painful or empty life if he is deprived of drugs. Even suicide would escape our scrutiny if we stipulate the unremitting misery the self-destroyed subject sees as his continued existence.

Before we face this sort of problem, we can try to dispose of one loophole we have left. We can resolve that an offender is unambiguously self-destructive when he behaves in a way which risks consequences he perceives as both probable and undesirable. But even this example, which seems straightforward, is not. We know that compulsive offenders, at the moment of their burgeoning resolves, feel *compelled* to act in ways that *at other times* meet our definition. (So do schizophrenics, whose controls may lapse sporadically and episodically, under protection of personality disjunctions such as blackouts and amnesias.) A person's perspective at the time of committing the offense must document, in some fashion, the case for offending. To diagnose subjective self-destructiveness, therefore, we must talk about the offender's *average* perspective, *excluding* his criminal resolve, and obviously *preceding* the advent of destructive consequences.

This description fits a category of offender who may be called *conflicted*, in that his disposition combines motives for offending with competing (law-abiding) premises. An offender of this kind is self-destructive on at least two counts: (1) because he finds himself doing things *some* of the time that *most* of the time strike him as undesirable, and (2) because he is the fulcrum of forces that coexist uncomfortably, even painfully, with each other. The image that comes to mind is that of the penitent skid-row tourist or the shamefaced exhibitionist on the "morning after." However, there are more prevalent and less dramatic versions of this syndrome among "main-line" offenders, including more young delinquents than most people suspect. According to one estimate (Palmer, 1970), more than half of all serious male delinquents and three-fourths of serious female delinquents are conflicted or neurotic. Warren (1977) writes that delinquents "so classified have a good deal of internal wear-and-tear involving anxiety, guilt, a 'bad me' self-image, 'negative life script,' distorted perceptions, and dysfunctional behavior." She believes that delinquency frequently involves a private meaning and represents more than merely "material gain or response to cultural pressure." The delinquent may be acting out "a family problem, an identity crisis, or a long-standing internal conflict" (p. 364).

In this connection, a distinction must be drawn between self-destructive personality *features*, self-destructive *persons*, and self-destructive *acts*. The unfortunate youths described by Palmer and Warren are delinquents whose behavior reveals self-destructive *features*, but these youths also have dominant personality traits that are anything but self-destructive. In fact, such youths respond more readily to treatment than do other delinquents (Palmer, 1975). By the same token, tragic, irrevocable self-destruction can reflect small, unrepresentative samples of offender behavior and personality. A man may kill the wife he loves in a fit of jealous rage, and may spend the rest of his life remorsefully digesting his tragic lapse in a prison cell. Such a man is not a self-destructive *person*, but is a person who has committed a self-destructive *act*. The same point holds wherever we see no *pattern* of self-destructive *conduct*, and this probably includes most completed suicides. When we think about self-destructive *personality* we think of stable traits or recurrent traits that produce stable or recurrent behavior. Several offender types come to mind in this connection. One such type is the *inadequate* offender. This type of person has achieved clinical respectability, in that offender dossiers prominently include diagnoses of "inadequate personality" or "personality with features of inadequacy." The American Psychiatric Association's *Diagnostic Manual* (second edition, 1968) officially defines the "inadequate personality" as "characterized by ineffectual responses to emotional, social, intellectual, and physical demands. While the patient seems neither physically nor mentally deficient, he does manifest inadaptability, ineptness, poor judgment, social instability, and lack of physical and emotional stamina."

We have facetiously characterized this type in a diagnosis of "shnookiness," with the caveat that it can be seen by clinicians as a dominant or subsidiary personality feature. Clinicians can thus speak of a "shnooky nut" (a dissociative personality with features of inadequacy), a "nutty shnook" (inadequate personality with dissociative features), a "crumby shnook" (inadequate personality with sociopathic features) or a "shnooky crumb" (sociopathic personality with features of inadequacy). Such labels recur very frequently in diagnostic workups on inmates.

It is obvious that inadequacy *as a clinical syndrome* is vulnerable to serious (as well as tongue-in-cheek) criticisms.[2] For one, the term is a blatant value judgment, a mixture of contempt, condescension, patronization, superciliousness, with a whiff of pity. The elements of the definition are also clearly too heterogeneous to reflect a common dynamic. As defined, an "inadequate personality" is a poor coper. But fate (as we all know) is a poor human engineer; we all find ourselves, from time to time, badly matched with environmental "demands." Moreover, though some of us may "respond ineffectually" to a wide range of "demands," our failures can have vastly different origins, even if we exclude "physical or mental deficiency" from our equation.

---

[2] Such criticisms may not apply to technical uses of the term to distinguish delinquents with extremely underdeveloped egos (such as those described by Redl and Wineman, 1962) from the more "advanced" neurotics such as 14s in the Warren-Palmer typology. For us, the advantage of such a distinction is that it identifies youths who are oblivious to their self-destructiveness and calls them "inadequate." The term, however, has undesirable connotations. As Aichhorn and Redl and Wineman have pointed out, among delinquents of this type extreme ego underdevelopment goes hand in hand with *effective* (but specialized) ego functioning. Though a youth may be helplessly sucked into destructiveness (and self-destructiveness), he is anything but inadequate in coping with adult reactions (including criminal justice reactions) to his misbehavior. Redl and Wineman talk about this effectiveness (in defense of delinquent impulsivity) as the "delinquent ego" (Redl and Wineman, 1962).

Inadequacy makes sense as a *behavioral* description, as a way of saying that a person, in retrospect, doesn't seem to have done very well in what he set out to do in his life. In this sense, offenders are sometimes inadequate offenders, as opposed to being effective offenders. This statement applies, for example, to the average felony murderer, who is often a robber who has shot people because he managed his robberies poorly, allowed himself to panic, became confused, or cut an otherwise unprepossessing figure as stage manager. A sex offender may similarly be a man who went about the preliminaries to lovemaking with unspeakable clumsiness. Unconscious motives can also sometimes contribute to inadequacy, as in the person who habitually consorts with the wrong mate and responds to arranged provocations with violence.

Contrary to popular impression, there are relatively few offenders who stand out as "pros"—as effective practitioners in careers such as burglary, armed robbery, or confidence-game management. (In this sense, offenders are probably no different from people in other occupations and professions.) John Irwin, in *The Felon,* classifies the most prevalent category of imprisoned offenders as "disorganized criminals . . . who pursue a chaotic, purposeless life, filled with unskilled, careless and variegated criminal activity" (Irwin, 1970, p. 24). The disorganized criminal is a man who is continually "doing wrong" or "fucking up." This means that he "shows bravado in the face of arrest or danger" and is given to "self-defeatism," believing "he is 'born to lose,' that he 'can't avoid trouble,' and that no matter how hard he tries, something will happen and things will go bad for him" (p. 25). Another offender category described by Irwin is that of "state-raised youths," who spend most of their lives in institutions of one sort or another. Such youths are (or see themselves as) fear-inspiring predators in prison, but they show limited competence on the outside. In several offender types, Irwin, like Miller (1958, 1965), highlights the person's faith in "fate" (which elsewhere in this volume is discussed as "external locus of control"). Since "fate" denotes abdication of agency, the belief in "fate" is correlated with ineffectiveness.

Another characteristic of ineffective criminals is their attitude toward postinstitutional adjustment. Though offenders may deplore prison, they may attribute their imprisonment to temporary carelessness or to arbitrary enforcement. This means that such persons are unlikely to increase their competence, not having "learned" their proverbial "lesson." Moreover, hope lurks eternal. The most ineffective of offenders may endlessly pursue the "big score" while engaging in flagrantly penny-ante criminality. If deluding oneself about the level of one's competence (or about one's prospects) is self-destructive, such patterns qualify as indirect self-destructive behavior (ISDB).

Prisons overrepresent inadequacy, because they contain offenders who have been caught. It is probably for this reason that early IQ studies concluded (mistakenly, it appears) that half of all imprisoned offenders were imbeciles or feebleminded (Sutherland, 1931). Habitual adaptive failure (which *descriptively* is self-destructive) is a particularly useful concept for explaining disproportionate recidivism in certain offenders compared to others in the same offense category. A drug pusher who gets arrested too often may be persisting in trade practices that have excessively high visibility. Such a pusher may be inadequate (hence self-destructive) because he is rigid, unimaginative, clumsy, or poorly advised. There is also the presumption that this type of offender has a limited capacity for profiting from experience.

A second self-destructive syndrome is *thrill-seeking*. Offenders may share this syndrome with such self-destructive nonoffenders as mountain climbers, drag racers, parachute jumpers, and schoolyard gladiators. A thrill-seeker is a person who knowingly courts predictable danger in order to reduce redundancy in his life, to arrange increased stimulation, and to show his disregard for probabilities.[3] The commodity sought by the thrill-seeker is "excitement," which implies a defiance of fate or danger. The direct self-destructive act that typifies thrill-seeking is the game of Russian roulette. A completed suicide may be an outcome of such an act, but is not its purpose. The purpose of the act is knowingly to *risk* suicide—a quasi-self-destructive act, because it is a marked departure from survival-oriented conduct.

Thrill-seeking offenses come in many forms. These include police-baiting, shoplifting, kidnapping, and daytime burglaries. The offender in question may be a youth rolling a stolen hubcap past a patrolling officer, an old lady carrying an expropriated fur coat (never necessities) out of a department store, or an airplane highjacker avid for publicity. Such persons do not desire the adverse contingencies they face, such as capture by the policeman, the in-

---

[3] In a sense, thrill-seeking is the other side of Miller's "fate" coin, in that the thrill-seeker defies fate or toys with it. Challenge mastery represents Promethean faith in one's sense of agency, which (as with Prometheus) invites the feast of buzzards when resentful gods—who are in charge of fate—claim their godly due. The point is not that fate is offended, but that it is there. The overreliance on fate (abdicating one's sense of agency) is also ISDB. "Macho" literature—Hemingway, for example—glorifies the Promethean stance, and denigrates the concern with survival, equating it with cowardice. Other authors—including the ancient Greeks and a good many Russian writers—stipulate the omnipotence of fate and characterize what seems to be self-destructive as inescapable.

tervention of the store detective, or the FBI sharpshooter at the airport. Their acts, however, gain meaning from the knowledge that destructive consequences are possible and *probably* from the hope of escaping such consequences.

Unless we take an overextended psychoanalytic perspective, we cannot argue that the thrill-seeker is self-destructively *motivated.* We can claim, however, that such an offender (like the inadequate offender) may be *descriptively* self-destructive, in that his destructive fate is a corollary of his strategy and his strategy is not a product of necessity.

The case for self-destructiveness is hardest to make where thrill-seekers escape their fate and do no harm to others. We must recall the popular adage that "Variety is the spice of life," whose corollary must be that an adventureless existence is insipid. In fact, the avoidance of excitement may be described as self-destructive, if we regard it as passive acquiescence to creeping entropy. Such, indeed, is the message of much of our literature, from *Major Barbara* to *The Matchmaker.* Psychologists have made an even stronger case in relegating safety concerns to the bottom of motivational hierarchies and in stressing the value of creativity, exploration, and risk-taking.

Though inadequacy has no literary or scientific proponents, it is also a priori innocuous. An inadequate professor may spawn disgruntled students, but—given tenure or a backdrop of mediocrity—his job is safe. An inadequate waitress may produce an exodus of gourmets, but (given the usual level of service in restaurants) she may risk little beyond reduced gratuities.

The syndromes are germane when we talk of offenders, because in a "cops-and-robbers" context thrill-seeking and inadequacy raise the probability of arrest. This is particularly the case when the syndromes are combined in the maladaptive risk-taker, who is self-destructive in any setting.

A third self-destructive syndrome is *compulsivity.* We have mentioned the compulsive offender in passing. Compulsivity often starts with thrill-seeking or even with carefree experimentation, and it may be the price paid for self-destructiveness, as well as being self-destructive in itself. Compulsivity can also be a derivative of inadequacy, and this is a sequence we infer in many sex offenders (Gebhart et al., 1965) and in some pyromaniacs.

In compulsivity the issue of motive is complicated, in that the offender tells us that he does what he does not want to do, yet the sources of his conduct are internal, while the consequences of conduct are flagrantly disregarded. Ascriptively and descriptively, the person is self-destructive, but he seems prescriptively innocent.[4] This fact (and the commonsense link between motivation and free will) makes us classify some such people as mentally ill (Szasz, 1961).

One legal definition of insanity is the "irresistible impulse" doctrine, which supplements a second definition (the McNaughton Rule) in many jurisdictions. A person's impulse is not "irresistible" merely because it *has not been resisted.* Rather, the test of irresistibility is that the offender persists knowing that his behavior is self destructive. As a prototypical query, we pose the case: "You are about to act, and you sense an alien presence. You look up and see a policeman at your elbow. Do you still act?" If the offender assures us smilingly that he would proceed, he "flunks" the "policeman-at-the-elbow test" and becomes insane. He also becomes certifiably self-destructive. In real life, however, we find: (1) that policemen rarely stand at the elbows of malefactors; and (2) when they do (as in presidential assassinations) there are hidden benefits (such as publicity) or an absence of alternate opportunities (presidents rarely are unguarded). The point is that though pure compulsivity is by definition blind to consequences, and hence self-destructive, limiting cases are hard to find.

Cynicism about the irresistibility of impulses leads us to invoke the personality model of the *malingerer,* the man who is by definition nonirrational. The more we assume that behavior is rational, purposive, instrumental, fraught with self-interest, and promotive of survival, the more we see malingerers behind every self-destructive facade. In such a perspective, self-destructiveness is the ever-presumptive alibi for egocentric and antisocial conduct. This undiluted (Darwinian) perspective has become increasingly outlandish as evidence of human irrationality and reluctant self-destructiveness accumulates, all of which becomes hard to interpret as a prevalence of incredibly good acting among otherwise unsophisticated men and women. Psychoanalysis, moreover, has furnished concepts that illuminate what are otherwise motivational paradoxes. We can now think in terms of ego processes which can

---

[4] According to Shapiro (1965), the "innocence" of impulsivity is not a corollary of impulsive personality but one of its goals. Impulsives can do what they want by ascribing responsibility for their acts to part of themselves (the hands that did the stealing) or to the external world (temptations, or tempters). Compulsives ascribe their behavior to their compulsivity, ignoring their role in programming their psychological computers to produce the motives to which they respond. In general, Shapiro argues, "the neurotic does not simply suffer neurosis, as, essentially, one suffers tuberculosis or a cold, but actively participates in it, functions, so to speak, according to it, and in ways that sustain its characteristic experience"; when a person says he could not help doing what he did, what he could not help is his "inclination, under certain circumstances of motivation, to feel 'I can't help it'" (Shapiro, 1965, pp. 20, 22).

fail to mediate reality or can become weak as controlling influences. More important, we know that there exist forces in all of us that seek ends (gratification) with utter disregard of anything other than the presence of juicy, tempting goals. Given such concepts, we can portray self-destructive patterns that involve the unchecked pursuit of short-term goals in defiance of predictable adverse consequences. Such self-destructive patterns involve *impulsivity,* which denotes the discharge of impulses that are unmediated by a decently functioning ego.

Compulsivity, however, is more than impulsivity. We speak of impulsive patterns when there is a seemingly overready response to all manner of temptations, ranging from ice-cream cones to sex and other people's money. The compulsive, by contrast, is specialized; he is fixated and ritualized, and his impulsivity is redundant. While impulsivity can be as destructive as compulsivity, compulsivity is more *self*-destructive.[5] This is the case in part because the compulsive is predictable, and he is thus at the mercy of his suppliers (in the case of drug addiction) or of predatory enemies such as members of vice squads.

One built-in characteristic of compulsivity is the inability to profit from experience, which becomes obvious to the offender, who knows he is self-destructive. Addicts arriving in jail, for example, are more likely than most offenders to sense their own contribution to their fates. Long-term addicts and "dead-end" alcoholics accept membership in self-blaming movements (such as Alcoholics Anonymous and Synanon) which make a fetish of recriminations. Such organizations, in fact, raise self-destructiveness to the status of the core feature of their personality theory.

Compulsive-personality theories highlight self-destructiveness as a defect or "fatal flaw" in character or personality. This perspective has its liability and its virtue. Its liability rests in the corollary that the person is fated to be self-destructive in the absence of continuing group or organizational support. Its virtue rests in the failure of alternate approaches to break the cycle of personal compulsivity and dependence. The "fatal-flaw" view, moreover, falls short of another, more dangerous conception, which derives from an early (justifiably discontinued) phase of Freudian theory. This view presumes the existence of unconscious motives (such as a death drive)

---

[5] Extreme impulsivity, of course, is very self-destructive, because it is blind to situational realities, and ignores consequences in pursuit of pleasure. For Freud, the ego develops to protect us from ourselves, rather than to protect the world from our depredations. Ego effectiveness is gauged in terms of how well we can achieve satisfactions in the face of social opportunities and constraints. The morality of our behavior (which has little to do with self-destruction) is the purview of the superego.

that have self-destruction as their goal. Compulsivity, from this perspective, represents a self-destruct mechanism run wild, which makes each compulsive person a pawn of a systematic campaign of self-annihilation, self-consumption, or terminal anesthetizing.

The teleological view of compulsivity is simplistic, because it reifies a hypothetical process (self-destructive unconscious intent) to explain a product (self-destructive behavior) which is otherwise hard to explain. Such proposed closure is dangerous, because it shuts off a challenging (though admittedly mind-boggling) area of inquiry. And while a descriptive conception of self-destruction is—by contrast—unromantic, it commends itself on the grounds of parsimony.

Minor compulsivity—the kind that sophisticated clinicians attribute to early toilet training and that the compulsive usually characterizes as "perfectionism"—is, if it is anything, anti-self-destructive. The everyday compulsive is a person who is sure that chaos must engulf him if a semicolon becomes a comma or an ashtray is inappropriately placed. The compulsive is thus waging a continuing battle against entropy, though his assignment of inappropriate priorities to minutiae may lead him to sacrifice goals. Though the compulsive's enemy is external, the dynamics of compulsivity center on *internal* chaos, which has to do with the person's runaway impulses. In this sense, self-destructiveness may be an antidote to destructive potential, which is ultimately self-destructive.

In criminal-justice contexts, the liabilities of compulsivity stem not only from the extremity of compulsive offender syndromes (drug and alcohol abuse, patterned sex offenses, pyromania, etc.) but from interpersonal (social) contexts of the system. It is these contexts (the cops-and-robbers game, the illicit sources of supply, the offender's vulnerability to exploitation) which—added to the inflexibility of addictive behavior—make the offenders self-victimizing. It is no coincidence that the drug user is arrest prone while the major drug dealer is comparatively immune; and it is not happenstance that laws aimed at "sex fiends" (i.e., sexual psychopath laws) are likely to victimize minor, *but compulsive,* offenders.

The relationship between context and self-destructiveness is even clearer for another category of offender, the man who is recurrently violent (Toch, 1969). Many violent offenders lack self-esteem, and they use violence as a defense or a compensatory tool, which helps them "prove" their own worth or protects them against "affronts." Some violent men are thus placed at the mercy of opponents who can make them explode by using appropriate verbal formulas or by behaving in a way that is certain to be offensive.

The "machismo syndrome" is a perspective that courts combat as a measure of self-worth. In noncrime areas (such as sports) it leads to "go-get-'em" lineup talks and homicidal cheers (Toch, 1977). Among offenders, it promotes escalations and confrontations with police, victims, and fellow offenders. Such strategies increase personal danger or risk. Members of fighting gangs, for example, are injury—and arrest—prone, and are in preferential line for hypertension. Self-destructiveness, here, is the price paid for an activity (fighting) that "works" because it requires no special skills, degrees, or liquid assets—which the person lacks—and because it yields power, pride, and status. Where these payoffs occur, future acts of violence (and their consequences) are promoted or reinforced through social learning (Bandura, 1973).

Self-destructiveness becomes even more probable when violence-prone people intersect, which is not unlikely, given the disproportionate prevalence of these men in "subcultures of violence" (Wolfgang and Ferracuti, 1967). A subculture is an ill-defined entity that contains people who have a great deal in common with each other. One thing such people have in common is the experience of growing up in the same parts of town, the same jungle clearings, granges, bazaars, bivouacs, oases, or teepees. Commonalities in life experience lead to similarities in beliefs, values, orientations, norms, and (to some extent) personalities. These similarities in turn are socially reinforced, because another thing that members of the subculture have in common is each other.

The term "subculture of violence" refers to people who share an acceptance of violent behavior. Such people take a relatively permissive view of violence that may range from punishing children, to defending the honor of loved ones, to responding to challenges, to protecting one's turf. The issue of self-destructiveness comes in through (1) subcultural reciprocity, in that victims (or their kin) are likely to retaliate or may engage in preemptive strikes; (2) the "objective" failure of violence to solve problems it addresses; and (3) the reactions of agencies in the dominant culture to deviant subcultural practices. A jealousy-motivated assault on a spouse may thus be deemed appropriate by the assaulter's peers, but may land the person in a hospital or morgue, a divorce court, and/or jail.

Other links between subcultures and self-destructiveness are found more directly in our culture. Among certain groups, such as skid-row alcoholics and drug users, there are norms that prescribe *directly* self-destructive conduct. The drunken bum's congenial peers are not only *unconcerned* about his rotting liver and wasted life but may underwrite his breakfast Muscatel (and its attendant toxicity) as a corollary of colleagueship. Drug addicts may similarly share their data about supply sources and may propagate beliefs (such as "nondrug addicts are boring squares") which reinforce addiction. One can plausibly talk about "subcultures of self-destructiveness" to describe social support for dysfunctional behavior (such as habitual drunkenness).

This statement does not imply that subcultures are merely in the social-norm and support business and are not relevant to our thinking about personal dynamics. Subcultural groups are no mere happenstance of geography. Few people were born on Skid Road or reared in the Bowery. Subcultural neighborhoods often comprise persons whose career patterns (or noncareer patterns) predispose them to their shared fate. An addictive alcoholic is likely to be a man who has failed, whereas a drug addict tends to be one who never tried. In both cases, the man's dysfunctional conduct was his own "solution" to his past problems, which are now so overladen with more recent problems that the syndrome is hopelessly compounded. This fact derives from the *cyclical* nature of many self-destructive patterns, in which "solutions" create new "problems" whose "solution" creates more new "problems."

There is a third tie between subcultures and self-destructiveness. This tie relates to personality *formation*. What is functional or dysfunctional is not only culturally relative but relative to dominant personality structures. To a nation of confirmed lotus eaters, work is a senseless departure from meaningful adaptation and the "good life." The Protestant ethic is a model which makes many of *us* comfortable, in that it is congruent with our goal-directed egos and superegos. When I say "our," I refer to the prototypical product of "middle-class upbringing." Different types of upbringing—more indulgent, depriving, uncertain, casual, harsh—can result in personalities whose orientation is different from ours, featuring different coping styles, ideologies, and conduct (Toch, 1971).

This argument does not lead to anarchic relativism, because we recognize that we live in a culture which poses tests not only for us but for persons (such as subculture members) with different ego structures. The lotus-eating ego must ultimately face our supermarkets and assembly lines, our standards and views of functional conduct. Outside of lotus-eating niches (such as food stamps), self-destructiveness may result from ill-fated results of honestly facing cultural tests.

An example of this process is risk-taking—a topic discussed elsewhere in this volume. The "main-line" ego is *low risk*. It has been raised in a fairly predictable world, which features cause and effect, work and reward, structure, promise, achievement. This world translates into the sort of personality that was described by Freud, which compromises and stores up, weighs, and takes charge. A child raised in inner-city streets, however, must often live with early uncertainty, risk, and threat. If the sun shines today, it is necessary and *appropriate* for such a child to make hay today. For the child, life *is* a gamble, fate *is* capricious, routine *is* deadly. Gambling, con games, "coolness," apathy, "high-life" and jail, cops and robbers, drugs and dreariness, can be adaptations to early autonomy, inhospitality, harsh survival. They are unfortunate lessons learned in jungle war by vulnerable youths.

Coping and self-destruction are almost never opposites. Our desperate efforts to survive today may incapacitate us tomorrow, or for life. Our struggles with one dominant problem may spoil us for another. To know self-harm means to understand the ways in which people strive and fail, without meaning to fail or wanting to fail.[6]

We must recall in this connection that our universe and our society are at best impersonal and at worst inhospitable. For law-abiding and non-law-abiding men alike, life entails trade-offs with options that variously destroy others and/or ourselves. The student of ISDB must have exquisite sensitivity to such options and nonoptions. He must control for his own hindsight, for his freedom from resourcelessness, from passion and pressure. To grasp tragedy (however unimpressive) we must have a sense of the tragic. We must never "diagnose" pathological constraints on coping when we deal—as we most often do—with men who have tried but failed.[7]

REFERENCES _____

American Psychiatric Association. *Diagnostic and Statistical Manual of Mental Disorders.* Washington, D.C., 1968.

Bandura, A. *Aggression: A Social Learning Approach.* Englewood Cliffs, N.J.: Prentice-Hall, 1973.

Gebhart, P. H., et al. *Sex Offenders: An Analysis of Types.* New York: Harper and Row, 1965.

Hendin, H. *Suicide and Scandinavia.* New York: Doubleday (Anchor), 1965.

Irwin, J. *The Felon.* Englewood Cliffs, N.J.: Prentice-Hall, 1970.

Miller, W. Lower-class culture as a generating milieu of gang delinquency. *Journal of Social Issues,* 14:5–19, 1958.

---

[6] In this connection, consider Hendin's (1965) discovery that motives for suicide are the corollaries of dominant cultural strivings.

[7] I am indebted to Gilbert Geis for this cautionary conclusion.

Miller, W. Focal concerns of lower-class culture. In L. A. Ferman et al., eds., *Poverty in America.* Ann Arbor: University of Michigan Press, 1965.

Palmer, T. *California Community Treatment Project. The Phase I, II and III Experiments: Developments and Progress.* California Youth Authority Research Report No. 10. Sacramento, 1970.

Palmer, T. Martinson revisited. *Journal of Research in Crime and Delinquency,* 12:133–152, 1975.

Redl, F., and Wineman, D. *Children Who Hate: The Disorganization and Breakdown of Behavior Controls.* New York: Crowell-Collier, 1962.

Shapiro, D. *Neurotic Styles.* New York: Basic Books, 1965.

Sutherland, E. H. Mental deficiency and crime. In K. Young, ed., *Social Attitudes.* New York: Holt, 1931.

Szasz, T. S. *The Myth of Mental Illness: Foundations of a Theory of Interpersonal Conduct.* New York: Dell, 1961.

Toch, H. *Violent Men: An Inquiry into the Psychology of Violence.* Chicago: Aldine, 1969.

Toch, H. The delinquent as a poor loser. *Seminars in Psychiatry,* 3:386–399, 1971.

Toch, H. *Police, Prisons, and the Problem of Violence.* A report of the National Institute of Mental Health. Washington, D.C.: U.S. Government Printing Office, 1977.

Warren, M. Correctional treatment and coercion: The differential effectiveness perspective. *Criminal Justice and Behavior,* 4:355–376, 1977.

Wolfgang, M., and Ferracuti, F. *The Subculture of Violence: Toward an Integrated Theory of Criminology.* London: Tavistock, 1967.

21

THE SELF-DESTRUCTIVE ROOTS OF DELINQUENCY

HERBERT HENDIN

Youngsters who are injured or killed in accidents in stolen cars or motorcycles, who drug themselves to the point of stupefaction or hospitalization, are likely to call attention to the self-destructive aspects of their behavior. Youngsters who break into houses to steal whatever they can sell, who set fire to stores or houses, who vandalize their schools, whose lives are a series of encounters with school authorities, police, and the courts, are likely to arouse enough irritation at the antisocial nature of their behavior to obscure its self-destructive aspects. Both groups contain youngsters who sabotage their schoolwork, alienate their families, and destroy their future prospects in ways that are perhaps the most self-destructive of all.

As the rate of suicide among the young has increased startlingly in the past twenty years, so the most dramatic increase in crime has been among "juveniles"—defined as anyone under eighteen years of age. From 1960 to 1975 there was a 144 percent increase in the number of juveniles arrested for all offenses listed as compared to a 12.9 percent increase during the same period in total number of arrests of persons eighteen and over (Federal Bureau of Investigation, 1975). Larceny (theft), burglary (breaking and entering), and motor vehicle theft (listed as a separate category) constitute the overwhelming majority of the offenses of the well over a million youngsters now arrested each year.[1]

The extent to which the environment of poverty and dissolving families encourages criminal behavior in the young has been explored, but as profound in its implications for society is the dra-

---

[1] Arrest figures, of course, include but a fraction of youngsters involved in such offenses. Nor are the figures for juvenile delinquency today inflated by the inclusion of "wayward," "disobedient," "truant," or "runaway" youngsters, i.e., status offenders. Juvenile delinquency is increasingly being defined as actions by youngsters that would constitute crimes if done by adults (Seller and Wolfgang, 1970).

matic increase in crime among youngsters from seemingly intact working-class and middle-class families (Bensing and Schroeder, 1960). During the past few years I have been seeing youngsters from intact families who break the law, abuse drugs, or run away from home.[2] What they and their families have to say is revealing of the character of the delinquent, of the self-destructive nature of his behavior, and of a failure of transmission of values from generation to generation.

The rejection of social ideals exists in the delinquent child not merely in overt acts of theft, arson, or other crimes. It is a way of relating to people and of perceiving the world. In the lives of the youngster and his parents it becomes a way of life in which the child is often, in effect, the con man the parents cannot resist.

Youngsters who con feel justified in promising anything to get what they want. They will lie to their families or steal outside, feeling entitled to do so and irritated at being caught. They will also tell their parents whatever they feel is necessary to avoid being "hassled" and will hide from their parents whatever can be hidden for as long as possible, i.e., difficulties with school authorities or the police.

Unlike the con man who goes on to another victim, delinquent youngsters who con are constantly hustling parents who have been burnt many times before—parents who are concerned that the youngster who is continually dishonest with them is likely behaving similarly outside the family. The need to provoke and frustrate their parents is also a significant part of such youngsters' intentions. They perpetually hustle the parents for money or the family car, both of which are then used to do things which provoke the parents. Money requested and given for a class trip will be used to buy drugs. A car requested for an evening will be kept out overnight.

One young man of seventeen with a long history of delinquency illustrated how pervasive is the need of such youngsters to exploit and frustrate their parents and to relate to the outside world in the same way. When his parents were going on vacation he was able to persuade them to let him have his mother's car while they were away. Their leaving him alone in the house and able to use her car when he liked was something he deeply wanted. But he had had keys made to his father's new car, which he planned to use surreptitiously. The keys would probably be discovered, which would lead to his being deprived of the use of both cars when his parents

---

[2] Although the overwhelming preponderance of male delinquents has made the word "delinquency" almost synonymous with male delinquency, female delinquency is now increasing. This chapter deals exclusively with male delinquency because two of the common problems among female delinquents—drug abuse and prostitution—are discussed elsewhere in this book.

came home. The motivation was not simply to take advantage of a situation or to express self-damaging defiance. In connection with this incident the young man related the satisfaction he and a friend derived from driving their cars parallel to each other at exactly the legal speed limit of fifty-five on a two-lane highway. Although he said they wanted to prove the legal speed limit made no sense, they clearly enjoyed the frustration of all the drivers honking behind them. Another young man, when asked if he had any pleasant memories of his early life, described an incident in which he provoked his father into wanting to hit him, and in frustration his father hit his fist into the wall.

While frustrating the motorists behind had no serious consequences, the need to frustrate the hopes and expectations of parents and teachers usually does. The delinquent knows his parents are more concerned about his reputation, his education, his future, than he is, and in this case his knowledge gives him power, even if he uses it in self-destructive ways.

Blackmail comes close to characterizing what happens between increasing numbers of middle-class parents and their children. A woman explains that since her son dropped out of college two years earlier he has done nothing but hang around the house or be with friends with whom he takes drugs. If she insists that he work to support himself or else move out of the house or tells him that she won't give him money, he threatens her that he will have to deal in drugs to support himself. Presumably more concerned about what will happen to him than he is himself, and guilty about her treatment of him as a child, she and her husband succumb to his blackmail. A couple whose son was arrested several times for burglary when he was under sixteen have been supporting him for several years, while he refuses to go to school or work, because of his threats to return to his former ways and his ability to arouse their fear of his going to jail. Another couple is quarreling about how to deal with their daughter, who announced at twenty-one that she was a lesbian, was taking an apartment with an older woman, and would have nothing further to do with them unless they accepted her lover as they would a husband and paid for the furniture she planned to buy, just as they might if she were getting married.

Such blackmailing behavior is psychologically akin to the coercive self-destructiveness seen in suicidal people—if you don't do what I want I'll kill myself—on the assumption that you will be more bothered than I by such behavior. The blackmailing delinquent's threat is not literally to end his life but to behave in ways that will effectively destroy it and any meaning, significance, and pleasure it may give to his parents.

Another common characteristic of the delinquent child reflects what has become a cultural theme, the intolerance of postponement of something desired, the sense that no future hopes or expectations warrant the exercise of any control. The infantile, grandiose quality of such expectations of immediate gratification, without regard to the needs or feeling of others, when accompanied by an equal lack of concern for the consequences to oneself, make self-destructive behavior a likely possibility.

One young man described his life like a series of events on a police blotter—a succession of encounters and difficulties with school authorities and the police. He had recently taken a teacher's car for a ride, thinking to return it before the teacher needed it. The teacher found the car missing and reported it to the police. A police car spotted the young man driving, but he would not stop for them and led them on a chase through several towns before he crashed the car into a telephone pole, this time fortunately not injuring himself or anyone else.

Partly because of this episode and partly because he had a prior history of having stolen television sets and other salable items from homes in his area, his father handled the situation by virtually confining his son to the house after school, except when he went bowling with the father or played on the school baseball team. The young man insisted this treatment of him was justified, and since his strongest complaint about his family life was the favoritism his father showed his sister (this was confirmed by the father), he derived pleasure from his father's interest. But he was also afraid of his father and reluctant to ask to be with his friends because of his father's objections. He would only half-jokingly insist that his father was stronger so he had better not argue. On one occasion when he was allowed to go to a dance, he drank himself to unconsciousness, had to be hospitalized, and seemed to prove to everyone that such tight control had to be reimposed.

The young man saw his mother as sympathetic to him but as having little to say in family decisions. He was disrespectful to her in ways that bothered the father, although the mother herself insisted she did not mind.

His mother revealed that she had felt depressed and exhausted after the birth of her son, born just one year after her daughter. She went to work, and her mother, who lived nearby, looked after the children. After a couple of years her mother told her that she had to stay home because the children were all calling the grandmother "Mommy." In recounting her story, she began to cry when she came to the point of telling how the grandmother moved back to Maine when the children were six and seven. Although the mother subsequently devoted herself to her children, neither of them appears to have forgiven her fully.

This youngster wanted his father's affection but resented the submissiveness he saw as the price of getting it. His anger was expressed in illegal activity which both defied his father and involved him intensely in his life. His early history and present behavior indicate a disturbance in his early relationship with his mother that had a great deal to do with the way in which he dealt with his life. He was aware of his envy and bitterness toward his sister but was out of touch with the anger toward both parents that seemed to underlie it. When his difficulties with the school authorities, the police, and his family became intolerable, his solution was to move to Maine to live with his grandmother. He had been there only a month when he took a motorbike that had been left with its key in for a ride, went through a stop sign, hit a car, and was killed.

Another young man, when his requests for money or use of the family car were turned down, became enraged and violent toward his parents. They could not understand why this seventeen-year-old was in so much difficulty in and out of the home, since he had been favored from birth as being better looking, brighter, and more artistic than his slightly younger brother, who was not having the same problems. It turned out that their mother's rigid, perfectionist demands on the older boy turned his being favored into a crippling disadvantage. He retaliated by making equally impossible demands of his parents. He could not accept his own limitations or those of a less than perfect world and consoled himself with fantasies of being marked for some singular destiny in life that revolved around using, obtaining, growing, and selling marihuana.

The frustration of such adolescents and their parents is enormous. "We're stalemated," said one youngster after one of the frequent intense arguments with his mother about his use or misuse of the family car. And stalemate—the image that each one blocks the other's freedom to move—is the image that best described their mutual entrapment.

The family car is often the tool with which parents and children play chess with each other. It may be the one thing everyone in the family has an investment in. The parents frequently use it as the last available symbol of their authority, a way of frustrating the youngster, to remind him that they have power over him and to deprive him of the means of getting where he wants to go. Ironically, by asserting themselves in this manner, the parents may only succeed in keeping the child who is an irritant near them. The child, when he obtains permission to use the car, often abuses it in some way or uses it to further behavior he knows will be objectionable to the parents. And, of course, "borrowing" other people's cars is one of the commonest offenses of delinquent youngsters.

School is another point of struggle between delinquent youngsters and their parents. From an early age, many of these youngsters show little interest in or aptitude for school, and school becomes a source of frustration and humiliation. Many express their resentment at being in school by destroying or defacing school property. Being the tough guy or the delinquent at school may be partly an attempt to repair the damage to their self-esteem caused by their painful difficulties with school. One young man, who was eventually expelled from his school, was secretly pleased and amused by the false rumors at school that an empty whiskey bottle had been found in a car that he had taken and cracked up while perfectly sober.

Some of the youngsters are bright enough to do their work well but are uninterested in doing so. Many rebel against parents and school, and manage not to graduate from high school after doing reasonably well up to that time. Middle-class parents usually hope their sons will go to college; working-class parents would often settle for high school graduation. But both see education as crucial to their children's future, and both are deeply disappointed by school failure. Both children and parents are aware that failure is more disturbing to the parents than to the youngsters.

Some of the other differences and similarities in the working-class and middle-class families whose children were in difficulty are worth noting. The desire to prove oneself by appearing tough, unafraid, and willing to take chances has been traditional among delinquent working-class children and continues to be prevalent. Such youngsters are easily humiliated by any wound to their masculine pride and will fight, be truant, or steal in order to strike back. One youngster, both emotionally and physically immature for his age, stole to impress older, bigger delinquent boys, to whom he turned over the profits.

While working-class families with delinquent children were usually not susceptible to the blackmail seen in middle-class families, the father's pride and honor were threatened by the child's difficulties with the law, and a power struggle with the youngster was the usual outcome, with varying results. Often the father reacted by physically punishing the youngster. The youngster perceives such punishment not in terms of physical pain but as humiliation, a fact which makes such measures counterproductive and almost forces the child to measure his worth by the magnitude of the trouble he creates.

The working-class mothers of delinquent children saw such children as more than they could handle and left serious efforts at control to their husbands. These mothers had little influence over the delinquent child and were treated with an indifference or contempt that they accepted with resignation, but which often disturbed their husbands.

Among working-class Catholic families one sees problems caused by the family having more children than the parents can cope with, emotionally or economically. In such families the child's position or role in the family may be crucial in his delinquency. One young man of sixteen had been caught several times robbing homes and cars in his suburban town. He was the youngest of four children, and neither his older sisters nor his brother had ever been in trouble. The mother was closer to the daughters than to the sons, but the father had, if anything, favored this particular young man.

The first time I met the young man and his parents, the father sat in the middle, and all dialogue was between him and his son or between him and his wife. After a few visits with the mother alone, it became clear that whatever she had to give her children had been exhausted by the time she had the fourth child. A religious Catholic who accepted large families as inevitable, she felt she had to practice contraception after the birth of this youngster, but it was evident that she wished she had begun at least one child earlier. Not surprisingly, from his birth she had seen him as too demanding, unwilling to listen to her, and arrogant. In a dream she reported that she visualized him as a small rat in her kitchen. While the rest of the family spent a lot of time together, this young man slept at home but was out of the house virtually all the time and was in a sense not part of the family. Most of his contact with them were arguments with his father about his staying out late, his truancy, or his delinquent behavior.

A boy of twelve who had been involved in burglary, theft, and arson was the fourth in a family of six children and the first in his family to be in trouble with the law. Yet it was clear that his two younger siblings were also going to have a harder time than the older children. His mother had tried vainly to persuade her doctor to sterilize her, but he refused until after her sixth child. After the birth of this young man, his father had to take a second job to support the family, and as a result even husband and wife had little time together. His mother cares for and respects her husband and does not complain about her life, but she admits that if she could live her life over she would not have had children and might not have married. Her twelve-year-old son had virtually no active relationship with the rest of the family. When he talked it was of his life outside the house and, like so many such youngsters, he merely slept at home and sometimes did not do even that. None of this seemed to disturb the family very much except when he got into trouble.

Much of the conversation in working-class homes centered on economic issues, and all of the youngsters were conscious of the family's economic problems. Most of the young men had fathers who worked hard, often doing two jobs to make ends meet. Some of the fathers of the delinquent children seemed to use work to escape from family life. Since the reality of their economic need is so apparent, such motivation is less obvious than it is in more affluent men who use work for the same purpose.

Fathers working at a second job in the evenings, or working a 4 P.M. to midnight shift, are removed from the flow of family life. Over and over, the effect of their absence is reflected in a disintegration of family life and structure. Few mothers today can cope with many children all by themselves. These women are often uncomplaining but perceive their lives as a burden. These families were not ungenerous with their children—most gave them whatever money they needed. But the sons as a group had a sense of the difficulty of obtaining money and of the harshness and unrewarding quality of their fathers' lives.

In the working-class families, family conversation was virtually never about feelings. Most of it was concrete, dealing with the reality of their lives. The youngsters from such families tended to be at a loss or uncomfortable when first encouraged to discuss their feelings and to be out of touch with their feelings about their families. Many could give no picture of their family relationships and did not describe families in response to Thematic Apperception Test pictures designed to elicit such relationships. They did not see any connection between their delinquency and their family situation, and indeed their delinquent behavior seemed to permit them to bury the pain and frustration of their family lives.

If the parents of working-class delinquents often seem uninvolved unless and until their sons are in difficulty with the police or school authorities, the parents of middle-class delinquents are often involved with the delinquent child in ways that are destructive and serve as an outlet for the parents' own discontent. One young man, whose mother saw only his failings, said perceptively that if he left home his father would begin to receive more of his mother's criticisms. It was a sentiment with which his father ruefully agreed.

Such youngsters retaliate in kind and let the parents know that whatever the parents give or do is not enough. The rising scale of needs and demands reflects both their anger and their sense of emotional loss. One such young man, who as a child was considered too dependent on his demanding, critical mother, was sent to summer camp at five with his older sister. On visiting day the family was surprised when his sister, who had been considered self-sufficient, cried while he did not. Instead he asked his parents insistently, "What did you bring me?" Whatever they subsequently gave him he rejected, abused, or was indifferent to, binding his parents in frustrating efforts at placation which was impossible to achieve.

Middle-class youngsters are less likely than their working-class counterparts to be involved in offenses like larceny or burglary that would bring them into direct conflict with the police and courts. They are more likely to be involved in stealing from the places where they work or from school organizations, or in forging checks. Shoplifting and dealing in drugs seem fairly evenly distributed among working-class and middle-class delinquents. So, too, is running away from home.[3]

Although the working-class youngster often leaves home much as he steals or burglarizes—without conscious anger toward his parents and conveying rather the sense that there is little at home to hold him—the middle-class youngster is articulately aware of his reasons for leaving. One young man, whose mother was furious with him for running away to another city for a week—the third time in two years—expressed the belief that she wished she could do the same. When I asked her about this, she laughed and said, "He must know me better than I realize." Outwardly content with her life, her dissatisfaction was expressed in finding fault with her family, and such thoughts were so unacceptable that despite her husband's encouragement she would not even take a trip without the family. For her son, running away was also his way of discharging the rage and frustration built up from constant arguments with his family. He would come home temporarily better able to deal with his family situation.

Some perspective on the efforts of young people to cope with antisocial impulses and their need to leave their families in order to do so is provided through considering the youngsters who deal with destructive and self-destructive impulses by joining religious cults. Whether the youngster's sense of self has been damaged through

---

[3] Approximately two million youngsters run away from home each year. They are classified as status offenders since in many states it is illegal to leave home before the age of fourteen to nineteen, depending on the particular state. Some runaways, like those discussed in this chapter, have a past history of delinquency; others become delinquents after leaving home. Many of these youngsters turn out to be not runaways but "throwaways," i.e., they were forced to leave their homes. And for some, running away from an impossible home situation can be more self-protective than self-destructive.

neglect or through the inability of his parents to permit his individuation, the need of such youngsters to feel special can be overpowering. Many believe that they have been intended for some singular mission in life. They tend to see portents of this in all sorts of chance occurrences—meeting people they were thinking of, things that they thought about coming to pass, etc. One such young man with a long history of delinquency described the difficulty he had in a small town finding a pen he could use to change the birthdate on his driver's license so he could get into a bar. As he emerged from a drugstore two young members of a religious cult approached him and asked if he had discovered Jesus. That they had spoken to him just as he was trying to change his birth-date—to be born again—renewed his sense of awe at this destiny and heightened his receptiveness to the cult.

The young person who feels he hears the tune of a different drummer often hears a modern form of the Pied Piper's song. The Pied Piper rids the town of rats by luring them away with his music. When the townspeople refuse to pay him as promised, he uses his powers to lure away their children. In any psychological interpretation of this story the rats are surely the bad or undesired aspects of the children. If youngsters grow up feeling that good behavior has no rewards, if they are made to feel ratty no matter what they do, then following the tune of any leader, whether he is the Pied Piper or the Reverend Jim Jones, may provide an alternative to destructive, delinquent behavior.

The religious sect may help the youngster control his destructiveness, although the price he pays may be a marked detachment from his emotions. The sect may also help its followers curb their exploitativeness, although it may be argued that this is accomplished by the youngster himself becoming the exploited. And the narcissistic needs of these young people are gratified by the grandiosity of the group in a way that makes some productive activity possible.

It is the mixture of destructiveness and self-destructiveness, exploitativeness and grandiosity that is so troublesome to delinquent youngsters, no matter what their socioeconomic class. One young man, who amiably and with some pride related how he stole from or cheated his employers, went from one grandiose scheme to another in his plans for instant wealth. His girlfriends were seen in the same context. He dreamt of himself as James Bond, but was unhappy that in the dream he did not have the same car James Bond drives. In another dream he saved his girlfriend's life, and her parents rewarded him by buying him a new car. Although he related his desire for the car to his desire to see his girl, who lived twenty miles away, and his parents accepted his desire to see her as one of the more reasonable justifications for needing the car, his dream more accurately expressed his feeling that the girl was the way to get a car rather than the reverse.

The most repetitive dream image I have seen among delinquent adolescents is that of King Kong. While in their dreams King Kong is an overwhelming aggressive threat and the source of considerable terror, the associations of the youngsters invariably indicate an identification of Kong with the anarchic destructive aspects of their own personalities over which they fear losing control. The image underscores the self-destructive aspects of their presumed aggressive behavior. And their self-image as Kong—a monstrous alien presence in a world he cannot shape and can only destroy—suggests the magnitude of their problems and ours.

The hidden gain—in excitement, released anger, or enhanced status—of his antisocial behavior keeps the delinquent repeatedly making attempts at crime. The need to treat his life carelessly, to define his freedom as being ready for anything, often leads to extraordinary risk-taking. The extent to which delinquents prize the experience of the joyride in the stolen vehicle underlines their inability to separate joy from danger, risks, or chances which are likely to end badly—in capture, physical disability, or death.

The depression and pessimism that underlie and reinforce such behavior are suggested by a feeling, common to many of the delinquent youngsters, that it did not matter what they did with their lives since they would probably die in ten years anyhow. None of the youngsters with this vision had any realization of how they were projecting their own inner sense of falling apart.

What bothers both the working-class and middle-class parents of delinquent youngsters is their sense that their children do not accept certain social and moral values to which they themselves subscribe, do not identify with them as they did with their own parents. Many of the parents of the delinquents could wonder why their sons were in trouble. Some of the parents who cared for their children had come from uncaring families and yet had not had the same difficulties as their children.

Given at least comparable difficulties, the parents' generation seems to have handled them in somewhat different ways. However troubled they were, they accepted a certain work ethic as the way to make a better life for themselves. Indeed, the fathers equated hard work and competence at work with being a man. Both the middle-class and working-class fathers of the young people I saw were extremely hardworking and law-abiding, and all had themselves strongly identified with equally hardworking fathers. While many of the fathers had been indifferent students or not very happy at home when they left school or home, it was to begin a working life. Some first joined the army, which provided them with a structure that helped them make the transition to adult life. Personal dissatisfaction or unhappiness was not a reason for not accepting certain socially definable goals.

In their confusion, guilt, or shame over their children's delinquent behavior, many of the families blame "bad company," "older boys," and "peer pressure." Many of the youngsters have an even greater stake in not knowing what they feel about their family structure, and they are more than willing to agree. And while it is true that many of the delinquent youngsters were led into crime by older boys, it is also true that they wanted to be liked by just those older boys, whose illegal activity appealed to them. The majority of the young, including siblings of delinquents, exposed to the same delinquent peer groups, do not become part of them. And even if they do, only the most vulnerable will center their lives on such behavior. Of course, the parents' own children are seen as the "bad peers" by other parents. Youngsters with similar inclinations tend to find each other, and drug-abusing, delinquent, or homosexual youngsters can in truth say that all the young people they know are doing what they are doing. And while the young find the peer group that satisfies their needs, the family dynamics determine what those needs are.

In most of the families I have been seeing, there is outwardly little to suggest that they would have a delinquent child. And indeed, it is frequently only one of a family's several children who has such problems. But in the course of several sessions, the impairment in the relations between the parents and the child who has become delinquent usually becomes evident. Certainly seeing the nondelinquent siblings of such youngsters one is powerfully impressed that only a youngster who has been profoundly hurt takes the antisocial route. Such siblings often have remarkable insight into their family situation. "Mom was more irritable as the years went by," said the oldest brother of one of the boys arrested for repetitive thefts. "It was easier on me, but my brother had it tough from the beginning." The fifteen-year-old brother of a drug-abusing seventeen-year-old was able to describe with a clarity not available to anyone else in his family how much more demanding his parents had always been of his delinquent older brother.

Although the special vulnerability in the family that produces a delinquent child is to some extent definable, there is a balance between the role of the family and the role of society in producing delinquency. Over two decades ago Albert Cohen postulated that working-class youths exposed to middle-class values that they cannot adopt because of social or psychological impediments resolve the dilemma by banding together and living counter to those values (Cohen, 1955). One would have to add that large numbers of middle-class youths also lack the ability, persistence, and determination to achieve contemporary middle-class goals.

For large numbers of youngsters, schools continue to be no solution. Not only are the schools unable to encourage socially cohesive values in delinquent youngsters, but the years of pain and failure, frustration and humiliation that they represent only foster social alienation. Social scientists have warned us for years that school is too rigid a requirement for countless adolescents with no aptitude for study or school work (Bloch and Geis, 1962). Many of them, if freed from these binds and provided with work, would find it less necessary to acquire what status they can from delinquent behavior.

And all of our necessary efforts to support and strengthen families should not prevent us from acknowledging when the family and adolescent would be better served by separation without stigma. Many adolescent youngsters are locked into situations with their families from which they find it hard to disengage but are proving destructive to all concerned. Psychotherapeutic intervention can often alleviate this conflict, but sometimes the best course lies in helping the disengagement process.

Although it is not difficult for delinquent youngsters to see the self-destructive aspects of their behavior, unless one can help them get in touch with the sources of their unhappiness and find some less destructive adaptation, it is difficult for them to stop. They are more likely to be aware of their anger at the police or school authorities with whom they come into conflict than of the anger and pain of their relationship with their families; and the delinquent behavior itself often permits them to express their frustration while enabling them to deny its origins. A rising tide of unfocused anger, tension, and depression are usually antecedents to the delinquent behavior, and the delinquent activity seems to provide an element of emotional release that makes a recurrence unlikely for several months.

We do not know what percentage of youngsters who are delinquent will remain so. Many drug-abusing teenagers are not drug abusers five years later, but the character and attitudes that led to their drug addiction remain, even if handled with less use of drugs. The delinquents I have seen who remain in a parasitic blackmailing relationship with their parents usually continue their self-destructive behavior. The conning, hustling character structure that has difficulty in sustaining effort or in accepting socially cohesive values is also less likely to remain a problem, whether or not the youngster becomes an adult criminal.

Society probably contributes to the encouragement of that character structure. The need to feel special, superior, different, which plays such a part in American life, divorced from a belief in the value of work or perseverance or achievement, is expressed antisocially by young people who seek status through drunkenness, through pushing drugs to their peers, through acquiring a reputation for delinquent toughness that can momentarily relieve their sense of failure and emptiness. Today such young people find a variety of marginally legal and illegal ways of feeling they are beating the system. Dealing in drugs or becoming a parasite on one's parents become ways of life for many. The delinquent who cons and extorts from his parents is also the product of a society in which the hustler is increasingly an ideal.

In the Pied Piper story it is the town elders of Hamlin who expose the children to the Pied Piper's song. It is also our society, and not simply the family, that helps to move young people down destructive and self-destructive paths or to take routes that will give them a narrow and partial life. It only seems to be paradoxical that some youngsters who wish to follow moral values feel they have to reject traditional familial and societal ties and join religious cults to do so. The impulse to become part of a new family in a youngster who has felt hurt in his original family is a powerful one and can be constructive. Society does not provide the large number of troubled young people with positive alternatives that can anchor them to productive lives and permit them to take charge of themselves in the real world.

REFERENCES _____

Bensing, R., and Schroeder, O. *Homicide in an Urban Community.* Springfield, Ill.: Thomas, 1960.

Bloch, H., and Geis, G. *Man, Crime and Society.* New York: Random House, 1962.

Cohen, A. *Delinquent Boys: The Culture of the Gang.* Glencoe: Free Press, 1955.

Federal Bureau of Investigation. *Uniform Crime Report for 1975.*

Seller, T., and Wolfgang, M. The legal basis of delinquency. In P. Lerman, ed., *Delinquency and Social Policy.* New York: Praeger, 1970, pp. 22–31.

22

SELF-DESTRUCTIVE BEHAVIOR AND ADAPTIVE STRATEGIES IN FEMALE PROSTITUTES

JENNIFER JAMES

Sexism—or sex-role stereotyping—dictates basic divisions in our society. With few exceptions, men and women are able to feel comfortable about themselves and successful in their relations with others only insofar as they perceive themselves as "masculine" or "feminine." This culture has placed so high a value on "proper" sex-role identification that many people virtually become addicted to the acting out of certain role-stereotyped behaviors in order to prove their normality and consequent acceptability. The political movement in defense of a homosexual sex role is attempting to legitimatize other options in a restrictive society. Women have also been politically active in order to establish sex-role freedom.

When a person's position in the social hierarchy makes it unlikely that he or she will be able to obtain the rewards of a successful sex-role performance through the "normal" channels of the majority culture, he or she often seeks those rewards through a sex-role performance modified according to the standards of an alternative peer group or subculture. These modified, alternative, or "abnormal" sex-role performances may seem to deviate from the societal norm, but they are actually adaptive variations of the same masculine-feminine theme.

Prostitution is a traditional variation of the female sex role which, in the past, has been seen by many not only as abnormal but as destructive to society and to the individual prostitute. Streetwalkers in particular have been stereotyped as "sick," degraded women, self-destructively abusing themselves through constant exposure to

Research was funded through the Department of Health, Education and Welfare Public Health Service Grants 1 RO1 DA 00918 and 1 RO1 MH 29968.

the risk of disease, drug-use problems, assault, men who "use" them, and imprisonment.

In this chapter we examine the life-style of female streetwalkers, some of whom are also drug addicts, in order to evaluate self-destructive behavior. Such behavior is reviewed in terms of its utility as an alternative, survival-promoting adaptation for the female sex role and as a self-protective reaction to the legal harassment of the profession.

Prostitution is an aspect of, not a contradiction to, the female sex role as it exists in this society. The spectrum of sex-role choices extends from madonna to whore and provides many options. The choice of prostitute obviously is heavily loaded with negative valuations according to the judgment of the majority culture. What, then, determines which individual women will act out the prostitution components of the female sex role? What factors enable or induce certain women to accept the deviant status conferred on them by their choice of prostitution? If prostitution inherently entails self-destructive behavior and potentially exposes women to drug abuse and criminality, why do some women choose a course which will contribute to their "own demise"? Explanations of the antecedents of prostitution have rarely been based on empirical research. Existing research has not evaluated the positive adaptive strategy nor reported the objective realities of "the life."

BACKGROUND

Our research at the University of Washington, completed in 1976, and a few other recent studies indicate that there are unreported factors which enable some women to accept the deviant status inherent in prostitution. These can be tentatively identified as: exposure to and acceptance of the prostitution life-style—through friends or through the existence of prostitution in their neighborhoods; certain patterns in child-parent relationships; and negative sexual experiences which lead to the development of a self-concept that includes a high degree of sexual self-objectification. The latter two of these three factors refer to evidence that prostitutes are women with histories of victimization predating their "choice," perhaps as women who have been "set up" to self-destruct in certain ways, and certainly as women whose perception of the alternatives available to them for fulfilling their sex-role expectations has been seriously modified.

Parental abuse or neglect is widely considered a typical childhood experience of women who become prostitutes. Jackman et al. (1967), Esselstyn (1968), Greenwald (1970), N. J. Davis (1971), and Gray (1973) all mention unsatisfactory relationships with parents as

a fact of life for these women. Whether the condition is simple neglect by absence or outright physical and/or psychological abuse,
the result is generally considered to be alienation of the child from
the parents and a consequent inability, depending on the child's
circumstances, adequately to internalize the conventional mores of
"respectable" society. Data from our study seem to reaffirm the
prevalence of parental abuse/neglect among female prostitutes. The
mean age at which the women in our study left home permanently
was 16.25 years. "Dispute with family" was one of the major reasons
given for leaving home, and physical and emotional abuse was also a
significant factor in separating many of them from their families. Of
the 136 prostitutes in the study, 65.4 percent had lived apart from
their families for some period before moving out permanently; 70.4
percent reported the absence from the family of one or more parents,
most often the father, during their childhood. Neglect, rather than
abuse, was the pattern for the majority of the subjects, although
abuse was reported by a significant number. Some typical comments about relations with parents were: "We had a lack of communication problem, me and my parents, for a long time. I didn't
even know how to approach them. I was scared to talk to them,
because every time I did something wrong, they'd yell at me." "My
mom didn't let us go out with boys. We were at home and always
working. If anyone called up, we got cursed out and then a beating."
"I felt isolated and that's why I ran away. I just felt that my mother
didn't care." "My stepfather, it's been negative since he's been
around. . . . He hits me 'till I'm all stiff."

One specific area of neglect on the part of the parents of the
women in this study was sex education. Compared to the 31 to 34
percent found by other researchers (e.g., Wittels, 1951; Sorensen,
1973) among normal female populations, only 15.4 percent of these
prostitutes had learned about sex from their parents. This lack of
parental guidance may help to explain why many prostitutes apparently are more sexually active at an earlier age than the majority of
women in the United States. A full 91.9 percent of the prostitutes in
our study were nonvirgins by the age of 18 (including 23 percent
who had experienced intercourse by the age of 13 or younger),
compared to 74.9 percent of the black subjects and 19.9 percent of
the white subjects studied by Kantner and Zelnik (1972). In a current study of juvenile female prostitutes the average age at first
intercourse is 13.3. Extensive interviews with the subjects revealed
a pattern similar to one found by N. J. Davis (1971, p. 301) in her
study of thirty prostitutes: "The 'technical virginity' pattern typical
of the middle-class female was not in evidence here. First sexual
contacts typically involved sexual intercourse." More than one-

third of the subjects in our study reported they had no further sexual relationship with their first intercourse partner; other studies have found 10 percent to 15 percent of their sample in this category (Eastman, 1972). That the superficial, nonemotional nature of the first sexual intercourse of many of these women initiated a series of such encounters is supported by the fact that the mean number of private (not-for-profit) sexual partners of the young adult subjects in our study was twenty-three. Making this figure even more signific-ant is the fact that the mean number of sexual partners with whom the subjects felt they had developed a "significant relationship" was only five.

When these women become sexually involved, they also run higher risks of abortion and illegitimate deliveries than do other women (James and Greene, 1977). Of the addict-prostitutes, 64 per-cent had at least one child, as did 60 percent of the prostitutes in our study; 40 percent of the addict-prostitutes and 43 percent of the prostitutes had experienced at least one elective abortion, and mul-tiple abortions per woman were not uncommon. Over one-fourth of the prostitutes and more than one-third of the addict-prostitutes failed to use contraceptives *ever*. The nonuse of contraception can be interpreted as ignorance, a desire to avoid "being prepared for sex" and therefore a clearly "bad" girl, the need for attention and the desire for "someone to love, someone to belong to." The possi-ble self-destructiveness of childbearing outside the nuclear or ex-tended family is not understood by women at such an early age.

Societal reactions to juvenile female sexual activity may also be an influence on some women's entrance into prostitution, especially on those young women who are more sexually active and less dis-creet than the majority of their peers, which appears to be the case with many prostitutes. "At what number of lovers is a girl supposed to lose the status of a decent person?" asks Choisy (1961, p. 1). Carns (1973, p. 680) explains: "A woman's decision to enter coitus . . . implies that she is creating for herself a sexual status which will have a relatively pervasive distribution . . . she will be evaluated downwardly. Such is the nature of the male bond."

Girls learn early society's moral valuation of their sexuality. It is clear that any open sexual expression outside of marriage is "self-destructive" in that it will provoke a negative societal response. For example, in discussing her childhood sex education, one street-walker said, "I think the basic theme of the whole thing was that it was a dirty thing but that it was a duty for a woman to perform, and if you fooled around, you were a prostitute." Female promiscuity, real or imputed, virtually guarantees loss of status in the majority culture: "I got pregnant and kicked out of the house and school." "I was accused of being promiscuous while I was still a virgin. They did that because I used to run around with a lot of guys." Such labeling, with its implied loss of status, may be an important step in the process by which a woman comes to identify with, and thus begins to see as a viable alternative, a deviant life-style such as prostitution. For its youthful victims, the labeling must strongly affect the development of an adult self-image. Loss of reputation through sexual activity is viewed as permanent, i.e., "Once a whore, always a whore." These women may attempt to rebuild their self-concept by moving into a peer group or subculture where the wider society's negative labeling of them will not impede their efforts toward a higher status—although that status itself will be perceived as negative by the wider society.

However negative or self-destructive the long-term effects of juvenile promiscuity on a woman's social status, the short-term effects of contranormative juvenile sexual activity may often appear quite positive to the young woman involved. Young women suffering from parental abuse or neglect, a common pattern for prostitutes, may be especially susceptible to the advantages of what Greenwald (1970, p. 167) calls "early rewarded sex—that is, . . . engaging in some form of sexual activity with an adult for which they were rewarded. [These women] discovered at an early age that they could get some measure of affection, of interest, by giving sexual gratification." This type of positive sexual reinforcement, particularly when coupled with the cultural stereotype of women as primarily sexual beings, may cause some women to perceive their sexuality as their primary means for gaining status.

"Sex as a status tool is exploited to gain male attention" (N. J. Davis, 1971, p. 304). Since all women in our culture must somehow come to terms with the fact that their value is often considered inseparable from their sexual value, it is not uncommon for female adolescents to use "sex as a status tool" through makeup, flirting, dating, petting, etc. Prostitutes, however, more often skip over the usual preintercourse sociosexual activities in favor of an active and more or less promiscuous intercourse pattern. Victimization results when "there is a 'drift into deviance,' with promiscuity initially used as a status tool, but later becoming defined by the individual as having consequences for the foreclosure of alternative career routes" (p. 300).

There is some evidence that prostitutes are women who have also been the victims of less subtle and perhaps even more destructive negative sexual experiences. Specifically, our study showed that prostitutes are disproportionately victimized by incest and rape compared to normal female populations (52.8 percent of the prostitutes had been raped and 18 percent had been victims of incest). The only study populations with comparable father-incest rates are those selected from the specialized sample of police reports or the case loads of child protection agencies (e.g., De Francis, 1969). The effect of incest on the child involved is virtually unknown. Some researchers, e.g., Jaffe et al. (1975, p. 691), prefer not to comment: "Little is known of the physical and emotional effects of incest." Ferracuti (1972, p. 179) notes that "Frequently victims of incest become sexually promiscuous after the end of the incestuous conduct." De Francis found guilt, shame, and loss of self-esteem to be the usual reactions of child victims of sex offenses. These feelings often led to disruptive, rebellious behavior, and some older (i.e., adolescent) victims later became prostitutes. Sexual abuse over a long period of time, as is usual with incest, was found by Gagnon (1965, p. 192) to be "extremely disorganizing in its impact" on the victim. Weiner (1964, p. 137) echoes Ferracuti in stating that "girls who begin incest in adolescence frequently become promiscuous following termination of the incest." In an early study (James, 1971) that included twenty incarcerated adolescent prostitutes, a full 65 percent of the adolescent subjects had been the victims of coerced sexual intercourse, 84.7 percent of the experiences occurring while the victim was aged fifteen or younger. Over half of our later adult prostitute population had also been raped; over a third of the women were multiple rape victims.

It is not possible, of course, to conclude that, because certain study populations of "deviant" or "self-destructive" women were disproportionately victims of rape and incest, these sex-related abuses were therefore the cause of deviance. On the other hand, the overfrequent victimization of these women, particularly in youth and childhood, is a fact—just as their status as "deviants" is a fact—and should not be lightly dismissed. We realize that incidents of sexual victimization such as incest do not occur in a social "vacuum" and are virtually always surrounded by a complexity of causal, mitigating, or aggravating factors. In fact, a large proportion of the available research on incest—like the majority of studies of other more common types of sexual experiences—focuses primarily on the family background of the victim. Study of the *causes* of sexual behaviors and experiences should not be our only concern, however. What we want to emphasize here is the importance of evaluating the *effects* of certain sexual patterns and experiences on the life of the individual.

Our experience supports the conjecture that early, traumatic sexual self-objectification may be one factor that influences some women to enter into prostitution or other "deviant" life-styles. To some degree, all women in this society experience sexual self-objectification, owing to the simultaneous cultural adoration and vilification of the female body and its sexuality (the familiar madonna/whore spectrum). It seems possible, however, that to be used sexually at an early age in a way that produces guilt, shame, and loss of self-esteem would be likely to lessen the victim's resistance to a perception of the female sex role as including the possibility of exploiting one's self as a salable commodity. The relationship between early sexual history—especially incidences of sexual victimization—and adult deviance or self-destructive behavior needs further study.

CONSCIOUS AND IMMEDIATE MOTIVATIONS _____

Despite its illegality, prostitution is an institutionalized occupational choice for women in this society. Because of its "immoral," illegal, "deviant" status, however, the choice of prostitution as an occupation has been surrounded by social scientists with an elaborate mythology of theory and analysis (e.g., "self-destructive behavior") far removed from our usual perception of occupational choices. It is true that "the conscious and immediate reasons that the prostitutes themselves are capable of giving . . . must be considered in conjunction with, and as overlaying other, more deeply hidden factors" (Pomeroy, 1965, p. 183). This same thing would hold, of course, if we were examining why some people become psychiatrists. Moreover, just because these conscious and immediate reasons are easily accessible does not mean they are not real. In the preceding section, we discussed some of the "more deeply hidden factors" which may influence certain women to become prostitutes. Now we will examine the more "conscious and immediate" motivations that influence women in their day-to-day lives as prostitutes. In isolating the self-destructive elements in the prostitute's lifestyle we discuss the risks taken versus advantages gained in four major areas: economics, at work "on the stroll," relationships with pimps, and use of drugs.

ECONOMICS

Economics is the pervasive theme of prostitution, and this reality is indicated by the fact that money is mentioned as a motive for prostitutes in virtually all of the literature, although some writers see the prostitute's emphasis on money as a symptom of, or less important than, certain sociological or psychological factors. One traditional stereotype of prostitutes represents them as wretched creatures forced into prostitution by extreme economic deprivation.

Opposing this stereotype is a body of research showing that the majority of prostitutes choose prostitution as the occupational alternative which affords them the highest attainable standard of living. In our study, 8.4 percent of the prostitute subjects claimed to have started prostitution because of economic necessity; 56.5 percent were motivated by a desire for money and material goods; 90.5 percent of the addict-prostitutes and 80 percent of the prostitutes stated that the advantage of continuing prostitution was money. It is, of course, very important in this context to recognize that money-making options are still quite limited for women in this society— especially for un- or low-skilled women. Recognition of this basic sex inequality in the economic structure helps us see prostitution as a viable occupational choice rather than as a symptom of individual immorality or "deviance." Pomeroy has noted that "the gross income from prostitution is usually larger than could be expected from any other type of unskilled labor" (1965, p. 175). Benjamin and Masters (1964, p. 93) were also aware of this sex-based economic differential and its relationship to prostitution: "The economic rewards of prostitution are normally far greater than those of most other female occupations." According to Esselstyn (1968, p. 129), "women are attracted to prostitution in contemporary America because the income is high and because it affords an opportunity to earn more, buy more, and live better than would be possible by any other plausible alternative."

Some researchers claim to find an abnormal, perhaps even neurotic, materialism among prostitutes. Jackman et al. (1967, p. 138), for example, state that "The rationalization by prostitutes violating social taboos against commercial sex behavior takes the form of exaggerating other values, particularly those of financial success, and, for some, the unselfish assumption of the financial burden of people dependent upon them." However, as Greenwald (1978, p. 142) more accurately points out, "Economic factors helped to mold the entire society, the family structure, and therefore the very personalities of these girls . . . the girls were caught up in the worship of material success." In what way is the economic motive of these women different from that of men who strive to attain a position on the executive level so that they can afford "the good life" and support the people dependent on them? The majority of Americans share the desire for financial success. Prostitutes are women who, usually with good cause, see prostitution as their only means, albeit illegal, for moving from an income of $3,000 to $6,000 a year to the style of living possible with $50,000 a year. It is obvious that in our culture money can buy respect.

A person's choice of occupation is not limited solely by external realities. One's self-image plays an important part in one's perception of alternatives. Traditionally, women's roles are those of wife and mother, both of which are exclusively biological and service roles. The emphasis on service carries over into the definition of "new" traditional women's roles, such as teaching children, serving food, and keeping track of appointments for the boss. The importance of physical appearance in many of these occupations (e.g., cocktail waitress, receptionist) reinforces women's self-image as physical/biological objects. As Rosenblum argues (1975, p. 169), "prostitution utilizes the same attributes characteristic of the female sex role, and uses those attributes toward the same ends; . . . the transition from non-deviance to deviance within prostitution requires only an exaggeration of the situation experienced as a non-deviant woman; . . . all women, to the degree to which they reflect the contemporary female sex role, are primary deviants." Greenwald, perhaps unwittingly, demonstrates this fact in his effort to prove that the economic motive is not the most important factor in the choice of prostitution as a profession. According to his report, eighteen out of twenty prostitutes he interviewed, none of whom "had skills to earn twenty to thirty thousand dollars a year in any other way," had had "chances either to marry or become the mistresses of wealthy men." In other words, if it's money you're after, why not be a "respectable" sexual object rather than a sexual "deviant"? The answer to this question lies in the other main advantages of the prostitute's life-style: the opportunities it offers for independence and adventure.

Financial independence is a possibility not included in traditional women's roles. In a sense, then, a financially independent woman is a "deviant" woman. These economic roles are beginning to shift and broaden now, but there are still virtually no occupations available to un- or low-skilled women which allow the independence, or provide the adventure, of prostitution. Data from our study support the assertion that independence is highly valued by many of the women who choose prostitution and/or independence from the strictures of family life. The responses to the question "Why did you leave home?" are first "desire for independence" and second "dispute with family." The two sets of responses to the question "What are the advantages of being a prostitute?" also reveal the value independence has for these women. The economic motive overwhelms all other categories in the first responses, but in the second responses independence has first place.

THE STROLL

For many women, the "fast life" of prostitution represents more than simply economic independence. The life-style of the prostitution subculture has itself proved very attractive to a large number of women over the years. "There is an abundance of evidence that on the conscious level it is the *excitement* of the prostitute's life, more than any other single factor, which works to frustrate rehabilitation efforts" (Benjamin and Masters, 1964, p. 107). Among the subjects in our study, the excitement, adventure, and life-style of the street prostitute were significant motives for becoming prostitutes. These same subjects listed the social life, the working conditions, the excitement and adventure of "working the stroll" as, next to independence, the most important advantages of their profession.

We believe the above facts provide a substantial response to Greenwald's (1970) implied question about marriage versus prostitution mentioned earlier. Neither marriage nor extramarital monogamy provides or allows for the economic independence, the excitement, the adventure, or the social life available through prostitution. The basic fact of sexual objectification may be the same in either case, but, for many women, prostitution obviously has benefits that outweigh the privileges—and limitations—of "respectable" women's roles. Winick and Kinsie (1971, p. 75) refer to a rehabilitation program for prostitutes in Japan in the 1950s which included such traditional women's activities as arts and crafts and homemaking. The program failed, they report, because the prostitutes simply were not interested. As Greenwald discovered (1970, p. 202), most prostitutes feel "overt hatred of routine, confining jobs." The traditional female occupation of housewife can be seen as one of the most "routine, confining jobs" of all, and thus has limited appeal for women who value the relative freedom of the "fast life."

There are also, however, many disadvantages to this life, especially for streetwalkers. Violations of the prostitution statutes account for approximately 30 percent of most women's jail populations. Convicted prostitutes serve long jail sentences compared to other misdemeanants such as shoplifters or those involved in larceny or assault. The judicial attitude represented by these sentencing patterns has no justification in the traditional legal concerns about danger to persons or property damage, nor does the large number of women arrested for prostitution (32,714 in 1976, according to the Uniform Crime Reports of 1977) indicate a commitment of the criminal justice system to an effective, realistic campaign to eliminate prostitution. Each act of prostitution, after all, requires at least two participants: a seller *and* a buyer. Despite this incontrovertible fact, the arrest rate for customers is only one per every eight prostitutes (Federal Bureau of Information, 1978). Kinsey and others have estimated that about 20 percent of the male population has some contact with prostitutes, and yet the prostitutes seem to be singled out to bear the weight of legal reprisals. Since the prostitution laws in almost every state are neutral on their face, holding the prostitute and her customer equally culpable, the above figures prove that prostitutes are victims of discriminatory law enforcement.

The traditional justification for discriminatory enforcement of prostitution laws was stated by K. Davis (1937):

> The professional prostitute being a social outcast may be periodically punished without disturbing the usual course of society; no one misses her while she is serving out her term—no one, at least, about whom society has any concern. The man [customer], however, is something more than partner in an immoral act; he discharges important social and business relations. . . . He cannot be imprisoned without deranging society. [p. 752]

This argument assumes a class difference between prostitutes and their customers: customers are middle- or upper-class "pillars of society," prostitutes are lower-class *lumpenproletariat*. While we may doubt whether law enforcement should discriminate on the basis of class, the characterization of customers as middle-class implied by Davis is accurate: most customers are middle-class, married, white, professionals or businessmen who live outside the urban core neighborhoods.

The class of prostitutes, however, is not as easily categorized. In our study, for example, 64 percent of the prostitute subjects reported their childhood family's income as middle- or upper-class. It is social mobility, as effected by societal application of the "deviant" label, that makes this common assumption of "prostitute–lower class" near absolute in fact. As Davis further stated, "The harlot's return is not primarily a reward for abstinence, labor or rent. It is primarily a reward for loss of social standing." The statistics on prostitutes' class standing as measured by income, education, etc., are not at issue here. We are merely pointing out that through "working the streets" as a prostitute a woman becomes defined by the larger society as "lower class" and thus gains all the liabilities appertaining to that social status. Moreover, the illegal, "deviant" status of prostitution means that the circle of those with whom a prostitute can form close associations is arbitrarily limited to a very small number of people, virtually all of whom are, or are considered to be, lower class. This limitation commonly closes off the possibility of upward mobility through social contacts or marriage, or through alternative occupations.

The life-style also presents the danger of physical injury. Although many studies have been made of "ancillary crimes" associated with street prostitution, the vast majority of these studies have concentrated on crimes committed *by* prostitutes, to the exclusion of the crime very commonly committed *against* prostitutes: assault by customers and police. Of addict-prostitutes interviewed, 68 percent had been so assaulted; of all prostitutes, 61 percent. The destructive impact of these assaults is aggravated by the fact that legal recourse usually is not available to these women. Prostitutes are not likely to be taken seriously by authorities, such as the police, to whom they turn for help. Faced with the attitude that she was "asking for it," or at least "had it coming to her," a prostitute who reports abuse from a customer to the police is liable to feel even more victimized by the discrimination of the legal system than by the violence of individual men.

Venereal disease (VD) and other vaginal health problems may also be destructive to prostitutes. Despite their high-risk status due to the large number of sexual contacts made, prostitutes account for only 5 percent of the venereal disease cases reported in the United States. These women are somewhat aware of the risks they are taking and, unlike the nonprofessional, promiscuous teenagers who account for the majority of VD cases, do try to take care of themselves. Yet even treated venereal disease can be a health problem. Pelvic inflammatory disease is a possible serious complication of recurrent venereal disease and can result in sterility. The importance prostitutes attach to the problem of VD was shown in our study, where VD placed fourth in the prostitutes' list of the disadvantages of being a prostitute (following "police/jail/legal expenses," "danger from customers," and "emotional stress").

Prostitutes seem to know what they want—money and material goods, independence and adventure—and they see prostitution, however unsuccessful, as the best available means for attaining these goals. The risks they take—legal sanctions, assault, VD, decreases in their own sexual enjoyment—are risks they choose to accept in return for the short-run opportunity to fulfill their life goals. These goals often result from a lack of opportunity to pursue "normal" goals successfully. The risks these women face are inherent in prostitution because the profession violates the "normal" female sex role and is therefore declared not only immoral but illegal. Owing to the limitations of the "normal" female sex role, however, it is only through violating that role that these women can see themselves as having any chance at all to get what they want and live the way they choose. Since prostitution is also conceptualized as a permanent violation, commitment to success in the alternative lifestyle becomes intense. The detrimental effects on the individual prostitute of such social crimes (noncompliance with sex-role expectations) are multiplied by institutionalizing her "deviance" as a legal crime (prostitution).

PIMPS

Not all prostitutes have pimps; among those who do, pimp-prostitute relationships range from business to deep emotional dependency. Here, we discuss the advantages and disadvantages of the latter because it is these relationships that are the basis of social stereotypes about the self-destructiveness of prostitutes involved with pimps.

Women in this society are socialized to feel they need a man for both security and self-respect. Prostitutes also desire a man to take care of them, to take care of business, to complete them, to love them, to make a home with them. This is part of the traditional female sex role; a woman without a man is a spinster in the larger society and an "outlaw" on the streets. Prostitutes are familiar with men in negative roles; many of them report negative or nonexistent relationships with fathers and stepfathers.

"Well, everybody wants a man, some kind of man," said one streetwalker. Explained another, "You can get lonesome. Even though they laugh and say, if you're with that many men how can you get lonesome. But believe it or not, it [prostitution] is much like getting up at eight o'clock in the morning, going to work, and coming home at five o'clock in the evening; it's just something you do to survive and that's it. There's no feelings involved."

For many of these women, a relationship with a pimp means "just knowing that you have somebody there all the time, not just for protection, just someone you can go to." Because of their involvement in a deviant life-style, however, prostitutes must share their lives with men who understand the dynamics and values of their deviant subculture—men who will accept their violations of the traditional female sex role. Any man who lives with a prostitute will be called a pimp, although usually the only factors which distinguish a prostitute-pimp relationship from a "normal" one, aside from the illegality of both roles, are the woman's status as sole "breadwinner" and, often, the man's overt maintenance of two or more similar relationships simultaneously.

Women's socialized need for men is reinforced by the fact that a women's status on the street is determined by that of her man. Prostitutes who can achieve a relationship with a "high-class" pimp have a higher standing in the subculture of prostitution. This higher status pays important dividends in her interactions with other members of the subculture: "If you have a pimp, other guys on the street, they kind of leave you alone." Thus, one often finds prostitutes actively seeking to attach themselves to those pimps whose patronage they feel will benefit them most in status and protection.

One of the most confusing aspects of the pimp-prostitute relationship is that while pimps strive to act out the male sex role completely and exclusively, the economics of the situation require prostitutes to violate as many norms of the female sex role as they fulfill. It is the job of the pimp to manipulate the prostitute's sense of reality so that she can feel like a "real woman": the pimp must convince her that in transgressing against her sex-role expectations she is really proving herself more of a woman than nonprostitutes. No pimp has to tell a prostitute that "every woman does it"; every woman "puts out" for men. Nor do most prostitutes need help in figuring out that their demand for direct payment makes them smarter than women who, in deferring payment, "do it for nothing." Prostitutes point out that sexual exploitation of women is an unalterable fact. Black prostitutes have the double rationalization of both sexism and racism. This natural, reactive rationalization is not sufficient, however, to resolve the prostitute's conflict between ends (fulfillment of sex-role expectations) and means (violations of sexual norms). This conflict is the pimp's opportunity. "Not only are you smarter than straight women," he tells the prostitute, "but you are more womanly; and your willingness to turn tricks for me proves it." It is every woman's duty to support her man. Prostitutes need emotional support in facing their sex-role dilemma; the opportunity provided by the pimp to perceive their "unfeminine" business transactions as motivated by love is a wonderfully womanly solution. Nothing is more universally acceptable as womanly than love—especially when expressed through self-sacrifice. Pimps, of course, state their understanding of woman's need to act out their support of men more simply: "Women are supposed to cater to a man, and this is just one way to do it."

The fact that many prostitutes enjoy their adventurous, potentially financially rewarding, and independent working lives does not mean they have not internalized much of the sex-role conditioning which programs them to be timid, passive, and dependent. For the prostitute, the pimp is the only man in whose company she can safely act out the traditional female sex role. Every man who is not a pimp is subculturally defined as a trick, with whom the prostitute must play a defensive, assertive, sometimes aggressive role. Only in relation to a domineering pimp does a prostitute have the opportunity to demonstrate her essential "femininity": her dependence on the male.

Pimps and prostitutes commonly agree that one of the pimp's important functions is "taking care of business"—handling the prostitute's earnings, arranging for living quarters, supplying bail bonds and other legal expenses, and arranging for child care when a prostitute is in jail. Protection is also a pimp function, but one which is usually provided by status alone; since pimps are not present "on the stroll," the amount of protection they can provide against assaults by customers or police is very limited. Prostitutes hand over their money for pimps to take care of for reasons similar to those of other career women who submit to the social domination of a man when work is over: in order to prove themselves "real women" within the dictates of their sex-role stereotype. Women are not "supposed" to be able to handle money, although many do (including many "housewives"). Moreover, since the ability to handle financial matters is not considered "feminine," a great many women never have the opportunity or the confidence to learn this skill.

Despite such business arrangements or personal needs, few prostitute-pimp relationships are desirable models of human social interaction. Some pimps are physically abusive. In some cases the woman sees this as appropriate male attention, a compliment to her role as the passive child-woman. Others fear abuse but expect it from all men. Prostitutes who experience abuse from their pimps are in a better position to leave them than nonworking wives with abusive husbands, in that prostitutes are at least financially more independent. On the other hand, because of their illegal deviant status, prostitutes, whether they are married to their pimps or not, are less likely than "respectable" married women to perceive the police and other social agencies as available sources of help in such situations. The illegality of prostitution, combined with the ethics of the deviant life-style, in effect give pimps a freer hand with the prostitutes they wish to dominate.

Prostitutes who have pimps usually do not keep the money they earn. Like many nonpimp men, pimps demand the right to control the finances of the relationship. This may not seem fair, but in fact many prostitutes consider it quite natural. In addition, many pimps and prostitutes agree, at least in general, about how the money should be spent. If she can have the flashy clothes she wants, if the pimp maintains a high-status car, if she can have the drugs she wants or needs, if the pimp will share with her a fantasy about the wealthy, respectable life they're going to lead sometime in the hazy future, the prostitute very likely will not feel inclined to complain about handing over her money. She may not be able to imagine that her life would be any different if she handled the money herself— except that she would be lonely without her man, and she would be faced with the unnerving prospect of "taking care of business" by herself.

In a functional pimp-prostitute arrangement, therefore, we see both constructive and destructive elements. Prostitutes receive emotional support from pimps, both in the form of "someone to love" and in the form of reassurance about their sex-role performance, assistance in "taking care of business," and the protection of being associated with a (more or less) successful man's status. In exchange, prostitutes give up the right to control the money they earn and risk the possibility of assault and/or coercion. The power pimps have over prostitutes is greater than the power other men have over the women they relate to because of the ethics and values of the life-style and because prostitution is illegal.

USE OF DRUGS

Drug use and abuse is considered to be a major category of self-destructive behavior in prostitutes. A major component of our research was an evaluation of the relationship between street prostitution and addiction. It is clear that a variety of drugs play a significant role in the business and recreational lives of prostitutes. Most, if not all, prostitutes interviewed in our research used marihuana, amphetamines, and barbiturates to increase their ability to work, and used cocaine as a recreational drug. A substantial number of women involved in prostitution are addicted to heroin. Approximately two-thirds of these women are addicts supporting their habit with prostitution, and one-third are women who became addicted after entering the business.

It is obvious why prostitutes get involved in drug use. Their life-style supports it as an escape mechanism, as a confidence booster, and as a normal part of "street consciousness." Prostitutes, because of the stress of a deviant, illegal life-style and the requirements of their occupation, work long hours and encounter many different potentially dangerous situations. These circumstances and the constant presence of drug users lead to drug abuse. The main reason is physical and emotional stress. Drugs help the prostitute relax and cope.

The negative consequences of drug use/abuse, whether they result from the direct toxic action of the drug, the effect of contaminants, hypersensitivity reactions, diseases contracted in the course of ingestion, or the myriad personal-social ramifications, are known to prostitutes. The women we interviewed were well aware of the potential destructiveness of drug use. In the combined interview group, 36.2 percent of the addict-prostitutes and 22.3 percent of the prostitutes said the worst thing they had ever done was get into crime and drugs. Over 65 percent of addict-prostitutes and 62 percent of prostitutes were involved in drug use as juveniles. Forty-one percent of all the women questioned felt that drug use had caused them health problems. But 64 percent of the addict-prostitutes indicated they would continue to use narcotics, and most of the prostitutes indicated that drug use was part of their life-style and did not foresee a time when they would stop using drugs.

The self-destructiveness of drug abuse is apparent to this population, but the stress of an illegal life-style and the values of the subculture override this concern. Drugs are accepted, as are the sex-role violations, as a part of the deviant life-style. Drugs facilitate membership in the subculture and in this sense are adaptive. The prostitute needs drugs to work and to relax; the addict needs to prostitute to support her habit.

SUMMARY _____

Traditional concepts or expectations of the female role in relation to sexuality contribute substantially to the development of some women's commitment to prostitution. The commitment grows out of the permanence of lost sexual status and the ambivalence surrounding entrance into a negative sexual status. Attempts to adapt to destructive circumstances can be seen as both constructive, i.e., finding an accepting peer group, and destructive, in the acceptance of a deviant consciousness.

Femininity seems to drive prostitutes in conflicting directions vis-à-vis the profession and the traditional view of woman as "doing for her man." His control is based on his ability to restore the femininity lost in the translation from "good woman" to "bad woman." The prostitute is often without alternative resources. She may have been labeled a "whore" early on and sought a life-style and subculture that would give her some measure of place and status. The loss of the normal peer group and family is counteracted by the development of an accepting peer group and family. The perceived permanence of this loss intensifies self-destructive behavior. She needs to keep "her man" or find another. She needs to earn money despite danger and arrest. Her fragile, constructed "deviant" self-respect requires her to be successful, at least in this life-style. The possibility of returning to the "straight" world does not become a reality until she is older and more aware of the dynamics of her situation. Until then the self-destructiveness of her situation is rarely perceived. The potential money, adventure, independence, and peer-group involvement inherent in prostitution are too attractive.

REFERENCES _____

Benjamin, H., and Masters, R. E. L. *Prostitution and Morality*. New York: Julien Press, 1964.

Carns, D. Talking about sex: Notes on first coitus and the double sexual standard. *Journal of Marriage and Family*, 36:677–688, 1973.

Choisy, Maryse. *Psychoanalysis of the Prostitute*. New York: Philosophical Library, 1961.

Davis, Kingsley. The sociology of prostitution. *American Sociological Review*, 2:744–755, 1937.

Davis, Nanette J. The prostitute: Developing a deviant identity. In J. M. Henslin, ed., *Studies in the Sociology of Sex*. New York: Appleton-Century-Crofts, 1971, pp. 297–322.

De Francis, V. *Protecting the Child Victims of Sex Crimes Committed by Adults*. Final Report, American Humane Association, Children's Division, Denver, 1969.

Eastman, W. First intercourse: Some statistics on who, where, when, and why. *Sexual Behavior*, 2:22–27, .1972.

Esselstyn, T. C. Prostitution in the United States. *Annals of the American Academy of Political and Social Sciences*, 376:123–135, 1968.

Federal Bureau of Information. *Crime in the United States, 1977*. Washington, D.C.: Government Printing Office, 1978.

Ferracuti, F. Incest between father and daughter. In H. Resnik and M. Wolfgang, eds., *Sexual Behaviors: Social, Clinical, and Legal Aspects*. Boston: Little, Brown, 1972.

Gagnon, J. Female child victims of sex offenses. *Social Problems*, 13:176–192, 1965.

Gray, Diana. Turning out: A study of teenage prostitution. *Urban Life and Culture*, January, 1973, pp. 401–425.

Greenwald, Harold. *The Call Girl*. San Diego: Decision Books, 1978.

Jackman, N. R., O'Toole, R., and Geis, G. The self-image of the prostitute. In J. Gagnon and W. Simon, eds., *Sexual Deviance*. New York: Harper and Row, 1967.

Jaffe, A., Dynneson, L., and Ten Bensel, R. Sexual abuse of children. *American Journal of Disabled Children*, 129:689–692, 1975.

James, Jennifer. *A Formal Analysis of Prostitution—Final Report*. State of Washington, Department of Social and Health Services, 1971.

James, Jennifer, and Greene, Avis. Female criminal involvement and its relationship to unusual pregnancy outcomes. Unpublished manuscript, 1977.

Kantner, J., and Zelnik, M. Sexual experience of young unmarried women in the United States. *Family Planning Perspectives,* 4:9–18, 1972.

Kemp, Tage. *Prostitution: An Investigation of Its Causes, Especially with Regard to Hereditary Factors.* Copenhagen: Levin and Munskgaard, 1936.

Pomeroy, Wardell B. Some aspects of prostitution. *Journal of Sex Research,* 1:177–187, 1965.

Rosenblum, Karen E. Female deviance and the female sex role: A preliminary investigation. *British Journal of Sociology,* 26:169–185, 1975.

Sorensen, R. *Adolescent Sexuality in Contemporary America.* New York: World, 1973.

Weiner, I. On incest: A survey. *Excerpta Criminologica,* 4:137–155, 1964.

Winick, Charles, and Kinsie, Paul. *The Lively Commerce: Prostitution in the United States.* New York: Quadrangle, 1971.

Wittels, F. *Sex Habits of American Women.* New York: Eton, 1951.

23

ALTRUISM, RISK-TAKING, AND SELF-DESTRUCTIVENESS
A Study of Interveners into Violent Criminal Events

GILBERT GEIS AND TED L. HUSTON

In-depth interviews with thirty-two persons who thrust themselves into criminal episodes laden with danger—events such as street muggings, armed robberies, and bank holdups—provide the empirical underpinning for this report. Members of our study population told us that they performed their acts of heroism with no preconceived idea that they might be rewarded. Thirty of the thirty-two maintained that they did not give serious thought to the possibility of injury when they acted, or else defined that possibility as unlikely. Our respondents typically said that they responded almost automatically to observed or signaled distress. All thirty-two interveners, however, suffered some personal loss or injury as a consequence of their behavior. They came to our attention when they filed claims under provisions of the California Good Samaritan statute (Geis et al., 1976; Holland, 1967).

The thirty-two interveners were drawn from a pool almost double that size, representing all persons who had received reparation payments from the state since the Samaritan Law was enacted in 1966. We selected for our interviews persons who met three criteria: they had intervened in criminal episodes rather than in emergencies (such as automobile crashes or fires); they had displayed personal initiative rather than being inadvertent participants in the

Work on the project on which this paper is based was supported by the Center for Studies of Crime and Delinquency, National Institute of Mental Health (MH 26667). The authors express their appreciation to the Institute, and to the persons who helped to arrange and conduct the interviews: Richard Wright, Mike Ripley, Jo Weiner, Duff Zwald, Howard Bidna, Chris Huston, Tom Garrett, and Jean Geis. Bob Meier and Robley Geis offered ideas on an earlier draft, and Rodney Cate was very helpful in the data analysis.

action; and, finally, their behavior had put them in jeopardy of life or limb. Three vignettes indicate the kind of activity which members of our sample engaged in:

1. Several men, apparently armed, were mugging a victim on a darkened residential street in East Los Angeles. The victim's scream brought a young man on the run from his apartment. The intervener plunged into the melee, scared off one of the assailants, but was knifed by the second before that person also fled the scene.

2. Two men, heading home from an evening at a roller-skating rink, suddenly came upon a pair of robbers emerging from a grocery store they had held up. One of the men started in pursuit, cornered a robber, and wrestled him to the ground. The robber escaped only after he fired his pistol directly into the mouth of the intervener who had trapped him.

3. A young man, coming upon the scene, took off after two robbers who had held up an ice-cream store where a friend of his was employed. The robbers drove several miles into a cul-de-sac adjacent to San Quentin prison, spun their car about, and trapped their pursuer behind them. They came up to the window of his car and fired two bullets at him.

The remaining twenty-nine episodes were no less dramatic, no less dangerous.

In this report, we compare our cohort of "altruistic," "risk-taking," and (in some cases perhaps) "self-destructive" persons with a matched group drawn from a 200-person population consisting of a stratified sample of people living in Los Angeles county. Only members of the general population survey who had not intervened in a crime were eligible for the matched group. The two groups were matched person by person for sex, ethnic background, age, and education; thereafter, they were compared on their attitudes toward criminal justice issues, competencies they might possess (such as first-aid or karate training), self-descriptions, and scores on personality scales that measure humanitarianism (Fischer, 1973), alienation (Srole, 1956), belief in a just world (Rubin and Peplau, 1975), fear of negative evaluation (Watson and Friend, 1969), social responsibility (Berkowitz and Lutterman, 1968), sensation-seeking (Zuckerman et al., 1964), and anger reactions (Novaco, 1975). We also gathered data on some physical characteristics of members of both populations.

A SEMANTIC FORAY

The concepts we employ in examining our interveners require further consideration. "Altruism," "risk-taking," and "self-destructiveness"—like all such labels—are, of course, merely shorthand, judgments based on social values and "objective" states, such as physical health and well-being. It might be argued that no behavior is truly altruistic; that humans always select from the available options the one that they believe will enhance their own self-satisfaction.

Some acts people perform may come to be defined as "altruistic" because benefactors or external observers view them as valuable to recipients and costly to the actor. An anonymous donor to the poor, though she herself may have only limited financial resources, may secretly revel in enhancing her own self-image, relieving guilt (Rawlings, 1968), or may delight in scorning the wretches who accept her charity. But, at least in a narrow sense, her act self-evidently benefits the donee and costs the donor. The recipient may, of course, use the money to buy a weapon to slay a socially valuable person (say a doctor who has just found, but not yet written down, the formula for a cancer cure). The "true" benefits of altruism, in the long run at least, may not be socially desirable, or even beneficial to the recipient (who may, for instance, in the case of the hypothetical killing, be executed for murder).

In short, without pursuing either semantic or hypothetical cases into deeper, even muddier waters, it seems unquestionable that acts that are said to fit concepts such as "altruism," "risk-taking," and "self-destructiveness" may reasonably be viewed in a variety of ways, depending on the referent (doer, recipient, microsociety, macrosociety, or combinations thereof) and depending on consequences that inevitably will remain unknown until they unfold—or forever. It may be true that the suicide of a healthy young man, such as Romeo, acting impulsively on a mistaken judgment that is readily remediable, constitutes needless and unfortunate self-destructive behavior. (For others, of course, the lesson conveyed by the act may have profound "positive" behavioral value.) The issues become more complicated when we consider the immolation of religious zealots, the incarceration of conscientious objectors (Gaylin, 1970), or the injury of intrepid pioneers into unexplored realms. Hunger strikes, as Gandhi demonstrated, can be dangerous to the health but invigorating to the cause. Judgments about altruism, risk-taking, and self-destructiveness, as Stephen Schafer (1974) pointed out in a monograph on political offenders, also often involve historical assessments, and can change with the vagaries of ideological currents flowing through a social system.

What, then, might be said about our thirty-two interveners into criminal events, persons who carried the moral of the parable of the Good Samaritan into more dangerous realms than their biblical precursor? Their motives may come under suspicion: they may have been impelled by fury at the criminal, lust for violence, or simple restlessness. But often they were enormously helpful to the beleaguered victims of criminal assaults, and sometimes they served to eliminate a depredator from society, at least temporarily. Unfortunately, we cannot know what might have happened had the intervener kept his (for, as we shall see, it almost certainly will be a "he" who intrudes into a crime) peace and bided his time. A robber is captured, for instance, but the intervener suffers an injury that could put him on the welfare rolls. The symbolic and modeling value of the Samaritan's act may be of inestimable worth, or the act may prove meaningless, even of negative value: others might find the heroism comic or naive. Most likely, indeed, both forms of reaction will ensue. How do we measure the intervention's overall significance?

In the final analysis, the foregoing issues come down to questions of public policy. Given our judgment that the interventions we are examining balance uncertainly in regard to the elements of altruism, risk-taking, and self-destructiveness, what is our judgment concerning public policy issues? Should laws be passed, such as those in European countries (Tunc, 1966), that failure to provide help to a person in need, even failure rooted in cowardice, itself constitutes a crime? Or should interventions be seen as smacking of vigilantism, obstructing the performance of persons who are paid and qualified to intervene, such as the police, and containing more individual risk and social harm than benefit to the victim and to the rest of us? These are matters to which we will return in our concluding section.

DEMOGRAPHIC PORTRAIT ——————————————————

The thirty-two interveners in our sample are by no means representative of the population at large. For one thing, an event permitting bystander intervention must take place before help can be proffered. Some persons—perhaps they might be dubbed the "voyeuristically vulnerable" (as against the "accident-prone")—clearly see a good many more criminal and emergency situations than their fellows. Part of this experience undoubtedly relates to where they live, where they work, and their other habits, much as sex-related activities makes men five times more likely than women to be struck by lightning. It is possible that other persons, located elsewhere in the social structure than the interveners, would do exactly as they did if faced with the same circumstances—but they never are, or at least they say that they never have been.

We asked how many times the respondent had witnessed a

holdup, car theft, assault, murder, or any other specific serious crime during the past ten years. The matched sample of noninterveners had seen an average of 0.6 such events, less than one serious crime per person. The interveners, on the other hand, said they had witnessed the listed crimes 122 times, an average of 3.8 per person. The last figure was inflated by one respondent who said he had seen 37 crimes, but even so, half of the Samaritans said they had seen two or more crimes compared to only three persons in the matched group with similar exposure ($t = 4.10, p < .01$, two tailed; eliminating the respondent who witnessed—so he said—37 crimes, $t = 3.50$, $p < .01$).[1]

Equally interesting are the interveners' reports of involvement in crimes other than those that triggered our interview with them. Eleven of the Samaritans reported that they had intervened at least one other time, and five of these said that they had done so on more than two other occasions.

We do not know, of course, how much the reported exposures have been influenced by memory quirks, reporting idiosyncracies, or distorted by the same set of characteristics that led to the interventions. Nor can we ascertain the extent to which the interveners might deliberately have placed themselves into crime-related situations. Whatever the explanation for this difference in exposure to crime, it seems that either the self-images or the reality (and we imagine the truth lies between the two) make interveners persons who often find or put themselves into perilous situations. Their responses seem to indicate an element of unusual risk-taking in a considerable number of them.

By far the most striking difference between the interveners and the population at large lies in the sex distribution. Thirty-one of the thirty-two interveners are males. The only female is an older woman who had looked through the peephole of her apartment door when she heard a loud rapping on the door of her eighty-three-year-old female neighbor. A minute or so later she heard a scream, and hastened to the rescue. The elderly neighbor was knifed almost a dozen times, but her life was saved by the old-fashioned steel corset she wore; the Samaritan suffered cut hand tendons.

The ethnic distribution of the interveners was twenty-seven whites, one black, three Chicanos, and one Oriental. The disproportionate involvement of whites may be a function of their relative willingness to use bureaucratic channels to obtain restitution for their losses. The interveners averaged somewhere in their mid-thirties at the time they offered assistance, and their average educa-

---

[1] The tests reported are all t tests for matched pairs.

tion was thirteen years. The matched group did not differ significantly in age ($t = 1.25, ns$) or education ($t = .14, ns$), and we matched exactly for sex and in all but two instances for ethnic background.

COMPETENCE TO INTERVENE

Of the many measures we used in our efforts to differentiate the interveners from their peers, the most significant results were yielded (unexpectedly: we had thought the personality measures would produce a rich harvest) by inquiries about the training the respondents had had which might assist them in an emergency. As Table 1 shows, there were no notable differences in first-aid training (a large majority of each group had such experience) or training in karate. But in terms of lifesaving, medical, and police training, the differences between the groups were statistically significant (lifesaving: $\chi^2 = 5.08$, significant at the .05 level; police training: $\chi^2 = 6.56$, and medical training: $\chi^2 = 6.62$, both significant at the .02 level). The lifesaving skills were not called into play in any of the interventions. Presumably, though, they symbolically reinforced the intervener's idea of himself as a person able to help others. In an earlier study, Clark and Word (1974) found that persons knowledgeable (as compared to naive) about electronics gave safer and quicker help to a man who was apparently endangered by an entanglement in electrical wires. A perceived ability to master a situation, therefore, seems to be related to intervention in it.

The difference in height of the members of the two groups approached significance. The Samaritans averaged 71.2 inches tall (SD = 3.16), whereas members of the matched sample averaged 69.8 inches (SD = 3.11), 1.4 inches shorter ($t = 2.00$, $p < .055$). Weight differences were tied to height: at an average of 176 pounds, the Samaritans were nine pounds heavier than the members of the matched group ($t = 1.55$, $p < .13$, ns).

The combination of training and physical attributes merits close scrutiny; it offers the best clues we were able to locate to the source

TABLE 1 Number and Percentage of Persons in Matched Groups Reporting Different Forms of Training

	Interveners		Matched Sample	
Skill	Number	Percent	Number	Percent
First aid	28	88	26	81
Lifesaving	20	62	11	34
Karate	17	53	12	38
Police	10	31	2	6
Medical	6	18	0	0

of intervention and risk-taking behavior in our study population. The Samaritans apparently possess a sense of capability founded on particular training and on personal strength. At slightly more than 5 feet, 11 inches, and 176 pounds, they are, compared to the average American male, relatively formidable (presuming, of course, that they are in good physical condition). They would therefore have reason to believe that they would be able to deal competently with situations into which they plunge and with the assailants they are likely to confront.

The training the interveners have acquired is, like all such social experience, difficult to interpret in causal terms. They might well have acquired such skills as lifesaving because of personal traits which also propelled the intervention—though it is important to note that our study did not uncover such traits, despite an intensive search for them. The training might also merely have complemented the physical attributes; police training, for example, can only be had by persons who meet minimum height and strength requirements. The medical training poses a different set of issues. Normally, no special physical attributes are required for such training. We would interpret the striking difference between the two groups as testimony that medical training carries with it indoctrination into an ethic (supplemented by some know-how) that impels the rendering of assistance to others. It should be noted, however, that only six of the interveners (compared to none of the matched sample) had such training. Parenthetically, the rather large number (at least in terms of our expectations) of respondents in both groups—seventeen interveners and twelve of the matched sample—who had had karate training is worth noting. We would be surprised were the figures so high for the population at large.

SELF-DESCRIPTIONS _____

We asked each person we interviewed to sort twenty-four cards, each containing a descriptive term, into one of three piles: (1) describes me; (2) undecided; (3) does not describe me. Such self-image measures obviously can be influenced by the interview situation; the insecure, for example, may want to camouflage their attributes. The interview exercise might be described as providing information about how the respondent believes or wants others to believe he perceives himself.

In the interveners, two traits reached statistical significance: *physically strong* ($t = 2.78$, $p < .009$) and *aggressive* ($t = 2.55$, $p < .016$). In the matched group, two other traits showed a trend toward significance: *shy* ($t = 1.89$, $p < .068$) and *conventional* ($t = 1.81$, $p < .08$). *Physically strong* was the fourth most pronounced trait found in the responses of the interveners, exceeded only by *happy* (also the primary self-descriptive trait of members of the matched group), *aggressive*, and *cooperative*, and equaled by *intelligent*.

The interveners' self-attribution of physical strength reinforces the material reported earlier. The ascription of aggressiveness could have emerged from their interventions; that is, their behavior could have inculcated a sense of their differentness and forcefulness that translated into the interview response. On the other hand, it is more likely that the trait of aggression constitutes a bulwark in the emerging portrait of the interveners: that they are persons of a commanding presence who actively move into physically challenging situations with confidence in their ability to handle such situations.

This profile is buttressed by responses given to a series of questions tapping attitudes toward criminal justice issues. Only one item yielded a significant result. Nonsignificant items included the seriousness of crime as a social issue, respect for the police and view of police power, and ideas about the sentencing and treatment of criminal offenders. The significant item concerned the kinds of things the respondent did out of a fear of crime. There were six specific subitems (Avoid walking at night; Generally lock your car; Avoid being out alone; Avoid talking to strangers; Install special locks or chains on doors and windows; Keep a watchdog) plus one subitem inquiring about any other specific preventive measures. The interveners did significantly *fewer* of these things than members of the matched sample ($p < .011$). They are *not* wary and cautious, but their "recklessness" seems to be born of confidence based on demonstrable self-sufficiency; though, like any nonneurotic who fails to check the fireplace flue each evening for possible intruders, they increase the likelihood of being harmed.

PERSONALITY SCALES _____

Several conditions had led us to hypothesize personality differences between the interveners and the matched group. We believed that previous research on bystander intervention (see, e.g., Latané and Darley, 1970) had failed to locate such differences because, among other things, the interventions the experimenters staged in the laboratory and, more rarely, in naturalistic settings, lacked compelling force. We also suspected that the nearly universal use of college students as subjects in intervention research failed to provide a varied enough study population to allow personality differences to become manifest.

Our results did not, however, support our expectation. Respondents were tested on scales that measured a plethora of traits, but we found no significant differences between the two groups, however much they may differ from the general population. The scales we used were shortened versions of standard inventories: a twenty-two-item humanitarianism scale (Fischer, 1973) with subtests on helping others, humanitarianism toward criminals, and social responsibility; a nine-item alienation scale (Srole, 1956, as modified by Christie; see Robinson and Shaver, 1973); a twenty-item "just world" inventory (Rubin and Peplau, 1975); an eight-item social responsibility test (Berkowitz and Lutterman, 1968); a ten-item scale measuring fear of negative evaluation (Watson and Friend, 1969); an eighteen-item anger reaction inventory (Novaco, 1975); and a thirty-three-item sensation-seeking scale (Zuckerman et al., 1974).

In the present context, the sensation-seeking scale is of particular interest. Of all the personality tests, it came closest to significance ($t = 1.50$, $p < .145$) and in the expected direction: the interveners were more likely to respond in a positive vein. An item analysis of the thirty-three questions, however, showed none of them approaching significance.

OVERVIEW OF CASE MATERIAL _____

A considerable literature on policemen, medical examiners, firemen, and similar people who routinely face emergencies indicates that such persons come to regard danger with a kind of indifference or nonchalance (see, e.g., Rubinstein, 1973; Manning, 1977). In part their attitude must stem from the repetitive nature of their experiences; the most exciting things become banal if encountered often enough. In part it probably arises from an introjected ethos: it's just part of the job, and we'd better get on with doing it. A similar kind of insouciance characterized our interveners. It was not that they were self-effacing or humble about what they had done; rather, they did not find their behavior particularly remarkable. In addition, they had a sense of obligation to do what they did. Egon Bittner (1974), in an excellent essay on police work, illustrates such an ethos with a vignette of a police officer directing traffic who espies an unusual event taking place nearby:

> . . . it is virtually certain that any normally competent patrolman would abandon the traffic post . . . without a moment's hesitation and without regard for the state of the traffic he was supposed to monitor, if it came to his attention that a crime was being committed somewhere at a distance not too far for him to reach in time either to arrest the crime in its course, or to arrest the perpetrator . . . even when the crime was of the sort which when reported to the police in the ordinary manner . . . would

> receive only the most cursory attention. . . . Yet there exists no law, no regulation, no formal requirement of any kind that determines that practice. . . . Why then should all concerned, inside and outside the police, consider it entirely proper and desirable that a patrolman abandon his post, exposing many people to serious inconvenience and the whole city to grave hazards, to pursue the dubious quest of catching a two-bit thief? [pp. 28–29]

Bittner's answer to his question fits both the policeman and our interveners. They see such events as *something that ought not to be happening and about which someone had better do something now!*

The attitudes of our interveners, they tell us, apply not only to themselves but to their male parents. We asked whether they believed their fathers would have done the same thing they had in a similar situation; twenty-two of twenty-eight thought so; three did not know; and one did not answer the question. We also asked the married interveners how their wives had responded to what they had done. They generally said that their spouses had been frightened and had warned them to be careful. Nine wives were said to approve of the intervener's action; six disapproved. This information was usually conveyed in a tone of tolerant condescension, the implication being that the women had done only what was to be expected of *them*, just as the interveners had done only what *they* had to do.

There was often a note of cynicism, however, about the behavior of persons other than the intervener and his family members, a note also found in studies of law enforcement officers (Rubinstein, 1973). The woman who had intervened to help her neighbor reported scornfully how others in the apartment house who undoubtedly had heard the scream had not come to the rescue. Several interveners told stories of being ignored in their own distress by passers-by at the time of the incident. The interveners were motivated, our interviews suggest, not by benevolence toward the victim they assisted— indeed, very often they ignored the victim in order to pursue the offender. Their expressed attitudes toward the offender were generally hostile, but primarily in the sense that he represented a foe, an opponent, rather than an evil being. In short, they view themselves rather blandly as different from most other people, as persons with a "duty" for which they have adequate training and prowess.

CONCLUSION _____

How does our empirical material about persons who intervene in criminal situations fit with the concepts of altruism, self-destructiveness, and risk-taking? The behaviors that our interveners engaged in are very dangerous. At the same time, these behaviors were voluntary. Nonetheless, altruism appears to be the concept most readily discardable. If the interveners were moved by humanitarian impulses, we were unable to uncover data to support such a thesis. They scored better (but not significantly so) than the matched group members on both the humanitarianism and the social responsibility scales; but we are inclined to write off this result as a function of the way in which they have been defined after their often well-publicized acts of intervention. They rarely expressed to us any sympathy for the persons they had assisted, or much satisfaction at having alleviated distress.

The risk-taking and the self-destructiveness (if any) of the interveners appear to be interrelated. As we noted, the interveners act out of a sense of duty and a feeling of competence. Any self-destructiveness in their behavior is similar to that which marks the acts of any human being who does not cocoon himself in an antiseptic milieu and try to postpone as long as possible his inevitable demise. The interveners take more risks than their fellows when they move into criminal events, but these risks are in a sense calculated, based on a balance of their competencies against the dangers of the events. Put another way, the chances of members of the matched group intervening successfully in similar episodes might be, say, 35 percent, compared to 65 percent for the persons who actually did intervene. Perhaps intervention can be regarded as a rational acceptance of challenge, just as moving outside a cocoon is an enabling—though a more dangerous—performance than remaining encapsulated. Obviously, had they done nothing to help others the interveners would have been spared hurt, and would have suffered nothing worse than the need to readjust their image of themselves and what they had thought was required of them. In short, it is our best judgment, in terms of our earlier foray into the semantics of the terms we are employing, that empirical and case study data support the proposition that intervention into criminal situations represents neither untoward risk-taking nor self-destructive behavior.

POLICY RECOMMENDATIONS _____

In regard to public policy, our findings indicate that persons who possess the ability to help their fellows in moments of distress ought to be encouraged to do so. The problem arises in regard to those who do not at the time feel obligated or, correlatively, competent to perform in this way. The simplest idea would be to offer training that would prepare members of the nonintervener group. We expect that such training would provide an impetus to intervene as well as the feeling of competence to do so.

Intervention might also be increased by sanctions against noninterveners, but we are inclined to regard such legislation as a last resort, unless a statute could be worded so delicately that only those qualified to act effectively would fall within its purview. A positive campaign providing highly visible rewards for persons who intervene would probably be valuable. Such a campaign should not dramatize encounters in which chance helped the intervener. Rather, it should stress attributes of the intervener that made his feat possible—his strength and skills—so that the unprepared might be inhibited from acting precipitously.

In summary, our work indicates that care should be taken to differentiate among human activities that involve components of risk-taking, altruism, and self-destructiveness. In particular, attention should be paid to the aims of the actor, the ethos that underlies the act, and the consequences of the behavior both for the actor and for those affected by his act. Few would dispute the nobility of an act of self-destructiveness that saved the lives of countless other persons (e.g., falling on a bomb in a crowded street). Acts committed in social isolation, such as using heroin, skydiving, and playing Russian roulette, may more readily be seen as acts of untoward risk-taking and self-destructiveness. The intervention into criminal events by bystanders, our work indicates, is risk-taking worth the risk.

REFERENCES _____

Berkowitz, Leonard, and Lutterman, Kenneth G. The traditional socially responsible personality. *Public Opinion Quarterly,* 32:169–185, 1968.

Bittner, Egon. Florence Nightingale in pursuit of Willie Sutton: A theory of the police. In Herbert Jacob, ed., *The Potential for Reform of Criminal Justice.* Beverly Hills, Calif.: Sage Publications, 1974, pp. 17–44.

Clark, Russell D., III, and Word, Larry E. Where is the apathetic bystander? Situational characteristics of the emergency. *Journal of Personality and Social Psychology,* 29:279–287, 1974.

Fischer, Edward H. Consistency among humanitarian and helping attitudes. *Social Forces,* 52:157–168, 1973.

Gaylin, Willard. *In the Service of Their Country: War Resisters in Prison.* New York: Viking, 1970.

Geis, G., Huston, T. L., and Wright, R. Compensating Good Samaritans. *Crime Prevention Review,* 3:28–35, 1976.

Holland, Lynwood M. The Good Samaritan laws: A reappraisal. *Journal of Public Law,* 16:128–137, 1967.

Latané, Bibb, and Darley, John M. *The Unresponsive Bystander: Why Doesn't He Help?* New York: Appleton-Century-Crofts, 1970.

Manning, Peter K. *Police Work: The Social Organization of Policing.* Cambridge, Mass.: M.I.T. Press, 1977.

Novaco, Raymond W. *Anger Control: The Development and Evaluation of an Experimental Treatment.* Lexington, Mass.: Lexington Books, 1975.

Rawlings, Edna I. Witnessing harm to others: A reassessment of guilt in altruistic behavior. *Journal of Personality and Social Psychology,* 1:377–380, 1968.

Robinson, John P., and Shaver, Phillip R. *Measures of Social Psychological Attitudes,* rev. ed. Ann Arbor, Mich.: Institute for Social Research, 1973.

Rubin, Zick, and Peplau, Letitia A. Belief in a just world and reactions to another's lot: A study of participants in the national draft lottery. *Journal of Social Issues,* 31(3):65–89, 1975.

Rubinstein, Jonathan. *City Police.* New York: Farrar, Straus and Giroux, 1973.

Schafer, Stephen. *The Political Criminal: The Problem of Morality and Crime.* New York: Free Press, 1974.

Srole, Leo. Social integration and certain corrolaries: An exploratory study. *American Sociological Review,* 21:709–716, 1956.

Tunc, André. The volunteer and the Good Samaritan. In James M. Ratcliffe, ed., *The Good Samaritan and the Law.* Garden City, N.Y.: Doubleday, 1966, pp. 43–62.

Watson, David, and Friend, Ronald. Measurement of social-evaluative anxiety. *Journal of Consulting and Clinical Psychology,* 33:448–457, 1969.

Zuckerman, M., Kolin, E. A., Price, L., and Zoob, I. Development of a sensation-seeking scale. *Journal of Consulting Psychology,* 28:477–482, 1964.

The excerpt on pp. 368–369 is reprinted from "Florence Nightingale in Pursuit of Willie Sutton: A Theory of the Police" by Egon Bittner in *The Potential for Reform of Criminal Justice,* Herbert Jacob, Editor, Volume III, Sage Criminal Justice System Annuals, © 1974, pp. 28–29 by permission of the Publisher, Sage Publications, Inc. (Beverly Hills/London).

PART SEVEN

STRESS-SEEKING AND HIGH-RISK SPORTS

24

THE SOCIETAL STAKE IN STRESS-SEEKING

SAMUEL Z. KLAUSNER

THE INTELLECTUAL SETTING
OF THE CONCEPT

Why Man Takes Chances: Studies in Stress-Seeking (Klausner, 1968) appeared a decade ago. The subtitle was a conference topic. I believe this was the first use of the term "stress-seeking," though certainly not the first expression of the idea. The National Institutes of Health dedicated a section to the study of stress. The physical metaphor "stress" was being borrowed to describe the condition of people encountering unusual environmental demands. Sometimes it referred to the response of the organism or the personality to pressure, a use close to the root meaning of the term in mechanics. The term also became an imprecise summary for the failures of an overexerted society to protect its members from a raging social and physical milieu. Semipopular interpreters grasped the concept to explain American military prisoners' cooperation with their North Vietnamese captors to a degree not condoned by the military code of conduct (Biderman, 1963). The imagery of stress rather consistently became that of coping with an evil located in the physical, interpersonal, or institutional environment. The clock hands passing 11:55, symbolizing the ultimate evil, fed the image. Orthodox Freudians and orthodox Christian theologians, almost alone, sought the source of stress within the person.

Anthropologists, social psychologists, and sociologists studied the group under stress.[1] As physiology and clinical psychology came to

---

[1] The conception of a group coping with imposed stress had its precursors before the 1960s. Anthropologists and social psychologists thought of international stability as a matter of managing international tensions (Klineberg, 1950). The maintenance of civilian morale (Watson, 1942) was a matter of managing tensions within nations. This work had its obverse in war-inspired studies of psychological warfare, of ways to increase a nation's tension (Linebarger, 1948; Lerner, 1949). Studies of natural disasters by sociologists (Baker, 1962; Barton, 1969) fell into the same mold. An unexpected attack by "nature" produced emergency social organizations which enabled communities to cope with the social disruption.

dominate the field of stress studies, research gravitated more and more toward concern with the stress of the individual. Hans Selye's *The Stress of Life* (1956) was the most widely read work at the time. The "adaptation syndrome," incorporating the image of coping, was its central, and best remembered, feature. The most authoritative statement among social and psychological investigators, the work of Basowitz et al. (1955), analyzed the issue from the perspective of the coping psyche and soma.

The concept of stress-seeking was introduced in this social and intellectual climate. It challenged the image of coping and the underlying equilibrium model of tension reduction, especially in its application to the theory of motivation. An image of man as an active challenger of the environment, as a creator of stress, was offered in its place.

INDIVIDUAL STRESS-SEEKING: DEFINING THE CONCEPT_____

The introduction to *Why Man Takes Chances* observed that even in times of tranquility people seek adventure, "look for trouble," "spoil for a fight," seek danger, search for problems resistant to solution, and "even seek the stress, fear, or anxiety engendered by such encounters" (p. vi). The revisionist image was set in the initial questions of the conference. "What types of men, what types of societies are more prone to seek stress by pitting themselves against a resistance?" "Under what conditions are they more apt to do so?" "What societal arrangements are made for promoting, facilitating and controlling stress-seeking behavior?" "When does this tendency ally itself with hostile emotions and eventuate in aggression, and when does it ally itself with a 'moral equivalent of war,' and advance the creative development of the individual or of his society?" (p. vi.).

Stress-seeking was introduced as a personality attribute, prompted or evoked by social conditions. Societies arrange for the encouragement and control of individual stress-seekers and the collective, itself, might be stress-seeking. Stress-seeking was not conceived as intrinsically good or bad for the individual or for society, but, like a drive, as something that might spend itself in the realization of diverse values.[2]

"Stress-seeking may be defined as behavior designed to increase the intensity of emotion or level of activation of the organism" (Klausner, 1968, p. 139). The concept has its cognates in other frames

---

[2] Selye's revised work (1976) recognized the stress-seeking component of human behavior, particularly in association with desirable values or self-enhancement—"eustress" (see below).

of reference, resembling, in some respects, Darwin's concept of "struggle," Freud's idea of Eros, Fenichel's (1939) counterphobic attitude, Berlyne's (1965) epistemic curiosity, McClelland's (1953) need achievement, Arnold's (1960) arousal-seeking, and risk-taking as used by Kogan and Wallach (1967). Unlike risk-taking, however, it is not bound to exposing the organism to dangers. Stress-seeking is related to striving and effort, to pushing against odds. Stress-seeking may be likened to voluntary tropistic behavior, stimulus-seeking, like a plant growing toward the sun.

The original approach to the concept was based on phenomenological descriptions of "fear and enthusiasm" among sport parachutists (Klausner, 1967). A basic reservoir of psychic energy, experienced as excitation, was posited. As this excitation level changes, it is experienced as a fearful or pleasant emotion depending on the contextual conditions which help define its meaning for the person. Stress-seeking behavior is carefully planned. The experience that elicits the stress, particularly if hazardous, may be controlled to assure maximum safety. Internal rather than external imperatives propel the stress-seeker. He/she returns again and again to the stress-producing situation. Failure to plan and control a stressful situation is to court self-destruction. Leaving loose ends or disregarding the threshold of danger characterizes the pathological stress-seeker, a masochistic or suicidal person.

The archetypical stress-seeker acts alone, or as part of a team. He/she is individualistic, acting autonomously, bringing individuality into relief. A complementary social type of stress-seeker acts as part of a crowd—shades of LeBon (1895/1960) and Freud (1921/1955). The group stress-seeker seeks to dissolve in crowd enthusiasm and, perhaps, in the aura of a charismatic leader. Individualistic stress-seekers may be narcissistic. The group stress-seeker shares in social narcissism. The social stress-seeker may also become pathologically self-destructive, perhaps with altruistic or even sadomasochistic ideation.

Societies encourage both their individualistic and their social stress-seekers. They are cheered on, applauded or, sometimes, goaded. Prevailing philosophies, myths, and ethical norms legitimate and even exalt them. Such social support suggests that stress-seeking has a social as well as a personality function. Stress-seekers may contribute to the constructive development of a society, offering a model of general optimism and of strength to achieve social goals. Societies also control their stress-seekers, a defense against the pathological association of stress-seeking with socially destructive aggression. Society's problem is to encourage enough stress-seeking to get the work of society done, while reining the tendency so that it does not become destructive—or burn itself out in mystic euphoria.

INITIAL VARIANTS OF THE CONCEPT _____

The several contributors to *Why Man Takes Chances* discussed the concept of stress-seeking from the perspectives of psychology, sociology, law, political science, military history, literature, and education. Working with slightly different images, each author elaborated on our understanding of the phenomenon. Jessie Barnard, sociologist, researcher on social conflict and sex roles, among other topics, envisioned a Dionysian, heroic, ecstatic and, above all, irrational stress-seeker. She explored "eudaemonism." Her term "eustress" caught the enjoyable side of stress-seeking. The eustress-seeker does not appear in those social classes that suffer hunger or threat. Among them, stress-seeking eventuates in no more than outlawry and brawling. The eustress-seeker appears among nobles and knights who seek to escape the routine, the stable, the fixed, to obliterate boredom and ennui. Capitalism and its rationalism were the death knell for the eudaemonistic hero; the new industrial society sought calculating risk-takers. Women's traditional role is in promoting stress-seeking in men. Yet women too may be eustress-seekers.

Charles Houston, a physician and mountain climber, examined a rational planner exposing himself to controlled risks—plotting, pulling, and stretching toward self-fulfillment. Rationality does not signal the "death knell," but becomes a characteristic of stress-seekers. Houston's winsome title, "The Last Blue Mountain," also projects an image of eustress, the bright thrill of danger. Climbers make ascents at night or in the winter or alone or deliberately in bad weather, and yet avoid uncontrollable dangers. The motive is "self-testing," a way of developing personal capacity.

A soldier's stress is a dramatic version of everyday life and, as such, is part of the nature of life. Thus wrote Samuel L. A. Marshall, military historian of many wars. His imagery was of the motives of males who seek stress as the alternative to indolence, relaxation, surcease. In modern society, these restful moments are commanded only at the rarest intervals in a lifetime. Stress-seekers emerge by natural selection. They are needed for survival of the species. Without them, Marshall believes, civilization would be eclipsed by another Dark Age or revert to a matriarchy.

Kenneth Burke, literary critic, saw stress-seeking as a response to a divided self, "homeopathically" calming troubled imaginings.

The stress-seeker creates actual troubles and then throws himself or herself into them. For Burke, as for Houston and Marshall, stress-seeking is rooted in a psychic need. That need may be exercised in sports, through horror stories, monastic disciplines, or excesses of ambition—as in the building of financial and political empires—or, in the right population, through juvenile delinquency.

For David Brion Davis, historian of moral consciousness, a student of American slavery, the stress-seeker lives like a tightrope walker, balanced between the death of conformity on one side and the death of excessive stress on the other. Theodore Roosevelt's strenuous activity takes precedence over sensual indulgence, domesticity, and intellectual discipline. Davis cited the image of the self-made man in American literature around the turn of the century. Stress is not intrinsically pleasurable, but it is virtuous. Strenuousness, however, has its attractive side. It is an escape from the immediate animal desires and impulses, but its reward is the immediacy and richness of experience. When strenuous activity brings wealth, it brings a contradiction, for wealth corrupts. Strenuosity is a form of redemption from that contradiction, a way of breaking out of the confining and demanding pattern set by society's equation of individual salvation with material success. Without this redemption, people would try to escape the pain of that conflict by self-punishing and self-defeating action.

Elton B. McNeil, clinical psychological researcher, compared political leaders with delinquents. Both are impulsive, want power, and suffer from defective egos. Stress-seeking is a visceral thing. It may be detrimental to the welfare of the rest of us. Stress-seeking may have violence as its handmaiden, as when leaders seek stress through war. McNeil recommended a study of the ego structure of leaders in order to identify this tendency.

E. Paul Torrance, known for his work in education and educational psychology, classified stress-seekers according to whether their behavior is a response to inner forces, outer challenges, or threats. Stress-seeking, an individual characteristic, varies with culture or subculture. Eminent high achievers, instead of merely adapting to their environment, deliberately expose themselves to stressful conditions. They commit themselves to goals that require sustained expenditures of intellectual and physical energy. A high-achieving subculture requires self-acting, stress-seeking persons and, to obtain them, offers social support to stress-seekers.

Society is the stress-seeker for Richard Falk. Concentrating on international law, he analyzed stress-seeking in the relations between states in terms of competition for dominance. Without the rule of law as a framework for this competition, it may escalate into destructiveness. External stress may be generated and consciously manipulated to promote law and order within the domestic society.

This variety of perspectives attended the concept as it entered the literature. Stress-seeking could be considered as an individual characteristic promoted and controlled by social and cultural forces. It might also be thought of as a characteristic of societies as collective actors. Rational planning seems associated with most contemporary stress-seeking, though here and there its Dionysian form may emerge. Stress-seeking is nurtured by society because it fulfills some social function. The content of that function depends on the values toward which the effort is directed and on the social positions in which individual stress-seekers are found (Coser, 1964).

THE LITERATURE ELABORATES
THE CONCEPT _____

Why Man Takes Chances was distributed as a technical monograph and adopted by a number of universities, typically as supplementary reading in psychology courses. The concept entered the popular psychological literature through Time-Life's volume on stress (Donovan et al., 1976). It also became part of the research literature—employed about equally by psychologists and sociologists. The interpretations this concept received in published research reports are instructive. Some students cited *Why Man Takes Chances* as they elaborated the concept of stress-seeking or applied it in some special circumstance. Palmer (1973) used the concept of individualistic stress-seeking to explain high suicide rates among the Hopi and depressive disorders among the Hutterites. Individualistic stress-seekers reject the tight social controls which characterize those societies. In groups that have a high degree of social integration, an individualistic stress-seeker "stirs things up" and creates tension. Palmer suggested that chancing life and limb in climbing mountains, shooting rapids, parachuting, and the like, as depicted in *Why Man Takes Chances*, are ways of escaping excessive social integration. The behaviors with which Palmer dealt were considered a pathology of stress-seeking in the original work. Palmer, though, enriched the concept by examining a relation between individual characteristics and an attribute of the social structure. His contextual analysis suggested that stress-seekers may serve different functions in societies with differing degrees of social integration. A society must be well integrated to support and benefit from the activities of individualistic stress-seekers. Yet if it is too rigidly integrated, perhaps too brittle, it may not be able to tolerate the stress-seeker. Highly individualistic types could not be allowed to appear too frequently in such societies.

Other authors have obliterated the revisionist attempt by incorporating the concept in the traditional frame of reference. Kolb and Straus (1974) related stress-seeking to problem-solving ability within the marital relationship. They used the concept to refer to an ability to balance tension in husband and wife interaction. Thus, they drew the concept into equilibrium theory. Knowles et al. (1973) wrote about risk-taking as a personality trait. They referred to the concept of stress-seeking to argue that attempts to approach as well as to avoid risky situations are ways of coping with arousal. This, again, undercut the intent of the original concept by relating it to tension reduction. The distinction is subtle, however. The concept was originally illustrated in connection with the counterphobic attitude—a matter of approaching risky situations in order to avoid some even greater stress. This psychoanalytic theory recognizes the tension-seeking thrust but places it within a larger tension-reduction context (Fenichel, 1939).

Some authors simply erred in their reading of the original. Ball (1972) described people deliberately seeking out and immersing themselves in situations of risk, injury, and danger, a form of stress-seeking. He took stress-seeking to be a biologically based instinct and cited *Why Man Takes Chances* as supporting that position. The societal problem then became, for Ball, one of designing social arrangements to constrain stress-seekers. The original notion allows that instinctual energies may feed the excitation associated with stress-seeking, but that the cognitive interpretation of the excitation is crucial. Thus it is not an unsocialized drive. Ball inferred the instinctual character of stress-seeking from Marshall's metaphorical references to it as a masculine biological drive. Marshall, however, was not writing as a psychologist would about a personality trait. His is a literary description of the drive and of its ubiquity in societies such as our own.

THE STRESS-SEEKING SOCIETY ————————————————

SOCIOLOGICAL QUESTIONS

The social-psychological perspective, investigating the influence of society on individual stress-seekers, has held the attention of researchers. The question of the societal functions of stress-seeking and the question of society as a stress-seeking actor—the sociological aspects of the idea—have not been pursued. An examination of these sociological questions will enable us to return, a bit better equipped, to deal with important social-psychological questions: How does a society, through its communal organizations and its families, socialize its members for stress-seeking? How does it encourage and how does it control stress-seeking? How is the manner of stress-seeking controlled? How are members of the society selected for the stress-seeking role? What norms govern social leaders who place others at risk? How does a group decide to risk itself for the sake of either the group or its members? This paper initiates the sociological elaboration of the concept of stress-seeking.

THE ENCOURAGEMENT OF STRESS-SEEKING

THE PROBLEM OF THE RISKY SHIFT. What are some social mechanisms by which a social group encourages, and controls, stress-seeking? The establishment of group norms about the propriety of, the occasion for, and the proper degree of stress-seeking is, perhaps, one mechanism for controlling the phenomenon. Research on risk-taking, a cognate phenomenon, has been moving toward such issues. One tradition in the study of risk-taking is to conduct experiments with contrived groups engaged in problem solving. Using a paper-and-pencil test, alternative courses of action selected by subjects are classified in terms of the relative risk they entail. Kogan and Wallach's (1964) scale for measuring risk-taking has been one of the most popular. In studying group consensus about risk, they observed a phenomenon which they called the "risky shift." A group decision tended to be more risky than the decisions of the typical members of the group. To account for risky shift, they suggested a mechanism of diffusion of responsibility (Wallach et al., 1964). A group taking responsibility jointly reduces the pressure on individuals. In their early experimental reports, they held that risky shift requires face-to-face group discussion. Later they discovered that the effect appears even when individuals talk over an "intercom" with simple voice communication (Kogan and Wallach, 1967).

Some psychologists had predicted an averaging effect. The deviant members, wanting to be more risky or more cautious than the average, would be pulled toward the mean. The group was, however, pulled in the direction of the deviant and was more likely to be drawn toward the more risky than the more cautious deviant (Siegel and Zajonc, 1967). The diffusion-of-responsibility hypothesis does not, however, explain why the risky shift is nearly always in the direction of greater risk or, in our terms, of stress-seeking.

Another explanation offered for the shift in the risky direction referred to cultural values. Risk has greater value than caution in the culture of the West. This finding has been confirmed in experiments with students in other Western cultures, including France,

England, New Zealand, Israel, and Germany (Zaleska and Kogan, 1971). Why, however, do certain societies sustain a norm encouraging risk? Social encouragement of stress-seeking would be likely if stress-seeking served some societal function.

The fact of social support for stress-seeking is revealed in the social rewards—power or money or prestige—offered by the society to its stress-seekers. King (1974), using small group experiments, showed that riskier occupations must offer entrants greater expected income in order to attract them. Income need not be thought of simply as an incentive, a "purse" for winning. The provision of income may rationalize the taking of the risk, not only for the risk-taker but for the society judging the act.

The extent of risky shift depends on the authority structure of the group, whether majority rule, oligarchy, or taking turns is the rule for obtaining consensus (Zajonc et al., 1970). Less authoritarian structures are associated with greater shift. The size of the group influences the extent of risky shift (Fraser, 1971). The larger the group, the greater the risky shift. Increase in size, Fraser holds, facilitates the group processes of both normative and informational influence.

SOCIAL SELECTION OF STRESS-SEEKERS. The manner of stress-seeking which is encouraged differs according to subculture and according to the status of the individuals in that subculture. The most striking stress-seeking activities, such as sport parachuting, draw a wide range of participants. Nevertheless, different social strata have their own tests. Few seem to cover all social groups. Unskilled laborers rarely engage in sport parachuting or skiing, a fact which cannot be explained only in terms of the cost of those activities. The levels of risk-taking vary within occupations. A "risk propensity" (Miskel, 1974) of the individual is weighed against the opportunity for risk-seeking in an occupation. Educational organizations place a premium on more reserved, less aggressive behavior in their recruits. Business, on the other hand, seeks managers with high risk propensity.

The noblesse oblige of particular status groups associates stress-seeking with position. Public servants, such as policemen or firemen, are obligated to expose themselves to danger. Selection of individuals for these roles depends on their personality characteristics. For example, Roberts and Wicke (1972) classified naval aviators as self-testers. High self-testers preferred games of chance and sought activities such as motorcycle riding, hiking, skiing, mountain climbing, skating, horseback riding, swimming, surfing, water skiing, sailing, gliding; and they also went into naval aviation. A general personality characteristic, a propensity to take risks, underlies both occupation and sport. Work and play do not stand in a compensatory relation, but in a relation of consistency—as alternative ways of seeking stress.

As people move through the life course, stress-seeking expectations change. Physical exertion is expected of young adults, political campaigning of those just getting into their stride, executive command is a burden of midlife, and later years bring increasing relief from these expectations. Precocious stress-seeking is an admired oddity. The maintenance of stress-seeking behaviors beyond the period in life when they are expected is also praised. Continuing too long beyond the appropriate age can lead again to an oddity, more foolhardy than admired. At worst, the elderly stress-seeker may be charged with covetousness for not relinquishing honor to the young.

That the degrees and forms of stress-seeking are a function of prescriptive norms is illustrated in a small group study by Rabow et al. (1966). By manipulating norms, they counteracted the forces that increase risk-taking in groups. Using a reverse logic, they concluded that the risk-taking itself must be normatively controlled. The norms provide social support for the person who exercises caution or takes risks.

The ability to contravene internalized norms is also a form of stress-seeking. Juvenile delinquency, unlike adult crime, tends not to be an instrumental activity aimed at profit. More often it is motivated by stress-seeking achieved by having the "guts" to break rules. Group consensus experiments have also shown that group discussion may facilitate unethical behavior such as stealing. Here, too, the risky shift phenomenon appears (Rettig, 1966). Stress-seeking behavior may thus be contrary to the established values. The larger society represses this form of stress-seeking whereas a subsociety may encourage it.

Stress-seeking is socially supported when it attaches to the realization of certain social goals. As in the above examples of norm violation, stress-seeking is not limited to an instrumental context. Stress-seeking may also be a symbolic act, a demonstrative, dramatic expression of commitment to a value. This expression is also subject to social sanctions. An analysis of the draft resistance movement of the 1960s showed how certain sectors of that movement encouraged their followers to assume such risks as exposure to arrest. Such a demonstration created an attention-attracting platform from which resisters could explain their motives and intentions. The voluntary assumption of risk demonstrated the individual's commitment to opposing the draft and the war (Thorne,1975).

Thus the experimental work has attributed the risky shift to the diffusion of responsibility and to the existence of norms encouraging stress-seeking. A more individualistic explanation for risky shift may also be examined. The tendency to seek stress may derive from the self-interests of members of a group. Military combat provides an extreme example of a contingently cooperative stress-seeking act. Risk-taking in combat units has been accounted for in terms of the primary-group character of the fighting unit. Moskos (1975) argues that it is more a matter of self-interest and ideological considerations than of primary-group ties. Under immediate life-and-death exigencies, individuals act pragmatically to maximize short-run advantages. With continual replacements, the units do not become socially integral. Individual self-interest remains the paramount basis for "solidarity." After individuals leave a combat unit they do not even correspond with their former buddies.

The normative encouragements described above would account for the rate of stress-seeking in various social groups. The norms are instructions to and permissions for members of those groups. The members, depending on their personality traits, may be more or less vigorous in seeking stress.

Rim (1964) studied the relationship of particular social attitudes to risk-taking behavior. He found that individuals who hold extreme views, either conservative or radical, tend to be more cautious in their initial decisions. After group discussions, conservatives become more cautious, while radicals shift in a risky direction. Tough-minded individuals, however, are more risky in their initial decisions than are tender-minded. The latter become riskier after group discussion.

In a fascinating study of bootlegging and selling moonshine in the Georgian Appalachians, Gordon (1970) attributed participation in the occupation of moonshining to a fundamental craving of the mountain personality for action and thrills, the antithesis of routine. Those who elect moonshining may say they do it for the money, but they do not. They spurn factory jobs in favor of this economically less secure activity.

Among social and demographic attributes, Cecil (1972) found that the risk-takers tended to be younger, from rural backgrounds, and to have lower incomes. Personal security is a predisposer to risk. King (1974) found that monetary risks are more likely to be assumed by those whose parents were wealthiest. Kogan and Wallach (1967) found that the subjects who had most test anxiety experienced the most risky shift, and those who were most defensive the least.

The ability to be a stress-seeker depends on intrapsychic controls which handle the extent of arousal. Fenz (1973) describes a gradient of anxiety and a gradient of inhibition of anxiety. Control of anxiety maintains arousal at normal levels and influences the quality of performance. The processes of inhibitional controls are learned. Learning to attend to external rather than internal cues is part of the control. This thesis is similar to Freud's early theory of anxiety. It is probably not the case that the inhibition of anxiety permits stress-seeking performance. Rather, a strengthening of the ego in the face of the affective rush probably inhibits the impact of anxiety on performance.

THE INSUFFICIENTLY STRESS-SEEKING PERSONALITY AS A SOCIAL PROBLEM. Some of the positions illustrated are "achieved statuses," such as that of the business manager or soldier. Society can consider these personality traits in its recruitment. Other illustrated statuses are "ascribed," such as those determined with respect to sex or age. Here, society may sanction performances which fall below or exceed its expectations. A few words about those who fall below expectations will contribute to our understanding of the social function of stress-seeking. The matter of controlling the overzealous will be commented on in the next section.

Society censures the insufficiently stress-seeking, those who do not perform at the level expected for their social position. If society's concern were merely to assign positions and ranks in society on the basis of stress-seeking propensity, the successful individuals and groups would have little concern for the downwardly mobile. The failures might only dramatize the triumph of the successful. However, society has an interest in the level of performance in each position. The upper strata cannot enjoy their rank without commanding the cooperation of the lower strata. Withdrawal from stress-seeking may imply not only imperfect role performance but withdrawal from role performance itself. In Western societies, a withdrawal into the self, taking the role of the "contemplative mystic" rather than participating in society as the "active ascetic," to use Weber's (1920–1921/1963) terms, elicits sanctions. Thus, societies tend to restrict the use of alcohol and psychotropic (among other) drugs when these are used to escape stress and to avoid social demands. Religious uses of alcohol are always a matter of social prescription and proscription (Klausner, 1964). The relation of drugs to withdrawal from performance was a basis for the Vietnam military drug programs (Sanders, 1973).

Social arrangements are established for inducing withdrawn members of society to reassume role responsibilities. Psychotherapy is one such arrangement which, on the surface, individuals select voluntarily. However, the suffering which leads to the decision to enter psychotherapy is due, in part, to the societal response to neurotic forms of adaptation. Religious support is offered to encourage members of society to risk themselves. This is one function of the military chaplains. Economic resources and other rewards may be denied to those who are insufficiently stress-seeking (Chaubey and Sinha, 1974). For instance, civil service advance is contingent on willingness to expose the self to successive examinations. Insufficient aggression is a rationale for censuring a military cadet and a reason for retarding the promotion of an infantryman. The social disapprobation of cowardice is quite general. Societies, in their collective expressions of sentiment, find it important to maintain an image that a high proportion of their members are stress-seekers.

EXCESSIVE STRESS-SEEKING AS A SOCIAL PROBLEM

The encouragement of stress-seeking along with the restraint of stress-seeking are two complementary movements in social control. That the term "social control" has more currency in the case of the excessive stress-seeker should not deceive us into thinking that different types of social mechanisms are involved. Stress-seekers may become socially or self-destructive. This was interpreted in *Why Man Takes Chances* as a pathology of stress-seeking. Societies can restrain recruitment to stress-seeking roles, the degree of stress-seeking permitted, and the values to which it may attach. Leaders, for example, are restricted in the degree of stress to which they may subject a society. Each society has some notion of acceptable loss. The measure of acceptable loss varies with social setting, with the cause and timing of the loss, and with the social positions of those to be risked. Acceptable losses are computed in battle plans, in immunization programs, and in policy decisions to expose a population to environmental risk—as in rail transport of radioactive materials. Such risk decisions arise with respect to any technological innovations subject to mechanical or human failure. The levels of acceptable risk are generally determined in the political process. The threshold of acceptability is not a constant. It may rise with the experience of loss.

The stress-seeker involved here is not ordinarily the potential victim—who may not even be aware of the level of risk. The risk is to society as a collective and to the leader who shoulders the experience. The leader who places others at risk may be an official in a bureaucratic role, such as safety officer on a ship or a jump-master for sport parachutists. The leader may have a particular relation to the subject at risk, as in the case of a parent controlling the behavior of a child. Stress-seeking is thus controlled by personal relations to the stress-seeker. A claim is made by those close to, especially those dependent on, the stress-seeker not to risk himself too much.

A study by Chang (1975) on military policy in the Taiwanese

military air force illustrates the last case. Chang examined the relationship between primary groups and risk-taking. That relationship differs, he found, according to the type of social control exercised in the group. When an organization is based on coercion and punishment, primary-group pressure acts to decrease risk-taking. People do not let their friends expose themselves. However, when the organization is reward-based, the primary groups act to increase risk-taking on the part of individuals. Groups expose themselves to risk by a consensus expressed in the group climate. Africa (1971) offered an interesting example of the way in which violence was conducted in Imperial Rome. Friends helped one another resist an assault or commit one. People assembled in the circuses as an occasion for communicating with the emperor. The roar of the crowd was political in tone, and the risky confrontation, which sometimes led to physical repression, was propelled by a petulant climate of opinion.

Constraint is exerted by legal means, rational control over stress-seeking behavior. The state proposes and enforces safety and licensing regulations, especially for the protection of nonparticipants. The pathological stress-seeker, meeting a complex of needs, some of which are neurotic, may be beyond social reach. A counterphobic defense, for example, as the grounds of stress-seeking, may become exagerrated and distorted. In a study of auto accident victims (Osman, 1968), counterphobic defenses were associated with risk-taking and with accidents. The mechanism suggested by the author is regression to an archaic conception of relationship to the world. This would tend to remove the individual from the influences of the agencies of social control. The counterphobic person is asocial.

This personality mechanism of stress-seekers acts to weaken the constraining influence of society. The social stress-seeker would, in contrast, be highly sensitive to social control. In the Le Bon (1895/1960) example, behavior in which individuality is submerged in crowd situations is almost entirely subject to social control, but the social, itself, is out of control.[3]

Social mechanisms emerge to discourage stress-seekers from engaging in undesirable roles. The criminal code does this. Local ordinances controlling daredevil performances focus on the boundary between normal sport activities and pathological stress-seeking. Private insurance companies that refuse to cover stress-seekers are

---

[3] In the military, with its hierarchical differentiation, risk-taking may be social, of the crowd variety, an altruistic melting of the individual into the group. The individual stress-seeker role is discouraged by the hierarchical and structured relations (Bridges et al., 1968). Hierarchical organization inhibits individual risk-taking, assuming broad control over behavior. Thus, as with all departures from routine, the military has a problem of providing for the heroic action so necessary to it at strategic moments.

imposing economic sanctions. Skydivers maintain their own insurance fund. People considered too dangerous to themselves may even be committed to mental hospitals.

Risk-taking seems to contain an inner dynamic drawing it toward the pathological, associating it with self-destruction and suicide. Jacobson (1973) explored this connection between risk-taking and suicide. Risk-taking, he found, may be part of a suicide plan. In that case, the two are associated. However, the proposition is not symmetrical. Those who are suicidal may resort to risk-taking, but risk-taking does not tend to lead to suicide.

Audiences control stress-seeking. There is a correct level of violence in hockey. The state, as gatekeeper, regulates the flow of individuals into stress-seeking positions. Licensing, for instance, controls who may hunt, when they may hunt, and what they may hunt. Peer judgment, as in parachute clubs, acts as a control. Admission to clubs is based on a peer judgment of the applicant's stability. Psychological screening is used in such fields as military aviation. State regulations control the nature of stress-seeking performances. Rules control boxing equipment, the length of rounds, and when the fight is to be stopped. Elaborate rules govern bullfighting. Socialization to most stress-seeking roles involves exacting safety training. Sport parachutists undergo careful instruction for packing the parachutes, for opening the second parachute when the first hesitates, and for accomplishing the parachute-landing fall without injury.

THE SOCIAL FUNCTIONS OF
STRESS-SEEKING _____

With such extensive societal involvement in stress-seeking, society must have some interest in the phenomenon beyond that of managing stress for the individual. The following thoughts on this question do not derive directly from the above documentation but suggest an extension of research on stress-seeking. One function of stress-seeking for the group is the maintenance of its ranking among groups of its type. This may be termed the assortative ranking of groups, a process leading to a system of group stratification. Societies seek to establish their rank along a variety of dimensions, promoting stress-seeking in various arenas. American stress-seeking is promoted in sports, as a quasi-military form, and in the economy. Hindu stress-seeking may involve contemplative mastery of the responses of the self to its environment—a radical individualism as an end in itself.

Stress-seeking also has an internal societal morale function. Champions acting in the name of the group may subserve this function. The stress-seeking function may become functionally autonomous, as in the development of sports. Structural arrangements for stress-seeking may become ends in themselves. This development may not detract from the morale function of stress-seeking. However, to serve an instrumental function for the society, stress-seeking must be bound to the goals of the society. Society may thus resist its becoming functionally autonomous. That resistance establishes a dialectical relation between the social organization for and of stress-seeking and the larger society. This is a good topic for another paper.

REFERENCES _____

Africa, Thomas W. Urban violence in Imperial Rome. *Journal of Interdisciplinary History*, 2:3–21, 1971.

Arnold, Magda. *Emotion and Personality*, Vol. I. *Psychological Aspects.* New York: Columbia University Press, 1960.

Baker, George W., and Chapman, Dwight W., eds. *Man and Society in Disaster*. New York: Basic Books, 1962.

Ball, Donald W. What the action is: A cross-cultural approach. *Journal for the Theory of Social Behavior*, 2:121–143, 1972.

Barton, Allen H. *Communities in Disaster: A Sociological Analysis of Collective Stress Situations*. Garden City: Doubleday, 1969.

Basowitz, H., Persky, H., Korchin, S. J., and Grinker, R. R. *Anxiety and Stress*. New York: McGraw-Hill, 1955.

Berlyne, D. E. *Conflict, Arousal and Curiosity*. New York: McGraw-Hill, 1965.

Biderman, Albert. *The March to Calumny: The Story of American POW's in the Korean War*. New York: Macmillan, 1963.

Bridges, E. M., Doyle, W. J., and Mahan, D. J. Effects of hierarchical differentiation on group productivity, efficiency, and risk-taking. *Administrative Science Quarterly*, 13:305–319, 1968.

Cecil, Earl A. Factors affecting individual risk taking attitudes. *Journal of Psychology*, 82:223–225, 1972.

Chang, Wen-lung. Primary groups and punishment-based control in an organization: An exploratory study. *Kansas Journal of Sociology*, 2:29–40, 1975.

Chaubey, Nageshwar P., and Sinha, Durganand. Risk-taking and economic development. *International Review of Applied Psychology*, 13:55–61, 1974.

Coser, Lewis. *The Functions of Social Conflict*. New York: Free Press, 1964.

Donovan, Hedley, et al. *Stress*. New York and Canada: Time-Life, 1976.

Fenichel, Otto. The counterphobic attitude. *International Journal of Psycho-Analysis,* 20:263–274, 1939.

Fenz, Walter D. Stress and its mastery: Predicting from laboratory to real life. *Canadian Journal of Behavioral Science,* 5:332–346, 1973.

Fraser, Colin. Group risk-taking and group polarization. *European Journal of Social Psychology,* 1:493–510, 1971.

Freud, Sigmund. Group psychology and analysis of the ego. *Standard Edition,* 18. London: Hogarth, 1955. (Originally published, 1921.)

Gordon, John L., Jr. Up top amongst none: Life in the Georgia Appalachians, part II. *Georgia Review,* 24:183–199, 1970.

Jacobson, Hanna Martina. An investigation of the relationship between risk-taking characteristics, belief in internal-external control, emotional reactivity, and the lethality of the suicide plan in women who have attempted suicide. Unpublished doctoral dissertation, New York University, 1973.

King, Allan G. Occupational choice, risk aversion, and wealth. *Industrial and Labor Relations Review,* 27:586–596, 1974.

Klausner, Samuel Z. Sacred and profane meanings of blood and alcohol. *Journal of Social Psychology.* 64:27–43, 1964.

Klausner, Samuel Z. Fear and enthusiasm in sport parachuting. In James A. Knight and Ralph Slovenko, eds., *Motivations in Play, Games, and Sports.* Springfield, Ill.: Thomas, 1967.

Klausner, Samuel Z., ed. *Why Man Takes Chances: Studies in Stress-Seeking.* Garden City: Doubleday Anchor, 1968.

Klineberg, Otto. *Tensions Affecting International Understanding: A Survey of Research.* New York: Social Science Research Council, 1950.

Knowles, E. S., Cutter, H. S. G., Walsh, D. H., and Casey, N. A. Risk-taking as a personality trait. *Social Behavior and Personality,* 1:123–136, 1973.

Kogan, N., and Wallach, M. Group risk-taking as a function of members' anxiety and defensiveness levels. *Journal of Personality,* 35:50–63, 1967.

Kogan, N., and Wallach, M. *Risk Taking: A Study in Cognition and Personality.* New York: Holt, Rinehart and Winston, 1964.

Kolb, T. M., and Straus, M. A. Marital power and marital happiness in relation to problem-solving ability. *Journal of Marriage and the Family,* 36:756–766, 1974.

Le Bon, Gustave. *The Crowd.* New York: Viking, 1960. (Originally published, 1895.)

Lerner, Daniel. *Sykewar.* New York: George W. Stewart, 1949.

Linebarger, Paul M. A. *Psychological Warfare.* Washington: Infantry Journal Press, 1948.

McClelland, David C. *The Achieving Society.* New York: Appleton-Century-Crofts, 1953.

Miskel, Cecil. Intrinsic, extrinsic, and risk propensity factors in the work attitudes of teachers, educational administrators, and business managers. *Journal of Applied Psychology*, 59:339–343, 1974.

Moskos, Charles C., Jr. The American combat soldier in Vietnam. *Journal of Social Issues*, 31:25–37, 1975.

Osman, Marvin P. A psychoanalytic study of auto accident victims. *Contemporary Psychoanalysis*, 5:62–84, 1968.

Palmer, Stuart. High social integration as a source of deviance. *British Journal of Sociology*, 24:93–100, 1973.

Rabow, J., Fowler, F. J., Bradford, D. L., Hofeller, M. A., and Shibuya, Y. The role of social norms and leadership in risk-taking. *Sociometry*, 29:16–27, 1966.

Rettig, Salomon. Group discussions and predicted ethical risk-taking. *Journal of Personality and Social Psychology*, 3:629–633, 1966.

Rim, Y. Social attitudes and risk-taking. *Human Relations*, 17:259–264, 1964.

Roberts, John M., and Wicke, James O. Flying and expressive self-testing: An exploratory consideration. *Journal of Safety Research*, 4:60–68, 1972.

Sanders, Clinton R. Doper's wonderland: Functional drug use by military personnel in Vietnam. *Journal of Drug Issues*, 3:65–78, 1973.

Selye, Hans. *The Stress of Life*. New York: McGraw-Hill, 1956.

Selye, Hans. *The Stress of Life*, rev. ed. New York: McGraw-Hill, 1976.

Siegel, Sheldon, and Zajonc, Robert B. Group risk-taking in professional decisions. *Sociometry*, 30:339–349, 1967.

Thorne, Barrie. Protest and the problem of credibility: Uses of knowledge and risk-taking in the draft resistance movement of the 1960's. *Social Problems*, 23:111–123, 1975.

Wallach, M. A., Kogan, N., and Bem, D. J. Diffusion of responsibility and level of risk-taking in groups. *Journal of Abnormal and Social Psychology*, 68:263–274, 1964.

Watson, Goodwin. Civilian morale. In Goodwin Watson, ed., *Second Yearbook of the Society for the Psychological Study of Social Issues*. Boston: Houghton Mifflin, 1942.

Weber, Max. *The Sociology of Religion*. Boston: Beacon Press, 1963. (Originally published, 1920–1921.)

Zajonc, R. B., Wolosin, R. J., Wolosin, M. A., and Loh, W. D. Social facilitation and imitation in group risk-taking. *Journal of Experimental Social Psychology*, 6:26–46, 1970.

Zaleska, Maryla, and Kogan, Nathan. Level of risk selected by individuals and groups when deciding for self and for others. *Sociometry*, 34:586–596, 1971.

25

HIGH-RISK SPORTS AS INDIRECT SELF-DESTRUCTIVE BEHAVIOR

JOHN L. DELK

We can get high on our own stress hormones. Stress stimulates our glands to make hormones that can induce a kind of drunkenness. Who would consider it prudent to check his conduct as carefully during stress as he does during the cocktail hour? He should. I venture to say that this sort of drunkenness has caused much more harm to society than the other kind.

Selye (1969, p. 25[1])

In this chapter, high-risk sports will be conceptualized as indirect self-destructive behavior (ISDB) and as addictive behavior. My focus will be on the analysis of sport parachuting (skydiving) as prototypic of high-risk sports. The addictive nature of the stress-production–stress-reduction cycle involved in high-risk sports will be discussed. I will also explore personality characteristics and unconscious motivations of skydivers, positive as well as negative outcomes associated with sport parachuting, and society's attitudes toward participants in high-risk sports. From this discussion will emerge a pattern of personality and behavioral characteristics which contrast with those of normative groups (nonparticipants in high-risk sports). Most interesting, however, are the similarities and

---

[1] In another publication, Selye gives a more technical description of the hormones produced in response to stress. He says there is "increased secretion by the hypophysis (a small gland at the base of the brain) of the so-called adrenocorticotrophic hormone (ACTH), which in turn stimulates the adrenal cortex to produce corticoids. Most important among the latter are the glucocorticoids such as cortisone (which influence glucose and, in general, organic metabolism) as well as the mineralocorticoids such as aldosterone or desoxycorticosterone (which regulate mineral metabolism)" (1977, pp. 17–18).

commonalities shared by skydivers and the indirectly self-destructive groups discussed in other chapters of this volume.

DEATH AND MAYHEM AT ONE'S LEISURE _____

Accident Facts, published by the National Safety Council (1976), contains statistics on accidental deaths and injuries in the United States for the year 1975. According to the figures reported therein, during that year 102,500 accidental deaths and 10,700,000 disabling injuries were caused by accidents. Between the ages of one and thirty-eight years, accidents are the leading cause of death, and for all ages combined, accidents are the fourth leading cause of death. Among workers, three out of four deaths and more than half the injuries suffered in accidents occurred off the job. That is, only 25 percent of accidental deaths and less than 35 percent of disabling injuries occurred at places of employment or during activities related to employment, such as commuting to and from work. It would be inaccurate, of course, to classify all time away from the structured environment of employment as leisure time.[2] But if one liberally adjusts the above statistics to include accidents in working around the home, during the running of errands, etc., the resulting figures still show that the majority of accidental deaths and injuries occur during *leisure* activities. One can see similar relationships between leisure time and homicide, suicide, encounters with legal authorities, and psychiatric crises. In addition, leisure time is often associated with alcohol and drug abuse, overeating, certain criminal and delinquent activities, and other self-destructive behaviors discussed in other chapters of this volume. The conclusion is inescapable—that in the pursuit of pleasure during leisure time, many people find, instead, death, mayhem, and emotional anguish. Psychologists over the years have rendered a valuable service to the public in the area of vocational guidance; however, *avocational guidance* appears to warrant at least as much attention from mental health professionals.

In the pursuit of pleasure,[3] many people, mostly males between the ages of fifteen and forty, engage in high-risk sports during lei-

---

[2] Leisure time tends to be regarded as a residual category that includes all nonwork social-institutional activities, as well as recreational pursuits. The individual may engage in many different behaviors during this time, including activities related to family life, religious life, domestic marketing, and recreation. Self-destruction, either direct or indirect, may occur within any of these social-institutional settings or while the person is apart from them.

[3] The concept of "pleasure" is admittedly too vague to account for the complex motivations of people who engage in high-risk sports. In later sections of this chapter, this concept and other motivations will be examined more closely.

sure time. It is impossible, however, to obtain reliable statistics on the number of participants in high-risk sports or the frequency of fatalities and injuries which result from those activities. A computerized search of the literature yielded few pertinent, reliable data. The available figures are mostly estimates and are difficult to verify because often no official records are kept, particularly of nonfatal injuries. Sport associations and manufacturers of sporting equipment have an interest in overestimating the popularity of (and the number of participants in) high-risk sports while minimizing the risk of fatality or injury. Some life insurance companies attempt to compile statistics on some of these sports but often have to rely on sports association estimates and newspaper accounts of fatalities. The Metropolitan Life Insurance Company (1975a, 1975b, 1976a, 1976b) reports the following statistics for the United States. In 1976 there were almost 400,000 motor vehicle racing drivers, of whom 145,000 were automobile drag racers, 115,000 were motorcycle racers, and 28,000 were stock car racers. During the years 1967 to 1976, inclusive, there were 436 fatalities from motor vehicle racing, including 104 from stock car racing, 77 from motorcycle racing, and 74 from automobile drag racing. In 1975 there were some 700 balloon pilots, and from 1964 through 1974, 16 fatalities resulted from balloon flying. By 1975, 30,000 people had flown delta kites (hang gliders) and 85 fatalities had resulted. According to one estimate, 7 percent of hang glider flights ended in injury or fatality. Glider plane pilots numbered 13,395 in 1973, and from 1960 through 1973, 73 deaths occurred in glider plane flying. Over 40,000 people have engaged in sport parachuting, and each year 10 to 12 fatal jumps are made. Klausner (1967) reported that when skydivers had jumped three or more years, 71 percent had suffered injury.

Skydivers voice objections to the general public's tendency to associate sport parachuting with the risk of death, asserting that skydiving is less dangerous than driving an automobile on the nation's highways. Statistically this may or may not be true, but skydivers as a group do admit that the thought of death as a result of sport parachuting does occur to them. In fact, Epstein (1962) and Epstein and Fenz (1962, 1965, 1971) have reported that skydivers experience considerable approach-avoidance conflict before a jump, reflected in both self-ratings and physiological (galvanic skin response) indices of arousal. Certainly the average automobile driver does not experience such a degree of fear, nor would he participate in sport parachuting. What prompts a person to jump, for sport, from an aircraft more than a mile above the earth, just to free-fall rapidly for some thirty seconds?

ANALYSIS OF SKYDIVING AS
PROTOTYPIC OF HIGH-RISK SPORTS _____

I have conducted a study of sport parachutists and skydiving activity (Delk, 1971, 1973), which may be viewed as prototypic of high-risk sports. The subjects of this study were forty-one adult male skydivers, volunteers from the southeastern United States regional sport-parachuting association. These subjects were administered: (1) a skydiver questionnaire, designed by the investigator to elicit personal and sociological data, as well as information pertinent to skydiving activity (for instance, the questionnaire inquired about age, education, number of jumps, thoughts of death, and at what times these thoughts occurred); (2) the Shipley Vocabulary Test, used to measure verbal intelligence; (3) the Minnesota Multiphasic Personality Inventory (MMPI), used in the analysis of personality characteristics. The analyses of the MMPI will be discussed in a later section.

The mean age of the sample of skydivers was twenty-eight years (range twenty-one to forty-nine years; SD 5.7). They tended to be about average in height and weight at 5 feet, 10½ inches, and 165 pounds. In terms of marital status, twenty-three were married, fourteen single, and four divorced. The average number of years of formal education was 14.3 years (range 10 to 18; SD 2.1). Of the forty-one, forty had received high school diplomas; eleven had graduated from college, of whom three had received advanced degrees. Occupationally, twenty-eight were skilled workers, six semiskilled workers, and seven college students. Analyzed another way, twenty-eight of the forty-one were in occupations requiring primarily mental activity, and thirteen were in occupations that involved mostly physical activity. Finally, thirty had had military experience, the United States Army being by far the most frequently listed branch of service.

In the sample of skydivers studied, the mean number of parachute jumps was no less than 546, of which the average number involving free-fall was 531. The range of free-fall jumps was 25 to 2,880. Only fourteen of the forty-one had attended military parachute school, and these fourteen had accumulated collectively a mere 139 jumps while in service, none of which involved free-fall.

The length of time the group had been sport parachuting averaged 309 weeks (slightly less than 6 years). The average number of jumps per week was 1.95, or virtually 2 jumps per week (range .1 to 12.8). In response to a question concerning the thought of death, thirty skydivers admitted having thoughts of death associated with sport parachuting. When the thought of death occurred, it was most likely to be before a jump (significant at the .01 level) rather than during or after a jump. If the thought of death occurred at either of the latter two times, it was more likely to occur during the jump (significant at the .05 level) than after it.

Skydivers tend to associate with each other. Thirty-four of the subjects said that at least half of their friends were also skydivers. Thirteen said that more than half of their friends were skydivers, and eleven claimed that almost all of their friends were sport parachutists. All forty-one expressed great enthusiasm for the sport, agreeing that "Skydiving is the most enjoyable sport imaginable."

Noncompetitive sport parachuting can be divided into ten distinct stages: (1) *anticipation A* (the takeoff and climb of the aircraft); (2) *anticipation B* (positioning of the aircraft); (3) *immediately before the jump;* (4) *the jump;* (5) *the free-fall;* (6) *the hookup of two or more skydivers during free-fall;* (7) *the chute opening;* (8) *landing safely;* (9) *immediately after landing;* and (10) *getting together with other skydivers after the jump.* The skydivers were asked to rank the various stages of skydiving in terms of the amount of anxiety provoked by each stage, assigning 10 points to the most anxiety-provoking stages, and so forth, down to 1 point for the least anxiety-provoking stages. They were also asked to rank the stages of skydiving in terms of the amount of pleasure they received from each stage, assigning 10 points to the most pleasurable stage and 1 point to the least pleasurable stage. The mean rankings for anxiety and pleasure during the various stages of skydiving are presented in Figure 1.

From Figure 1, it can be seen that anxiety during skydiving is moderately high at the onset (*anticipation A*), increases to the highest peak *immediately before the jump,* falls with *the jump,* increases to a secondary peak at the point of the *chute opening,* and steadily falls thereafter. Pleasure, on the other hand, is low at the outset, rises to a sharp, high peak *during free-fall,* declines below anxiety during the time of the *chute opening,* and from that point on rises again and remains above anxiety. Looking at the pleasure and anxiety curves together, one can see that, in general, the fall of anxiety during skydiving is accompanied by an increase in pleasure. This inverse relationship between anxiety and pleasure is especially pronounced from the point of *immediately before the jump* to the point of the *chute opening,* all of which, including the *free-fall* and *hookup* of parachutists, may require less than thirty seconds to complete. Each of the other stages of skydiving may involve several minutes or even hours. This means that the fall of anxiety with the jump occurs very rapidly and is accompanied by a rather intense state of pleasure. These same curves for skydiving were independently discovered by Klausner (1967).

FIGURE 1 *Pleasure and Anxiety Curves for the Various Stages of Skydiving*

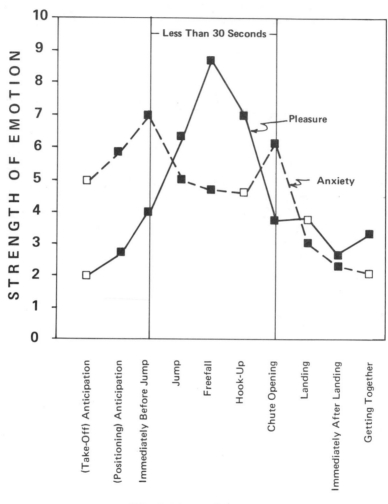

Note that pleasure increases as heightened anxiety (stress) falls. Also note the relationship between anxiety and pleasure at the point of the chute opening. (At each stage of skydiving, the points on the graph *between* curves are statistically significant at or beyond the .01 level. On either curve, ■ denotes statistical significance at or beyond the .01 level between that particular point and the immediately preceding point, and □ denotes nonsignificance.)

Source: Delk (1971).

In the science of psychology there is a well-known postulate, the tension-reduction hypothesis, which states that a decrease in above-normal tension (especially when the decrease is rapid) produces a pleasurable state. For example, heightened hunger tension (produced by deficiencies of nutritive substances in bodily tissues and mediated through innervation of the lateral hypothalamus of the midbrain) is reduced by ingestion of food, which is accompanied by pleasurable feelings. Likewise sexual arousal is a kind of neurovascular tension which can be further heightened through sexual activity and can be suddenly and explosively reduced with orgasm, a very pleasurable form of tension reduction.

The tension-reduction hypothesis does not rule out self-induced tension, which when later reduced leads to a pleasurable state. Self-induced tension for later reduction and accompanying pleasure is quite common in our society. Who has not gone to a "horror" movie purposefully to scare himself, i.e., to heighten anxiety, so that he would find pleasure when the anxiety was ultimately reduced? Or who has not climbed aboard a carnival roller coaster for the same purpose? Tension reduction involved in skydiving is essentially of the same nature, but appears to be on a grander scale.

One stage of skydiving, the *chute opening*, deserves special consideration. As can be seen from Figure 1, anxiety rises above pleasure at this point. This increase in anxiety and fall of pleasure appears to be caused, in part, by a concern about whether the chute will open and deploy correctly. There is also the anticipation of the physical impact of the parachute as it opens and jerks, sometimes quite hard, on the harness of the skydiver, producing considerable discomfort. More important, however, is the fact that the opening chute signals the end of the skydive. Tragic accidents occasionally occur at this point in skydiving because the sport parachutist delays pulling his ripcord for too long, perhaps to prolong the pleasure of the free-fall. Ostensibly, the skydiver, by delaying the pull of his ripcord, is also attempting to avoid, as long as possible, the increase in anxiety that is associated with the chute opening. Presumably, if one could find some way of reversing the anxiety and pleasure curves at the point of chute opening, fewer mishaps in skydiving would occur.

It should be noted that pleasure remains above anxiety at the end of the skydiving, which means that sport parachuting is a rewarding experience to the participants and will probably be repeated once it has been done. Certainly, if the relationship between anxiety and pleasure were reversed at the very end of skydiving (i.e., if anxiety were higher than pleasure), one would expect skydiving to be viewed negatively and not repeated.

As stated earlier, all skydivers in the sample said that "Skydiving is the most enjoyable sport imaginable." It will also be recalled that the average number of free-falls performed by these skydivers was 531, and that they average 2 jumps per week. These facts attest to the addictive nature of the stress-production–stress-reduction cycle. Rapid reduction of self-induced heightened stress is accompanied by intense pleasure (see Figure 1). It appears that skydivers can get hooked on their own stress hormones (Selye, 1969), becoming "adrenalin freaks" and needing a fix every few days. It also seems possible that a tolerance develops, inducing the skydiver to "push the limits" in order to maintain the same level of stress and, hence, the same level of pleasure through stress reduction.

It is probable that each high-risk sport has its own characteristic anxiety and pleasure curves. The number and the elevation of peaks in anxiety and pleasure surely must vary from sport to sport. Some sport participants, such as automobile racers, may or may not experience an intense acceleration of anxiety at one given stage of their sport, culminating in rapid stress reduction (i.e., pleasure). Stress for these sport enthusiasts may be moderately high and sustained over a longer period of time. However, the stress-production–stress-reduction cycle appears to operate in all high-risk sports. The buildup of stress and the concomitant release of stress hormones along with the ultimate reduction in stress would account for the apparent addictive nature of all high-risk sports.

UNCONSCIOUS MOTIVATION AND THE PSYCHODYNAMIC INTERPRETATION OF SKYDIVING _____

From a classical Freudian or psychodynamic view, sport parachuting would be seen as a compromise between conscious, rational forces (the ego) and unconscious, irrational forces (the id and the conscience of the superego). According to this theory, a skydiver is attracted to heights and enjoys jumping because of the ever-present, powerful death wish, and because his guilt feelings *may be* alleviated thereby. He wears a parachute and deploys it at the appropriate time because of the (usually) more powerful forces of the conscious, rational ego. However, the ego may be tricked, caught napping, or rendered drunk on stress hormones, leading to serious injury or death. Since skydiving does not usually result in death, the unconscious, irrational, and destructive forces are not fully satisfied and will soon again wax in strength, causing the activity to be repeated over and over again. This is what Freud (1926/ 1959) called the *repetition compulsion,* a kind of *psychological addiction.*

Many neo-Freudians and contemporary personality theorists

question the existence of the death wish. Modern psychoanalytic theory places greater emphasis on other unconscious motives and mechanisms. Two similar unconscious defense mechanisms, reaction formation and counterphobia, are most cogent in interpreting skydiving activity. Karl Menninger (1963, p. 144) explains the two concepts:

> In what is called in psychoanalytic theory *reaction formation,* by some curious internal somersault of overcompensation, aggressive impulses appear externally in a form exactly opposite to that in which they set out. A man irritated by a troublesome stray cat and bent upon destroying it ends up by feeding, sheltering, and protecting it against indignant neighbors. The *counterphobic mechanism* is similar; instead of being avoided and run away from, danger is eagerly sought and even produced. One sees it in a childish form in the defiance of feared danger, "whistling in the graveyard." This symptom is of particular social importance in adolescents when the temptation to overcome fear by bravado is uncontrolled by mature judgment, with the result that the laws of reality and of the community are apt to be flouted, not so much in contempt of law as in fear of cowardice.

Menninger's concept of the counterphobic defense can be easily related to skydiving and other high-risk sports. Rather than being driven by an unconscious death wish, the skydiver, according to this view, is compelled to jump because of an unconscious fear of cowardice. His fear of being labeled a coward, by others or *himself,* is stronger than the fear of death. Over and over the skydiver must engage in counterphobic defiance of death in order to prove repeatedly to himself that he is no coward. Skydivers would probably resent this interpretation of their sporting activity. Consciously they view themselves as "macho"; people who do not participate in high-risk sports would, in the thinking of skydivers, deserve the label "coward" more than they. Their interpretation of the following lines from Shakespeare would be quite different from that of Menninger:

> Cowards die many times before their deaths;
> The valiant never taste of death but once.
> *Julius Caesar,* Act II, Scene 1, line 32

PERSONALITY CHARACTERISTICS OF SKYDIVERS _____

The Minnesota Multiphasic Personality Inventory (MMPI) was administered to the subjects to determine what personality characteristics differentiated skydivers from nonskydivers.

In accordance with chi-square procedures outlined in Siegel (1956), an analysis of MMPI items was performed comparing the skydivers to the MMPI Adult Male Normative Group (Dahlstrom and Welsh, 1960). To ninety-four items, skydivers' responses were significantly different from those of the normative group, at or beyond the .01 level of statistical significance. Examination of the content of these ninety-four items suggest that they can be grouped under nine headings, each representing a personality trait more characteristic of the skydiver sample than of the normative group. These nine traits, with the number of items contributing to each, are the following:

1. *Freedom from anxiety, phobia, and depression* (thirty-six items): Compared to the normative group, skydivers are relatively free from psychological conflict which manifests itself in neurotic anxiety, phobia, or depression. The absence of neurotic conflict in the skydiver may be due to an underdevelopment of the superego (conscience), which appears likely in view of other personality characteristics listed below, especially those immediately following.

2. *Social deviance, anticonvention* (eleven items): Sport parachutists are less inhibited and more impulsive than the normative group. They tend to be less constrained by social custom and convention, which sometimes leads to their breaking rules and regulations. A significant number of skydivers admitted to having been in trouble with the law, having engaged in petty thievery as children, having been suspended from school because of misconduct, and having used deception to further their own ends. As will be noted next, skydivers are more open and less defensive than others tend to be, so it is likely that they would more readily admit having engaged in deviant behavior.

3. *Openness, lack of defensiveness* (eleven items): Sport parachutists present themselves more forthrightly and openly than do members of the normative group, apparently having less concern about how others view them. Perhaps this reflects the positivism and self-confidence noted below.

4. *Rejection of traditional religious beliefs* (ten items): There was a stronger tendency in these skydivers[4] than in the normative group to disavow belief in a supreme being, a life after death, factualness of the Bible, and general theological tenets.

---

[4] These skydivers were from the southeastern United States and were largely of Christian (Protestant) backgrounds. Their average age and years of education were twenty-eight and 14.3 respectively. The normative group, from pre-World War II Minnesota, averaged thirty-three years in age and 9.7 years in education.

5. *Positivism, self-confidence* (seven items): Self-doubt and caution are not descriptive of sport parachutists. They appear to be bold, optimistic, and sanguine in their approach to life, probably because most of their past efforts have met with success. They seem accustomed to favorable outcomes, especially in regard to short-term goals, and are prepared to experiment and try new things.

6. *Orientation toward action, impulsiveness* (five items): Sport parachutists are not passive spectators of life. Instead, they are action oriented, wanting to be up and doing. Skydivers have a rather strong urge to act, a need to engage in physical activity. Consequently they attempt to resolve problems, when they develop, through physical action, and, as noted above, sometimes act on impulse.

7. *Hedonism, pleasure-seeking, risk-taking* (five items): To a greater degree than the normative group, skydivers appear to be primarily motivated by the pursuit of pleasure and the avoidance of discomfort. Sensual gratification is very important to them, and they readily participate in activities that satisfy their desires. For instance, a significantly large number of skydivers admitted to having indulged in unusual sex practices, doing dangerous things just for the thrill involved, and using alcohol to excess. Skydivers, more than the normative group, seem to seek immediate gratification rather than pursuing long-term goals. Because they are action oriented, they appear to be better equipped for dealing with immediate problems and desires than they are for laying careful, long-range plans that require patience and prudence. They tend to choose the proverbial bird in the hand, the path of least resistance, the easy way out. Consequently their ultimate accomplishments are seldom commensurate with their ability and potential.

8. *Sociableness, extroversion* (five items): Skydivers are gregarious people. They enjoy parties and get-togethers, especially when the fun is loud and ribald. They readily join in the fun and games and make friends easily. Apparently most people like skydivers because they seem natural and at ease, not as inhibited as other people are. However, their relationships with others tend to be somewhat superficial and shallow.

9. *Freedom from health worries* (four items): Although only average in physical size, skydivers appear to be above average in physical fitness and health. They do not experience somatic discomforts as often as the normative group, whether these somatic complaints are of physical or psychological origin.

In addition to the above MMPI item analysis, the mean MMPI

profile and the Welsh A (Anxiety) and R (Repression) scales were computed. The mean T scores[5] for these latter scales were 44 and 51, respectively, indicating neither an anxious nor a repressive personality structure (Dahlstrom and Welsh, 1960). These A and R scores are consistent with the above-listed personality characteristics of skydivers.

The mean MMPI profile for the skydiver was composed of T scores (K corrected) of: L (46), F (52), K (58), Hs (52), D (51), Hy (56), Pd (63), Mf (57), Pa (53), Pt (57), Sc (57), Ma (63), and Si (44). Thus peaks were on the Pd and Ma scales and a low point on the Si scale. Consistent with the above-listed personality traits derived from item analysis, Dahlstrom and Welsh (1960, p. 192) say of the Pd-Ma peak scores:

> Persons with this profile pattern show clear manifestation of psychopathic behavior, the hypomania seemingly energizing or activating the pattern related to scale 4. That is, these people tend to be overactive and impulsive, irresponsible and untrustworthy, shallow and superficial in their relationships. They are characterized by easy morals, readily circumvented consciences, and fluctuating ethical values. To satisfy their own desires and ambitions, they may expend great amounts of energy and effort, but they find it difficult to stick to duties and responsibilities imposed by others. In superficial contacts and social situations they create favorable impressions because of their freedom from inhibiting anxieties and insecurities. They are lively, conversational, fluent, and forthright; they enter wholeheartedly into games, outings, and parties, without being self-conscious or diffident. However, their lack of judgment and control may lead them to excesses of drinking, merrymaking or teasing. They may be prone to continue activities so long that they exceed the proprieties, neglect other obligations, or alienate others.

Other researchers (Gilberstadt and Duker, 1965; Marks and Seeman, 1963) have found essentially the same personality structure in the Pd-Ma peak scorer. However, in regard to the sample of skydivers under study, it should be pointed out that their peak scores on Pd and Ma were both at T score 63, moderately elevated positions. These are average T scores, which, of course, means that there were skydivers in the sample who fell toward the extremes of T score 63. Those who peaked higher than T score 63 on these two

_____

[5] The T score is a standardized score with a mean of 50 and a standard deviation of 10 for the normative group. The basic MMPI profile consists of three validity scales (L, F, and K) and ten clinical scales. The latter are Hypochondriasis (Hs), Depression (D), Hysteria (Hy), Psychopathic Deviate (Pd), Masculinity-femininity (Mf), Paranoia (Pa), Psychasthenia (Pt), Schizophrenia (Sc), Hypomania (Ma), and Social Introversion (Si) scales.

scales would probably be more like the description of Dahlstrom and Welsh quoted above than those who peaked below T score 63.

One would anticipate some minor group differences in personality traits between skydivers and those who engage in other dangerous sporting activities. However, it seems most reasonable to believe that all participants in high-risk sports share some common personality characteristics, particularly those traits associated with the Pd-Ma peaks described above. Since risk-taking and thrill-seeking are associated with the Pd-Ma profile, it appears likely that all high-risk sports enthusiasts share these personality characteristics to some degree. The Pd-Ma profile is, moreover, indicative of a predilection toward alcohol and drug abuse. People who become addicted to their own stress hormones—i.e., people who engage in high-risk sports—are likely to share these personality traits.

POSITIVE GAINS _____

Up to this point I have made much of the danger inherent in high-risk sports and some of the negative personality characteristics of participants. In fairness, the positive gains associated with participation in high-risk sports should also be mentioned. On an intrapersonal or subjective level, the participant experiences many positive emotions, some of which are requisite to mental health. There is a sense of mastery, achievement, and personal worthiness which derives from being expert at a high-risk sport. The participant experiences a degree of exhilaration not often felt by a nonparticipant, and these feelings may act as a defense against boredom and depression. Some high-risk sports entail aesthetic, almost spiritual, experiences. For instance, skydivers often speak of the beauty of the earth as they descend and of the awed reverence they feel for the totality of the universe. They feel that they have temporarily escaped the bonds of earth and have transcended the existence of earth-bound mortals.

Interpersonally, participation in a high-risk sport yields many dividends. In these sporting activities one can attain peer recognition and acceptance. Opportunities are afforded for social interaction with people of similar interests and characteristics. It should be recalled that 83 percent of the skydivers studied said that at least half of their friends were also skydivers. Most important is the feeling among participants in high-risk sports that they belong to an "elite" group. Identification with and belonging to an "in" group is extremely important to most adolescents and young adults.

ATTITUDES OF NONPARTICIPANTS _____

I have asked many nonskydivers why sport parachutists pull their ripcords at the appropriate time. Answers invariably concern the prevention of death. The skydivers to whom I informally put this question answered quite differently. They responded, usually without hesitation, that if they did not deploy their parachutes, *they would not be able to skydive any more.* The skydiver's answer is not concerned (at least overtly) with death but with the pleasure they get from skydiving and with the desire to continue sport parachuting. As noted earlier, however, the thought of death as a result of skydiving does, at least occasionally, perturb them.

Death is the common denominator of all people; it is the ultimate equalizer. Fear of death is an extremely powerful emotion which influences, in one way or another, everyone's cognitive and behavioral patterns. In some people, fear of death manifests itself in conscious anxiety, phobic avoidance behavior, and extremely restrictive life-styles. In others, as discussed above, it leads to denial and to a counterphobic defiance of death. Becoming aware of one's own mortality and ultimate (and possibly impending) demise is one of the most fundamental and important events in the developmental process of each human being. The modes and mechanisms developed in an attempt to cope with this knowledge of mortality have a profound influence on one's life-style and on one's attitudes toward risk-taking. The attitude of most people toward death is ambivalent, balanced between fear and attraction.

Klausner, in this volume, discusses his thesis that each society attempts to develop and maintain its own societal level and distribution of risk-taking. For the overall good of society, both the person with too great an inclination toward risk-taking and the person with too little inclination toward risk-taking are encouraged to adjust their attitudes and behavior in the direction of the "optimal" societal balance. The risk-takers whom society tolerates (and perhaps encourages?) may provide a *psychological* service to society as well. Participants in high-risk sports may fulfill certain psychological needs of other, nonparticipating members of society. From the relative safety of the spectator's position, or via television, the nonparticipant may view a high-risk sport or stunt performance. Many of these performances draw huge audiences. The spectator is thereby provided an opportunity to identify with participants and through them vicariously defy, or even experience, death. Circus acts, whenever possible, it seems, are labeled "death-defying" to maximize their appeal to the public. This suggests that the greater the risk of death to the performer, the more the spectator is attracted to the event. A very daring but successful "defiance" of death may vicariously impart to the observer a feeling of elation and well-being, and even a momentary sense of immortality. After such a performance the observer would probably view the risk-taker with positive, or at least ambivalent, feelings. But how would the observer feel, and how would he view the performer, after an unsuccessful event which resulted in death to the risk-taker?

Since a review of the literature revealed no research concerning the public's attitudes toward participants in high-risk sports, I conducted a small study on the topic. An adjective checklist questionnaire was administered to thirty-two middle-aged subjects of middle to lower-middle socioeconomic class. None of the subjects (sixteen male and sixteen female) had engaged in high-risk sports. They were skilled and semiskilled workers, and their average age was forty-three years. All the subjects had observed, either in person or on television, high-risk sporting events, but none had actually witnessed death during such an event. The questionnaire asked about their interest in viewing high-risk sports; their feelings during the performance; their feelings after a successful performance; their evaluation of a successful performer; what their feelings would be after an unsuccessful performance which resulted in the death of the risk-taker; and how they would evaluate an unsuccessful performer who died as a result of his high-risk sporting activities.

The questionnaire revealed strong ambivalence in the subjects. There were individual differences, as one would expect; group trends, however, were quite pronounced. Moderately high interest in viewing high-risk sports was expressed by the subjects as a group, males indicating a slightly higher interest than females. Younger male subjects would probably show an even greater interest, since young males are noted for their risk-taking behavior. The adjectives "excited," "fearful," "uneasy," "drawn to watch," and "suspenseful" were most often chosen as representing the subjects' feelings during the viewing of a high-risk sport. These adjectives, plus the moderately high interest in viewing high-risk sports, suggest a fairly strong identification with the performer during the sporting activity. Their feelings after the successful performance were most frequently "relieved," "joyful," "refreshed, more alive," and "happy for him," again indicating identification with the successful performer. After completion of a successful performance, the risk-taker was most often described as "brave," "heroic," "smart," and "worthy of admiration." Some negative adjectives, such as "foolish" and "immature," were recorded, however.

Almost uniformly, the subjects indicated that their feelings after viewing an unsuccessful performance in which the risk-taker was killed would be negative or strongly ambivalent. Adjectives such as "disgusted," "disappointed," "sorry for him," and "angry" were endorsed most frequently. Written responses showing contempt and hostility, such as "tough shit" and "glad he got what he deserved," were sometimes recorded. The adjectives chosen to describe a performer who dies during a high-risk sport were most often "foolish," "self-destructive," "a bad example," and "immature." An occasional "brave" was also endorsed.

These data, although admittedly impressionistic, suggest that nonparticipants are ambivalent about participants in high-risk sports. Observers tend to identify with participants when they are successful, viewing them with predominantly positive feelings and experiencing vicarious satisfaction in their counterphobic defiance of death. If the effort is unsuccessful and results in death to the risk-taker, the observer must then make adjustments in his emotional ties to the participant. Positive feelings give way to negative ones as the spectator is compelled to dissociate himself from the "foolish," "immature," and "self-destructive" performer. Feelings of disappointment, disgust, contempt, and even anger are vented at the unsuccessful risk-taker for having vividly reminded the observer of his own mortality and vulnerability.

Behavioral patterns inherent in high-risk sports, like the people who engage in them, are complex and many-faceted. There are multiple determinants of these behavioral patterns, which have been conceptualized in this chapter as indirectly self-destructive and as addictive. It is most interesting and significant that the personality characteristics found among participants in high-risk sports—tendencies toward denial, elation, mania, and sociopathy— are also shared by the indirectly self-destructive groups discussed in other chapters of this volume.

REFERENCES _____

Dahlstrom, W. G., and Welsh, G. S. *An MMPI Handbook*. Minneapolis: University of Minnesota Press, 1960.

Delk, J. L. Why they jump: A psychological study of skydivers. *Parachutist*, 12:12–15, 1971.

Delk, J. L. Some personality characteristics of skydivers. *Life Threatening Behavior*, 3:51–57, 1973.

Epstein, S. The measurement of drive and conflict in humans: Theory and experiment. In M. R. Jones, ed., *Nebraska Symposium on Motivation*. Lincoln: University of Nebraska Press, 1962, pp. 281–321.

Epstein, S., and Fenz,W. D. Theory and experiment on the measurement of approach-avoidance conflict. *Journal of Abnormal Psychology*, 64:97–112, 1962.

Epstein, S., and Fenz, W. D. Steepness of approach and avoidance gradients in humans as a function of experience: Theory and experiment. *Journal of Experimental Psychology*, 70:1–12, 1965.

Epstein, S., and Fenz, W. D. Fear in sport parachutists. In J. Kagan et al., eds., *Psychology: Adapted Readings*. New York: Harcourt Brace Jovanovich, 1971.

Freud, S. Inhibitions, symptoms and anxiety. *Standard Edition*, 20. London: Hogarth, 1959. (Originally published, 1926.)

Gilberstadt, H., and Duker, J. *A Handbook for Clinical and Actuarial MMPI Interpretation*. Philadelphia: Saunders, 1965.

Klausner, S. Z. Sport parachuting. In R. Slovenko and J. A. Knight, eds., *Motivations in Play, Games, and Sports*. Springfield, Ill.: Thomas, 1967, pp. 670–694.

Marks, P. A., and Seeman, W. *The Actuarial Description of Abnormal Personality*. Baltimore: Williams and Wilkins, 1963.

Menninger, K. *The Vital Balance: The Life Process in Mental Health and Illness*. New York: Viking, 1963.

Metropolitan Life Insurance Company. Accident mortality among men at the working ages. *Statistical Bulletin*, 56:3–5, 1975a.

Metropolitan Life Insurance Company. Flying in balloons, blimps, gliders, and kites. *Statistical Bulletin*, 56:5–7, 1975b.

Metropolitan Life Insurance Company. Cycling accident fatalities in the United States. *Statistical Bulletin*, 57:3–4, 1976a.

Metropolitan Life Insurance Company. Fatalities in motor vehicle racing. *Statistical Bulletin*, 57:2–4, 1976b.

National Safety Council. *Accident Facts*, 1976 ed.

Selye, H. Stress: It's a G.A.S. *Psychology Today*, 3(4):25–26, 56, 1969.

Selye, H. Creativity in basic research. In F. F. Flach, ed., *Creative Psychiatry*, Vol. 11. Ardsley, N.Y.: Geigy Pharmaceuticals, 1977, pp. 1–32.

Siegel, S. *Nonparametric Statistics for the Behavioral Sciences*. New York: McGraw-Hill, 1956.

26

THE LURE OF THE DEEP
Scuba Diving as a
High-Risk Sport

THEODORE H. BLAU

By the sea, by the sea, by the beautiful sea
You and me, you and me, oh how dead we could be.

This paraphrase of Joe Howard's hit of the early 1900s might well be true in 1978. Scuba (self-contained underwater breathing apparatus) diving has the highest fatality rate of any sport practiced in the world today. Instructors' training emphasizes the importance of reassuring students that diving is a safe sport (Tzimoulis, 1971). Much ado is made of the fact that although there were almost 200 deaths in 1975 (Schenck and McAniff, 1977) and similar numbers in those years for which statistics are available (see Table 2 below), these figures must be viewed in respect to the estimated 9 to 11 million dives made each year.

Accidents and fatalities in both skin and scuba diving have many causes (Kindwall et al., 1971; Bachrach, 1970; Bodner, 1967; Cross, 1967; Irwin, 1968; Max, 1968; Brown, 1976; Dueker, 1977; Smith, 1970; Graver, 1976; U. S. Department of Commerce, 1975). Table 1 presents some of the dangers encountered by skin divers and scuba divers. Many things can go wrong for humans in the underwater world. For someone not familiar with diver training and conditions of diving, this list may be awesome. The same list, to some extent, applies in the world above water, but we take these things for granted, since we are all trained in avoiding most of the hazards. This, of course, is not true for our highways, where we lose about 60,000 people per year. When a scuba diver has been properly trained, the chances of accidents and fatalities are greatly reduced. Basic scuba training requires between twenty-eight and forty-two hours of classroom and water work designed to instill skills and safety consciousness. Additional open-water training and supervision are necessary to ensure competence.

TABLE 1 *Some Circumstances, Conditions, and Situations Encountered by Skin and Scuba Divers Which Can Lead to Injury or Death*

Condition	Cause	Treatment and outcome	Prevention
Carbon dioxide poisoning	Breath-holding, using rebreathing apparatus.	Fresh air. Rest. Treat for water aspiration. Can be fatal.	Don't use rebreather.
Carbon monoxide poisoning	Carbon monoxide in air tank.	Fresh air, oxygen. Treat for secondary conditions. Can be fatal.	Fill air tanks at reliable air stations.
Oxygen toxicity	Breathing pure oxygen compressed to more than two atmospheres or air at ten atmospheres.	Treat for shock and neurologic sequellae. Can be fatal.	Do not use oxygen breathers. Do not dive below 296 feet.
Shallow water blackout	Breath-holding while free diving.	Resuscitate. Can be fatal.	Be very cautious with hyperventilation before free diving.
Lipoid pneumonia	Air tanks filled from compressor using oily lubricant.	Appropriate inpatient and outpatient medical management. Can be fatal.	Fill tanks at reliable air stations.
Bacterial pneumonia	Aspiration of sea water (usually near shore).	Appropriate inpatient and outpatient medical management. Can be fatal.	Dive only in water conditions which can be safely managed.
Ear and sinus squeezes	Recent nasopharyngeal condition prevents inner pressure equaling ambient pressure.	Clear. Use decongestants. Abort dive.	Do not dive when congested; predive anticongestants.
Nitrogen narcosis	Diving below 100 feet.	Return to depths above 100 feet or abort dive. Can be fatal.	Keep close contact with buddy. Do not dive below 100 feet.
Cardiac arrest	Basic physical condition inadequate for stress.	Abort dive; immediate medical management.	Annual physical for all divers over thirty-five. Avoid stressful dives.
Seasickness	Predisposition to nausea in a moving or rocking boat.	Abort dive. Vomit. Rest. Cool fresh air. Return to land. Can be fatal in water.	Use of appropriate antimotion-sickness medication.

TABLE 1 *(Continued)*

Condition	Cause	Treatment and outcome	Prevention
Toxic responses	Touching various corals, sea plants, and dangerous sea life.	Antihistamines, papain, medical management of severe reactions. Can be fatal.	Proper training and practice.
Predatory marine creatures	Bites by shark, barracuda, moray eels.	Immediate medical management. Can be fatal.	Proper training and practice. Avoid hunting and antagonizing such creatures.
Lung expansion injuries (barotrauma)	Breath-holding while ascending or sudden breath exhalation while ascending.	Recompression and medical management of injuries. Can be fatal.	Proper training and practice.
Decompression illness (bends)	Nitrogen coming out of solution in blood when diver overstays time limits or does not decompress properly.	Recompression and medical management of neurological sequellae. Can be fatal.	Proper training and practice.
Vertigo	Ruptured ear drum. Diver has not cleared properly.	Abort dive. Early medical management. Can be fatal.	Proper training and practice.
Hypothermia	Diver stays too long in cold water.	Treat for exposure. Can be fatal.	Proper training. Avoid fatigue. Proper suiting. Avoid cold-water diving.
Drowning	Fatigue, panic injury, weather conditions, current and wave action; loss of air supply.	Resuscitation and immediate medical management.	Proper training and practice. Good physical condition. Good judgment.

Diving is unusual in that there are relatively few minor accidents in comparison to reported fatalities (Schenck and McAniff, 1977). This might be compared with the recently popular skateboarding, which in 1976 caused 27,000 hospitalizations and 9 fatalities (Zarudiski, 1977b; National Safety Council, 1977). Surfboarding, a fairly "dangerous" individual sport, accounts for approximately a dozen deaths a year in California alone (California Bureau of Vital Statistics, 1977). There are considerable problems in data collection for all sport injuries and deaths, since the sources of reported accidents are not always indicated (National Safety Council, 1972).

DIVING ACCIDENTS AND FATALITIES _____

The number of skin divers and scuba divers is unknown. It has been estimated that there are almost 2 million trained and untrained scuba divers in the United States. There are at least five national and international organizations which train instructors and sanction the instruction of divers. It is estimated that between 9 and 12 million dives took place in 1977. Obviously diving is a popular sport.

The lure of the deep is compelling. Water covers five-sevenths of the earth's surface and can be considered "the last frontier." Exploration and adventure are a part of even the most elementary kind of diving. It is exciting and fulfilling. Even those who say they would not go underwater agree that they are interested and curious. The underwater world and its reality easily rivals the more lurid fantasies and temptations of television. Would Kojak really stand a chance against Jacques Cousteau?

Only recently have diving fatality statistics been available. For this, credit must be given to H. V. Schenck, Jr., and J. J. McAniff of the University of Rhode Island for their unstinting and invaluable pioneering work in identifying and classifying diving fatalities. They and their staff have provided the most significant and challenging research in the field of scuba safety (Schenck and McAniff, 1971, 1972, 1975, 1976, 1977; Schenck et al., 1972). In spite of the great difficulty in collecting reliable accounts of diving accidents and fatalities, a fairly accurate picture has emerged over the years. The following tables are largely based on the data provided by these various studies.

Table 2 presents fatalities recorded between 1970 and 1975, by

TABLE 2   Skin Diving and Scuba Fatalities, 1970–1975

	1970		1971		1972		1973		1974		1975	
Diver/Status	M^1	F^2	M	F	M	F	M	F	M	F	M	F
Skin diving	26	3	17	0	15	1	23	1	26	1	14	1
Scuba (professional and semipro)	3	0	1	0	1	0	4	0	4	0	8	0
Scuba (sport)	101	8	106	7	107	12	113	6	126	15	124	8
Total	141		131		136		147		172		155	

[1]M = male
[2]F = female

TABLE 3   Location of Skin and Scuba Fatalities

	1970	1971	1972	1973	1974	1975
Salt water	66	66	72	76	79	83
Cave	11	8	19	18	25	18
Fresh water; other	32	39	26	25	37	31

Note: Most accidents occur in water under 100 feet deep, and many occur near the surface.

sex, training status, and scuba versus skin diving (masks, flippers, and snorkel only). Table 2 shows that more males than females die in the underwater world. This probably reflects the ratio of male to female divers. Since there are a fair number of professional divers, the table suggests that experience counts in preventing fatalities. All fatality data must be viewed in the light of the annual fatality rate for all water-related deaths, which for 1976 was 7,200 in the United States and 636 in California' (California Bureau of Vital Statistics, 1977).

Table 3 presents some information about the location of skin- and scuba-diving fatalities. Cave-diving deaths should be assessed in the light of the relatively small number of divers who pursue this specialized form of diving. Cave diving requires training, supervision, equipment, and experience far beyond open-water scuba diving. The majority of accidents occurred in water under one hundred feet deep, and many occurred near the surface.

Table 4 presents the point of origin of the dive. A fatality is most likely to occur when the diver enters from a shore, beach, or pier. This is supported by the data suggesting that a rough environment and cold water are primary sources of diving accidents and fatalities.

Although much diving takes place from charter boats, the fatality rate is much lower than when the dive originates from a private recreational vessel. This may mean that charter boats generally carry more experienced divers, more knowledgeable about safety

TABLE 4   Point of Origin of the Dive (Platform: Skin and Scuba Combined)

	1973	1974	1975
Shore, beach, pier	94	112	95
Shore with surface float	3	5	1
Charter boat	13	14	10
Private recreational vessel	29	32	28
Other	4	5	12

TABLE 5   *Experience and Training of Divers in Fatal Occurrences*

	Fatalities (%)					
Experience	1970	1971	1972	1973	1974	1975
First dive in scuba	12	14	6	3	11	9
First open-water dive	9	12	6	5	2	4
Early open-water dive	15	19	21	31	31	19
Some experience	29	28	29	32	32	35
Considerable experience	21	20	32	23	22	13
Very experienced	14	7	6	6	2	10

and rescue techniques. Charter-boat dive-masters may require proof of certification. Most professional charter boats require adherence to safety standards.

Table 5 presents some information about the experience and training of divers who were involved in fatal accidents between 1970 and 1975. The data suggest that many divers with a great deal of experience become fatalities. There is a heartening downward trend in the number of fatalities during the first open-water dive, suggesting that our training is somewhat better than it was at one time. The rest of the data are certainly a matter for concern.

One of the myths about diving is that having a buddy on a dive makes you relatively safe. The data presented in Table 6 raise some real questions about this belief, as a significant number of fatalities occurred when one or more diving buddies were present.

Table 7 presents the available autopsy findings for diving deaths between 1970 and 1975. Drowning was obviously the primary cause of death. Many conditions may lead to drowning, as will be dis-

TABLE 6   *Partner Status during Fatal Accident*

	Number of accidents					
Number with victim	1970	1971	1972	1973	1974	1975
None	13	12	11	10	21	13
One	47	54	41	60	60	51
Two or more	40	47	57	41	51	58
Unknown	9	0	10	8	8	10

TABLE 7   *Autopsy Findings for Fatalities, 1970–1975*

Primary cause	1970	1971	1972	1973	1974	1975
Asphyxiation or drowning	25	26	22	32	29	39
Lung barotrauma	9	12	9	8	12	12
Injury (usually head)	5	2	2	0	2	0
Heart attack	5	1	3	6	5	4
Decompression illness	0	0	1	1	1	0
Other	3	1	3	1	2	2

cussed later. It is of interest that one in five deaths in the over-thirty-five age group was attributed to cardiac arrest. This finding suggests that more thorough physical evaluation of divers over thirty-five should be required.

During diver training, every diver is instructed in the use of a personal flotation device. This device can be inflated manually, by blowing through a tube, or by pulling a cord and releasing a carbon dioxide cartridge. Supposedly, it will save the diver from drowning if all else fails. Table 8 presents some data on flotation devices in respect to fatal diving accidents. In a number of fatalities the flotation device was not used. A significant number of the devices were found to be faulty or without an inflation cartridge. One can only speculate whether lives would have been saved if the divers involved in these fatalities had been trained to blow their flotation devices automatically at the first sign of difficulty.

In an effort to pinpoint the conditions which resulted in fatalities during scuba diving, a careful analysis was made of all data available and applicable for the year of 1975. Table 9 presents this information. Medical injuries and environmental causes shared the top ranking as causes of death in diving accidents in 1975. A significant

TABLE 8   *Personal Flotation Devices Status of Fatalities*

	Number of cases					
Situation	1970	1971	1972	1973	1974	1975
Flotation device not used	16	14	18	23	33	26
Flotation device inflated during accident	6	9	15	10	14	14
Flotation device faulty or malfunctioned or no cartridge	7	7	7	2	5	6

TABLE 9   *Causes of Fatalities, 1975*

A.	Medical and injury	
	1. Air embolism	12
	2. Heart attack	4
	3. Exhaustion, panic, or possible embolism	28
	4. Other	8
		52
B.	Environmental	
	1. Lost or out of air in cave	15
	2. Out of air at depth	11
	3. Dangerous waves, surf	6
	4. Carried off in strong current	2
	5. Tangled in kelp	4
	6. Lost under ice	4
	7. Other	4
		46
C.	Equipment	
	1. Unsafe air	1
	2. Overweighted	1
	3. Excess water in tank	1
	4. Oxygen seizure	1
		4
D.	Undetermined	30

number of deaths were of undetermined cause. The data are enough to suggest the desirability of increased training and precautionary activity to prevent fatalities.

PSYCHOLOGICAL FACTORS AND DIVING ACCIDENTS

MYTHS

The sea has always been mysterious. Diving, although an exciting idea, has always been fraught with speculations about danger. Concern about being bitten or eaten by a shark is perhaps the predominant fear of novices. Recent fictional accounts and motion pictures portray shark attacks as commonplace and frequent. In the 1940s and 1950s, motion pictures about the South Seas usually featured the dangers of being trapped by a giant clam. The myth of the danger of the barracuda is still current among many divers.

Reported shark attacks more often involve people bathing in the surf than divers. Fatalities from shark attacks are extremely rare. In almost every case, the diver who was killed by a shark was fishing in the shark's feeding ground or diving in waters known to be shark infested and therefore dangerous. No recorded account of a barracuda attack has been substantiated. The giant clam myth is exactly that.

In spite of the realities represented by data collected over the past ten years, a great deal of training and attention is devoted to the nature of sharks (or in point of fact to the little we know about the nature of sharks). Thousands of special shark weapons are manufactured and purchased each year. Many diver-training manuals still describe the barracuda as a dangerous marine predator.

The moray eel, too, is considered an extremely vicious and dangerous creature of the deep. This belief, like so many others, is more fancy than fact. Certainly the moray eel is a tenacious and voracious creature, but it stays in its own hole and does not bother anyone who does not bother it. Some professional divers take pride in feeding a moray eel that nests in a crevice of an often-visited reef.

It is possible that the perpetuated myths about the danger of predatory marine animals make diving a more attractive sport. Those of us who dive regularly find a certain degree of reinforcement in the wonder and awe of the nonpractitioner who considers us extremely brave and intrepid to be risking ourselves in the underwater world. Encouraging the myths might well represent a desire of divers to be considered "special" and daring.

WHY DO PEOPLE DIVE?

Throughout history, much literature and art have been devoted to the lure, excitement, danger, and adventure represented by the sea. Many divers feel that the underwater world is the last frontier and thus represents the last chance to be an individual. Divers involved in treasure hunting and salvage often express such beliefs. Diving can be a healthy exercise. One should be in good physical condition to dive safely. It is a sociable sport, since one never dives alone. It is certainly a heterosexual sport, and more women are participating than ever before. It has been suggested that scuba diving meets individual needs for identity, stimulation, and security (Worrick, 1968).

PANIC—THE ULTIMATE DANGER

Panic and all it implies may well be the primary cause of diving accidents and fatalities (Bachrach, 1970). Training seems to go out the window when panic occurs, and even the most experienced divers are subject to serious errors of judgment and fatal consequences (Egstrom and Bachrach, 1971). Panic is essentially a condition of fear that results in loss of control (Egstrom and Bachrach, 1971; Stelnicki, 1972). Various attempts have been made to help divers during training to learn to face and avoid panic situations (Fead, 1974; Blaue, 1976).

If apprehension leads to panic, the diver loses control. The ability to cope is severely affected, and even the most trained diver can become a danger to himself. When panic occurs, reactions usually include increased physical activity and greater fatigue, which in turn leads to more panic. Although good physical capability and open-water experience are necessary preventives, panic can come to divers at all levels of experience (Bachrach and Egstrom, in press). The frequency with which panic occurs in diving depends almost entirely on the risks taken by the diver.

RISK-TAKING

Risk-taking occurs when a diver does not follow the rules. Training, under sanctioning national and international organizations, provides the diver with a broad range of carefully graduated experiences, designed to build a capability for coping with whatever conditions he or she may meet in the real underwater world. Supervised experience beyond the initial training period is necessary to ensure that the diver is indeed comfortable in a variety of circumstances. But in spite of careful training, divers at all levels of experience tend to make some decisions which are contrary to their training and good practice. Diving when tired, diving too soon after an illness, diving in strange waters, diving with an inexperienced buddy, and so forth, tend to occur at one time or another in the experience of all divers. It is rare indeed to find a diver (or for that matter a diving instructor) who can honestly say, "I always follow the rules, and never take a risk." A great deal of preparation is involved in getting ready for a dive. Bad weather or surf conditions, slight illness, fatigue early in the dive, all demand that further diving be canceled. This is a difficult thing to do if one has made many preparations and has high expectations of the dive. By and large, it would be difficult to attack the view that all scuba divers are to some extent risk-takers. Some, however, seem to take more risks than others.

PERSONAL EXPERIENCES

Divers seem willing to describe some of the experiences that demonstrate their own risk-taking behavior. A diver recently reported a dangerous situation involving a shark (Murphy, 1975). This diver freely admitted having made a number of serious mistakes in judgment, including entering the water before his buddy was ready, waiting for the buddy at depth for fifteen minutes, proceeding with the dive without the buddy, coming close to running out of air, and finally facing a fairly large shark with no preparation and much panic. Fortunately, the diver survived.

A diver under the ice for the first time reported details of a near fatality (Max, 1968). The diver was poorly equipped, had little experience, lost his buddy early in the dive, and committed a variety of errors of judgment. The diver survived and wrote the story. Panic was kept at a minimum, but it was really through sheer accident that he survived. The account includes a variety of references to the errors made and the risks involved.

Reports of shark attacks usually reveal that the victim was diving in an area that was considered the shark's feeding ground, or that the victim was spearing fish (Zarudiski, 1977a). Professionals have reported their accidents and risk-taking behavior (Johnson, 1976; Beloso, 1972), and fatal accidents have been described (Desautel, 1971) in vivid detail, showing that the victims did not follow the rules and that the most experienced divers made fundamental errors of judgment. The "rules of the road" for safe diving are well known and constantly being reaffirmed (Brown, 1976; Fead, 1975; Bangasser, 1976; Tzimoulis, 1971).

There are risks in the underwater world. Some of them are quite unexpected and unusual for professional divers, such as a giant swordfish's attack on a small research submarine which resulted in an electrical failure (Zarudiski, 1967). Reports of accidents involving amateur or semiprofessional divers suggest that the risks taken were generally unnecessary, and some fundamental training rules were almost always ignored.

The statistics suggest that very experienced divers sometimes get themselves into dangerous and potentially self-destructive situations. In an effort to determine whether there is a tendency to ignore well-known danger signs and to be self-destructive, I interviewed several diving instructors. They were asked the question, "Do you always follow the rules? If you ignore basic safety precautions, do you ever get into trouble?" The first instructor said the following:

> I have been free diving for twenty years, and scuba diving for about fifteen. I have been an instructor for twelve years. I frequently snorkel alone and feel comfortable in areas that I know well. It is certainly nothing that I would allow my students to do. Sometimes I make a third, fourth, or fifth dive that I shouldn't make. It is usually okay, but five years ago I got clipped. I was taking a group of divers through their first open-water dive, two at a time. The dive involved descending to approximately sixty-five feet in a very open cave in fresh water. I've always prided myself on giving students individual

attention, and I carefully calculated my time so that I could take five pairs of students through and still be within the No-Decompression dive limits of the Navy Tables. One pair of students ran into trouble clearing their ears at about fifteen feet down. They returned to the surface, to take some decongestant. When it came time to take them down again, I realized that I was coming close to my time limits, but I decided to "risk it." I took them through with no trouble. I was perhaps one minute over my No-Decompression time limit.

About fifteen minutes after the dive ended my hands began to tingle and feel numb. I realized I was showing some initial symptoms of decompression illness [the bends]. I began to make preparation to have myself driven by the State Police to the nearest recompression chamber. The symptoms began to subside and I realized that the "skin bends" were very minor. I have watched my decompression time limits very carefully since then, but I realize I am subject to errors in judgment.

There is probably nothing that every experienced diver knows so well as the Navy Dive Tables. They were constructed so that less than 3 percent of the Navy's divers, in excellent physical condition, would develop a case of decompression illness. Sports divers ordinarily add an additional safety margin to protect themselves. This very well trained and experienced diver cannot explain why he stretched the limits other than that he wanted to finish up his class. He admits that for several weeks he had been quite hurried and was somewhat depressed before the dive.

Another diving instructor reported:

About eight years ago I was diving in relatively shallow water to salvage on one of the old Spanish wrecks. I had a diving partner who was well trained. The water was extremely murky and small fish were running. We came up and boarded the salvage boat, but then developed some problems underneath. My partner and I descended again, to fix the drive shaft. We were enclosed in a kind of a cage around the equipment under the boat. We saw the shapes of sharks circling us. We fixed what we had to fix and waited for about thirty minutes. We were getting close to the end of our air supply. We finally decided we'd best go up and quickly went to the surface. Our dive mates were very concerned about us because a number of large sharks had been circling. We probably shouldn't have entered, knowing that it was dangerous territory. We could have fixed the trouble later, since it had nothing to do with any work that had to be done at the moment. I can't really explain why we took this risk. I guess we do this several times a year.

We have lost five persons during the last six years on this particular salvage operation. Two of them were very experienced divers.

On further inquiry the same experienced salvage diver told the following story:

My partner and I made a long automobile trip to dive on an old cannon in order to assess the territory for a possible salvage operation. When we arrived we found the surf quite turbulent. We had traveled four hours to make this dive and so we decided to go in. We made a proper beach entry, timing the waves as best we could. We were very badly tumbled back on the beach, losing some of our equipment. Both of us suffered bruises and contusions. At this point we decided not to try the dive again. There is no question it was an extremely dangerous entry. We both knew that we had little experience with surf entries. Most of our diving had been done from a fairly stable platform. We laughed about the experience, but we also realized that we had come close to being in serious trouble.

A very experienced instructor revealed the following:

I consider myself extremely safety conscious. My students must make three supervised open-water dives, including a beach entry. I know surf and I know how to read it. I have a well-developed sense of "safe water" and "dangerous water."

I recently made a trip to do some snorkeling on a very good shallow reef. My partner and I had planned to spend three days at this particular point. Extremely bad weather prevailed for two days, and it was impossible to dive. The day before we were to leave, the weather broke, and although the surf was heavy and the drift very strong we decided to snorkel out to the reef. My partner made it across the reef even though he was much less experienced than I. For reasons I cannot explain, I was caught by an unexpected swell, tumbled into the reef, was badly bruised, and managed to lose some equipment. I aspirated some of the seawater and within two days was suffering a fairly severe bacterial pneumonia with high fever. It took me ten weeks to recover from this.

I can't explain this accident. I wouldn't expect one of my students to make that mistake. I know the waters thoroughly, and I know that surf entries can be extremely dangerous with the kind of reef structure in that particular place.

I am a safety-conscious instructor, but I realize that on various occasions I will take risks that would be unacceptable to me if done by my students or my assistants. I can't really tell you what my feelings were like at the time. I was angry that we had spent this time waiting for the weather to clear and really didn't want to go home without diving on the reef. This is not a sensible attitude at all. I am afraid I make this kind of decision two or three times a year. This, in spite of the fact that I have had friends die after making a relatively senseless decision contrary to their own knowledge of the water conditions.

An extremely talented, sensible, and successful woman instructor told the following story:

I have been taking classes through this particular open-water dive for years. I know the territory thoroughly. At the end of the day's diving I suddenly suffered numbness in one leg. This can be a symptom of decompression illness, and I arranged to be transported to a recompression chamber. Once I was put into the recompression chamber, I came closest to dying. There was a malfunction in the oxygen system and I nearly asphyxiated.

We have never been completely sure whether I had decompression illness or not. I may have had a pressure on a spinal nerve as a result of handling heavy tanks. I have handled heavy tanks all of my diving career. I'm not really sure what happened.

This diving instructor could not relate details of recent events that would indicate any kind of self-destructive tendencies.

All of the diving instructors interviewed agreed that they take unnecessary risks. Some of them associated such risks with being fatigued, having had a bad situation at home or work recently, or simply "not giving a damn." All agreed that such behavior is foolish and self-destructive. The range of seriousness represented by the risks taken ranged from very minor to exceedingly serious.

There are no data or body of opinion to explain risk-taking behavior in the underwater world. Some suggested dynamic concepts included:

1. The psychoanalytic concept that the water represents the mother, and suicidal activity in the water therefore represents repressed rage toward the mother coupled with a desire to return to the womb.
2. Underwater deaths have a tremendous impact on other divers and on society in general. Underwater fatalities are carefully and rather vividly reported in the news. It may be that suicidal activity underwater expresses the wish to "hang one's skeleton in someone else's closet" (Shneidman and Farberow, 1957).

3. There is much "macho" about diving. Many divers are continually "testing" their own strength, their own worth, and their own bravery. Self-destructive behavior underwater may be a result of this kind of dynamic testing of self together with the will to fail.

At the present time, all of these hypotheses tend to be rather thin soup.

DECREASING FATALITIES IN THE UNDERWATER WORLD_____

Diver training has been developing for almost one hundred years. A good many safety skills are built into diver training. Diving could be more dangerous than it is. But the fatality data suggest room for improvement. Based on the review of current statistics, it seems worthwhile to consider adding or reemphasizing some safety principles and developing new equipment. The following are recommended:

1. Specialists in the field should develop stress-tolerance exercises to indicate limits of divers, so that judicious choices of dive areas and diving limits can be made.
2. Training to cope with panic should be introduced into the basic scuba course.
3. Understanding and gauging wave action and tide should be introduced into scuba training at an early point.
4. A regulator should be developed which sounds a five-second interval signal when breaths are not being taken.
5. A safety-check certification system for equipment rental shops and air stations should be developed, and recertification should be required every year.
6. Specific training in how to identify and avoid turbulent and dangerous waters.
7. Teach students to dive new areas only with a very experienced diver.
8. Teach students to take a backup flotation or rescue device with them on all beach or pier entries.
9. Post detailed descriptions of unique and dangerous aspects of tide and current at popular or dangerous diving areas.
10. Increase the amount of lifesaving and rescue training required for certified divers. Require renewal.
11. Increase the training emphasis on steady regulator breathing during emergencies and during water turbulence.
12. Improve indicators of operational status of bouyancy vests.
13. Eliminate 12- and 16-gram cartridge safety vests.

14. Encourage more training in thermal exchange data and the proper suiting for cold water.
15. Develop longer and more graduated training periods.
16. Increase the emphasis not only on "never dive alone," but on always diving with an experienced buddy. The buddy should be trained in rescue methods. Visual contact should be maintained at all times.
17. Require annual cardiac surveys for divers over thirty-five years of age in order to renew certification.
18. Emphasize the rule of no diving within ten days of any kind of airway infection.

To some extent all of the above appear in training. The question is one of emphasis.

FURTHER RESEARCH NEEDS _____

It is obvious that we know very little about personality correlates of risk-taking behavior in diving. Some efforts in this direction have been started (Bachrach, 1970; Bachrach and Egstrom, in press). More focused and supported research is necessary. We know practically nothing about nonfatal occurrences. Whether there is a "funneling" of nonfatal occurrences toward fatalities is a question that ought to be answered. This might well help us to identify "divers at risk." Research methods in psychological autopsy are very applicable to diving fatalities. This would be an extremely important area for research (Shneidman and Farberow, 1957). There is no question that the world under water is magnificent and offers great opportunity for pleasure, sport, and personal fulfillment. It would be unfortunate if conscious and unconscious risk-taking continues to be a part of the world below.

REFERENCES _____

Bachrach, A. J. Diving behavior in human performance and scuba diving. *Proceedings of the Symposium on Underwater Physiology.* La Jolla, Calif.: Scripps Institution of Oceanography, 1970, pp. 119–138.

Bachrach, A. J., and Egstrom, G. H. Apprehension and panic. In *British SubAqua Diving Manual* (in press).

Bangasser, R. P. SDM diving doctor director. *Skin Diver,* 25(8):46–47, 1976.

Beloso, R. H. First person account: I survived a deep-sea diving accident. *The Undersea Journal,* 5(5):8–10, 1972.

Blaue, W. Panic underwater. *The Undersea Journal,* 9(4):11–12, 1976.

Bodner, J. Thermal protection: Physiological aspects of cold water submergence. *Skin Diver,* 16(11):48–50, 68, 1967.

Brown, C. V. Medifacts: Arterial embolism. *Skin Diver,* 25(5):20, 1976.

California Bureau of Vital Statistics. *Death by Drowning in 1976.* A report of the State of California Public Health Department. Sacramento, Calif., 1977.

Cross, E. R. Technifacts from a master diver. *Skin Diver,* 16(8):49, 1967.

Desautel, D. Cave diving—not a sport for the inexperienced. *Florida Skin Diver Association Bulletin,* July, 1971, p. 16.

Dueker, C. W. Decompression sickness. *The Undersea Journal,* 10(1):20–21, 1977.

Egstrom, G. H., and Bachrach, A. J. Diver panic. *Skin Diver,* 20(11):20, 111, 1971.

Fead, L. Stop, get control, think, act. *The Undersea Journal,* 7(3):9–10, 1974.

Fead, L. Relax: Dive within your limits. *The Undersea Journal,* 8(1):7, 1975.

Graver, D. *Professional Association of Diving Instructors Training Course—Information Booklet.* Santa Ana, Calif.: PADI, 1976.

Irwin, A. Seashore diving dangers. *Skin Diver,* 17(4):62, 67, 1968.

Johnson, R. The long road back: A personal account of the agonizing recovery of a bends victim. *Skin Diver,* 25(9):40–41, 1976.

Kindwall, E. P., Schenck, H., and McAniff, J. J. Nonfatal, pressure-related Scuba accidents, identification and emergency treatment. *Scuba Safety Report Series, Report No. 3.* Kingston, R.I.: University of Rhode Island, 1971.

Max, B. Ceiling of ice. *Skin Diver,* 17(12):53–55, 1968.

Murphy, D. A Bimini experience. *Florida Skin Diver Association Bulletin,* Nov., 1975, pp. 12–13.

National Safety Council. *1971 Surfboarding Fatalities in U.S.* Chicago: the Council, 1972.

National Safety Council. *Report of Skateboard Accidents, 1975–1976.* Chicago: the Council, 1977.

Schenck, H., Jr., and McAniff, J. J. Skin and scuba diving fatalities including a complete summary of fatal accidents for 1970. *Scuba Safety Report Series, Report No. 6.* Kingston, R.I.: University of Rhode Island, 1971.

Schenck, H., Jr., and McAniff, J. J. Mortality risks for skin and Scuba divers. *Scuba Safety Report Series, Report No. 7.* Kingston, R.I.: University of Rhode Island, 1972.

Schenck, H., Jr., McAniff, J., Schenck, M., and Schenck, H. Diving accident survey, 1946–1970, including 503 known fatalities. *Scuba Safety Report*

Series, Report No. 5. Kingston, R.I.: University of Rhode Island, Department of Ocean Engineering, 1972.

Schenck, H. V., and McAniff, J. J. *U.S. Underwater Fatality Statistics, 1973.* U.S. Department of Commerce Report No. 11 (URI-SSR-75-9), 1975.

Schenck, H. V., and McAniff, J. J. *U.S. Underwater Fatality Statistics, 1974.* U.S. Department of Commerce Report (URI-SSR-75-10), 1976.

Schenck, H. V., and McAniff, J. J. *U.S. Underwater Fatality Statistics, 1975.* U.S. Department of Commerce Report (URI-SSR-77-11), 1977.

Shneidman, E. S., and Farberow, N. L. *Clues to Suicide.* New York: McGraw-Hill, 1957.

Smith, J. R. Medical notes. *Florida Skin Diver Association Bulletin,* July, 1970, pp. 8–9.

Stelnicki, P. Panic. *The Undersea Journal,* 5(4):31, 1972.

Tzimoulis, P. J. How far is alone? *Skin Diver,* 20(3):3, 1971.

U.S. Department of Commerce. *National Oceanic and Atmospheric Administration Diving Manual: Diving for Science and Technology.* Washington, D.C.: U.S. Government Printing Office, 1975. Stock #003-017-00283.

Worrick, R. S. Why do we dive? *Skin Diver,* 17(11):16–19, 1968.

Zarudiski, E. F. K. Sub and swordfish in underwater duel. *Skin Diver,* 16(12):3, 1967.

Zarudiski, E. F. K. "I felt a tugging," shark victim says. *Ventura County Star Free Press,* August 16, 1977a, p. 1.

Zarudiski, E. F. K. Whee! Wham. *Time,* November 14, 1977b, p. 33.

NAME INDEX

A

Abram, H. S., 91–94
Achté, Kalle A., 5, 20, 41–56
Adler, G., 276
Africa, Thomas W., 388
Aisenberg, P., 197
Aitken, R. C. B., 53
Alexander, Franz, 119
Alexander, J., 199
Anderson, K., 94
Anderson, M. M., 90, 94
Anslinger, H. J., 163
Anstee, B. H., 272
Arlow, Jacob A., 119
Arnold, Magda, 377
Asch, S. S., 262–264, 266, 267, 271, 273
Atkinson, M., 52
Attardo, N., 193

B

Bach-y-Rita, G., 266, 267, 269, 271
Bachman, J. A., 258
Bachrach, A. J., 410, 418, 419, 425
Bacon, Catherine, 118
Baden, M. M., 194
Bahnson, C. B., 119
Baker, George W., 375n.
Balint, M., 236
Ball, Donald W., 381
Ballinger, B. R., 259
Balster, R. L., 144
Bandura, A., 323
Bangasser, R. P., 420
Banker, Lem, 303
Barglow, P., 267, 270
Barnard, Jessie, 378
Barraclough, B. M., 53
Barter, J. R., 258, 259
Barton, Allen H., 375n.
Barton, E., 289
Barton, W. I., 149, 174
Bashkin, E. A., 269, 272
Basowitz, H., 376

Battacharyya, N. N., 258
Beard, B. H., 93
Beavers, R., 58
Beck, A. T., 38, 58, 172, 174, 210, 212
Beckett, Samuel, 58
Beigel, A., 260
Belfer, M. L., 224
Beloso, R. H., 420
Benjamin, H., 348, 350
Bensing, R., 328
Benson, R. A., 147
Bergler, E., 304
Berkowitz, Leonard, 361, 368
Berlyne, D. E., 17, 310, 377
Bernstein, Douglas A., 9, 243–253
Bespalec, D. A., 246
Bettelheim, B., 264
Bibring, E., 38, 211
Biderman, Albert, 375
Billings, J. H., 151
Bittner, Egon, 368–369
Blachly, Paul H., 17
Blank, H. R., 269
Blau, Theodore H., 12, 410–427
Blaue, W., 419
Blitzer, J., 236
Bloch, H., 339
Blum, H. P., 235
Blum, R., 196
Blumberg, H., 176
Blumer, H., 59
Bodner, J., 410
Borges, P., 271
Borkenstein, R. F., 288
Bors, E., 99
Boswell, J., 171
Boszormenyi-Nagy, I., 191
Bourestom, N. D., 113
Bowlby, J., 36
Braconnier, A., 148, 178
Bratter, T. E., 152, 181, 182
Braucht, G. N., 177
Bridges, E. M., 388
Brodie, D. C., 147
Bron, B., 179

429

SUBJECT INDEX

A

Abortion, 344
Accidents, 9–10
  automobile:
    alcohol abuse and, 165
    causes of, 287–288
    one-car, 28, 32–34
    personality and, 284–285, 292–295, 388
    suicide and, 54
    (*See also* Drunken driving)
  fatal, 165, 207, 288
  during leisure activities, 394
  purposive, 171
  stressful life events and, 285–288, 291–292
Acting out, 23, 44–45, 53, 158, 262
Addiction (*see* Drug abuse; Sports, high-risk)
Adolescents, 158, 193, 247
  alcohol use of, 176
  dreams of, 336–337
  drug abuse of, 8, 170–186, 339
  drug education for, 147
  parental blackmail by, 329
  peer groups, 338
  runaway, 335
  school and, 339
  suicidal, 8, 174
  (*See also* Delinquents)
Aerosol, 168
Aggression, 37, 39, 43, 46, 48, 51
  alcohol and, 213, 295
  coronary symptoms and, 119
  in interveners, 367
  self-mutilation and, 263, 273
Alcohol:
  adolescent use of, 176
  barbiturates and, 159, 167, 172, 174
  physical effects of, 171, 220
  poisoning by, 52
  society and, 157, 296–297, 386
  violence and, 160, 165–166

Alcohol abuse, 5, 7–8, 171, 199, 207–219, 233, 244
  accidents and, 165, 207, 288–296
  case studies of, 214–217
  comparison with diabetes, 212–213
  cost to society of, 208
  definition of, 208
  incidence of, 208, 223
  life expectancy and, 207
  by offenders, 222
  parental, 148, 192
  personality and, 51–52
  by self-mutilators, 263
  sex differences in, 221–225
  by skydivers, 403
  in spinal cord injury patients, 100, 109, 112
  stress and, 291–292
  suicide and, 210–211, 225
  treatment of, 217
  by women, 220–231
  (*See also* Drinking; Drunken driving)
Alcoholics Anonymous, 210, 217, 233, 321
Alcoholism (*see* Alcohol abuse)
Alienation, 58
  in coronary illness patients, 117–118
  in drug users, 178, 179
Altruism, 361–362, 369–370
  (*See also* Interveners)
Amphetamines, 140, 148, 157, 160, 163, 166, 180, 183, 263, 356
  death from, 175–176
Amyloidosis, 107
Angel dust (*see* Phencyclidine)
Anger:
  in coronary patients, 123–125
  expression of, 123–124
  indirect self-destructive behavior and, 6, 25
  masochism and, 43
  physical illness and, 117, 122
  in self-mutilators, 265
  suicide attempts and, 211